MILTON STUDIES

V

MILTON STUDIES

V

Edited by

James D. Simmonds

UNIVERSITY OF PITTSBURGH PRESS

MILTON STUDIES

is published annually by the University of Pittsburgh Press as a forum for Milton scholarship and criticism. Articles submitted for publication may be biographical; they may interpret some aspect of Milton's writings; or they may define literary, intellectual, or historical contexts—by studying the work of his contemporaries, the traditions which affected his thought and art, contemporary political and religious movements, his influence on other writers, or the history of critical response to his work.

Manuscripts should be upwards of 3,000 words in length and should conform to the *MLA Style Sheet*. They will be returned only if sufficient postage is enclosed (overseas contributors enclose international reply coupons). Manuscripts and editorial correspondence should be addressed to James D. Simmonds, Department of English, University of Pittsburgh, Pittsburgh, Pa. 15260.

Milton Studies does not review books.

Within the United States, *Milton Studies* may be ordered from the University of Pittsburgh Press, Pittsburgh, Pa. 15260.

Overseas orders should be addressed to Media Directions Inc., One Park Avenue, New York, New York, 10016, U.S.A.

Library of Congress Catalog Card Number 69–12335

ISBN 0–8229–3174–5 (Volume I) (out of print)

ISBN 0–8229–3194–x (Volume II)

ISBN 0–8229–3218–0 (Volume III)

ISBN 0–8229–3244–x (Volume IV)

ISBN 0–8229–3272–5 (Volume V)

US ISSN 0076–8820

Media Directions Inc., London

Manufactured in the United States of America

CONTENTS

MILTON STUDIES
V

PARADISE LOST:
"TRAGICAL—COMICAL—
HISTORICAL—PASTORAL"

Roger B. Rollin

Paradise Lost is more than a highly dramatic poem: it is "an epic built of dramas," an encyclopedic work composed of three distinct yet interlocking plots, each of which approximates the theoretic form of a different genre of Renaissance drama. That drama of which Satan is the protagonist fulfills Aristotle's chief criteria for tragedy, and, as a dramatic character, Satan conforms to Aristotelian, Renaissance, and modern conceptions of the tragic hero. Adam is less a tragic hero than the protagonist of a pastoral tragicomedy whose *crisis* is the tragic incident of the Fall, but whose *climax*—his reconciliation with his spouse and with his God—is essentially comedic. Framing both these plots is the drama of the Son of God, which parallels the theoretic form of the Renaissance history play until it trails off into mere narrative in Books XI–XII. A fourth dramatic form is the monodrama of Milton the narrator. Its subject is the composing of an epic poem and its tension arises out of the question, can the poet-hero, against great odds, complete his magnum opus? Mainly played out in the great invocations, this monodrama remains unfinished. Its climax must be supplied by the reader of *Paradise Lost* himself as he experiences the triumphantly theatrical conclusion of Book XII.

WHEN so distinguished a Miltonist as Douglas Bush begins to wonder if "it is possible that there has been too much emphasis on the dramatic character of *Paradise Lost*," any student of that epic must be given pause.[1] And when another scholar, after surveying the umbrageous grots and caves of Milton criticism, charges that the very term *dramatic* has been so overused therein that it "has been drained of

3

meaning if not of imaginative energy," one who intends not only to employ that term but to reopen the whole question of the dramatic character of *Paradise Lost* runs the risk, it would seem, of violating a new prohibition.[2] Nonetheless, this essay proposes that *Paradise Lost* becomes more accessible if it is viewed, not merely as a vaguely dramatic poem, but specifically as an encyclopedic drama-epic.[3] More precisely, it argues that Milton's vast design becomes more comprehensible if his poem is analyzed in terms of the theoretic forms of three genres of drama—tragedy, tragicomedy, and history play. Such an examination, it also suggests, leads to the conclusion that *Paradise Lost* is most successful when it adheres most closely to these three theoretic forms and comes closest to failure when it most deviates from them. To support these contentions this essay examines Milton's handling of plot, character, and theme in the light of selected theories of drama and the dramaturgical practices of playwrights both ancient and modern.

To take such a critical approach, however, is not to imply that *Paradise Lost* is the result of Milton's deliberate imposition of dramatic forms upon the epic. Rather it is to suggest that, of all the literary forms which this great poem subsumes or transubstantiates, the major dramatic modes of Milton's age (comedy only excepted) are among the most important. Thus, whenever this essay makes statements about *Paradise Lost* which utilize terms out of the lexicon of dramatic literature and criticism, such statements are meant to be taken metaphorically rather than literally. The sole justification for making them at all is that essentially pragmatic justification of metaphoric language in general: though a comparison will inevitably be inexact, it will be proper so long as it illuminates without distorting.

The record of Milton's involvement in dramatic literature need only be summarized here, yet even in summary that involvement is remarkably extensive for one who is usually thought of as a nondramatic poet. His "Vacation Exercise," "Arcades," and *A Mask* were actually performed and, despite Milton's intentions, *Samson Agonistes* has been. Furthermore, his prose as well as his poetry is studded with allusions to dramatists, dramatic literature and criticism, and the production of plays. Finally, as William Riley Parker has suggested, although Milton was of the party that closed the theaters, as one whose longstanding attitude toward drama was strongly positive though not uncritical, he must have opposed the move.[4] Thus it is hardly surprising that his projected major work on the Fall of Man first took shape in Milton's mind as a drama, or that Satan's soliloquy (Book IV) was remembered by Edward Phillips as having been extracted from a verse tragedy begun years before the composition of the epic was undertaken.[5]

Almost from the moment of its publication Milton's epic seems to have struck readers as being the stuff from which drama is made. That early Miltonist, John Dryden, sought and received permission to "tag" Milton's verses for the libretto of his opera, *State of Innocence, and Fall of Man*, and three hundred years later The Living Theatre displayed a contemporary response to Milton's epic in a production entitled *Paradise Now* (October 1968).[6] Thus, when Merritt Hughes observes that "a reader coming to *Paradise Lost* for the first time, and going rapidly through it to the end of Book X, is likely to get the impression that he is reading drama" (p. 173), he appears to be describing a common reaction to the poem. And when Hughes remarks that the reader, "looking back [after completing Book XII,] will see a series of dramas composing the epic plot," he makes explicit a response which lies behind a great deal of Milton criticism. Finally, when he concludes that "*Paradise Lost* is not drama; it is an epic built of dramas," Hughes suggests, but does not pursue, the major thesis of this essay.

The reason why *Paradise Lost* as a whole "does not profoundly trouble, profoundly satisfy us, in the manner of great tragedy," is that it is *not* a tragedy.[7] It is an epic which *contains*, among other things, a tragedy, that of Satan. When the narrator of *Paradise Lost* proclaims, "I now must change / These Notes to Tragic" (IX, 5–6) he has to be referring to those "Notes" with which he will describe the Fall of Man, but not necessarily to all the remaining notes of the poem. As will be shown in more detail below, the term *tragic* does apply to the *catastrophe* of Satan's drama and to the *crisis* of what will be classified as the tragicomedy of Adam and Eve, but it does not apply to all that transpires in Books IX–XII. For these books embody the resolution of the plot of a kind of history play—that of the Son of God. This drama contains, integrates, and unifies Satan's tragedy and Adam and Eve's tragicomedy, but is itself contained within the outer framework of the epic form. This structure of interlocking dramatic units can be crudely diagrammed as follows:

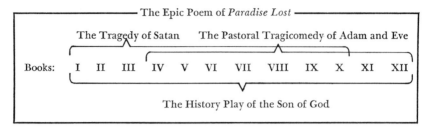

One need not be a purist to be disconcerted by the use of terms like tragedy, tragicomedy, and history play in connection with an epic poem, but as Lily B. Campbell has noted, in the seventeenth century such terms "were applied to nondramatic as well as dramatic writing."[8] Furthermore, since the time of Aristotle students of the drama have had difficulty in agreeing upon their terminology. Thus, in this essay the emphasis will be less upon definitions than it will be upon the assumptions about art and life which lie behind these genres of drama and upon the types of character and situation through which such assumptions are worked out.

I

Although plot may well be the soul of tragedy as Aristotle claims, it is not self-evident that it is also the soul of the epic.[9] For the plot of *Oedipus Rex* Sophocles selected certain incidents concerning the famous king and ordered them into "an imitation of an action that is complete, and whole, and of a certain magnitude" (p. 65). The plot of *Paradise Lost,* on the other hand, is in a sense God's Providence itself, that is, every action that has occurred or will occur within or beyond the time-space continuum. But even if we regard the Fall of Man as Milton's main plot, that plot involves two subplots, the fall of Satan and the elevation of the Son of God, and this complex relationship is further complicated by Milton's artful dislocations of chronology. Nonetheless, for purposes of analysis, it is possible to normalize the order of the incidents which comprise the three plots and to separate each plot from the others.

For example, the incidents in which Satan figures prominently have been arranged by Milton so that, taken together, they make up an action which in its wholeness, completeness, and magnitude satisfies Aristotle's requirements for a tragic plot. This Satan-plot consists of a few incidents selected from the many legends about him and these incidents in combination comprise an action which has a recognizable beginning, middle, and end. From the scene on the burning lake in Book I to that in the hellish garden in Book X, Milton develops a plot of unerring if complex unity. The War in Heaven of Book VI, for example, is technically only a part of Raphael's narrative, yet in both its conception and execution it rises to such heights of dramatic spectacle that a reader is to be forgiven if he forgets that he is responding, not to an "imitation of an action," but to an imitation of an imitation. Milton thus has his material both ways, as poetic narrative and as drama, as he manages to do throughout much of *Paradise Lost*.

The *catastrophe* or climactic incident of Milton's Satan-plot—the seemingly victorious hero's metamorphosis into a serpent (Book X)—fulfills Aristotle's requirement of a "Scene of Suffering" (p. 73). Like most tragic plots Satan's is a series of variations on the theme of suffering, and like most tragic protagonists Satan achieves a kind of release from suffering at the moment of catastrophe. But Satan agonistes is not Samson. He is liberated to an extent from circumstance (the pressures of his role in Hell), but is still held fast in the iron grip of necessity (his continued punishment in other shapes and, eventually, in other dimensions). His fate resembles that of Oedipus, for whom necessity is continued existence in a reality dominated by the inexorable will of implacable fortune or pitiless gods.

Whether Satan's final metamorphosis is accompanied by that "change from ignorance to knowledge" which Aristotle requires (p. 72) is left ambiguous by Milton. Satan speaks only in indecipherable hisses after this point, and with his customary accuracy Milton describes the reactions of all the newly hatched serpents more in terms of instinct than of intellect. Yet the implication that Satan achieves tragic recognition can be inferred, for the fallen angels are "Yearly enjoin'd, some say, to undergo / This annual humbling certain number'd days, / To dash thir pride, and joy for Man seduc't" (X, 575–77). They become their own object lesson, which, to be effective, requires their recognition.

But does the fate of Satan himself arouse and purge the "fear and pity" Aristotle deems essential to the dynamics of audience response to tragedy (p. 78)? While there can be little doubt that the catastrophe of the Satan-plot is well calculated to make an audience "thrill with horror," whether it will also cause them to "melt with pity" (p. 78) depends upon their previous reactions to Satan. Milton's readers have reported a variety of such reactions, often conflicting; however, it may not be necessary to take sides in the Satan controversy to determine if Milton has satisfied Aristotle in his shaping of Satan's character.

It is obvious that the standard myths of Satan as God's adversary, as the enemy of mankind, as the father of lies, enter into Milton's characterization. It is also obvious that the poet attempts to reinforce the stock responses to those myths. On the other hand, students of *Paradise Lost* from Blake to Empson have, if nothing else, compelled readers to be wary of making *only* such responses. As Hughes implies (pp. 177–79), the question, "Is Satan hero or villain?" is so simplistic that any response to it must be a reductive one.

"Good and evil we know in the field of this world grow up together almost inseparably," says the Milton of the *Areopagitica* (p. 728), and it is this kind of moral realism that has gone into the creation of Satan's character. This realism, to be sure, is heightened by Milton's art so that both the good and the evil in Satan are larger than life, as he is. The moral point still holds, however, for from his descriptions of Satan (such as I, 591–94) it is evident that Milton accepts the psychology of evil implicit in the rhetorical question of Socrates: "do you fancy that great crimes and unmixed wickedness come from a feeble nature and not rather from a noble nature that has been ruined?"[10] With Satan's metamorphosis into a serpent in the black pastoral groves of Hell, his form finally loses all its original brightness. But nine and one-half books have largely failed if the reader regards this involuntary reenactment of Satan's willed metamorphosis in the Edenic groves as *merely* the "downfall of the utter villain," which for Aristotle would be "alien to the spirit of Tragedy" (p. 75).[11]

II

A statement in *Of Education*, the epigraph to *Samson Agonistes*, and the play itself, all suggest that the *Poetics* and its Italian commentators contributed to Milton's sense of the decorum of drama.[12] The *Samson* epigraph, however, with its attack on the tendency of playwrights to intermix "Comic stuff with Tragic sadness and gravity," also establishes Milton's sensitivity to the "new" tragedy. According to Alfred Harbage, the basic premise of this uniquely Renaissance form can be summed up in the cry of Richard II: "For God's sake, let us sit upon the ground / And tell sad stories of the death of kings" (act 3, scene 2, lines 155–56).[13] Although it seems overly broad and simple, such a concept allowed the likes of Shakespeare to create plays of such power as to impress even a confirmed neoclassicist like young Milton. The mature poet's polemical condemnation of the moderns need not be taken as evidence that Aristotelian theory and English dramaturgical practice were wholly incompatible. If it is possible to accept Milton's Satan as a great tragic character in both the Aristotelian and the Renaissance conceptions, it is also possible to be persuaded by Helen Gardner that for his characterization Milton was much indebted to Elizabethan and Jacobean dramatists.[14]

Gardner explains that a prevailing theme of tragedy in this period is the "deforming" of such a mighty figure, "in its origin bright and good, by its own willed persistence in acts against its own nature." Thus, "it is on the tragic stage that we find the idea of damnation in English literature before *Paradise Lost*" (p. 206). Like Faustus, Macbeth, and Beatrice-Joanna, Satan commits "an act against nature . . . a primal sin, in that it contradicts the 'essential fact of things,' and its author knows that it does so" (p. 207). Satan then, like most tragic figures, is an inveterate romantic. The world of tragedy, however, is essentially a realistic one in the sense that it accepts human limitations, transiency, and death as facts; thus, the tragic figure, who tends to seek transcendence, pays a high price for becoming a realist. Satan, for example, performs his "act against nature" for his "imagined good," but finds that retributive justice grants that good only ironically: the would-be king is exalted, but only to a "bad eminence." The irony pervading the Satan-plot arises less from Milton's artistic (or his God's metaphysical) manipulations than it does from the discrepancy between the poet's realism and what he perceives as Satan's romanticism.

The tragic protagonist's romantic agony is heightened by his "incapacity for change to a better state, or repentance" (p. 207). Satan is possessed by the kind of rigor we often associate with the archetypal Puritan, and this lends a deterministic aura to his acts. Though his character is not intended by Milton to be his fate, the programming of that character to his fate is so precise as to raise theological questions which Milton is less able to avoid than is, for example, Shakespeare.

Although Gardner's argument is persuasive, it is, like the argument of this essay, a qualified one: "Satan is, of course, a character in an epic, and he is in no sense the hero of the epic as a whole. But he is a figure of heroic magnitude and heroic energy, and he is developed by Milton with dramatic emphasis and dramatic intensity" (p. 208). She also contends, however, that Milton's treatment of Satan's character and plot results in a tragedy so great that it destroys the poem's unity, overwhelming the "secondary epic" of Adam and Eve (p. 214). Succeeding sections of this essay will argue that this is not the case by indicating how Adam and Eve function as the protagonists of a tragicomedy that is itself artistically successful. This tragicomedy complements and is complemented by the tragedy of Satan, who is at once the protagonist of his own drama and the antagonist of theirs. To understand fully the relationship between these two dramas, however, it will be necessary to go beyond Aristotle for additional evidence that Milton's Satan-plot is indeed a tragedy and that his Adam-plot is not. That analysis will be based upon the formulations of tragedy devised by Northrop Frye and Richard Sewall.[15]

III

Sewall does not discuss "tragic flaws," "recognition scenes," or similar subjects which have proved so vexing to Aristotle's commentators. He concentrates, not upon tragedy's "technical form," but upon its "theoretic form"—"the dominant feelings, intuitions, [and] insights that we meet in so-called tragic writings" (p. 347). For example, Sewall perceives that "basic to the tragic form is its recognition of the inevitability of paradox, of unresolved tensions and ambiguities, of opposites in precarious balance" (p. 349). Milton's Satan-plot is a case in point: its horrendous catastrophe in Book X is as mysterious to its protagonist and those about him as are Hamlet's and Lear's. The difference is that *Paradise Lost* provides its audience with a view of Satan's tragedy and ultimate fate *sub specie aeternitatis*, whereas the audiences of Shakespeare's tragedies are largely left to their own spiritual resources.

Sewall's profile of the tragic protagonist also more closely approximates Milton's Satan than his Adam:

Like the cosmos which he views, tragic man is a paradox and a mystery. He is no child of God; yet he feels himself more than a child of earth. He is not the plaything of Fate, but he is not entirely free. He is "both creature and creator" (in Niehbuhr's phrase)—"fatefully free and freely fated" (in George Schrader's). He recognizes "the fact of guilt" while cherishing "the dream of innocence"

(Fiedler), and he never fully abandons either position. He is plagued by the ambiguity of his own nature and of the world he lives in. (p. 352)

Milton's Satan can publicly deny the fatherhood of God—"We know no time when we were not as now" (V, 859)—yet in private he can admit the truth to himself; torn by regret that he has elected to play God and to plague God, he can cry: "Ah wherefore! he deserv'd no such return / From me" (IV, 42–43). The soliloquy from which these lines come has the traditional dramatic purpose of laying bare an inner life. In Satan's case, this inner life, like that of the typical tragic protagonist, is not only alienated from itself by conflicting impulses and attitudes, but from the character's outer life as well. Like many of his counterparts on the tragic stage, Satan's personality is so paradoxical as to border upon spiritual (if not psychological) schizophrenia.

If the tragic protagonist's feelings are invariably complex and contradictory, so too are those of the audience toward him. They are so, Frye argues, not so much because of the audience's moral perspective, their approval or disapproval of this character, but more because of "the inevitability of the consequences" of his situation and his actions:

Aristotle's hamartia or "flaw" . . . is not necessarily wrongdoing, much less moral weakness: it may be simply a matter of being a strong character in an exposed position, like Cordelia. The exposed position is usually the place of leadership, in which a character is exceptional and isolated at the same time, giving us that curious blend of the inevitable and the incongruous which is peculiar to tragedy. (p. 38)

Thus, whether one views Satan as the ultimate sinner or as one more sinned against than sinning, he remains a tragic figure, for his strength is manifest, his position supremely dangerous, and his ultimate fate seems both inevitable (given Divine Providence) and incongruous (given Divine Irony).

Milton's Adam fails to measure up to these expectations. In spite of Satan's gradual deterioration throughout *Paradise Lost*, to the final scene of his tragedy he remains every inch a king—at least to the extent that Lear is—as well as a champion and a general. Adam, although he is "our first Father" (IV, 495) and is initially described by such adjectives as "Godlike" and "Divine" (IV, 289, 291), is soon eased into his role of Everyman as pastoral swain. Milton's portrait in Book IX, which shows Adam weaving a garland while his nymph is in the process of losing her innocence, is in every way appropriate for one whose "place of leadership"—unlike that of Oedipus or Othello—is circumstantial rather than earned. Furthermore, as Frye observes, the tragic protagonist "is usually vested with supreme authority, but is often in the more ambiguous position of a *tyrannos* whose rule depends on his own abilities, rather than a purely hereditary or *de jure* monarch (*basileus*) like Duncan" (p. 217). From the very beginning of *Paradise Lost* Satan is the complete *tyrannos*, and most of his actions in Books I and II are motivated by his need to consolidate his shaky political position as defeated leader. Milton's own political instincts are displayed to good advantage in his dramatization of Hell as a Fascist state with all of its ludicrousness and terror, and of Satan as a great dictator who must employ all his talents for guile, cheap rhetoric, mass psychology, and strong-arm tactics before he is sure enough of his authority to delegate it temporarily. Adam, however, is by nature a setup, a *basileus*, one more suited to become the victim of a tragic event than its perpetrator.

Adam is isolated by his position of leadership over Eve, but less so than, for example, Macbeth. Both Eve and Lady Macbeth are partners to their spouses in virtue as well as in vice, but Eve is deceived by a third party and on the whole she shares more of her husband's inner life than does Lady Macbeth. And in the end, Macbeth has only his sword to clasp; Adam has the hand of Eve—which in the finite world of art makes all the difference.

Such expressions of reconciliation and dependency do not sort well with the streak of recalcitrance that is so conspicuous in the make-up of the typical tragic protagonist. The dynamic of this recalcitrance, Sewall suggests, is pride. "It sustains his belief, however humbled he may become by later experience, in his own freedom, in his innocence, and in his uncommon sense" (p. 352). Adam is not without his pride, of course. And this quality, "like everything else about tragedy, is ambiguous; it can be tainted with arrogance and have its petty side; but it is not to be equated with sin or weakness" (p. 352). In Adam's case, however, it is not pride that goes before his fall but his lack of it:

> Was shee thy God, that her thou didst obey
> Before his voice, or was shee made thy guide,
> Superior, or but equal, that to her
> Thou didst resign thy Manhood, and the Place
> Wherein God set thee above her made of thee?   (X, 145–49)

At the moment of crisis, when Adam must choose to sin or not to sin, it is not pride but "The Link of Nature" (IX, 914) which impels him. This is of course a moment of exquisite pathos—"the best word," says Frye, "for low mimetic or domestic tragedy"—for pathos "presents its hero as isolated by a weakness which appeals to our sympathy because it is on our own level of experience" (p. 38). Only after the fact, when Adam attempts to rationalize his decision, does he approach tragic hybris, envisioning himself and Eve become "Gods, or Angels Demi-gods" (IX, 937). But both his pride and his recalcitrance are short-lived.

It is different with Satan. From the beginning he resembles those tragic protagonists who are marked by "a proud, passionate, obsessed or soaring mind which brings about a morally intelligible downfall" (Frye, p. 210): "He trusted," says the narrator, "to have equall'd the most High" (I, 40). Throughout the poem Satan exhibits hybris in his deeds and in his words, including his last ones: "What remains, ye Gods, / But up and enter now into full bliss" (X, 502–03). The way in which tragedy "mingles the heroic with the ironic" (Frye, p. 37) is exemplified in the shocking reversal of this scene. Here a tragic protagonist who, according to Frye, is usually an impostor "in the sense that he is self-deceived or made dizzy by hybris" (p. 217), is suddenly revealed for what he is, and is punished even beyond the punishment of that revelation. It is reality as well as Divine Justice which squashes Satan into the shape of a snake; but reality can quash neither his pride nor his recalcitrance.

This "Scene of Suffering," the culmination of numerous such scenes and the prologue to others, to suffering unmitigated by hope, also confirms Satan as a tragic figure, one who

suffers because he is more than usually sensitive to the "terrible dislocations" he sees about him and experiences in himself. He is more than usually aware of the mighty opposites in the universe and in man, of the gulf between desire and fulfillment, between what is and what should be. This kind of suffering is suffering on the high level, beyond the reach of the immature or brutish, and forever closed to the extreme optimist, the extreme pessimist, or the merely indifferent. (Sewall, pp. 353–54)

Before the Fall Adam sees and experiences no "terrible dislocations" nor does he show himself especially sensitive to the "mighty opposites" in his universe—in spite of the fact that Raphael has informed him of their existence. Even after the Fall his immaturity is still so marked that he must be instructed by Michael so that he will be able to suffer more appropriately. Satan, however, is more than once wracked by the necessity of living in divided and distinguished worlds. Adam's prelapsarian world is really a unitary system, and though his sin will make separate if related systems of heaven and earth, it is promised that they will eventually become one again.

Except for a single brief moment, Adam also lacks that consciousness of his "simultaneous guilt and guiltlessness" which causes much of the tragic protagonist's suffering (Sewall, p. 354). Adam is *guilty*, and not for long is he permitted the luxury of doubting it. On the other hand, from his soliloquy in Book IV we know that the Hell within Satan is stoked by his polarized moral sense of himself. In his agony Satan is at bottom the tragic protagonist who

knows nothing of grace and never glories in his suffering. Although he may come to acquiesce in it partly and "learn" from it . . . his characteristic mood is resentment and dogged endurance. He has not the stoic's patience, although this may be a part of what he learns. Characteristically, he is restless, intense, probing and questioning the universe and his own soul. (Sewall, p. 354)

While the fallen angels do "know" of grace—Mammon at least holds it out as a theoretical possibility (II, 237–39)—it is clear from Satan's strategy in the Grand Consult and from his soliloquies that for him grace might as well not exist: he could never sue for it nor ever accept it unsought. Adam of course will settle for either.

It might seem that, contrary to Sewall's definition, Satan does glory in his own suffering—he reminds his followers that, as their leader, he is the one condemned "to greatest share / Of endless pain" (II, 29–30)—but this is a statement for popular consumption, more the political rhetoric of one upon whose head the crown lies uneasy than an expression of a born masochist's ecstasy.

Nor could The Readiness is All be his motto as it is for that archstoic, Belial. Satan endures, not to endure, but to prevail. His case makes the point that in discussions of tragedy it might be more appropriate (if less dignified) to speak of the "tragic itch" than of the "tragic flaw," for the protagonist of tragedy is the last one to let well enough alone. He sees himself as born to set things right. Thus Satan must set off on his impure quest for the holy grail of the human soul and is, in the process, doomed to explore the wasteland of his own blasted soul.

Although the tragic protagonist normally is an establishment figure, it seems as if within him there is a radical crying to get out. For him (and perhaps only for him) the times are out of joint, and, "rising in his pride, he protests: he pits himself in some way against whatever, in the heavens above and in the earth beneath, seems to him to be wrong, oppressive, or personally thwarting" (Sewall, p. 355). It is Eve who is *human* society's first revolutionary, though she does so at the instigation of an outside agitator. Adam's revolutionary fervor, on the other hand, fades with his first feelings of guilt for by-passing the political process. With his conversion he, like many reformed revolutionaries, swings to the opposite extreme: "Henceforth I learn, that to obey is best" (XII, 561), and his commitment binds himself, Eve, and their progeny to a theocracy. Satan's protest, however, is the original radical act, and to a greater degree than Eve's and Adam's it is a tragic act, one which makes a difference to society or to history (Sewall, p. 358). It does so, of course, with a vengeance, being the first cause of what is to become the human condition. In a perverse way then Satan mediates between the human and the divine. Both Frye (p. 207) and Sewall (p. 357) assert that the authentic tragic protagonist normally serves a mediatorial function simply because he is very great in terms of the human but small in terms of the divine. Here again Milton's Adam does not measure up. Before the Fall Adam is scarcely more than a statuesque and sober adolescent to whose purity and innocence postlapsarian readers can respond more with nostalgia than with empathy. The possibilities for his eliciting our empathy are increased after the Fall, but, paradoxically, to too great an extent for Adam to function well as a tragic figure: he has become all too much like us. Intensely aware of both his guilt and his limitations, he surrenders to cosmic power and says that it is good. Rather than transcending the human condition, as the tragic protagonist does, he all too accurately defines it. He has become Everyman.[16]

Satan is *not* Everyman although everyone can recognize something of himself in Satan. Like other tragic protagonists he is larger than life, but in him polarities of evil and good exist in a state of tension that is lifelike. They exist, however, at a much higher degree of intensity than they do in us because his powers and his power are greater than ours. For this reason, and because the tragic protagonist and his society have more to gain or to lose than we and our society, through his predicament we transcend ordinary existence and perceive it on the kind of overarching cosmic or historical scale that can be discerned in daily life only with difficulty.

In tragedy then "all who are involved have been witness to new revelations about human existence, the evil of evil and the goodness of good" (Sewall, p. 358). It must be stressed, however, that in tragedy these revelations tend to be just that—revelations rather than resolutions, for "the action of tragedy will not abide our questions" (Frye, p. 208). It might have been Milton's recognition of this that led him to abandon his plan for writing a tragedy about the Fall of Man and to turn instead to a form which could accommodate history and comedy as well as tragedy, answers as well as questions.[17]

IV

One advantage to be gained by analyzing *Paradise Lost* in terms of the theoretical forms of drama is that it becomes less possible to succumb to the sense that with Book IX Milton's poem is to all intents and purposes over, that the rest is epilogue. Books X through XII can scarcely be regarded as of only minor significance when one realizes that they contain the catastrophes of all three of the poem's dramatic plots. Thus, it becomes important to determine precisely what it is the narrator means when he proclaims that he must "change / These Notes to Tragic" (IX, 5–6). Possibly the reference is to the tragedy of Satan, but the anguish and reluctance of the narrator provide a different cue: they lead his audience to anticipate the Fall and its aftermath—specifically the advent "into this world" of "a world of woe, / Sin and her shadow Death, and Misery / Death's Harbinger" (IX, 11–13). These lines describe accurately enough Books IX through XII up to the prophecy of Christ's coming midway through Book XII, but are less appropriate (as will be shown below) to the last half of Book XII. Nonetheless, even though Milton conceived of the Fall as tragic and succeeded in implementing that conception in Book IX, one tragic incident does not a tragedy make.[18] Whether dramatic structure determines conclusion or vice versa, the way in which a literary work terminates must profoundly affect reader response to that work as a total aesthetic experience. Discovering how it all turns out satisfies more than idle curiosity: resolution is to literary structure as the double helix is to living form.

Michael's vision of human history from the Garden to "the World's great period" (XII, 466) is grim, but not unrelievedly so. Men famous for their faith and justness—Enoch, Jonah, Abraham, Isaac, Joseph, and Moses—present themselves to Adam's view with almost cyclical regularity. These types of Christ function as affirmations of human goodness just as Christ himself is an affirmation of cosmic goodness. Milton means to ensure his readers' positive response to Michael's vision and narration through their participation in Adam's reactions: "O goodness infinite, goodness immense! / That all this good of evil shall produce, / And evil turn to good" (XII, 469–71). Whether or not every reader shares in Adam's exultation in the divine comedy he has witnessed and his exaltation of its author, it is clear enough that the whole drama is intended to make a kind of metaphysical affirmation which normally is foreign to the spirit of tragedy.

On the other hand, it is possible to argue that the actual banishment of Adam and Eve from the Garden changes these notes to tragic once again. But banishment as a climactic act lacks the finality and, consequently, the simplicity and universality of death. Thus each fictive instance of banishment must be examined separately to determine its unique meaning and the tone and mood by which that meaning is orchestrated. There is, for example, the profoundly pessimistic existentialism of the conclusion of *Oedipus Rex*:

> Make way for Oedipus. All people said,
> "That is a fortunate man";
> And now what storms are beating on his head!
> Call no man fortunate that is not dead.
> The dead are free from pain.[19]

At best Sophocles' chorus is recommending a rigorous Stoicism, at worst, an almost nihilistic fatalism. The last two books of *Paradise Lost*, on the other hand, "present a drama in which the character of Adam is molded into an example of Christian fortitude," a blend of moderate Stoicism and Christian positivism.[20] As Adam explains to Michael, he has learned that "suffering for Truth's sake / Is fortitude to highest victory, / And to the faithful Death the Gate of Life" (XII, 569–71). Adam has become emotionally and philosophically ready for his exile; Oedipus can only accept the inevitability of his. God has said to Michael, "So send them forth, though sorrowing, yet in peace" (XI, 117), and it is with just such mixed yet balanced emotions and attitudes—in Adam and (hopefully) in Milton's audience—that *Paradise Lost* is brought to a close.

This scene merits particular attention. With near Shakespearian bravado Milton begins his serious poem's final moment with an incident (enlivened by stage business) that could almost be comic, as Michael is forced to take physical measures to evict Adam and Eve from the Garden:

> In either hand the hast'ning Angel caught
> Our ling'ring Parents, and to th' Eastern Gate
> Led them direct, and down the Cliff as fast
> To the subjected Plain; then disappear'd.   (XII, 637–40)

Then with another bit of stage business Milton shifts the delicate balance of his mood towards the serious: he has Adam and Eve, in an archetypally human gesture, look back at the home to which they can never go again (XII, 641–44). Finally, in one superb line Milton permanently fixes the emotional tenor of his long poem's conclusion: "Some natural tears they dropp'd, but wip'd them soon" (XII, 645). Tragedy also ends with tears, but seldom is the audience left with the sense that they will be wiped away, and soon, for the denouement of tragedy initiates a period of mourning, a time of stasis more than of action.

The vale of tears that is the world closes in on the survivors of tragedy, but the situation is far different with Adam and Eve: "The World was *all* before them, where to *choose* / Thir place of rest" (XII, 646–47, italics mine). These lines have none of the naiveté but some of the optimism of "O brave new world" about them. And the fact that Adam and Eve have not only free choice but also divine guidance contrasts with that keen sense of restriction and of man's aloneness before unknowable gods which characterizes the final moments of so many tragedies. As Frye has pointed out, tragedy tends to isolate its protagonist from his society (p. 219), but Adam and Eve *are* society. Although they have been excluded from the geographical Garden and have become to some extent spiritually distanced from the heavenly city, they will comprise their own community. Tragic protagonists either make their final exits alone and largely loveless or find that in the grave all are alone and none do embrace. Adam and Eve, however, have each other and a newly tempered love for each other. "They hand in hand with wand'ring steps and slow, / Through *Eden* took thir solitary way" (XII, 648–49). Here again Milton conveys his meaning through a precise and artful use of stage business: the hands which Michael separated to usher the pair out of the Garden are once again joined to become symbol. When Milton's audience first sees Adam and Eve they are "hand in hand" (IV, 321), and the parting of their hands much later—"from her Husband's hand her hand / Soft she withdrew" (IX, 385–86)—foreshadows the Fall. It is comedy, not tragedy, whose major thrust is in the direction of the physical and spiritual union of the lovers and this union implies the crystallization of a new society around them.[21]

This is not in contradiction of the point made earlier that the Fall, as dramatized by Milton, is tragic; for the Fall is not the catastrophe (climax) of the Adam-plot, but its crisis or turning point, the incident determining the direction which that plot will take. Its true climax is less a catastrophe than it is an *anastrophe* or upturn.[22] Depending on whether one takes a theological or a theatrical point of view, the anastrophe of Milton's Adam-plot is that passage in Book XII referred to above in which Adam is confirmed in Christian fortitude—his "recognition scene"—or the final scene of exile. It is evident then that the Adam-plot of *Paradise Lost* must be approached from a different critical angle than Milton's tragedy of Satan.

V

In his discussion of the six phases or types of tragedy, Frye explains that the second phase corresponds to "the youth of the romantic hero, and is in one way or another the tragedy of innocence" (p. 220). He cites Iphigenia, Jephthah's daughter, Romeo and Juliet, Hippolytus, and Saint Joan as examples, but also says that this phase "is dominated by the archetypal tragedy of the green and golden world, the loss of innocence of Adam and Eve. . . . In many tragedies of this type the central character survives, so that the action closes with some adjustment to a new and more mature experience" (p. 220). But of the examples cited only Adam and Eve may reasonably be said to inhabit a "green and golden world," and only they survive to adjust to a new reality. Thus it would be more consistent of Frye to place the Adam-and-Eve myth into another of his categories—that of a comedy which contains "a potential tragedy within itself" (p. 215).

On the other hand, Frye also seems to be thinking of *Paradise Lost* and of Milton's portrait of the Garden in his description of the milieu of "romance"—"a pastoral and Arcadian world . . . full of glades, shaded valleys, murmuring brooks, the moon, and other images closely linked with the female or maternal aspect of sexual imagery" (p. 200). Romance, comedy, tragedy: Milton's Adam-plot is all of these and none of these, a hybrid form whose nearest equivalent in literature is pastoral tragicomedy.

In his preface to *The Faithful Shepherdess* (ca. 1608) John Fletcher bluntly announces that "a tragie-comedie is not so called in respect of mirth and killing, but in respect it wants deaths, which is inough to make it no tragedie, yet brings some neere it, which is inough to make it no comedie."[23] Yet, as Eugene M. Waith has pointed out, Fletcher's dramaturgical theory is deceptively simple, for in his practice "tragicomedy is not a mechanical combination of the attributes of tragedy and comedy but a subtle fusion in which each loses its identity" (p. 44). The flowering of tragicomedy took place during Milton's youth and it is possible to see his first important dramatic work, *A Mask*, as a response to that phenomenon. *Comus* is typically Miltonic in that it is a highly personal adaptation of an established genre. That this work is set in an Arcadian world, that it is a serious comedy which contains "a potential tragedy within itself," and that it concludes with a kind of resurrection of its protagonists, all suggest that it can be viewed as a masque whose conception has been broadened and deepened by a vision of pastoral tragicomedy.

It is unlikely that anyone so interested in dramatic literature as Milton would have been unaware of the tradition of tragicomedy and of its wide acceptance in England. Possibly Milton knew of Macropedius' *Adamus* (1552), described by Marvin T. Herrick as "a serious play which exhibits the errors and sufferings of Adam and Eve and their sons."[24] This play is brought to a conclusion by a deus ex machina—Christ—who, as the prologue explains, "comes to save mankind, removes the confusion, and by means of this comic event the outcome is a happy one."[25] Milton's intention of justifying the ways of God to men was foreshadowed in a tragicomedy written by the Huguenot, Henry de Barran, *Tragique Comedie Francoise de l'homme iustifié par Foy* (1554), whose argument recounts "how Man is led astray by Satan, Sin and Concupiscence, abandoned by Roman Catholicism, but rescued by Paul the Protestant preacher. Faith and Grace were revealed in Act 4, and in Act 5, after a debate between Paul, the Law, and Grace, Man was assured of salvation."[26] But it was John Fletcher whom Herrick credits with being "the first English dramatist to rescue the term 'tragicomedy' from its 'mongrel' status and to restore its standing in the world of letters" (p.

261). His *Faithful Shepherdess* (ca. 1608), *Philaster* (with Francis Beaumont, ca. 1609), *The Prophetess* (1622), and *Maid in the Mill* (1623) have pastoral settings amid which the protagonists are, like Adam and Eve, placed in jeopardy, but survive. Fletcher's achievement opened up the field for dramatists like Middleton, Heywood, Massinger, Ford, and Shirley, all of whom attempted the tragicomic form during the period of Milton's maturation as an artist.

Milton's nephew, Edward Phillips, described tragicomedy as "half tragedy and half comedy," a definition which, despite its crudity, is accurate enough as a quantitative analysis of the Adam-plot of *Paradise Lost*: the "tragic" portion of that plot consists of Books IX through XI and part of XII and its "comic" portion of Books IV, V, VIII, and the conclusion of XII.[27] The qualitative parallels between this plot and the theoretic form of tragicomedy go considerably deeper.

VI

The late sixteenth century in Italy saw an increasing emphasis being placed upon two elements of particular relevance to this essay's approach to Milton's tragicomedy—love and the pastoral (Herrick, p. 124). In *Paradise Lost* these two elements receive such extensive elaboration that they seem far removed from their technical source, Genesis ii–iii. The Biblical account of Adam and Eve, which attains at best the level of primitive pastoral, is transfigured by Milton into nothing less than the ultimate pastoral, a bucolic poem into whose creation has gone all that English, European, and Middle Eastern literature comprehended as pastoral. From his magnificent descriptions of that "happy rural seat of various view" (IV, 247), to his loving portraits of Eve as pastoral goddess or nymph (IX, 386), to his delineation of Adam as a pastoral swain (IX, 838), Milton's poem is steeped in the bucolic mode.[28] And by developing a full-blown love story of Adam and Eve the poet simultaneously modifies significantly the sacred text (the term *love* does not appear in Genesis ii–iii) and conforms to the secular tradition of pastoral (in which love has always been a dominant factor).

Readers accustomed to think of pastoral literature as at best trivial forget that modes of the bucolic—the most notable being the image of Christ as the Good Shepherd—permeate the texture of the Bible and that these modes exerted a continuous influence upon medieval and Renaissance art. (Milton himself, in Book II of *The Reason of Church*

Government, classifies the Song of Solomon as "a divine pastoral Drama.") Sometimes forgotten as well is the line of classical pastoral which
begins with Theocritus and Bion and which down through literary history, in the hands of almost every poet of note, has passed through modi-
fications ranging from *Lycidas* to "West-running Brook." Archetypal
critics have proposed that the myth of the pastoral may not only be
central to human art and culture but also to the human psyche, which
seems to yearn deeply for a life close to nature. Pastoral and high seriousness then are far from incompatible. As a dramatist from Milton's era,
Thomas Heywood, observed, "there is neither tragedy, history, comedy,
moral, or pastoral from which an infinite use cannot be gathered."[29]

Most pastoral literature is characterized by two fundamental tensions of the human condition—that between primal good and primal
evil, and that between the state of childlike (sexless) innocence and
what Robert Burton called "this Tragi-Comedy of Love."[30] Milton's
Garden, like most Arcadias, initially seems a world of stasis, where divine reason manifests itself in a stable and contented human society
and in a natural world which ministers to that society. Such a world
contains all the elements of the good life, which is, of course, the moral
life. It is also a safe world, or seems to be. Milton himself goes to some
lengths to emphasize his Garden's security arrangements. Security, however, implies a threat, for, given the human condition, it is impossible
for an audience to respond to utopia without being at least semicon-
sciously aware of its converse, nonutopia, or the world as it is. The evil
in the world adjacent to Arcadia (symbolized frequently by the court
or the city) exerts a constant pressure upon the pastoral from without.
From within, the bucolic equilibrium often is in danger of being disturbed by another force, that of love. Whether that disturbance is
merely a ripple caused by a singing contest among shepherds, a per-
turbation like that brought on by the affair of Orlando and Rosalind,
or a cataclysm such as that initiated by Adam's decision to align his
destiny with Eve's, love can be destructive of the rational and moral
order of Arcadia. Materialism or megalomania are the ruling passions
which threaten the pastoral world from without; eroticism becomes a
ruling passion which can threaten it from within. All of these forces
come into play in Milton's Adam-plot.

That plot parallels the typical action of tragicomedy. In the *protasis*
or *exposition* (Acts I and II) the pastoral situation is established and

characters are introduced (Books IV, V, and VIII of *Paradise Lost*). In the next phase of the plot, the *rising action* or *complication*, the bucolic good life is threatened by an antagonist (like Milton's "satyr," Satan) who poses a challenge so serious that the play's idyllic aura takes on the semblance of tragedy. Called *epitasis* in tragicomedy and usually comprising Acts III and IV (Herrick, p. 32), in *Paradise Lost* this phase takes place during the latter portion of Book VIII and throughout Book IX. Within this phase occurs the *crisis* or *turning point*, where the pastoral world and the life style it represents hang in the balance. Because both are in fact lost in Milton's poem, the crisis of the Adam-plot evokes the pity and terror associated with tragedy. Following the crisis is the phase of *falling action*, in which the complications of the plot move towards some kind of resolution. In *Paradise Lost* this phase takes the form of the deliberately sordid scene out of domestic drama at the close of Book IX, the miracle-play scene at the beginning of Book X, and the historical pageant which takes up most of Books X through XII. The plot's final resolution comes in the anastrophe of the tragicomedy's fifth act (the last third of Book XII, discussed in section V above). It is followed by the *denouement*, in which something like the original pastoral situation of the play's beginning is reestablished. In Milton's denouement Arcadia is abandoned, as it sometimes is in pastoral tragicomedies, yet the importance of the Arcadia within and the promise of the outer Arcadia that is yet to come are stressed, and these truths mitigate the pastoral protagonists' sense of loss. They also give the Adam-plot psychological and metaphysical dimensions which are rarely approached by conventional pastoral tragicomedies.

VII

For Northrop Frye the Bible presents "a gigantic cycle from creation to apocalypse, within which is the heroic quest of the Messiah from incarnation to apotheosis" (p. 316). This cycle and this quest loom in the background of every passage of *Paradise Lost* but come to the foreground only occasionally. Whether or not he is physically present in a scene, the Son of God is always Satan's antagonist. In theater terms however the Son is not one of the principals in the tragedy of Satan: the only "onstage" confrontation between the two takes place in Book VI. Likewise, in Milton's tragicomedy, the Son appears to Adam and Eve only in the judgment scene of Book X. Nonetheless he is the hero of the scenes set in Heaven, and in Raphael's and Michael's visions he appears at both the Creation and the Apocalypse. Since the Bible was, for Milton, history, the Son has to be that history's preeminent hero. And since that history ends happily, the drama of God's Son is also a comedy.[31] During the Renaissance, Herrick notes, "history became a legitimate basis for comedies as well as tragedies" (p. 314), but in order to show how the plot of God's Son can be viewed as a kind of history play within *Paradise Lost*, it will be necessary to examine briefly Renaissance conceptions of history and of the history play.

Lily B. Campbell suggests that "Saint Augustine may be reckoned a precursor of the Reformation writers about history" because like them (and like Milton) "he used an account of universal history to justify the ways of God to men" (pp. 33–34). The didactic thrust of Renaissance historiography is illustrated in Thomas Blundeville's summary of the reasons for studying history: "First, that we may learn to acknowledge the providence of God; Second, that we may learn how to act wisely in public and in private affairs . . . ; Third, that we may learn by example to follow the good and flee the evil" (quoted in Campbell, p. 50). That Milton, himself a historian, remained under the influence of this tradition of Christian historiography even while fulfilling his function as an epic poet becomes evident when his stated intentions concerning *Paradise Lost* are compared with Irving Ribner's characterization of that tradition:

It was anti-nationalist, emphasized world history, and began usually with the creation of Adam. It treated history as above all the illustration of the working out of God's judgment in human affairs, and thus it tended to ascribe little to the independent judgment or to the will of humanity. And . . . it saw in history an intelligible and rational pattern which was inevitably good and which always affirmed the justice of God.[32]

Milton, of course, ascribes much to "the independent judgment" of humanity, but as Ribner explains, the tradition of Christian historiography was modified during the Renaissance by an assumption derived from the Italian humanists—that "man had some measure of control over his own destiny" (p. 18). Poetry then for Milton was, as John Hollander has put it, "an instrument for bringing to bear the thought of history, as well as some of the history of thought, upon the problems of a rich and turbulent present."[33]

According to Herrick there was during the English Renaissance "a tendency to call any *drama libre* which did not fit either comedy or tragedy or which fell somewhere between these two forms, a history" (p. 215). Nevertheless, Ribner regards history plays as forming "a continuous dramatic tradition which extends from the Middle Ages to the closing of the theatres in 1642" (p. vii), one that "by its very homogeneity constitutes a separate dramatic genre" (p. 14). Coleridge saw the history play as "the transitional link between the epic poem and the drama," and Tillyard connects Milton and Shakespeare in his hypothesis that the latter's history plays constitute his version of the epic.[34] Thus, given the Renaissance view of history and of literature based upon history, *Paradise Lost* could be regarded as a historical poem containing three distinguishable historical poems.

The problem of defining the history play is compounded by the fact that dramatists often have points of view and thus their history plays tend to veer towards tragedy, comedy, tragicomedy, or romance. For the purposes of this paper the history play will be defined as one which treats an event presumed to have actually taken place, which orders and interprets that event, and which tends to emphasize that event's public effects and implications rather than its effects upon the private lives of its principals.[35]

While the public and private lives of noted leaders, the usual subjects of history plays, are closely intertwined, the dramatist writing a tragedy or tragicomedy based upon history will contrive to make most of his scenes serve as revelations of his principals' moral, spiritual, and psychological lives, whereas the comic or the historical dramatist will be more likely to display his principals' lives in the social or political arenas. Thus, approached as drama, *Paradise Regained* could be treated as a tragicomedy; the story of God's Son in *Paradise Lost*, however, bears more resemblance to the history play because most of its scenes are public ones and convey little sense of the Son's inner life. Milton's Son as hero is closer to Hal than to Hamlet; though he has no Falstaff, his Hotspur is Satan. The incidents in which he figures most importantly—the War in Heaven, the Creation, his intercession on behalf of mankind —have historical implications.

Beneath the history play's sociopolitical surface, the underlying source of its dynamics is the tension between order as a manifestation of God's reason and disorder as a manifestation of human (or Satanic) passion. Milton's version of the history play in *Paradise Lost* in a sense reverses this formula: on its surface the plot of God's Son is metaphysical and moral but underneath it is political, having to do with power, its distribution and uses. It is inevitable then that the cosmic common-wealth of *Paradise Lost* bears some resemblance to the English common-wealth of Renaissance history plays. Monarchy becomes metaphor, and Milton, locked into his myth, must make the best of it. He does so with such success that it is doubtful whether the reader who happens to be unacquainted with the poet's life in politics would perceive much dif-ference between the political implications of *Paradise Lost* and those of most English history plays. In both the epic and these dramas the images of the ideal state and the ideal statesmen are expressed through the dramatization of disorder. Milton's Heaven is utopia, which makes its ruler the ultimate political being—and, inevitably, less attractive than the Son, who is the ultimate social being.

In the crown policy of Tudor England "rebellion, no matter what the cause, was the worst of all possible sins. A healthy society must ob-serve 'degree' and 'order' just as the heavens observed them, with every citizen keeping his proper place . . . in the social hierarchy" (Ribner, p. 157). Milton continuously reminds his audience that Satan's aims are political: "He trusted to have equall'd the most High" (I, 40). He rebels against what he fancies to be divine nepotism: "by Decree / Another now hath to himself ingross't / All Power" (V, 774–76). The Church of England's attitude toward political rebellion as revealed in its Book of Homilies is that rebels reenact this crime of Satan: "Let every soul submit himself unto the authority of the higher powers; for there is no power but of God; the powers that be, be ordained of God. Whosoever therefore resisteth the power, resisteth the ordinance of God: but they that resist shall receive unto themselves damnation"[36]

History plays like Shakespeare's then afforded their audiences not only delight but political instruction. A Renaissance apologist for the wicked stage might add that they afford moral instruction as well, for on the authority of Polybius, exposure to history was "the surest and indeed the only method of learning how to bear bravely the vicissitudes of fortune."[37] And it is the inculcation of such Stoicism in Adam that is the main purpose of the final act of Milton's history play, Michael's revelation of the future: "I am sent," the angel says, "To show thee what shall come in future days . . . thereby to learn / True patience . . . equally inur'd / By moderation either state to bear, / Prosperous or adverse" (XI, 356–64). Since Stoicism entails the acceptance of things as they are and the suppression of inward or outward rebellion, the pious fortitude Adam learns enables him to become both the ideal leader of the earthly community and the ideal subject of the heavenly community. Adam's faith, however, enables him to transcend classic Stoicism, to go beyond mere equanimity to tempered optimism. When he can rejoice, at the conclusion of Michael's narrative, at how God "all this good of evil shall produce, / And evil turn to good" (XII, 470–71), he expresses a theme of not only Milton's history play but of Renaissance history plays generally. The famous victories of Henry V, for example, resemble the famous victories of the Son of God in that they are not only martial and political triumphs but the victories of Truth, Righteousness, Reason, and Order. Without this kind of *felix culpa*, a serious play based upon history (for example, *Richard III, Samson Agonistes*) almost inevitably takes on the shape of tragedy.

Another good that emerges out of evil in history plays is their definition and exemplification of heroism.[38] Heroism can be hypothesized amid order (as in Book III) but realized only amid disorder (as in Book VI). That the heroics of Book VI stand in apparent contradiction to the narrator's snide dismissal of "Battle's feign'd," "tilting Furniture," and "gorgeous Knights" (IX, 31, 34, 37) is so plain that it is safe to assume it did not pass unrecognized by Milton himself. He may have rationalized his way out of the predicament by regarding Book VI as metaphorical only or as having Biblical authority, and thus not open to the same criticism as conventional fictive heroics; or he may have felt that the sequence was more necessary to his grand scheme than the maintenance of small-minded consistency. That need, Arnold Stein has argued, is basically a satiric one. He holds that the purpose of Book VI is to make Satan look ridiculous, which is why to some it reads like a comedy or even a farce.[39] To refute this thesis in detail would require more space than is available here, but it can be argued that a close examination of the structure of Book VI will show that it pivots upon its dramatic challenge (the threat to the Father and the Son), its crisis (the third-day appearance of the Son), and its anastrophe (the Son's victory). The main function of Book VI then is to present the Son as hero, to demonstrate and glorify his power.[40] Another function, it is true, is the denigration of Satan, but this is only one more instance of a process that has been continuous throughout the poem. For Milton the exaltation of the Son has to be a serious purpose, one for which farce—even epic farce —would be unsuitable.

Because of the physical limitations of stages, battle scenes in history plays tend to come off only indifferently well. In Book VI, however, Milton's technical resources are comparable to those of a film director, and he takes full advantage of them. His focus ranges from close-ups of individual combatants to wide-angle images of mass engagements, and by both methods the horror, more than the humor, of war is graphically communicated. Milton dramatizes war as hell within as well as without, and this hell in Heaven of Book VI effectively parallels the hell in Hell of Books I and II and the hell on Earth of Books IX through XII.

Book VI is by no means the only incident in *Paradise Lost* which calls the history play to mind. The first half of Book III, for example, is generally thought of as being theological in content and so it may strike the earthbound reader. But in Heaven reality and theology are identical. Thus, in heavenly terms at least, the discussion which takes place there is (as was suggested above) in essence political. The scene itself is one of the staples of the history play—the convening of the royal court to consider a threat to the kingdom. In the course of this scene the characters of the king and his various courtiers are defined and their relationships to each other established. The point at which the Son volunteers for his desperate mission resembles that moment in the history play when the protagonist announces his intention to act heroically.

In Book IV further heroic action seems promised but the promise is not kept: the confrontation between Satan and the angelic guard turns out to be only a preliminary skirmish—preliminary, that is, to the action of Book VI, which dramatically *follows* Book IV though it *precedes* Book IV in strict chronology. The flyting that takes place in IV and before the battles in VI, the individual combats in VI, its surprising tactics and new weapons—all are stock devices of the history play. Finally, Milton's dialogue in Books IV, V (Abdiel's scene), and VI has that mixture of the serious and the flippant, the sincere and the hypocritical, the dignified and the desperate, that characterizes the speeches of so many of Shakespeare's scenes of combat. It is an uneasy mixture but an authentic one, the emotion-ridden dialogue of men at war.

Whatever it is in real or historical time, in terms of reader-time or dramatic time (the sequence in which incidents are encountered as one reads through a book or views a play), the victory of the Son in Book

VI is the anastrophe of his plot in *Paradise Lost* and all that follows is denouement. The account of the Creation, for example, though remarkable for its beauties, is dramatic only as spectacle. It lacks a focal character, for the Son is only a vague presence. The latter's intercession on behalf of Adam and Eve in Book XI is the final scene in which he has both dialogue and action. His plot trails off into narrative. The vision Michael sets forth in Book XI could have had the effect of a play-within-a-play and occasionally does. But even these vestiges of the dramatic disappear when Michael shifts into direct narrative in Book XII. This lack of fully realized action and expressive dialogue among characters in confrontation helps to explain why Books XI and XII have often failed to please. (Shakespeare occasionally reverts to a prologue or chorus for his exposition, but his estimation of his audiences' attention span is more conservative and more accurate than Milton's.) Thus, in his handling of the plot of God's Son, Milton makes a more radical departure from his dramatic analog, the history play, than he does in the case of the tragedy of Satan or the tragicomedy of Adam and Eve. And therein lies his tactical error.

VIII

It would overextend this essay to explore further parallels between various scenes and incidents in *Paradise Lost* and some of the lesser genres of the theatre, for example, courtroom drama (the Grand Consult, Book II); morality play—domestic melodrama—sex farce (the confrontation between Satan and Sin and Death, Book II); burlesque (the Limbo of Vanities sequence, Book III); comedy of manners (the scene between God and Adam, Book VII). By way of conclusion then this essay will briefly take note of only one other important dramatic element of the poem and one that has not always been recognized as such—the monodrama of Milton's narrator.

Of all the dramatis personae of *Paradise Lost*, the narrator is the only one whose role remains the same in each of the poem's three main plots: like the narrator of Wilder's *Our Town* he serves as a kind of stage manager. He contributes expositions of character and situation, sets moods, and even explicates the moral dimensions of particular incidents. Thus, he also resembles the prologues, choruses and epilogues of Renaissance drama.[41] Like them he is less an objective announcer than he is a kind of actor-priest who interprets the ritual which has been or will be performed, and he ensures that his audience will not overlook that ritual's instructional aspects.

The involvement of Milton's narrator in the action he narrates is continually felt though seldom intrusive because his presence is deliberately dramatized. He is a well-developed character, not so much in the three dramas contained by the poem nor even in the framing epic itself, but in still another drama—one which might be entitled "The Famous Victory of the Epic Poet." The subject of this drama is the composing of *Paradise Lost* itself. Milton the poet takes the fact that he is in the process of writing *Paradise Lost* and transforms this fact into a fiction, a drama in which he is the sole character, the protagonist, and indeed the hero.

Because the distinction has not always been made and because it is of special importance here, it must be pointed out that Milton and the narrator of *Paradise Lost* are not identical. The latter is a created character, a persona for John Milton, and we know about him only what John Milton the poet wishes us to know and when he wishes us to know it. For example, that the narrator is blind is not definitely established by the blind poet until Book III (ll. 22 ff.); that the narrator is, like the poet, an oppressed person, is not established until Book VII, line 25. The point is that Milton develops the monodrama of his narrator organically and gradually, giving it the kind of careful treatment he gives to the other dramas of his poem. Readers of *Paradise Lost* do not need to know Milton's biography in order to respond to the poem's narrator. Enough information about him is supplied for them not only to know him and to believe in him *as a character*, but ultimately to empathize with him as a hero committed to a quest for "Things unattempted yet in Prose or Rhyme" (I, 16).

It is chiefly in the invocations that this miniature drama is acted out. It begins with the reference to "my advent'rous song" (I, 13), a phrase which does not mean that *Paradise Lost* will be a romance, but that the *writing* of such a poem is a kind of romance. Like many heroes of romance the narrator cannot accomplish his quest unaided, so he calls upon Urania to be his guide and companion. The unprecedented nature of his quest and his supposed lack of fitness for it are then proclaimed (I, 14–24). Finally the great goal which will crown the mission's success is revealed: "I may assert Eternal Providence, / And justify the ways of God to men" (I, 24–25). The narrator then gradually retires from center stage, and with the adverb "now" (I, 54) the action of Satan's tragedy gets under way. Although the narrator is never completely offstage, for the remainder of Books I and II he remains largely out of dramatic focus. He is, nonetheless, quite active, describing center stage action; providing exposition (for example, the catalog of devils); making transitions between speeches; commenting upon characters; and in general guiding audience response.

With Book III the narrator's monodrama emerges as a distinctive phase of the dramatic *Paradise Lost*. The Invocation to Light becomes a spotlight into whose beams the narrator himself now moves. His prayer is not only a plea for illumination but a dramatization of the desperate situation which justifies that plea. It is also a vivid description of the creative process itself, a process which for Milton entails the imaginative *enactment* of the fictive event he is composing. In the theater of the Miltonic imagination, the poet becomes a participant, an actor, in a drama of his own making. Like the man of faith engaging in the act of formal religious meditation (and, as Louis Martz has explained, like the metaphysical poet), his mind calls upon memory to recreate vividly and concretely a particular event into which he then mentally projects himself.[42] Through this "composition of place, this vicarious but felt experience," the poet Milton and the narrator meet and to some extent merge—though they can never merge completely.

In Books I and II Milton has written of Hell and through his narrator he explains that to have written of Hell was to *be* in Hell. Addressing Light, he announces: "Thee I revisit now with bolder wings, / Escap't the *Stygian* Pool, though long detain'd / In that obscure sojourn" (III, 13–15). The experience of literary creation and the created literary experience have in effect been one. Satan's flight "Through utter and through middle darkness" (III, 16) has also been the narrator-poet's flight, although these two are not one. The latter blesses light and is blessed by it—"thee I revisit safe, / And feel thy sovran vital Lamp" (III, 21–22)—while Satan curses Light and thus himself—"O Sun . . . how I hate thy beams" (IV, 37). Milton's counterpointing is as precise as his irony: the narrator-poet is blind, but with God's grace he will see with the mind's eye—"thou Celestial Light / Shine inward, and the mind through all her powers / Irradiate, there plant eyes" (III, 51–53). Satan has eyes, but cannot see; within him burns no light, only fire—"Which way I fly is Hell; myself am Hell" (IV, 75). The narrator-poet is irradiated by grace; sunk beyond grace, Satan is darkness visible. Thus, through the more than tour de force that is his invocation to Book III, Milton largely completes what he began in Books I and II—the creation of a persona who is a fully dramatic character. This role is delineated with remarkable virtuosity. The persona's uniqueness is evoked by the presentation of precise medical details about his blindness and by what approaches literary gossip—the fact that he composes at night, for example. Yet at the same time the archetype within is evoked through references to other blind men, great poets and prophets, and to the nightingale, symbol of the poet. This mythic distancing is followed by a bold attempt to close that distance again by eliciting empathy through the use of irony: we, his audience, are blessed with the "sight of vernal bloom, or Summer's Rose, / Or flocks, or herds, or human face divine" (III, 43–44), but he who will shortly recreate Eden before our mind's eye is surrounded by "cloud . . . and ever-during dark" (III, 45). Yet it is the blind narrator-poet who, paradoxically, will be the guide of us, the sighted, if Heaven grants that he "may see and tell / Of things invisible to mortal sight" (III, 54–55).

The invocation to Book III is the crisis of the narrator-poet's monodrama. From this point on until the invocation to Book VII he withdraws from stage center, content to follow the rising action of the three dramas within the epic. In this long sequence he performs the same functions of stage manager and chorus that he did earlier, but with the notable addition of his role as social critic and sexologist in the famous passage on marriage in Book IV (741–73). The invocation to Book VII serves to remind his audience once again that he is also a hero on an adventurous quest—"above th' *Olympian* hill I soar, / Above the flight of Pegasean wing" (VII, 3–4)—yet that proud boast is tempered by Christian humility—"Up led by thee / Into the Heav'n of Heav'ns I have presum'd, / An Earthly Guest" (VII, 12–14). The return of his story to earth and the fact that the midpoint of the poem has been reached provide an opportunity for reminding his audience that the narrator-poet and hero is also a mere mortal, beset by troubled times and troubling enemies, both of which imperil his artistic quest.

The final scene in which the narrator-poet is the principal is that which opens Book IX. Although at this point the narrative is moving inexorably towards the tragic crisis of the Adam-plot, this last main appearance of the narrator-poet can be regarded as the anastrophe of his own monodrama. The tension implicit in this moment has also been the source of the dynamics of the invocations. It is expressed in the question, will the Heavenly Muse continue to inspire an aged and oppressed poet so that he may obtain "answerable style" (IX, 20), the artistic power to pursue an "argument / Not less but more Heroic than the wrath / Of stern *Achilles*" (IX, 13–15) through to its completion? The question is answered only by the poem itself, for the narrator-poet makes but one more noticeable intrusion into the drama after this—to bewail the action of "much deceiv'd, much failing, hapless *Eve*" (IX, 404). Although he remains on stage to the end, acting out his self-defined role, he never again focuses upon himself as character. The catastrophe of Satan and the anastrophes of the Son and of Adam and Eve serve as the denouement of the narrator's own drama. This is yet another reason why Books X through XII have found less favor than their predecessors. The monodrama of the narrator-poet is one whose complications are of intrinsic interest, and its protagonist has been effectively developed. Furthermore, the invocations in which he figures so prominently are significant and artistically successful moments in the poem. That the lines which begin Book IX are *not* cast in the form of an invocation and that a portion of them are devoted to a gratuitously quarrelsome and even contradictory condemnation of traditional epic heroics diminishes their dramatic force. Even the poignancy of the narrator-poet's situation—his blindness, his advanced age, and his enemies—is dissipated when to these ills he querulously adds the discomfort of a "cold / Climate" (IX, 44–45).

Clearly Milton's strategy of dramatizing the act of writing an epic poem within the epic poem itself has created a problem for him. To provide his narrator-poet's quest with a highly dramatic anastrophe could be considered superfluous, for the finished poem is itself the demonstration of his triumph. Furthermore, such an addition could weaken the dramatic impact of the intertwined resolutions of his three other plots. Milton's refusal to compromise the conclusion of his poem can be regarded as an artistic mistake or as an act of heroic artistic restraint. In any case, the great poem has, against heavy odds, been completed, and this fact alone confirms the narrator-poet, among all the epic's dramatis personae, as being the one incontestable hero of *Paradise Lost*.

Franklin and Marshall College

NOTES

1. Douglas Bush, "The Isolation of the Renaissance Hero," in *Reason and the Imagination: Studies in the History of Ideas*, ed. J. A. Mazzeo (New York, 1962), p. 185.

2. Roger B. Wilkenfeld, "Theoretics or Polemics? Milton Criticism and the 'Dramatic Axiom,' " *PMLA*, LXXXII (1967), 515. This prohibition regarding the "dramatic *Paradise Lost*" has already been violated in two excellent essays which I encountered well after the main outlines of this paper had been set down—John T. Shawcross, "The Style and Genre of *Paradise Lost*," *New Essays on "Paradise Lost*," ed. Thomas Kranidas (Berkeley, 1969), pp. 15–33; and F. T. Prince, "Milton and the Theatrical Sublime," *Approaches to "Paradise Lost*," ed. C. A. Patrides (London, 1968). By "theatrical sublime" Prince means "Milton's use of organized and enacted spectacle . . . which leaves us with the impression of having witnessed a consciously complete *performance*, on the part of both the poet and his poem" (p. 55). Since my main concern here is with the form and structure of *Paradise Lost*, I have chosen not to substitute Prince's term *theatrical* for *dramatic*, even though I agree with him that Milton's epic is "not only more dramatic, but more 'theatrical' than [*Adam Unparadiz'd*] could have been," and that "Milton created what was in form a narrative, but in feeling and content a drama . . . for 'the Theatre of the Soul' " (p. 62).

3. Shawcross calls *Paradise Lost* a "dramatic epic," that is, a work which "is neither drama nor epic in an unrelenting classic definition. . . . By casting his work in epic form, while deriving it from drama and retaining dramatic sections, Milton acquired greater scope for the inexplicable and obtained answerable style" (p. 25).

4. William Riley Parker, *Milton: A Biography*, I (Oxford, 1968), pp. 81, 218.

5. Merritt Y. Hughes, ed., *John Milton: Complete Poems and Major Prose* (New York, 1957), pp. 175–76. Subsequent citations of Hughes's commentary and all quotations from Milton are taken from this edition and will be noted in my text. James Holly Hanford, *A Milton Handbook*, rev. ed. (New York, 1933), p. 45.

6. David Masson, *The Life of John Milton*, VI (Oxford, 1880), pp. 708–12.

7. A. J. A. Waldock, *"Paradise Lost" and Its Critics* (Cambridge, 1966), p. 145.

8. Lily B. Campbell, *Shakespeare's "Histories": Mirrors of Elizabethan Policy* (San Marino, Calif., 1947).

9. *Aristotle's Poetics*, trans. S. H. Butcher, introduction by Francis Fergusson (New York, 1961), p. 63. Subsequent citations of Aristotle and references to Fergusson's introduction will be identified in my text.

10. Quoted by Hughes, *Complete Poems and Major Prose*, p. 179.

11. In his Ph.D. dissertation, "The Elements of Aristotelian Tragedy in *Paradise Lost*" (Tulane University, 1967), J. Patrick Tyson argues that Milton's Satan-plot does indeed " 'depict the downfall of the utter villain,' " yet tragic "pity and fear for this downfall" are nonetheless elicited from the reader (p. 55). It is not necessary, however, to accept such a contradiction if it is recognized that unless Satan is viewed simplistically, his catastrophe has every potential for evoking the mixed emotions whose catharsis Aristotle saw as essential to the paradoxical pleasures of tragedy.

12. "I mean not here the prosody of a verse . . . but that sublime art which in Aristotle's *Poetics*, in Horace, and the Italian commentaries of Castelvetro, Tasso, Mazzoni, and others, teaches what the laws of a true epic poem, what of a dramatic, what of a lyric, what decorum is, which is the grand masterpiece to observe" (Hughes, *Complete Poems and Major Prose*, p. 637).

13. Alfred Harbage, *William Shakespeare: A Reader's Guide* (New York, 1963), p. 299.

14. Helen Gardner, "Milton's 'Satan' and the Theme of Damnation in Eliza-

bethan Tragedy," in *Milton: Modern Essays in Criticism*, ed. Arthur E. Barker (New York, 1965), pp. 205–17. Subsequent references to this essay—originally published in *English Studies*, N.S. 1 (1948), 46–66—will be identified in my text.

15. Northrop Frye, *Anatomy of Criticism: Four Essays* (Princeton, 1957); Richard B. Sewall, *The Vision of Tragedy* (New Haven, 1959); subsequent references to both of these works will be identified in my text.

16. For Shawcross "there is no hero in the poem although Adam and Eve constitute a protagonist as representatives of Mankind in the drama of life . . . that kind of protagonist one finds in a morality play" ("Style and Genre," p. 18). The point is well taken, though it goes somewhat too far. As characters Adam and Eve are too complex to be quite like the protagonists of the conventional morality play, and while they may not be adequate to serve as the dual hero of *Paradise Lost* as a whole, they are sufficient to perform that function for at least a part of the poem.

17. I have found that a similar conjecture was advanced more than fifty years ago by James Holly Hanford in "The Dramatic Element in *Paradise Lost*," *SP*, XIV (1917), 93:

> Milton's ultimate decision to adopt the epic form must have resulted from a perception that neither [the human nor the divine aspect of his story] could receive its full development within the contracted limits of tragedy. In epic there was ample scope for all. But the epic which should include them would differ radically from any that Milton had previously contemplated on typically heroic themes. For it would retain a core of drama inherited from the original conception and would be subject to the influence of the dramatic quite as much as of the epic tradition.

18. Gardner contends that Milton fails to make the Fall tragic. She contrasts Satan's rebellion with that of Adam and Eve, which she sees as only "a great symbolic act," different not only in kind from the usual tragic act but different in dramatic quality: "The plucking of the apple is not in itself imaginatively powerful. . . . The temptation and fall of Eve . . . lacks the shock of dramatic situation . . . [and] the scenes between Adam and Eve are deeply human, but they lack the terror and dreadful exaggeration of tragedy" ("Milton's 'Satan'" p. 209). But these are distinctions without differences. Even a symbolic act of rebellion is still an act and still rebellion, as both Antigone and Creon recognize and as Adam and Eve will to their sorrow learn.

19. *Sophocles' King Oedipus*, trans. William Butler Yeats, in *The Collected Plays of W. B. Yeats* (New York, 1935), p. 517.

20. Lawrence A Sasek, "The Drama of *Paradise Lost*, Books XI and XII," in *Milton: Modern Essays in Criticism*, ed. Arthur E. Barker, p. 355. This essay originally appeared in *Studies in English Renaissance Literature*, ed. W. F. McNeir, Louisiana State University Studies, Humanities Series, no. 12 (Baton Rouge, 1962).

21. See Frye, *Anatomy of Criticism*, pp. 163–64; Shawcross, "Style and Genre," p. 17; and Virginia R. Mollenkott, "Milton's Rejection of the Fortunate Fall," *Milton Quarterly*, VI, no. 1 (March 1972), 2.

22. Northrop Frye, *A Natural Perspective: The Development of Shakespearian Comedy and Romance* (New York, 1965), p. 73.

23. Quoted in Eugene M. Waith, *The Pattern of Tragicomedy in Beaumont and Fletcher* (New Haven, 1952), p. 44. Subsequent references to this work will be identified in my text.

24. Marvin T. Herrick, *Tragicomedy* (Urbana, Ill., 1962), p. 24. Some of the

subsequent references to this work, to which this section of my essay is heavily indebted, will be identified in my text.

25. Ibid. Milton may also have been aware of Hieronymous Ziegler's *Protoplastus* (1543), a "comitragedy" dramatizing Genesis from the creation of man to the expulsion from Eden (ibid., pp. 57–58). Plays like *Protoplastus* were mainly written by schoolmasters for the instruction of students; in them "the formal structure of classical comedy" was imposed upon "the loosely-made medieval drama, the mysteries, moralities, [and] farces," and the result was "a drama that was neither pure comedy nor pure tragedy, but a mixed form" (pp. 61–62).

26. Ibid., p. 175. At least six French tragicomedies appeared in the sixteenth century and others were to follow in the seventeenth century, the high point of English tragicomedy (p. 176).

27. Phillips is quoted in ibid., p. 317.

28. For a full discussion of this point, see John R. Knott, Jr., *Milton's Pastoral Vision: An Approach to "Paradise Lost"* (Chicago, 1971).

29. Quoted in Herrick, *Tragicomedy*, p. 283.

30. Robert Burton, *Anatomy of Melancholy*, ed. Floyd Dell and Paul Jordan-Smith (New York, 1927), p. 617 (III.1.1.1.).

31. In "The Balanced Structure of *Paradise Lost*," *SP*, LXII (1965), 696–718, John T. Shawcross argues that Milton's poem as a whole is in both its mode and its main effects a "divine comedy."

32. Irving Ribner, *The English History Play in the Age of Shakespeare* (Princeton, 1957), p. 22. Subsequent references to this work will be identified in my text.

33. John Hollander, *The Untuning of the Sky* (Princeton, 1961), p. 316.

34. Coleridge is quoted in Campbell, *Shakespeare's "Histories"* p. 9. E. M. W. Tillyard, *Shakespeare's History Plays* (New York, 1946), pp. 262–63, 320–22.

35. Campbell's conception of the history play, which suggests that tragedy deals with ethics and history plays with politics (*Shakespeare's Histories*, pp. 16–17), seems simplistic, whereas Ribner's definition seems rather limiting, especially for the Renaissance: "if a play appears to fulfill what we know the Elizabethans considered to be the legitimate purposes of history, and if it is drawn from a chronicle source which we know that at least a large part of the contemporary audience accepted as factual, we may call it a history play" (p. 27).

36. Quoted in Tillyard, *Shakespeare's History Plays*, p. 66.

37. Quoted in Ribner, *English History Play*, p. 25.

38. In his invocation to Book IX Milton claims that his poem will redefine true heroism, but it is possible to take the view that he failed to do so, for Adam is a protagonist but hardly a hero, Satan is a hero in only the traditional and therefore "false" sense, and the Son displays an uneasy mixture of "false" and "true" heroism—the former in his victory over Satan (Book VI), the latter in his Incarnation. Milton's decision to write *Paradise Regained* could suggest that he recognized that his redefinition of heroism in *Paradise Lost* had been insufficiently dramatized.

39. Arnold Stein, *Answerable Style: Essays on "Paradise Lost"* (Minneapolis, 1953), pp. 17–37.

40. In *The Moral Paradox of "Paradise Lost"* (The Hague and Paris, 1971), John E. Seaman charges that the Son is "as much a Homeric Warrior as Satan, and the epic paraphernalia thus seems incompatible with the passive virtues which are commonly thought to represent Milton's ideal of heroic virtue: endurance, other worldliness, humility, and suffering" (p. 19). Like the protagonists of romantic epics

the Son is "the untested young hero who must prove that his merit is equal to his great birthright" (p. 42).

41. In *Milton's Epic Voice* (Cambridge, Mass., 1967), pp. 14–16, Anne Davidson Ferry implies that the very existence of the narrator in *Paradise Lost* makes the poem "undramatic" to some extent, and thus not a work which lends itself very well to the kind of criticism exemplified by this essay and others referred to above. But no student of theater, I think, would accept her argument. From its beginnings to the present the theater has regularly made use of narrators and narrational devices of various kinds. Ferry also seems to overlook the extent to which the narrator and his story are dramatized by Milton.

42. Louis Martz, *The Poetry of Meditation* (New Haven, 1954) and *The Paradise Within* (New Haven, 1964).

MILTON AND THE EPIC EPITHALAMIUM

Gary M. McCown

In *Paradise Lost* Milton alludes to conventions of the classical epithalamium both to praise the wedding of Adam and Eve and, ironically, to adumbrate its desecration. Book IV shows his positive
imitation of images and plot from Catullus 61, undoubtedly the
most influential lyric epithalamium revived in the Renaissance. For
his epideictic style, however, Milton draws upon traditions of the
epic epithalamium whose topics of "proemium," "praise of the love
that rules the world," and "praise of the nuptial couple" he develops to elevate proper marital virtues. Comparison of Milton's
epithalamium for Adam and Eve with others composed by hexameral poets such as Du Bartas, Andrew Ramsey, and Jacob Cats
reveals how Milton's version follows Christian humanists' qualification of certain topics found in secular epithalamia. Especially significant is the humanists' dispraise of material splendor and their
substitution of a new topic glorifying the natural simplicity manifested in the Edenic setting for Adam and Eve's wedding. A final
qualification of the pagan genre is located in Michael's presentation of the fallen world in Book XI. Here Adam is shown a pagan
wedding in progress so that he may learn how it desecrates Christian marital virtues.

L IKE MANY poets John Milton aspired to be a playwright. Although
he never sought to write for the public theatre, over a period of
years he accumulated in the "Trinity Manuscript" some one hundred
subjects for a projected drama. Of all these Milton was most fascinated
by the Fall of Man since four versions are developed there. In the first
of these the characters "Heavenly Love" and "Chorus of Angels" appear
at the head of the dramatis personae immediately following "Michael."[1]
In an expansion Milton added "Hesperus the Evening Starre" while re-

taining "Heavenly Love" and the "Chorus of Angels." In a third draft
we find the action of the Fall clearly divided into five acts, the second of
which is devoted entirely to the wedding of Adam and Eve:

Act 2

Heavenly Love
Evening starre
Chorus sing the mariage song and describe Paradice.

In Milton's fourth plan both "Heavenly Love" and "Hesperus" are
omitted and drama yields to narrative as Gabriel merely relates to a
chorus of angels "what he knew of man as the creation of Eve with thire
love, and mariage." Clearly, then, an extended celebration of Adam and
Eve's wedding occupied a central place in the poet's plans for his un-
written drama.

What is not so clear, however, is the relation these early plans for
dramatizing a "mariage song" bear to the narrative poem Milton actually wrote. It seems evident to me that Milton thought of his "mariage
song" in terms of the classical epithalamium and that, moreover, he continued to do so when he came to convert his drama into epic. While some
critics have described one part of Book IV as an epithalamium, none has
revealed the extent to which this genre determines the subject matter,
imagery, and structure of that book.[2] Furthermore, no one has yet
pointed out how widely Milton uses epithalamic motifs for ironic purposes in other parts of *Paradise Lost*. This essay will examine how Milton
uses varieties of this genre, Christian as well as classical, epic as well as
lyric, to celebrate an ideal potential in every human marriage, an ideal
which he finds first manifest in the angelic "mariage song" presented
for the nuptials of Adam and Eve.

I

The tradition of the epithalamium which Milton inherited from
the Renaissance revival of classical learning was a rich one. Preeminent
among Latin models were, of course, the two lyric epithalamia of Catullus, the semidramatic 61 and the amoebaean 62. By the seventeenth century this tradition included (besides thousands of neo-Latin versions)
dainty pastoral contributions by members of the Pléiade, madrigal and
canzone adaptations by Italian poets such as Tasso and Marino, and
lyric versions by nearly all major poets of the English Renaissance: Sidney, Spenser, Donne, Jonson, Herrick, Carew, Marvell.[3]

Several of Milton's early poems reveal a thorough acquaintance with the conventions of this lyric tradition. In his Latin Elegy V on the advent of spring, Milton employs at least three motifs from the epithalamium: the invocation to Hymen as the god of marriage, the collocation of spring with marriage rites, and an hymeneal refrain interjected by wedding guests, "Marmoreas iuvenes clamant Hymenaee per urbes; / Litus io Hymen et cava saxa sonant."[4] "An Epitaph on the Marchioness of Winchester" also includes epithalamic elements. Referring to the Marchioness's marriage Milton writes:

> The Virgin choir for her request
> The God that sits at marriage feast;
> He at their invoking came
> But with a scarce-well-lighted flame.[5]

As Merritt Hughes points out, the "scarce-well-lighted flame" alludes probably to the wedding of Orpheus at the beginning of Ovid's tenth book of the *Metamorphoses* (one of the model epithalamia cited by Julius Caesar Scaliger in *Poetices libri septem*) where Hymen appears not with the "felix taeda" ("lucky torch") requisite for any auspicious marriage, but with a sputtering torch suggesting bad omens.[6] *L'Allegro* manifests Milton's acquaintance with the portrait of Hymen in Catullus 61 where the god is asked to come clad in the bride's marriage veil ("flammeum"):

> There let Hymen oft appear
> In Saffron robe, with Taper clear,
> And pomp, and feast, and revelry,
> With mask, and antique Pageantry.[7]

The pomp, feast, and revelry here reflect both Roman and English custom, but the "mask, and antique Pageantry" suggest that Milton has in mind the nuptial masques created for weddings at court by Jonson, Campion, and others.

Despite his "Trinity Manuscript" plans to dramatize an epithalamium, Milton found when he came to convert these plans into his epic that the time scheme he had adopted ruled out the possibility of presenting an epithalamium at the actual wedding of Adam and Eve. Since we are introduced to them at some unspecified time after their marriage, we can never be present at the occasion when such a poem would be appropriate. Eve indicates this time differential when she reminds Adam of their first encounter: "That day I oft remember, when from sleep / I first awaked" (IV, 349–50); and Adam's account of the nuptial day to Raphael in Book VIII (485–520) reveals that the event has taken place before we meet them in Book IV.

Nevertheless, Milton retained much of his original dramatic plan in order to present Adam and Eve to us *as if* celebrating their wedding day. This can be seen in the poet's adaptation of features from Catullus's two epithalamia, 61 and 62, the most influential lyric models for the Renaissance revival of the genre.[8] According to Catullus 62, it is Hesperus the evening star who is to be invoked as the appropriately auspicious deity for nuptials.[9] Such an address functioned also as part of the poem's structure: the entirety of Catullus 62 dramatizes the contrasting emotions of hope and anxiety voiced by choirs of young men and women awaiting the arrival of Hesperus. As the young men know, only the appearance of Hesperus allows them to begin the hymeneal song which will usher in the bride: "Vesper adest, iuvenes, consurgite: Vesper Olympo / expectata diu vix tandem lumina tollit. / surgere iam tempus" ("The evening is come, rise up, young men. Vesper from Olympus now at last is just raising his long-looked-for light. Now is it time to rise").

Hesperus, we recall, was a central figure in Milton's plans for dramatizing his epithalamium. In Book IV he suggests the time-marking function of the star by conflating repeated references to it with an echo of the familiar refrain "dies abit" ("the day departs") from Catullus 61 where it shows the groom's impatience. As Adam and Eve sit feasting, Milton presents his first stellar time-marker:

> the Sun
> Declin'd was hasting now with prone career
> To th' Ocean Isles, and in th' ascending Scale
> Of Heav'n the Stars that usher Evening rose.   (352–55)

After Satan has observed Adam and Eve discoursing, Milton reminds us once more of time's passage with the approach of evening:

> the setting Sun
> Slowly descended, and with right aspect
> Against the eastern Gate of Paradise
> Levell'd his ev'ning Rays.   (540–43)

Following Uriel's encounter with Gabriel, Milton refers again to passing time as measured by the heavenly bodies:

Now came still Ev'ning on, and Twilight gray
Had in her sober Livery all things clad;

. . . .

now glow'd the Firmament
With living Sapphires: *Hesperus* that led
The starry Host, rode brightest. (598–606)

Another epithalamic image Milton imitates from the lyric Catullan tradition is the *fax* or marriage torch which Hymen traditionally carried. The Cupid of "wedded Love," Milton writes, kindles in marriage "His constant Lamp, and waves his purple wings, / Reigns here and revels" (763–65). Since Spenser had referred to Hesperus as the "Fair child of beauty! glorious lamp of love!" Milton may imply here that the lamp is the evening star. A. W. Verity, however, cites a parallel action in Book XI "They light the *nuptial torch*" (590) and identifies the "constant lamp" with the classical *fax*.[10] In either case Milton draws upon epithalamic imagery explicitly to correlate his narrative version with classical tradition.

But Book IV of *Paradise Lost* recalls the tradition of the lyric epithalamium in more than its imitation of imagery. Peculiar to the epithalamium is the role its speaker performs: he is, at various times, spokesman for the god Hymen, director of ceremonies (or choragus), or representative of a community of well-wishers at the wedding. The speaker in Catullus 61, for example, uses language magically to make things happen: the god is beseeched to leave Mount Helicon to appear at the nuptials; the guests assembled before the bride's house are enjoined to start the procession; the matrons are ordered to prepare the nuptial couch and the groom is cued when to enter. By using such a language of decree, the poet-speaker translates the ideal potential of the event into actuality: he bids the matrons close the doors to the bridal chamber and, lo, they *are* closed. At the most climactic point of Book IV when he addresses the deity presiding over these nuptials "Hail wedded Love" and catalogues the god's powers, Milton assumes just this stance. Later as choragus he addresses Adam and Eve directly: "Sleep on, / Blest pair; and O yet happiest if ye seek / No happier state, and know to know no more" (773–75).

Much of the narrative structure too of Book IV is based upon Catullus's two lyrics, especially the semidramatic 61, although Milton, to be sure, may only allude to this structure obliquely rather than incorporate it directly. The first scene of 61 is laid before the house of the bride's father. The core of this part constitutes an encomium of Hymen as the marriage god: his invocation (1–35), an appeal to join in a hymn of praise (36–45), and the hymn itself (46–75). Since this part clearly corresponds with the climax of Book IV, the famous paean to "wedded Love" (750–75), I reserve discussion. The urban scene before the bride's house in Catullus 61 is, for Milton of course, inappropriate; but not so the more generalized one of 62. Here natural images (the evening star, the flower in a garden, the grapevine entwining a tree) provide the matter for extensive elaboration at the wedding feast. Poets of the Pléiade preferred a pastoral setting for their courtly epithalamia and so did many of their successors in England beginning with Sidney's epithalamium in the third eclogue of the *Arcadia*. When he introduces Adam and Eve as a nuptial pair amidst a lush "sylvan scene" and "happy rural seat" (205–87), Milton is writing, then, within the popular Renaissance tradition of a pastoral epithalamium, a tradition derived ultimately from Catullus 62.

Like Catullus before him, Milton praises his nuptial couple, mentioning their external beauty while emphasizing virtues of character such as fidelity (289–318). In 61 Catullus had cited the pliant vine entwining the tree as an instance of mutual love (102–05); Milton incorporates this pastoral motif into his epic encomium as an emblem of proper marital hierarchy: Eve's "golden tresses" wave "As the Vine curls her tendrils, which impli'd / Subjection" (304–11).[11]

After these static portraits of Adam and Eve, Milton increases the tempo of his narrative to show the couple walking hand in hand to "a fresh Fountain side" where they eat their evening dinner. In Catullus 61 the tempo accelerates in its second part as the bride is coaxed from her father's house to join the procession to the wedding feast at her husband's home. Throughout this lively *deductio domum* (117–51) emphasis falls on rapid movement, hilarity, and badinage in the form of risqué jokes about the couple's sexual obligations—the customary Fescennine jesting. There is no chorus of youths to observe the stately *deductio* of Milton's bridal pair, but the poet does introduce God and the Angels as an approving chorus of well-wishers at this point:

> So pass'd they naked on, nor shunn'd the sight
> Of God or Angel, for they thought no ill:
> So hand in hand they pass'd, the loveliest pair

That ever since in love's imbraces met,
Adam the goodliest man of men since born
His Sons, the fairest of her Daughters *Eve*.   (319–24)

Both Milton and Catullus present next the wedding feast. In Catullus the bridegroom reclines ("accubans") on his couch, lost in a revery of love. Milton too depicts his couple feasting Roman style ("side-long . . . they sat recline") on nectarine fruit as they enjoy "youthful dalliance . . . linkt in happy nuptial League" (325–355). Just as Junia and Manlius are besieged by hilarious shouts of "io Hymen Hymenaee!" so Adam and Eve are entertained at their feast amidst festivity appropriate to the pastoral setting: "About them frisking play'd / All Beasts of th' Earth, since wild, and of all chase / In Wood or Wilderness, Forest or Den" (340–42). The "Sporting" lion "ramp'd" and "Dandl'd the Kid"; large animals "Gamboll'd before them," and the "unwieldy Elephant / To make them mirth us'd all his might, and wreath'd / His Lithe Proboscis." The comic diction here, especially the verbs, suggests Milton's search for an alternate, more innocent humor to replace the ribald Fescennine joking required by epithalamic tradition.

After the feast in Catullus, Junia enters the *thalamus* or bridal chamber followed by her husband. Here begins the third part of the poem (177–231) including the preparation of the chamber, the poet-priest's advice to the married couple (*allocutio sponsalis*), and his prayers for long happiness and illustrious progeny. Following Satan's interruptive and invidious comments from the periphery of the feast, Milton depicts Adam and Eve moving together (not separately as in Catullus) toward their "Blissful Bower." They offer before retiring an evening prayer (724–35) whose recollection of several psalms has long been noted. What has not been pointed out, however, is the inclusion of several epithalamic topics. The "gift of sleep," for example, is a topic frequently included in Renaissance epithalamia. In England Spenser, Donne, and Herrick write particularly noteworthy versions.[12] More importantly, the conclusion of this mutually offered prayer is a version of the final topic in all classical epithalamia—the request for children:

But thou hast promis'd from us two a Race
To fill the Earth, who shall with us extol
Thy goodness infinite, both when we wake,
And when we seek, as now, thy gift of sleep.   (732–35)

Taken in conjunction with the central phrase "our mutual help / And mutual love," the passage demonstrates Milton's conscious imitation of epithalamic convention.

At this climactic moment in his narrative Milton presents his justly famous "Hail wedded Love." These verses resemble in a number of ways the opening section of Catullus 61. Both constitute a hymn to the Deity since both employ the second person vocative of address and the repetitive syntax characterizing liturgy. In praising the god, moreover, both hymns enumerate his specific offices and powers. Catullus invokes Hymen by celebrating his genealogy and titles: "Collis o Heliconii / cultor, Uraniae genus" ("O dweller on Mount Helicon, Urania's son"). Milton invokes and specifies his marriage god by the title "wedded Love." Catullus validates Hymen's authority by distinguishing proper from improper love: Hymen is "dux bonae Veneris, boni / coniugator amoris" ("the herald of chaste Venus, the coupler of honest love") and condones no adultery. Milton validates his deity in a series of appositives: "mysterious Law, true source / Of human offspring, sole propriety / In Paradise of all things common else" (750–52). Catullus catalogues at length Hymen's powers: he is the object of old men's prayers for their children; he receives the loosened cestons of young girls; he holds the power of handing over marriageable girls to husbands; he legitimizes children. Milton too enumerates the beneficent powers of his "wedded Love":

> By thee adulterous lust was driv'n from men
> Among the bestial herds to range, by thee
> Founded in Reason, Loyal, Just, and Pure,
> Relations dear, and all the Charities
> Of Father, Son, and Brother first were known.   (753–57)

Catullus evokes the aura of religious liturgy by repeating words and syntactical constructions: "huc / huc veni, niveo gerens / luteum pede soccum" ("hither, come hither, wearing on your snow-white foot the yellow shoe"). Milton's invocation depends likewise upon the rhetoric of liturgy: "By thee adulterous lust was driv'n . . . by thee . . . all the Charities . . . were known"; or, "here Love his golden shafts imploys, here lights / His constant Lamp, and waves his purple wings, / Reigns here and revels."

For Milton the marriage god is obviously less the anthropomorphic personality he is in Catullus; rather, he is a compendium of moral principles drawn from Christian thought. It seems clear, nevertheless, that

Milton is here imitating an important convention of the lyric epithalamium, the hymn to Hymen. Not only does he recall rhetorical and topical conventions of the hymn, he places it precisely where an epithalamium in antiquity was presented: following the feast and before the bedding of the nuptial pair. It is sung literally *at* the nuptial chamber, *epi thalamou,* or, as George Puttenham puts it in his *Arte of English Poesie,* "at the chambre dore."[13]

II

While Milton does base his hymn on Catullus, it is equally clear that his "Hail wedded Love" is written in a different, more elevated key. To understand why Milton goes beyond the lyric "Catullian formula" here we need to recognize how the epithalamium had been revamped by poets and rhetoricians subsequent to Catullus. By the second and third centuries A.D. lyric epithalamia yielded their popularity to epic versions. For poets such as Statius, Claudian, or Sidonius the genre served as a useful vehicle for flattering their imperial patrons. The skeletal plot for all their epic epithalamia is standard. The bridegroom and/ or the bride-to-be groan from wounds which Cupid has laughingly inflicted. In an idyllic garden setting (usually Venus's bower) Venus and Cupid relate the history of the love affair lauding throughout the beauty and merits of the imperial pair. Upon Cupid's request Venus and her entourage wing their way over the sea to persuade the bride to yield to her suitor. Numbers of gods bearing gifts attend their wedding and the poem closes with acclaim for the union.[14]

Although the plot is simple, the epideictic style developed for such poems is not. In his *Peri Epideiktikon,* the rhetorician Menander divided the poem into four parts, each of which was to be expanded using devices of heightening such as *ekphrasis.* The purpose of the *proemium* (προοίμιον) was to state the specific occasion for the nuptial poem as ornately as possible. The *peri gamou* (περὶ γάμου) "about marriage," glorified the love which rules the world by celebrating marriages of the elements which brought order out of chaos. The third topic, *encomium tôn gamountôn* (ἐγκώμιον τῶν γαμούντων), "praise of the nuptial couple," was, of course, the central one and tended to absorb the others. Finally came the *ekphrasis tês numphês* (ἔκφρασις τῆς νύμφης), a description of the actual wedding festivities, the topic most closely drawn from the lyric tradition.[15]

The continuing importance of this style for Renaissance poets is manifest in an encyclopedic essay on the epithalamium which Scaliger published in his influential *Poetices libri septem*. His catalogue of epithalamic topics (largely lifted from classical rhetoricians) demonstrates how central to poetic practice had become the epideictic style. During the Renaissance, as O. B. Hardison, Jr., points out, it served a "theory of praise" designed to promote virtue by celebrating the good and castigating the bad.[16] From first to last Scaliger insists that the aim of all occasional poetry is praise—*laus*. The epithalamium should praise, first of all, "the renown of the groom's songs, sports, arms, and all the deeds done for the sake of his bride whose good heart you allude to by concealed hints and hidden intimations rather than acknowledging openly." Secondly, "praises must be presented for both of them on the basis of their country and race, mentioning their sharpness of intellect and excellency of body." In the third part of the poem the poet must prophesy good omens for the wedding while in the fourth he must dramatize "wantonness and dalliance." In the fifth part he should promise offspring and in the last part exhort all except the bridal couple to sleep. Incidentally, the poet should praise the bridal couch, examples of illustrious marriages of the gods, and how, from the nuptials of heaven and earth, all species proceeded. He concludes his meandering catalogue with a list of classical models. These include, besides the lyric examples of Catullus, epic versions by Musaeus, Ovid, Statius, and Claudian.[17]

Since its scope and epideictic style was obviously more "heroic," it was this latter tradition, the epic, which came to be regarded in Renaissance Europe as the most appropriate for celebrating royal weddings. With the exception of a few genuine masterpieces such as the stirring epithalamium Buchanan contributed for the marriage of Mary Queen of Scots to Francis II, the typical epic epithalamium composed for state occasions, whether in neo-Latin, French, or English, was bombastically overwritten and shamelessly derivative.[18] More interesting are the epic versions written in the late sixteenth century and seventeenth century by those zealous poets whose intention was to reclaim the province of poetry for the Christian religion.[19] These fervent humanists may have taken their cue from Patristic interpretation of the Song of Songs and Psalm 45 as allegorized epithalamia, or they may have discovered their model in Avitus's depiction of the nuptials of Adam and Eve in Book I of *Poematum de Mosaicae historiae gestis libri quinque*.[20] Whatever

their source, poets such as Du Bartas, Jacob Cats, and Andrew Ramsey
began to appropriate epithalamic material for their epic poems on the
Creation and the prelapsarian life of Adam and Eve.

The humanist and Protestant sympathies of these poets were consonant with Milton's own; his admiration for their works is well documented.[21] Since, I submit, Milton's own version of an epithalamium in
Paradise Lost depends significantly upon this Christian tradition, we
would do well to glance at the content and emphasis of a representative
hexameral epithalamium: Book II, "De beata hominis conditione," of
Andrew Ramsey's *Poemata Sacra*.[22]

Although Ramsey's epithalamium for Adam and Eve is written in
heroic hexameters, it eschews the mythological fiction of a love match
perpetrated by Cupid and elaborates, instead, the four topics recom-
mended in rhetorical theory. Ramsey begins his *proemium* by invoking
God as the priest ("pronubus") at these joyful nuptials. He explains the
occasion of his epithalamium by tracing the history of Eve's creation
from Adam's side (an act which symbolizes the closeness of their union).
When God himself carefully places the nuptial bed in Eden, all Nature
gives its approval through the voice of a fiery bird ("flammeus Ales")
who chants a sacred lyric praising marriage. This long lyric constitutes
the second epideictic topic, *peri gamou*. Like Catullus, Ramsey reaffirms
the value of marriage by pointing out how men would enjoy no chaste
kisses nor the gift of children without it. Society benefits from marriage
too for continuing repopulation encourages trade. In the passage beginning "Commoda quanta ferent Hominum Connubia genti!" ("How
many satisfactions do the marriages of men bring to the race!"), however,
Ramsey gives a decidedly Puritan emphasis to the benefits of marriage:
"In commune bonum, communia vota, precesque, / Jungant, et cura
communi pignora tollant" ("May they be joined for a common good,
by common vows and prayers, and may they raise children under a
mutual discipline"). Resounding throughout this *peri gamou* is Ramsey's Christian transformation of Catullus's refrain: "Adsis! O Hymenaee Trias! Hymen Hymenaee!" ("Be present, o Triune Hymen! Hymen
Hymenaee!").

The phoenix then turns from his encomium of marriage to address
directly the nuptial pair in an *allocutio sponsalis* commending passionate love and the perdurability of the marriage bond. Eve is to recognize
the paternal authority of her husband but this adjuration is balanced

by a reemphasis on "Mutua cura domus, res mutua" ("mutual household responsibilities, property in common"). Ramsey concludes his advice to the couple with a praise of God as "Connubii, Genitor!" ("Creator of marriage!") and a hope that the couple will fill heaven with souls to replace those fallen through wickedness into Hades. At this point the phoenix yields to an entire chorus of birds who raise their voices to heaven praising the kingly couple in an extended *encomium tôn gamountôn*. All the rhetorical devices of the epideictic style such as the outdoing conceit and comparisons with the pantheon from antiquity are called upon to render praise to these sovereigns of creation. The epithalamium closes with cries of good wishes to these first and most perfect lovers, wishes only slightly qualified by allusions to those ills— bad weather, sickness, death—which not yet ("nondum") have entered the world.

III

As Milton pondered how to render his earlier dramatic plans into narrative form, the epic epithalamium as purified by Christian humanist poets like Ramsey must have seemed to him an attractive option. Like the hexameral poets he wished to raise the status of matrimony so long obscured by the church's preference for virginity; like rhetoricians urging an epideictic style for the epithalamium, he too saw the subject matter of this genre as the marriages of princes or other such grand persons requiring heroic poetry of an appropriate magnitude.[23] Indeed, as I shall show, *Paradise Lost* depends heavily upon a number of topics from the epic tradition, specifically the *encomium tôn gamountôn*, Venus's bower, and the *peri gamou*.

When we first see Adam and Eve in Book IV we see them through the heightened rhetoric of an epideictic *encomium tôn gamountôn*:

> Two of far nobler shape erect and tall,
> Godlike erect, with native Honor clad
> In naked Majesty seem'd Lords of all,
> And worthy seem'd, for in thir looks Divine
> The image of thir glorious Maker shone,
> Truth, Wisdom, Sanctitude severe and pure,
> Severe, but in true filial freedom plac't;
> Whence true authority in men; though both
> Not equal, as thir sex not equal seem'd;
> For contemplation hee and valor form'd,

> For softness shee and sweet attractive Grace,
> He for God only, shee for God in him:
> His fair large Front and Eye sublime declar'd
> Absolute rule; and Hyacinthine Locks
> Round from his parted forelock manly hung
> Clust'ring, but not beneath his shoulders broad:
> Shee as a veil down to the slender waist
> Her unadorned golden tresses wore
> Dishevell'd, but in wanton ringlets wav'd
> As the Vine curls her tendrils, which impli'd
> Subjection, but requir'd with gentle sway,
> And by her yielded, by him best receiv'd,
> Yielded with coy submission, modest pride,
> And sweet reluctant amorous delay.   (288–311)

Scaliger had insisted that "praises must be presented for both [the bride and bridegroom] on the basis of their country and race, mentioning their sharpness of intellect [*notatio*] and excellency of body [*effictio*]." Like all hexameral poets Milton cannot celebrate country and race. Caspar Barlaeus (or van Baerle) who translated with epic additions the *Gront-Houwelick* of his fellow Dutch humanist, Jacob Cats, as *Paradisus, sive Nuptiae primorum parentum, Adami et Evae,* however, provides an ingenious version of the topic which Milton can follow.[24] The marriage of Adam and Eve in Barlaeus takes precedence over any subsequent story ("fabula") about wanton Venus since God himself ordained the nuptials from heaven ("summo placuere Jovi, juratque coelo / Foedera"). In *Paradise Lost*, Milton suggests such a pedigree by noting how "in thir looks Divine / The image of thir glorious Maker shone." In the *notatio* and *effictio* of this *encomium* every adjective, every noun works to ennoble the pair: they are of "far nobler shape," "Godlike erect," "looks Divine." Even Satan from the sidelines must join in the praise of these "high advanc't / Creatures of other mould, . . . to heav'nly Spirits bright / Little inferior" (359–62). Throughout this passage the private virtues of "Simplicity and spotless innocence" consonant with the idealized pastoral world of Eden replace the customary public virtues of country and race.

Because Milton intends his epic to teach as well as to delight, he insists, like Ramsey and Barlaeus before him, upon the worthiness of Adam and Eve as models for emulation. Although most secular epithalamia stressed the "Equality of Persons" (as Donne does for the Earl of Somerset), Milton recurs to the more purely Christian concept of marital hierarchy by insisting that Adam and Eve are "Not equal." Like Ramsey's Eve, Milton's is the heart of man ("For softness shee and sweet attractive Grace"), while Adam remains the head of the conjugal relationship ("His fair large Front and Eye sublime declar'd / Absolute rule").

Scaliger's central topic had been praise of the desires of the bridal couple, their wantonness and dalliance ("lascivia lususque"). As Adam and Eve watch the animals frisking about, Milton describes their dalliance:

> Nor gentle purpose, nor endearing smiles
> Wanted, nor youthful dalliance as beseems
> Fair couple, linkt in happy nuptial League,
> Alone as they. (337–40)

Later he expands this topic:

> So spake our general Mother, and with eyes
> Of conjugal attraction unreprov'd,
> And meek surrender, half imbracing lean'd
> On our first Father, half her swelling Breast
> Naked met his under the flowing Gold
> Of her loose tresses hid: hee in delight
> Both of her Beauty and submissive Charms
> Smil'd with superior Love, as *Jupiter*
> On *Juno* smiles, when he impregns the Clouds
> That shed *May* Flowers; and press'd her Matron lip
> With kisses pure. (492–502)

But the emphasis here is on something other than wantonness. Eve's hair is not merely yellow; it is like "flowing Gold," hence of great worth and value. Adam does not merely smile, he smiles like Jupiter, an epideictic comparison which justifies Milton's estimation of him as a sovereign. Milton's epic similes do not merely describe, then; they compliment and evaluate. In presenting Adam and Eve to us, Milton succeeds in heroicizing them into epic exemplars of marital virtue.

Scaliger's remarks on the nuptial consummation grow out of the conclusion to Catullus 61 where the couple's final embrace is alluded to. These lines mention the propriety of the husband's feelings ("bonum amorem"), and bid the couple *ludite ut lubet* ("play as it pleases you"). Secular neo-Latin and Renaissance vernacular epithalamia of the seventeenth century grew increasingly bold in depicting what Secundus had called the "hora suavicula" ("the sweet hour"). While Milton frankly alludes to the consummation of nuptials, he qualifies it with an epic dignity and reticence absent from more explicit descriptions in Continental baroque and Cavalier versions:

> into thir inmost bower
> Handed they went; and eas'd the putting off
> These troublesome disguises which wee wear,
> Straight side by side were laid, nor turn'd I ween
> *Adam* from his fair Spouse, nor *Eve* the Rites
> Mysterious of connubial Love refus'd.   (738–43)

Like Barlaeus whose Adam glows with ardor for Eve but "non lasciva tamen" ("but not wantonly"), Milton is content to suggest the physical encounter in a delicately negative Vergilian syntax. Although such delicacy has annoyed certain modern readers, the poet's rendition shows him, in fact, well within the tradition of the hexameral epithalamium. Barlaeus concludes his epithalamium, for example, with Night as the sole witness to the couple's love-making: "Nox pronuba donec / Stellantes depicta sinus, tangensque iacentes, / Omina perpetuo genitalia foedere [*sic*] sanxit" ("While Night as matron of honor, her bosom painted with stars, touching the reclining lovers, has sanctified with an eternal bond their solemn union"). Milton's reticence in depicting the sexual act, then, affirms the Christian humanists' conception of it as a private and natural rather than a public or ceremonial occasion.

Some modern scholars, indeed, have assumed that Eve's "coy submission" and "reluctant amorous delay" reveal the poet's uncertainty about the propriety of the sexual act itself.[25] Such doubts vanish when we read this passage in the light of other Christian versions and recognize it as the epithalamic convention that it is. As Scaliger explains, the bride must always be depicted as a modest virgin so that her yielding can suggest no sexual lightness; it is to be excused by commemorating the bridegroom's virtues. When Milton writes that Eve "Yielded with coy submission, modest pride, / And sweet reluctant amorous delay," he is following this tradition. The last phrase, in fact, recalls precisely the feminine delay which Catullus dramatizes in 61: "tardet ingenuus pudor" ("noble modesty slows her steps"). Milton's Eve is not playing the vamp, then, but behaving strictly according to the epithalamic convention of bridely *pudor*.

Prominent in the tradition of the epic epithalamium was the topic of vernal nature's congratulation. In secular versions this usually took

place within Venus's bower, the prototype for which, as A. Bartlett
Giamatti has pointed out, is the goddess's evocative bower in Claudian's
epithalamium for the emperor Honorius.[26] Milton imitates this topic
in Book VIII when Adam describes his first meeting with Eve:

> the Earth
> Gave sign of gratulation, and each Hill;
> Joyous the Birds; fresh Gales and gentle Airs
> Whisper'd it to the Woods, and from thir wings
> Flung Rose, flung Odors from the spicy Shrub,
> Disporting, til the amorous Bird of Night
> Sung Spousal.   (513–19)[27]

This topic was favored by hexameral poets since it allowed them to
expatiate in the popular pastoral mode. In Ramsey's version the rivers
of Paradise echo watery applause ("liquido . . . plausu") as the fields
laugh. After "Mighty Pan" has married the couple in a version by Nathaniel Baxter,

> *Tellus* and *Flora* kep't it holy-day,
> Attired in their moste gorgeous array.
> And all the Orbs and Spheres gave looking on,
> When Princely *Adam* tooke his Paragon.[28]

By placing his wedding within the context of congratulatory nature,
Milton makes of it, as Thomas Greene remarks, a universal and "cosmic
experience, an event so marvellous that nature has to demonstrate its
complicity, but also an event somehow of a piece with the loveliest acts
of nature."[29]

Another related epithalamic topic was praise of the nuptial couch.
Extrapolating from Catullus's fragment in 61 apostrophizing the bridal
couch ("o cubile"), Scaliger had urged poets to praise the bed on which
sacred rites were to be consummated. For Christian poets the tasteless-
ness to which treatment of this topic led in baroque poets like Marino
confirmed their belief in a fall into luxuriance from Eden's originally
innocent nuptial bower. In Barlaeus's version God insists that the love
of Eden's nuptial couch is chaste: "legesque maritis / Fixit, et innocuo
scripsit sua iura cubili" ("He established laws for the bridal couple and
wrote them on the guiltless bed"). Milton happily conflates praise of the
classical nuptial couch with a depaganized paradisiacal garden to emphasize innocent sexuality rather than wanton luxury. Like Ramsey,

Barlaeus, and Du Bartas before him, he banishes from his bower any
assistance from Venus or Cupid in order to demonstrate the consonance
of human sexuality with nature's unpolluted fertility.

> it was a place
> Chos'n by the sovran Planter, when he fram'd
> All things to man's delightful use; the roof
> Of thickest covert was inwoven shade
>
> .   .   .   .
>
> each beauteous flow'r,
> *Iris* all hues, Roses, and Jessamin
> Rear'd high thir flourisht heads between, and wrought
> Mosaic;
>
> .   .   .   .
>
> Here in close recess
> With Flowers, Garlands, and sweet-smelling Herbs
> Espoused *Eve* deckt first her Nuptial Bed.   (690–710)

Despite this lush *ekphrasis*, Milton does not conclude his epithalamium here. Rather, he follows the precedent of hexameral poets like
Barlaeus whose *Paradisus* ends with a grand version of "Laudate Dom-
inum" directed to "Magne Deus, sine patre pater, sine fine perennis"
("Great God, fatherless Father, endless Eternal").

> Thou also mad'st the Night,
> Maker Omnipotent, and thou the Day,
> Which we in our appointed work imploy'd
> Have finisht happy in our mutual help
> And mutual love, the Crown of all our bliss
> Ordain'd by thee.   (724–29)

As Milton had written in the *De Doctrina*, "the prime end and form of
marriage, as almost all acknowledge, is not the nuptial bed, but conjugal
love, and mutual assistance through life." [30] As manifested by the reiterated "mutual help . . . mutual love," stressing rewards not punishments,
Milton stands ideologically with other Christian humanist poets and
thinkers like Erasmus and Cats who sought to free marriage from the
contempt heaped on it during the medieval period.

For this reason, Milton's version of the *peri gamou*, "Hail wedded
Love," comes at the climactic point of his epic treatment of the epithalamium. In this he resembles Du Bartas whose "Epithalamie, or Wedding

Song" clearly constitutes a *peri gamou*, a praise of the Author of marital
love:

> Source of all ioyes! sweet Hee-Shee-Coupled-One
> Thy Sacred Birth I never thinke upon,
> But (ravisht) I admire how God did then
> Make Two of One, and One of Two againe.[31]

Milton too praises not the individual participants in this union but
"mysterious Law, true source / Of human offspring," stressing its preeminence as a type of divine love by virtue of its establishment in Eden
prior to the Fall.

His *peri gamou* is divided, as we might expect in an epideictic epithalamium, between praise (*laus*) of proper love and dispraise (*vitupera-
tio*) directed against perversions of it.

> Far be it, that I should write thee sin or blame,
> Or think thee unbefitting holiest place,
> Perpetual Fountain of Domestic sweets,
> Whose bed is undefil'd and chaste pronounc't,
> Present, or past, as Saints and Patriarchs us'd.   (758–62)

By reminding his readers in the last phrase that many of the church
fathers were married men, Milton refutes attacks made against matrimony by the Council of Trent and other Counter-Reformation organs.
Like Barlaeus before him, he realized that the weight of Patristic writing
was against him here, especially as it concerned praising the marriage of
Adam and Eve. Nowhere among the hexameral writings of Basil the
Great, Gregory of Nyssa, or Ambrose do the church fathers celebrate
this marriage.[32] This may suggest why Renaissance hexameral poets felt
obliged to return to classical models of the epithalamium to find support
for their panegyrics on Adam and Eve. In the light of earlier hostility
compounded by the extreme antifeminism of the medieval period,
Milton's praise of the marriage bed as "undefil'd and chaste pronounc't,
/ Present, or past," must be recognized as part of the radical revision of
orthodox Christianity to which humanist poets directed themselves.

In the second section of his *peri gamou*, Milton turns from the more
abstract "Law" to praise its manifestation on earth: "Here Love his
golden shafts imploys, here lights / His constant Lamp, and waves his
purple wings, / Reigns here and revels" (763–65). It may be surprising

to find Cupid here, even a chastened one, since few other hexameral poets had assigned him any positive role. It is true that Du Bartas has him play a major role in the epithalamium for Solomon in *Devine Weekes* [*sic*], but the French poet does so ironically since he prefaces his narrative with a warning to the king to avoid the "strange Bone, a barbarous Rib, a Peece / Impoysoned all with Memphian Leprosies."[33] In his earlier epithalamium for the marriage of Adam and Eve which Sylvester labels "The commodities of Mariage," Du Bartas had distinguished proper love from earthly lust by castigating Cupid:

> By thee, we quench the wilde and wanton Fiers,
> That in our Soule the *Paphian* shot inspires:
> And taught (by thee) a Love more firme and fitter
> We finde the Mel more sweet, the Gall lesse bitter.[34]

Milton too distinguishes Love's proper revels from false imitations in a polemic directed against all forms of sex which do not culminate in marriage:

>   not in the bought smile
> Of Harlots, loveless, joyless, unindear'd,
> Casual fruition, nor in Court Amours,
> Mixt Dance, or wanton Mask, or Midnight Ball,
> Or Serenate, which the starv'd Lover sings
> To his proud fair, best quitted with disdain.
> These lull'd by Nightingales imbracing slept,
> And on thir naked limbs the flow'ry roof
> Show'r'd Roses, which the Morn repair'd.   (765–72)

This passage exemplifies what undoubtedly is the most important Christian topic for the humanist hexameral epithalamium. In traditional secular epic versions, the illustriousness of the bridal pair is manifested by troops of pagan gods who come to honor them with gorgeous gifts. The arrival of the gods at the wedding of Peleus and Thetis in Catullus 64 provides the *locus classicus* for such a procession. Aware of the traditional *ekphrasis* elaborating the material splendor of nuptials, Barlaeus inverts the topic to insist upon superiority of natural gifts:

> Scena thori iam prima patet, Deus autor amandi est,
> Terra locus, sunt astra faces, spectator Olympus,
> Nos testes, dos orbis, amor foecundus amoris,
> Lectus ager, fructus epulae, spes una nepotes.

(Now the first scene of the marriage couch opens;
  God is the author of the loving,
Earth the setting, the stars the lighting, Heaven the
  spectator,
We the witnesses, the world the dowry, love begets love,
The field is the marriage couch, the fruits of the field
  the banquet, and the one hope—posterity.)

Barlaeus replaces the sumptuous feast with simple fruit, "pompous Hymen" and a host of quickly disappearing gods with the eternal God, and
the fastidiously prepared couch with the good earth itself. In this epi-
grammatic *oppositio*, everything that man has made through his artifice
is weighed and found wanting when compared with what God has first
made. Much of the epideictic heightening of secular occasional epithalamia is thus undercut by the moral virtues implicit in the pastoral
mode. In a prose dialogue which Barlaeus translates, Cats had described
similarly the simple virtues of the earth's first wedding:

Hic sine pompa, sine fastuoso apparatu confecta omnis et peracta res est. Nisi
illud ad celebritatem maxime faciat, tanto negocio adfuisse Angelicas mentes,
adspectasse naturam omnem humani generis primos parentes, et applausisse
novis imperatoribus quicquid in aere volatilium, in aquis piscium, in terris
ceterorum animalium fuit.

(Here, without fanfare, without pomp, all things are made ready and completed. If God had not taken particular care with this celebration, then all the
angelic beings would have been present for such an event, all nature would
have come as spectators to observe the first parents of the human race, and
whatever birds were in the air, whatever fish were in the waters, or whatever
animals were on the earth would have come to applaud their new rulers.)

Although at the wedding in Cana there had been wine-induced hilarity,
"Hic in sobrietatis et temperantiae sede Paradiso, sine Libero incaluit
sanctissima Venus" ("Here in the sober and temperate seat of Paradise
most holy Venus grew hot without a need for Bacchus").[35]

    Milton's version of Cats's *oppositio* indicts an entire spectrum of
sexual behavior which he finds besmirching the chastity of Edenic love:
prostitution or "Casual fruition," courtly nonplatonic Platonism of the
variety Queen Henrietta Maria had popularized, and, finally, the sterile
literary Petrarchism of the "starv'd Lover" whose desire remained forever unsatisfied. Such an attack is not found, to be sure, in most secular
epithalamia. It is thoroughly in line, as we have seen, with the humanist
hexameral tradition which used *oppositio* to contrast fallen love with

the austere virtues of simplicity, chastity, temperance, and sobriety which it located in Adam's nuptial bower.

IV

It is clear, then, that Milton has drawn not only upon the lyric tradition of Catullus but upon the epic tradition as well, especially as it was adapted by Christian humanist poets writing on hexameral subjects. Moreover, in imitating such models he has adhered to an epideictic poetic in which praise of the good and castigation of evil constitutes the goal of *imitatio*. Some important peculiarities in Milton's version of the epic epithalamium, however, remain to be considered. Where, for instance, are comparisons between the bridal pair and the illustrious marriages of the antique gods which Scaliger recommends?

They are here, but their effect is not so much complimentary as sadly ironic:

> In shadier Bower
> More sacred and sequester'd, though but feign'd,
> *Pan* or *Silvanus* never slept, nor Nymph,
> Nor *Faunus* haunted. Here in close recess
> With Flowers, Garlands, and sweet-smelling Herbs
> Espoused *Eve* deckt first her Nuptial Bed,
> And heav'nly Choirs the Hymenaean sung,
> What day the genial Angel to our Sire
> Brought her in naked beauty more adorn'd,
> More lovely than *Pandora*, whom the Gods
> Endow'd with all thir gifts.   (705–15)

While seeming to praise the bride, Milton's "outdoing" simile adumbrates the manner in which the impending catastrophe will occur. Like the lustful forest deities, Eve will seduce Adam; like Pandora she will bring into the Christian world all its evils. Following Scaliger's advice to prophesy a happy future for the marriage, Milton does mention in Book VIII the "selectest influence" of the stars for the wedding day. But in Book IV where he simulates dramatically the action of an epithalamium and acts as choragus, he prophesies the opposite: "O for that warning voice, which he who saw / Th' *Apocalypse*, heard cry in Heav'n aloud." It is Satan's presence within the garden, of course, which makes the poet anxious for the future. And it is through Satan's eyes, moreover, serving as a kind of sin-tinted glass that we observe the couple's danger throughout the epithalamium. Twice he interjects sardonic remarks which bode ill. His first intrusion begins "O Hell! what do mine eyes with grief behold" and is spoken, ironically, following Milton's *encomium tôn gamountôn*. Having concluded a chilling speech which inverts the epithalamic request for children by promising to provide a home in Hell for the "numerous offspring" of Adam and Eve, Satan "alights among the sportful Herd" to rejoin innocent Nature's festivities honoring the nuptials.

But Satan is more than an ill-mannered, uninvited wedding guest. In a brilliant stroke Milton makes of him a surrogate choragus directing the proceedings and thereby undermining Milton's performance of that role! At the conclusion of his second speech (505–35) Satan cynically substitutes in this *allocutio sponsalis* the pleasures of a brief *carpe diem* for Catullus's "play as it pleases you" with its promise of pleasures endless as the African sands:

> Live while ye may,
> Yet happy pair; enjoy, till I return,
> Short pleasures, for long woes are to succeed.

Milton's epic epithalamium thus creates tragic irony by placing its innocent bridal couple between rival choragi who vie to control the outcome of their wedding.

Another topic which Milton fails to mention in Book IV is the traditional Fescennine jests. Frolicking animals and flowers wafting fragrant odors replace Claudian's soldiers indulging in the permitted freedom ("permissisque iocis . . . licentior") of bawdy humor. The immediate reason for their omission, of course, is the absence of human wedding guests! Yet I think Milton decided not to allude to this ancient custom because he realized the essential conflict between the license of Fescennine revelry and the firm basis in rational control of his own "wedded Love." A close reading of the epic reveals, in fact, that Milton *does* include Fescennine revelry. He reserves it, however, for his picture in Book XI of the fallen world. Michael's vision includes, indeed, a miniature epithalamium. Here all topics excluded from the marriage of Adam and Eve are alluringly and temptingly presented for Adam's inspection:

> they on the Plain
> Long had not walkt, when from the Tents behold
> A Bevy of fair Women, richly gay
> In Gems and wanton dress; to the Harp they sung

Soft amorous Ditties, and in dance came on:
The Men though grave, ey'd them, and let thir eyes
Rove without rein, till in the amorous Net
Fast caught, they lik'd, and each his liking chose;
And now of love they treat till th' Ev'ning Star
Love's harbinger appear'd; then all in heat
They light the Nuptial Torch, and bid invoke
Hymen, then first to marriage Rites invok't;
With Feast and Music all the Tents resound.
Such happy interview and fair event
Of love and youth not lost, Songs, Garlands, Flow'rs,
And charming Symphonies attach'd the heart
Of *Adam*, soon inclin'd to admit delight
The bent of Nature.   (580–97)

Adam's immediate response to this vision of earthly delight is to follow his inclination and he exclaims "Here Nature seems fulfill'd in all her ends." But as Michael points out, pursuance of appetite is not the best guide for holy living. Moreover, as we perceive, Adam's definition of nature contrasts radically with our vision of it unfallen in Book IV. These women are, in fact, bred only "to the Taste / Of lustful appetence" and they are "empty of all good wherein consists / Woman's domestic honor and chief praise." Michael does not object to the joyousness of the wedding revelry but, rather, to that same irrational abandon that had led an earlier Christian humanist to write in his pastoral epithalamium: "But thou foule *Cupid*, syre to lawlesse lust, / Be thou farre hence with thy empoyson'd darte."[36] The men watching the procession allow their eyes to "Rove without rein"; they forgo their male sovereignty by becoming passively caught "in the amorous Net"; and "They light the Nuptial Torch" all "in heat" rather than in "Reason, Loyal, Just, and Pure." If Milton's "Hail wedded Love" celebrates the marital ideal of which man is capable, then this passage represents, in its depiction of the way men are wont to behave, his antiepithalamium.

Michael's discomfort at the sensual license encouraged by the wedding is not eccentric, as we now can see, but part of a Christian hexameral tradition stressing natural pleasures ordered by a temperate and mutually shared love. As his hymn to "wedded Love" reveals, Milton's concern is with the specific contemporary abuse in "Mixt dance . . . wanton Mask . . . [and] Midnight Ball." In his own day he had witnessed the degeneration of a genre championed once by his "better teacher than Aquinas." No longer did a poet like Jonson pray modestly for fruitful issue "But dared not aske our wish in Language fescennine."[37] Instead, libertinism so ruled the genre that Thomas Randolph could facetiously pervert Erasmus's censure of monastic overpraise of virginity into a mockery of the ideal of marital chastity: "Virginity (whereof chaste fooles doe boast); / A thing not known what 'tis, till it be lost."[38]

A final modification of epithalamic convention—and the most telling of them—is Milton's special handling of Scaliger's topic encouraging the poet to represent the bride overcome ("coactam") by the force of Venus or Cupid. This is the topic which baroque poets like Marino and Crashaw as well as elegant Cavaliers such as Suckling and Carew were fond of elaborating. Milton too treats this topic; not, however, in his presentation of Adam and Eve *before* the Fall but, rather, in a bitterly ironic fashion, *after* it:

> hee on *Eve*
> Began to cast lascivious Eyes, she him
> As wantonly repaid; in Lust they burn:
> Till *Adam* thu 'gan *Eve* to dalliance move.
> *Eve*, now I see thou art exact of taste,
> And elegant, of Sapience no small part,
>
> .   .   .   .
>
> So said he, and forbore not glance or toy
> Of amorous intent, well understood
> Of *Eve*, whose Eye darted contagious Fire.
> Her hand he seiz'd, and to a shady bank,
> Thick overhead with verdant roof imbowr'd
> He led her nothing loath; Flowers were the Couch.   (IX, 1013–39)

Adam and Eve do not here fulfill proper "wedded Love" but pervert it; their mutual but unthinking submission to the power of Venus breeds only mutual suspicion, mutual hatred, and misery before God.

The epithalamium which Milton in the "Trinity Manuscript" planned to dramatize was never written, but his preparation was utilized, as we have seen, to splendid purpose in *Paradise Lost*. Whether he imitates epideictic topics such as the *encomium tôn gamountôn* or *peri gamou* from the epic epithalamium, or the dramatic plot of Catullus 61, or Christian adaptations by hexameral poets, Milton transcends his models to create from such epithalamic elements a complex poem fraught with the tragic tension between the glory that married love once was and our despair at what man has made of it. Milton's imitation of the classical epithalamium was never an uncritical one. The pagan glorification of "the dark knowledge of the blood" that overrides man's reason in its drive to satisfy appetite he simply could not, as a Christian humanist, tolerate. As his epithalamium presenting the fallen world in Book XI and, even more, his depiction of Adam's lust shows, the unrestrained force that drives a young man's green age is indeed also his destroyer. The love which Milton rather chooses to celebrate is a "Perpetual Fountain of Domestic sweets . . . Founded in Reason, Loyal, Just, and Pure."

Guilford College

NOTES

1. Quotations from the "Trinity Manuscript" are taken from facsimile reproductions included by Harris Francis Fletcher in *John Milton's Complete Poetical Works*, II (Urbana, 1945), pp. 16, 26.

2. George Coffin Taylor, *Milton's Use of Du Bartas* (Cambridge, Mass., 1934), p. 79; J. B. Broadbent, *Some Graver Subject: An Essay on "Paradise Lost"* (New York, 1960), pp. 186–87; Marjorie Hope Nicolson, *John Milton: A Reader's Guide to His Poetry* (New York, 1963), p. 243.

3. For a history of the epithalamium in European poetry see Robert H. Case's engaging introduction, pp. vii–lx, in his anthology, *English Epithalamies* (London, 1896). For a more succinct survey see Cortlandt Van Winkle's introduction, pp. 5–26, to his edition of Spenser's *Epithalamion* (New York, 1926). More specialized studies include E. Faye Wilson, "A Study of the Epithalamium in the Middle Ages: An Introduction to the *Epithalamium Beate Maria Virginis* of John of Garland" (Ph.D. diss., University of California, 1930); Thomas Greene, "The Epithalamium in the Renaissance" (Ph.D. diss., Yale University, 1954).

4. "Through marble cities the youths are chanting *Hymenaee*; the shores and the caverns echo with the cry, *Io, Hymen*." *John Milton: Complete Poems and Major Prose*, ed. Merritt Y. Hughes (New York, 1957), p. 40. All references to Milton's early poems, his prose, and *Paradise Lost* are to this edition; further citations of *Paradise Lost* are included in the text. All translations throughout the text are mine.

5. Ibid., p. 66.

6. Cf. Seneca, *Medea*, edited with English translation by Frank Justus Miller in *Seneca's Tragedies*, I (London, 1938), p. 232: "et tu, qui facibus legitimis ades, / noctem discutiens auspice dextera" ("And do you, Hymen, who attend the torches of lawful marriages, dissipate the night with propitious hand").

7. Hughes, *Complete Poems and Major Prose*, p. 71. All references to the poems of Catullus are taken from the edition and translation of F. W. Cornish in *Catullus, Tibullus, and Pervigilium Veneris* (London, 1918).

8. Of Catullus's influence, John Bernard Emperor has written in *The Catullian Influence in English Lyric Poetry, Circa 1600–1650*, University of Missouri Studies, III, no. 3 (Columbus, 1928), p. 15: "There arose what one might call a 'Catullian formula' in the making of epithalamia, a formula which became so much a part of

English poetic tradition that we may see a poet apparently otherwise oblivious of Catullus, making an epithalamium on the model of the famous sixty-first carmen, that of the nuptials of Vinia [*sic*] and Manlius."

9. Cf. Seneca, *Medea*, p. 232:

> et tu quae, gemini praevia temporis,
> tarde, stella, redis semper amantibus,
> te matres, avide te cupiunt nurus
> quamprimum radios spargere lucidos.

> (And you, Hesperus, forerunner of twilight,
> who return so slowly for lovers,
> you mothers, you brides eagerly await, to see you
> scattering your bright beams.)

10. *Paradise Lost: Books III and IV by John Milton*, ed. A. W. Verity (Cambridge, 1954), p. 100.

11. See Peter Demetz, "The Elm and the Vine: Notes Toward the History of a Marriage Topos," *PMLA*, LXXIII (1958), 521–32.

12. See Case's *English Epithalamies* for a convenient collection of the best examples of the genre.

13. George Puttenham, *The Arte of English Poesie*, ed. Gladys Doidge Willcock and Alice Walker (Cambridge, 1936), p. 53.

14. Although Catullus 64, an epyllion for the wedding of Peleus and Thetis, displays certain features of the epic epithalamium, the version that Statius presented for the wedding of Stella and Violentilla more nearly represents the late Latin tradition. For a good survey of these late Latin epithalamia see Camillo Morelli, "L'Epitalamio nella tarda poesia latina," *Studi Italiani di Filologia Classica*, XVIII (1910), 319–432.

15. For discussion of these four topics see Wilson, "Study of the Epithalamium," pp. 4–6, and Henri Frère's notes to the Budé edition of Statius's *Silves*, trans. H. J. Izaac (Paris, 1961), pp. 19–20. For general background see Theodore Burgess, *Epideictic Literature*, University of Chicago Studies in Classical Philology, III (Chicago, 1902).

16. In chapter 2, "Rhetoric, Poetics, and the Theory of Praise," from *The Enduring Monument: A Study of the Idea of Praise in Renaissance Literary Theory and Practice* (Chapel Hill, 1962), pp. 24–42, O. B. Hardison, Jr., demonstrates how the separate disciplines of rhetoric and poetry became entwined in the late classical period and how this new amalgam was transmitted into Renaissance theory.

17. Julius Caesar Scaliger, *Poetices libri septem*, 2d ed. (n. p., 1581), pp. 381–82.

18. For a lively summary of heroic epithalamia composed for state weddings, see Case's introduction to *English Epithalamies*.

19. Lily B. Campbell describes this aggressive movement in *Divine Poetry and Drama in Sixteenth-Century England* (Berkeley, 1959).

20. Origen, for example, refers to the Song of Songs as a "little epithalamium" in *The Song of Songs: Commentary and Homilies*, trans. R. P. Lawson, in *Ancient Christian Writers*, XXVI, ed. Johannes Quasten and Joseph Plumpe (Westminster, Md., 1957), p. 21. The following passage from Avitus's *Poematum de Mosaicae historiae gestis libri V* in *Opera* (Paris, 1643), p. 221, may be the first to employ epithalamic details in conjunction with the nuptials of Adam and Eve:

> Taliter aeterno coniungens foedere vota,
> Festinum dicebat hymen, castoque pudori

Concinit angelicum iuncto modulamine carmen.
Pro thalamo paradisus erat, mundusque dabatur
In dotem, et laetis gaudebant sidera flammis.

(Thus, joining their vows in an eternal pledge,
The marriage god was chanting joyously, and with a chaste demeanor
Was singing an angelic song of blended harmony.
Paradise was their bridal chamber, the whole world was given
As their dowry, and the stars rejoiced in happy flames.)

In his *The Celestial Cycle* (Toronto, 1952), p. 505, Watson Kirkconnell points out how widely popular were Avitus's *Poemata* in the Renaissance.

21. See Taylor, *Milton's Use of Du Bartas* and Geoffrey Bullough, "Milton and Cats," in *Essays in English Literature from the Renaissance to the Victorian Age Presented to A. S. P. Woodhouse*, ed. Millar MacLure and F. W. Watt (Toronto, 1964), pp. 103–25.

22. Andrew Ramsey, *Poemata Sacra* (Edinburgh, 1633); the *Poemata* were reprinted in *Delitiae Poetarum Scotorum* (Amsterdam, 1637), ed. Arthur Johnston.

23. I paraphrase Alessandro Carriero, *Breve et Ingenioso Discorso contra L'Opera di Dante* (Padua, 1582), pp. 49–50, 55. See also Minturno's *De Poeta* (Venice, 1559), pp. 417–18, as well as Puttenham, *Arte of English Poesie*, and Scaliger, *Poetices*.

24. Caspar Barlaeus, *Paradisus*, in *Faces Augustae, sive Poematia, Quibus Illustriores Nuptiae, a Nobili et Illustri viro, D. Jacobo Catsio, Jam A Caspare Barlaeo et Cornelio Boyo Latino Carmine celebrantur* (Dordrecht, 1643), p. 3 ff. Roger Williams's claim to have taught Dutch to Milton notwithstanding, I believe Milton knew Cats's work through this Latin translation. Since this heroicizes the original poem into epic proportions, I treat the *Paradisus* as a work of Barlaeus.

25. C. S. Lewis, in his *A Preface to "Paradise Lost"* (New York, 1961), p. 124, writes, "Eve exhibits modesty too exclusively in sexual contexts, and [Milton's] Adam does not exhibit it at all. There is even a strong and (in the circumstances) a most offensive suggestion of female bodily shame as an incentive to male desire."

26. In *The Earthly Paradise and the Renaissance Epic* (Princeton, 1966), p. 50, A. Bartlett Giamatti writes that the Venus's bower passage "exerted great influence on succeeding generations of Christian paradise poets, for the fact that Claudian's description coincided with Christian versions of the earthly paradise behind or upon a mountain meant he could safely be read as a secular (and pleasurable) analogue to what was religiously acceptable."

27. Compare the second prefatory verse to Claudian's epithalamium for Honorius in *Works*, ed. Maurice Platnauer, I (London, 1963), pp. 232–34, especially these lines:

> omne nemus cum fluviis,
>   omne canat profundum
> Ligures favete campi,
>   Veneti favete montes.

> (Sing, woods and rivers all,
>   sing, deep of ocean.
> Give your blessing, too, Ligurian plains,
>   and yours, Venetian hills.)

28. Nathaniel Baxter, *Sir Philip Sidney's Ourania* ... (London, 1606), M3ᵛ.
29. Thomas Greene, "The Epithalamium in the Renaissance," p. 53.

30. Hughes, *Complete Poems and Major Prose*, p. 1004.

31. *Du Bartas, Devine Weekes and Workes*, trans. Joshuah Sylvester (London, 1611), p. 172. Cf. the "Lodi del Matrimonio," in Gasparo Murtola's *Della Creazione del Mondo Poema Sacro* (Macerato, 1618), Giorno Sesto, Canto Vigesimo primo, pp. 601–02. In his forthcoming *Catalogue of Milton's Library*, Jackson C. Boswell includes the works of Murtola along with those of Avitus, Cats, and Du Bartas among the books which Milton probably had available to him.

32. These basic writings include Saint Basil, *Hexameron* and *III Orationes*; Saint Gregory of Nyssa, *De hominis opficio*; Saint Ambrose, *De Paradiso liber unus*, *Hexameron libri sex, De Dierum Creatione Hymni VI*.

33. Sylvester, trans., *Du Bartas, Devine Weekes*, p. 568.

34. Ibid., p. 173.

35. Barlaeus, *Dialogi. Aliquot Nuptiales, . . . a Nobilissimo Jacobo Catsio . . .*, in *Faces Augustae*, beginning with the second pagination, p. 18.

36. *The Poems of Sir Philip Sidney*, ed. William A. Ringler, Jr. (Oxford, 1962), p. 92.

37. *The Complete Poetry of Ben Jonson*, ed. William B. Hunter, Jr. (New York, 1963), "Epithalamion . . . [for] Hierome Weston," p. 236.

38. *The Poems and Amyntas of Thomas Randolph*, ed. John Jay Parry (New Haven, 1927), "An Epithalamium to Mr. F. H.," p. 121.

THE TYPOLOGICAL STRUCTURE OF MILTON'S IMAGERY

John C. Ulreich, Jr.

The seeming abstractness of Milton's imagery results from its intellectual structure, particularly from the way metaphors are re-created through typological fulfillment. The letter of a pagan or Hebraic type is first analyzed, then reconstituted in a Christian spirit which contains it, as "the spiritual and rational faculty contains the corporeal." Milton's imagery is not sacramental; neither is it simply abstract, for Milton re-creates his own incarnational symbolism by a process of analysis, purification, and reembodiment. Images function typologically according to the law of Coleridge's secondary Imagination, which first "dissolves, diffuses, dissipates, in order to re-create." In Sonnet 23, the shadowy image of Alcestis is transformed, through typological allusions, into a Christian reality. The same pattern recurs in Samson's final reply to the Philistine Officer and in Christ's Incarnation of the Word in *Paradise Regained*. The basis of analogy in Milton's poetry is moral and psychological. His images are often difficult to apprehend immediately, because their effect depends largely on a conscious awareness; they are, nonetheless, concretely metaphorical, because they are grounded in the psychic activity of the protagonist. By this means the dead letter of imagery is reborn in the spirit, whose active and saving faith embodies itself in works of poetry.

M ODERN CRITICISM—the school of Eliot and Pound, at least—holds that poetry ought to be concrete, dramatic, immediate, and intense. Milton's poetry has been called abstract, remote, and diffuse; it lacks, we are told, the tension of drama and the life of human experience; it is dissociative rather than creative. To borrow an aphorism from F. R. Leavis: Milton "exhibits a feeling *for* words rather than a capacity for feeling *through* words; we are often, in reading him, moved to comment that he is 'external' or that he 'works from the outside.' "[1]

Less often, apparently, do we observe that he is working inward, from the surfaces of words to their substance.

Despite a withering away of the polemical spirit, T. S. Eliot's strictures continue to influence the critical imagination; no student of Milton's language can afford to ignore J. B. Broadbent's opinion that "the language of Milton's poetry is . . . deficient in body," that the tendency of his imagery is "away from the incarnate towards the ideate," hence toward abstractness and dissociation.[2] Attempts to defend Milton's style have not, for the most part, dealt directly with this crucial problem of metaphoric quality. What is needed, however, is not another reassessment but a reexamination of the nature and function of Milton's figurative language. Toward that end, I propose to consider the intellectual structure of Milton's imagery, to argue that his language is not simply dissociative but reassociative, and to suggest that his re-creation of metaphor can best be understood as a process of typological fulfillment.

I

The dissociation of imagery is generally understood to be a consequence of rationalism[3]—whose disruptive influence on seventeenth-century poetry can be felt as much in the *discordia concors* of the metaphysical conceit as in the abstractness of Miltonic imagery. Ultimately, the analytical impulse destroyed the harmony between inner and outer worlds of experience which had animated Elizabethan imagery. In the objective macrocosm, "new Philosophy cals all in doubt"; the microcosm in subject to the same disorder: " 'Tis all in pieces, all cohaerence gone."[4] Similarly, the objective, perceptual (or conceptual) surface of imagery becomes divorced from its emotional and spiritual content. As Malcolm Ross suggests, the struggle between outer and inner worlds of experience tends to disintegrate poetic images as it does religious symbols. Radical Protestantism especially destroys images "in an urge to purify the idea"; under the influence of rationalism, sacramental analogies tend to become mere figures, shadows of an idea rather than embodiments of it.[5] And so it would seem in Milton's poetry: as he matures, his imagery becomes increasingly abstract and dissociative; the sensuous richness of *Comus* and *Lycidas* is sacrificed to the Puritan austerity of *Samson Agonistes*, sacramental imagery to rationalism.[6] This view of Milton's development, however, does not do justice to the complex function of his mature symbolism. As Ross has suggested, the process of externalization and abstraction is not final, for Milton revives desiccated images by recreating his own symbolism: he "uproots" images from their conventional ground and "rearranges them" so that "they come somehow to cohere in living and novel patterns."[7] Defining that process of revitalization is crucial for an understanding of Milton's poetry.

Perhaps the readiest way to apprehend Milton's re-creative symbols is to examine them in the historical context of typological symbolism. To be sure, Milton does not make extensive use of conventional types; nonetheless, as William Madsen has persuasively argued, the assumptions of typological theory can be used to illuminate Milton's symbolic practice.[8] My concern is not so much with particular types as with the distinctive structure of typological symbolism.

Typological interpretation assumes a precise theological formulation of the relationship between Old and New Testaments, whereby Christ's actions *fulfill* the law and the prophets (Matthew v, 17). In theory, any event in the Old Testament may be regarded as prefiguring the Incarnation; indeed, the Old Testament *must* be so interpreted, for its significance cannot be fully apprehended until it has been revealed in Christ. Without weighing all the implications of this view, one can see immediately that it has certain poetic advantages, the most striking being its unremitting historical concreteness. Most forms of symbolism assume a dualism, whereby a phenomenal *sign* is taken to imitate or represent a noumenal *significance*. In Platonic idealism, for example, signs (images) are apparent reflections of noumenal reality (ideas or forms); in Aristotelian realism, the phenomena (material forms) are real, the noumena (intellectual forms) abstract; in both, however, the analogical relationship is between concrete and abstract. Typological symbolism, on the other hand, is radically monistic: both sign and significance are inseparably concrete.[9] If history is God's allegory, then the literal, objective reality of both the Old and New Testaments is intrinsically noumenal. It is this view of history which sustains sacramental symbolism, in which sign and significance are not merely like but identical. It is this typological perspective, primarily, which gives the incarnational symbolism of the Fourth Gospel its extraordinary power: "And the Word was made flesh, and dwelt among us" (John i, 14).

Given the occurrence in Milton's poetry of certain crucial types (Samson is an obvious, though very complex, example), together with his emphatic monism, one might be tempted to suppose that Milton's imagery is sustained by such a sacramental view of history.[10] But the evidence will not support such a hypothesis. On the contrary, Milton's use of types consistently undercuts their literal significance. When Moses, for example, is related typologically to Christ as Mediator, he is denied actual possession of that Office: *"Moses* in figure bears" (*PL*, XII, 241).[11] The verb suggests that the significance of Moses's role is not so much *in* him as *on* him, figurative *rather than* literal. And it is even arguable that the historical reality of Christ in *Paradise Regained* is sacrificed to his moral and spiritual significance.[12] At the very least, Milton's understanding of typology is complicated by his rationalistic attitude toward analogies of any kind. He generally eschews the sacramental attitude; he is, in Madsen's words, strongly bent "away from the material and toward the spiritual," away from the sign to its significance.[13] His approach to scripture is accordingly spiritual rather than historical, and (in the *Christian Doctrine*, at least) abstract rather than concrete. Many Protestants had favored the use of sacramental imagination:

> Whilst the soul is joined with the body, it hath not only a necessary but a holy use of imagination, and of sensible things whereupon our Imagination worketh. What is the use of the sacraments but to help our souls by our senses, and our faith by imagination?[14]

But Milton will allow no such expedient. In his view, the soul has no need of the "weak, and fallible office of the senses."[15] He admits in sacraments a "peculiarly close relation between the sign and the thing signified," but only to avoid the confusion of identifying letter and spirit.[16] He insists that the relation is only an analogy, a figurative representation, and the only sacraments he recognizes are Baptism and the Eucharist. And he is equally skeptical of typological analogies; "under the name of Christ" he admits "Moses and the Prophets, who were his forerunners," but he twice qualifies the value of such associations: "if an argument . . . can be derived from allegory and metaphorical expressions"; "if we may reason by analogy respecting spiritual things, from types of this kind."[17] In general, he is not much inclined to draw analogies between flesh and spirit: "All corporeal resemblances of inward holiness & beauty are now past."[18]

If, then, we are to conclude that Milton does not share the historical assumptions of medieval typology and that the analogical basis of his imagery is not sacramental, how are we to interpret his shadowy types? What *is* the basis of analogy in his poetry, and in what sense is it useful to describe his symbolism as typological? The answer to the second question, I believe, implies an answer to the first. What Milton preserves from the medieval world view is not the sacramental type but the structure of typology, not the literal type but the spirit of typological interpretation. His symbolism enacts a movement forward in time which is both upward, from body to spirit (*PL*, V, 478), and inward, from the letter which kills to the spirit which gives life:

> From shadowy Types to Truth, from Flesh to Spirit,
> From imposition of strict Laws, to free
> Acceptance of large Grace, from servile fear
> To filial, works of Law to works of Faith.   (*PL*, XII, 303–06)

Milton's typology is based on the fundamental Pauline analogy between the old Adam and the new: "For if through the offense of one many be dead, much more the grace of God, and the gift by grace, which is by one man, Jesus Christ, hath abounded unto many. . . . For as by one man's disobedience many were made sinners, so by the obedience of one shall many be made righteous" (Romans v, 15, 19). We are saved not by literal observance of the law but by submission to faith: "For Christ is the end of the law for righteousness to everyone that believeth" (x, 4).[19] But Paul's doctrine of justification by faith implies a fundamental paradox. He argues: "Do we then make void the law through faith? God forbid: yea, we establish the law" (iii, 31). But if that is the case, how can we also hold that "now we are delivered from the law" (vii, 6)? Milton addresses himself directly to this point. He argues that the literal injunctions of the law have been abrogated by Christ, who came to free men from slavery to sin and death under the law.[20] However:

The sum and essence of the law is not . . . abrogated; its purpose being attained in that love of God and our neighbour, which is born of the spirit through faith. . . . Matt. v. 17. *think not that I am come to destroy the law, or the prophets; I am not come to destroy, but to fulfil.* . . . it is the tablet of the law, so to speak, that is alone changed, its injunctions being now written by the Spirit in the hearts of believers.[21]

The letter of the Old Testament has died in order to be reborn in the spirit of the New, just as (in Paul's words) "our old man is crucified . . . that the body of sin might be destroyed, that henceforth we should not serve sin" (Romans vi, 6). Thus "we are delivered from the law, that being dead wherein we were held; that we should serve in newness of spirit, and not in the oldness of the letter" (vii, 6).

Typology, the analysis of the literal type and its subsequent recreation by the antitype of the Word *made flesh*, is a paradigm of the imaginative process in Milton's poetry. The letter of his imagery is destroyed in order to be reborn in the spirit of his symbolic intention; his imagination works first to abstract meaning from the letter (in effect to destroy images) and then to reembody that meaning. He interprets a sign and then re-presents it as inseparable from the significance which he has developed discursively; he re-creates concrete meaning.[22] Perhaps the most explicit embodiment of this process—a kind of imaginative self-illustration—occurs in Raphael's ode on Creation (*PL*, V, 469–505). The poetry is first ratiocinative; action is described abstractly: things *proceed* and *return* (470); they are *endued* (473) and *refined* (475). As each thing strives to realize its proper form, the "bounds proportioned to each kind" (478–79), it must be transformed in order to achieve a higher degree of perfection. Body must work up to spirit (478), the corporeal body be transformed into the spiritual and imaginative body which it is potentially. These philosophical abstractions are then embodied in verbs which are both concrete and universal, specific in context but general in their possible reference. The stalk *springs* (480) and *breathes* (482); flowers and fruit *aspire* (485). The concept of spirit is fleshed out in the *Spirits odorous* of the plant (482) and in the *vital spirits* of man (484). The hierarchy of natural forms is reenacted in man, in life and sense, in fancy and understanding, and finally in Reason. The incarnation of the rational spirit in the image of the growing plant gives life to the abstract formulae which precede and follow so that Reason itself becomes concrete. The activity of the verse is an image of the imaginative process; in fact, the lines *are*, "substantially expressed" (III, 140), the action they imitate, the reincarnation of meaning.

Milton's poetry works according to Coleridge's law of the secondary Imagination, which first "dissolves, diffuses, dissipates, in order to re-create . . . to idealize and to unify."[23] Coleridge, in fact, uses Raphael's exposition as a preface to the thirteenth chapter of the *Biographia Literaria*, "On the Imagination, or Esemplastic Power," and his distinction between primary and secondary imagination can help to define the peculiar quality of Milton's imagery. The primary imagination, which Coleridge calls "the living Power and prime Agent of all human perception," is essentially receptive; it becomes all things.[24] The secondary imagination, which half perceives and half creates, is projective; it makes all things of itself, abstracts life from objects and then *re*embodies that life in metaphor. It is this distinction which underlies Coleridge's comparison of Milton's poetry with Shakespeare's. Shakespeare

> darts himself forth, and passes into all the forms of human character and passion. . . . [Milton] attracts all forms and things to himself, into the unity of his own IDEAL. All things and modes of action shape themselves anew in the being of MILTON; while SHAKESPEARE becomes all things, yet forever remaining himself.[25]

Shakespeare "is the Spinozistic deity—an omnipresent creativeness. Milton is the deity of prescience: he stands *ab extra*"—outside even himself as he *meditates* the muse.[26] As Milton himself observes in his poem *On Shakespeare*, Shakespeare's "easy numbers flow," whereas Milton's "slow-endeavoring art" is much more insistently *wrought*. The mind • of one finds itself naturally in objects, becomes all things; the other draws all objects into itself, digests, analyzes, and reshapes objects to the reality it makes.

Milton has "the allegorizing fancy of the *modern*, that still *striving* to project the inward, contradistinguishes itself from the seeming ease with which the poetry of the ancients reflects the world without."[27] Symbols, which reflect, are "always *taut*egorical, that is expressing the same subject, but with a difference, in contradistinction from metaphors and similitudes, that are always *alle*gorical, that is, expressing a different subject but with a resemblance."[28] Milton's "allegorical" imagery works *through* the rational principle. As Owen Barfield has suggested, "the rational principle . . . is above all that which produces self-consciousness. It shuts off the human ego from the living meaning in the outer world, which it is for ever 'murdering to dissect', and encloses that same ego in the network of its own, now abstract, thoughts."[29] And as the rational, apprehensive principle abstracts the mind from objects, thought turns in on itself; "reality" shapes itself according to the self-conscious structure of human experience. Shakespeare's imagery is ordinarily symbolical rather than allegorical; Milton is more subjective, and his poetry is inventive, a projection of his consciousness into objects. Borrowing a very useful distinction from Barfield's discussion of poetic diction, we might describe Shakespeare's language as primarily *figurative*, Milton's as *metaphorical*. Figurative meaning is original and intrinsic, a direct reflection of objective nature in the subject. Conscious metaphor, on the other hand, is a *re*-creation (by the secondary imagination), a revitalization of concrete meaning in a word which the rational principle had made abstract; a metaphor *re*unites object and subject, letter and spirit.

In order not to mistake this metaphorical quality, it is necessary to distinguish between *allegory* (in Coleridge's sense) and mere *personification*. Both are projective, but the former is truly metaphorical, the latter primarily conceptual. Personification projects thoughts *onto* images, clothing significance with images, whereas allegory projects thinking *into* images, infusing them with significance. Personifications are a product of thought; allegories embody the process of thinking. Personifications, which reflect *natura naturata*, nature made, are essentially inert; allegories are alive because they embody *natura naturans*, nature making. The difference between these modes is not always clear-cut in practice, but the predominance of one over the other can usually be felt. In *L'Allegro*, for example, the lark (41–43) is primarily a personification of cheerfulness; images in this poem are often felt to be conventional because they do not possess a high degree of imaginative life; like the lark, they are images of thought rather than embodiments of thinking. In *Il Penseroso*, however, poetic meditation transforms the lark into Philomel (56–58), not a bird merely but the translation of a human spirit into the nightingale. In the first poem we merely hear the song; in the second we share in the imaginative activity of the poet, embodied in the mythic bird who will deign a song "In her sweetest, saddest plight" (57).

II

This process of transformation and reembodiment, the movement through analysis to synthesis, recurs throughout Milton's poetry—in *Comus*, for example, through the gradual subliming of the body into the "soul's essence" (462) and in *Lycidas* through the typification of Orpheus.[30] But perhaps the structure of such transformations can be most readily observed in Milton's twenty-third sonnet, to his "late espoused Saint." In much the same way that typological symbolism is used in Books XI and XII of *Paradise Lost* to organize Milton's vision of history, the pattern of allusions in the sonnet enacts an emergence of images from literal types to spiritual truth. Interpretation of the sonnet depends, to a considerable extent, on understanding Milton's reference to "Purification in the old Law."[31] The phrase is invariably glossed as an allusion to Leviticus xii, which describes the rite of purification after childbirth.[32] There is, however, another even more appropriate scriptural allusion in the New Testament, for which the "old Law" is a source:

And when the days of . . . [Mary's] purification *according to the* [old] *law of Moses* were accomplished, they brought him to Jerusalem, to present him to the Lord. . . . And [in the words of Leviticus] *to offer a sacrifice . . . a pair of turtle doves.* (Luke ii, 22, 24)[33]

The ritual offering is spiritually received, and its promise of salvation is fulfilled, in the Gospels.

Upon this allusion the typological structure of the whole poem turns. The phrase "old Law" identifies the Old Testament and implies the New by distinguishing the old letter from the new spirit. The allusion is ironic rather than literal, for the law is powerless to save; it "can discover sin, but not remove" (*PL*, XII, 290).[34] Milton's saint comes *as* one saved because real purification is spiritual and figurative, not literal and ceremonial; the law is *old* because it has been transcended by the new covenant of faith. One function of the law, however, is to inform "by types / And shadows" (XII, 232–33). Because the old letter prefigures its fulfillment by the new spirit, typological allusions invariably require double vision. Moses, for example, was a *literal* type of the law, "who could not bring the children of Israel into the land of Canaan."[35] In his office of Mediator, however, Moses is a *spiritual* type of Christ: "Mediator, whose high Office now / *Moses* in figure bears" (*PL*, XII, 240–41). The allusion in the sonnet is likewise twofold: "as whom . . . Purification in the old Law did save" refers both to "one whom ritual purification could not save from original sin ('child-bed taint')" and to "the one (Mary) who *was* saved, not by law, but by Christ's sacrifice."

Once the function of *Purification* is clearly apprehended, other images in the poem fall into coherent perspective. The development of images, classical, Hebraic, and Christian, is dialectical—in accord, approximately, with a division into quatrain, quatrain, and sestet. The poem moves from a dimly shadowed possibility, through purification and redefinition, to a final realization; from simile (*"like* Alcestis," *"as* whom") to concrete, metaphorical presence; and from the mere outward shape of a dream to the inward reality of vision.

Like Old Testament history, pagan myths are to be understood as shadows of Christian truth. Typologically, Alcestis's self-sacrifice and resurrection are associated with Christ's; her subsequent need for purification foreshadows Leviticus and Luke. In the same way, "Jove's great Son" suggests Christ, the Son of God; Hercules' obscurely fabled descent into Hell is an analogue of true Christian redemption. But these associations are merely apparent; like the classical Muse in *Paradise Lost*, the image of Alcestis is only "an empty dream" (VII, 39), a pagan fable, *pale and faint*. The allusion points to the reality of salvation, but indirectly; the image is merely external and physical, a literal shadow of inward meaning.

Movement inward begins in the second quatrain; the allusion to *Purification* in the Old Testament initiates a moral redefinition of the pagan type, a purging of literal illusion necessary to achieve spiritual vision. The law cannot *save*, but it can *discover* sin and in this way help effect man's "natural regeneration," whereby "the natural mind and will of man" are "partially renewed by a divine impulse" so that "those in whom it takes place are said to be enlightened, and to be endued with power to will what is good."[36] And this recovery from natural corruption makes possible man's supernatural regeneration, "whereby the old man being destroyed, the inward man is regenerated by God after his own image, insomuch that he becomes as it were a new creature."[37] By this means the purified shadow of Alcestis is transfigured, remade in the spirit of "Love, sweetness, goodness." Pagan, Hebraic, and Christian images are thus characterized respectively as physical (literal), moral (allegorical), and spiritual (symbolic); the poem works typologically to transform the emotionally charged pagan image into a fully significant Christian one.

The transformation is not yet complete, however, for the New Testament antitype not only fulfills its Old Testament type, but also foreshadows the resurrection into eternal life, "such as yet once more I trust to have." Milton's saint is still veiled, "For now we see through a glass, darkly; but then face to face" (1 Corinthians xiii, 13). Once again the syntax is double: the parallel clauses, "Mine as whom . . . And such as" indicate both (1) similarity: "*like* one purified (in but not *of* the old Law) and *like* one whom I hope to see again (since she has been saved in Christ)" and (2) difference: "*as though* purified but not yet *such as* I hope to see fully (at the Resurrection)." As Alcestis prefigures Milton's veiled saint, and as the myth of Hercules, half man, half god, prefigures the Incarnate Word, so the Incarnation itself prefigures the Resurrection into eternal life. Consequently, there are not three typological levels in the poem but four. On the literal, emotional level, Alcestis is apparently *saved* by Jove's great Son and *restored* to her husband. Real salvation begins on the moral level and is completed on the spiritual; Milton's saint is *saved* by the Son of God. Her *restoration*, however, can take place only on the substantial level. Leviticus specifies that "a lamb of the first year" be offered as a sacrifice; in Luke the ceremonial law is fulfilled, morally by Mary, spiritually by Christ; in Revelation, Christ himself becomes the sacrificial lamb, as well as the "glad husband" of his purified bride, who is Milton's "espoused Saint."[38]

In the structure of its images and allusions, the sonnet closely resembles *Lycidas*. In each poem, an initially classical image is redefined, through a series of allusive transformations, as a Christian one; a shadowy pagan type becomes a substantial Christian reality. As Alcestis becomes, through Mary, redeemed Christianity, so Orpheus and Phoebus become, in "the Pilot of the Galilean Lake" (109), Peter and Christ; the pastoral shepherd Lycidas becomes the Good Shepherd. And the classical image does *become* Christian: potential spiritual meaning, already latent in the type, is drawn out, refined, and realized in Christian form. The original image is not merely analyzed; rather, the pagan type is reintegrated into a Christian context. The letter is subsumed in the spirit, given new life in a spiritual body: "For spirit being the more excellent substance, virtually and essentially contains within itself the inferior one; as the spiritual and rational faculty contains the corporeal, that is the sentient and vegetative faculty."[39] And so the sensible letter is contained in the rational spirit and by it reinfused with substantial life. Spiritually and by analogy, Lycidas becomes the "day-star" (168), Christ—the "greater Sun" of the *Nativity Ode* (83)—but concretely he becomes also the pagan "Genius of the shore" (183). Pastoral imagery is redeemed and fulfilled by the poet's Christian vision. In the same way, the image of Alcestis is transformed, not negated, so that she becomes the embodiment of a spiritual vision, a living presence rather than a mere shadow.

III

Typological fulfillment, then, is not merely a process of analysis and redefinition; it is also a rebirth of the spirit *in* the letter, a reembodiment of abstracted meaning. The process of reintegration is difficult to define—especially since it works by synthesis rather than analysis. But since the transformation is analogical, further illustrations may help not only to suggest its quality but to provide a clearer idea of how it works, through the spirit. For the analogical basis of Milton's poetry is to be found, not in a literal pattern of images, but in their spiritual coherence.

The irony of the twenty-third sonnet is similar to that which occurs at the climaxes of *Samson Agonistes* and *Paradise Regained*, and the process by which imagery is transformed in these poems is similarly typological. In Samson's terse reply to the Public Officer, paradox transforms the literal reality of the lines into the spirit of the Incarnate Word:

> Masters' commands come with a power resistless
> To such as owe them absolute subjection;
> And for a life who will not change his purpose?   (1404–06)

The dramatic irony is clear: Samson goes with the messenger of his own volition, not out of servile fear. But to whom does he owe "absolute subjection"? The allusiveness of the reference draws us irresistibly inward, to participate in the consciousness of the speaker (as the typological allusion in Sonnet 23 invited us to share the poet's inward vision). Only one Master commands absolute submission, in whose will is perfect freedom. Samson does not simply "change" his purpose; his will is recreated by the "resistless" clarity of his insight. He quits himself (1709) to find himself, loses life to accomplish eternal life. Dramatic irony is subsumed in paradox. The Word embodies itself and crucifies the flesh in order to be reborn in a spiritual body. Language is metamorphosed to express an inward reality which has completely transformed the outward and visible significance of the words.

Similarly, in *Paradise Regained*, when Satan suggests that Christ cast himself from the temple, the Son of man replies: "Tempt not the

Lord thy God" (IV, 561), meaning "I will not tempt God—You, Satan, cease tempting me." For the first time we—and Christ Himself, as He utters the words—learn who He is. The Incarnation is made manifest.[40] When the divine Word enters flesh, the natural relation between matter and spirit is completely transformed. Christ, like Samson, withdraws into himself, through a spiritual death, to the source of His being; at the consummation of this action, he returns to life *in* but not of the world. Samson's *anagnorisis*, like Christ's epiphany, is imitated by the word of poetry, made flesh in order to assimilate the human letter in the divine spirit.

The basis of typological reincarnation is moral and psychological. As Rosemond Tuve has suggested:

> when myths are allegorized, the first [i.e., concrete] term is not an historical Circe or Red Crosse who existed . . . like Samson, something which historically took place like the leading of the Jews through the wilderness. . . . The first term's historical and literal reality consists in its being a true account of every man's innumerable encounters with unregenerate natural man as he meets him in himself.[41]

Milton's Samson is allegorical in this sense. The moral imagination works, first to analyze experience, then to re-create it; first to understand, then to enact. Milton first defines the analogy between every man and Samson, the *internal* significance of Samson's action; like Moses, he had originally been a type of the law, but in *Samson Agonistes* he is transformed into a conscious type of Christ. His regeneration transforms the letter into the spirit, so that his visible enactment of his renewed "intimate impulse" (223), his destruction of the Philistine temple, becomes the paradoxical *sign* of his spiritual rebirth: "For whosoever will save his life shall lose it; but whosoever shall lose his life for my sake . . . the same shall save it" (Mark viii, 35). Samson must die in the covenant of works to be reborn in the covenant of faith.

So it is that the concreteness of Milton's imagery derives, not from its literal coherence, but from the spiritual experience of the protagonist —and of the audience. Such analogies will seem to a reader abstract precisely to the extent that he has failed to realize their significance *within* himself. The imagery of Milton might more accurately be called "self-conscious," for it makes the reader consciously participate in the spiritual activity which substantiates images. His poetry is thus allegorical, in Coleridge's sense, a projection of consciousness rather than a reflection of objects, but it is not merely rationalistic. When we are aware of dissociation, the effect is usually intended. Sin and Death, for example, have troubled many critics since Addison, who objected to their "chimerical" implausibility, and Johnson, who felt that the allegory suffers from "a confusion of spirit and matter," that it is unskilful because personifications are made to interact with the real personality of Satan.[42] But that is precisely the point: Sin and Death are personified because they do not exist until they are given substance by man's fallen imagination; "once actual now in body" (X, 587), they are a grim parody of God's creation. As Arnold Stein has observed, they are only "a mechanical metaphor cut off from true reality."[43] And Satan more and more comes to live in their world, the Hell of his own imagination; he loses his reality and becomes a caricature of himself. The "steady drift towards allegory" which A. J. A. Waldock deplores is the visible manifestation of Satan's degeneration, the evacuation of his failed angelic self.[44] Allegory is the proper mode of existence for creatures who inhabit Hell, "a universe of death," made (or unmade) by the diseased imagination in which "death lives" (II, 622, 624).

When it is fully realized, however, Milton's imagination is alive and concretely metaphorical—although at times its vitality is difficult to feel because one's participation must become explicit. One of Johnson's strictures against *Samson Agonistes* illustrates this difficulty very well. He objects that "sometimes metaphors find admission; even where their consistency is not accurately preserved." As an illustration he cites:

> How could I once look up, or heave the head,
> Who like a foolish Pilot have shipwreck't
> My Vessel trusted to me from above,
> Gloriously rigg'd; and for a word, a tear,
> Fool, have divulg'd the secret gift of God?   (197–201)

"Thus," Johnson argues, "Samson confounds loquacity with a shipwreck."[45] And even Christopher Ricks agrees. He suggests that the incongruity results from an ill-advised attempt to imitate Shakespearean dramatic idiom; the mixture fails because it does not create new meaning. But the comparison with Shakespeare is inappropriate, for Milton's technique is altogether different. The incongruity *is* dramatic; the analogy which supports the juxtaposition, however, is intellectual and structural rather than associative. It is true, as Ricks observes, that "pilots don't shipwreck because they divulge secrets," but we must press the analogy much further.[46] The pilot is Samson's rational will; the "Vessel . . . Gloriously rigg'd" is his "glorious strength" (36). From the beginning, Samson has associated his internal confusion with the "popular noise" (16), as if, could he only win escape from his enemies, he might find the purpose he lacks. The lines in question, by suggesting that the noise issues from himself, are a tentative step toward self-realization. The immediate disparity of the metaphors emphasizes the diffuseness of Samson's consciousness at the same time that a fundamental analogy hints at the possibility of reorganization. Johnson's "loquacity" is not well chosen; the emphasis in *divulges* is not on speech but on the act of making public, of giving oneself up to the common ruin. Samson *divulges* himself by making himself common, one with the "popular noise." The *gift* he casts away is himself, his integrity. The connection between disparate images is suggested primarily by the verbs and participles—*shipwreck't-trusted-divulg'd*. The first and last, morally analogous, are opposed to the second. Only by regaining *trust* (both his trust in God and his own trustworthiness) can Samson repair the ruin of himself. These associations are perhaps tenuous, but they are meant to be; imagery will not be fully integrated until Samson himself has been transformed and has reorganized the shape of his own experience. Images will cohere only when they have been illuminated from within and recreated, their "virtue rous'd / From under ashes into sudden flame" (1690–91).

The Miltonic image is a paradox, a re-union of the mind with objects, of what is inwardly vital with what is outwardly fixed and dead. Figurative meaning is a product of mythic consciousness, of the instinctive mind which becomes all things; the subject shares in the life of objects. Samson has lost this original participation, which had united him instinctively with God and with himself.[47] He sees himself—"this great Deliverer" (40)—as purely objective, "the scorn and gaze" of his enemies (34); his sense of blind impotence is dissociated from any real metaphorical awareness of his spiritual plight, because his active, rational mind has abstracted life from objects—including himself—so that they no longer possess meaning. It is only when he rediscovers himself *as a subject* that he can reinvest his blindness with metaphorical significance. Then, "with inward eyes illuminated" (1689), he consciously re-creates symbolic meaning by sacrificing himself in order to purge the idolatry of the Philistines: "And behold, the veil of the temple was rent in twain from the top to the bottom; and the earth did quake, and the rocks rent" (Matthew xxvii, 51).[48]

So it is that Milton revives dessicated images, the "old-cast rudiments" of Jewish law, the vestments of "sensual idolatry."[49] His language "reflourishes, then vigorous most / When most unactive deem'd" (*SA*, 1704–05), for his iconoclasm is prophetic:

> They that make a graven image are all of them vanity. . . . they see not, nor know; that they may be ashamed. . . . He maketh a god, and worshippeth it; he maketh it a graven image, and falleth down thereto. . . . They have not known nor understood: for he hath shut their eyes, that they cannot see; and their hearts, that they cannot understand. (Isaiah xliv, 9,15,17–18)[50]

The prophet objects, not to the materiality of idols, but to their emptiness. And not only the idols are empty but those who make them: "unto them that are without, all these things are done in parables: That seeing they may see, and not perceive; and hearing they may hear, and not understand" (Mark iv, 11–12). To the literal-minded all is literal; there is no salvation in works, for external forms of worship are dead, vanities of man's creation—unless they are animated from within.

An active and saving faith, however, embodies itself in works, which are the outward sign of inner grace. And the works of poetry are images. The active mind makes all things; instead of sharing passively in the life of objects as formerly, consciousness gives life to the objects in which it finds itself reflected. In Raphael's paradigm, imagination first contracts, dissolves, abstracts, and then expands to create the rhythms of life that it shares, consciously, with all growing things. What begins in abstraction and dissociation ends in the resurrection of images. Literal, objective reality, is first digested and purified and then reanimated in a spiritual body. The secondary imagination actively re-creates objective meaning and, by reshaping objects to the mind's reality, enables us to "regain the blissful seat" (*PL*, I, 5) by possessing "a paradise within" (XII, 587).

The University of Arizona

NOTES

1. *Revaluation: Tradition and Development in English Poetry* (London, 1947), p. 50. Eliot's remarks on the "dissociation of sensibility" (in "The Metaphysical Poets"

[1921], *Selected Essays* [New York, 1950], pp. 241–50) and his detailed objections in the two essays on Milton (in 1936 and 1947, collected in *On Poetry and Poets* [New York, 1957], pp. 156–83) scarcely need another rehearsal here. The critical issues and their historical development are anatomized by Patrick Murray in *Milton: The Modern Phase (A Study of Twentieth-Century Criticism)* (London, 1967), pp. 31–49.

2. "The Nativity Ode," in *The Living Milton: Essays by Various Hands*, ed. Frank Kermode (New York, 1960), pp. 17, 23.

3. A good deal of evidence to substantiate this view has been sifted by Herschel Baker, *The Wars of Truth: Studies in the Earlier Seventeenth Century* (Cambridge, Mass., 1952), and Basil Willey, *The Seventeenth-Century Background: Studies of the Thought of the Age in Relation to Poetry and Religion* (New York, 1934).

4. John Donne, *The First Anniversarie*, ll. 205, 213, in *The Complete Poetry of John Donne*, ed. John T. Shawcross (Garden City, 1967).

5. *Poetry and Dogma: The Transfiguration of Eucharistic Symbols in Seventeenth-Century English Poetry* (New Brunswick, 1954), p. 157.

6. Cf. G. S. Fraser, "Approaches to *Lycidas*," in *The Living Milton*, ed. Kermode, p. 41.

7. Ross, *Poetry and Dogma*, p. 219.

8. *From Shadowy Types to Truth: Studies in Milton's Symbolism* (New Haven, 1968).

9. See Erich Auerbach, "Typological Symbolism in Medieval Literature," in *American Critical Essays on the Divine Comedy*, ed. Robert J. Clements (New York, 1967), pp. 107–08: "in a figural relation both the signifying and the signified facts are real and concrete historical events."

10. On Samson as a type, see Madsen, *From Shadowy Types to Truth*, pp. 181–202, and F. Michael Krouse, *Milton's Samson and the Christian Tradition* (Princeton, 1949). On monism, see, for example, *PL*, V, 469–505 (discussed below) and *Christian Doctrine*, I, 7 (on Creation).

11. References to Milton's poetry are from *John Milton: Complete Poems and Major Prose*, ed. Merritt Y. Hughes (New York, 1957).

12. See Malcolm Ross, *Poetry and Dogma*, p. 188: "Milton's Christ becomes a symbol of abstract values rather than a person." Christ bears a striking resemblance to the radical formulation of John Everard: "External [that is, literal and historical] Jesus Christ is a *shadow*, a symbol, a figure of the *Internal*: viz. of him *that is to be born* within us" (*The Gospel-Treasury Opened* [London, 1659], The First Part, p. 55; cited by Madsen, *From Shadowy Types to Truth*, p. 41).

13. Madsen, *From Shadowy Types to Truth*, p. 70.

14. Richard Sibbes, *The Souls Conflict with Itself* (1635), ed. A. B. Grosart, in *Works, Nichol's Standard Divines*, 6 vols. (London, 1863), I, 185; cited by Madsen, *From Shadowy Types to Truth*, p. 80.

15. *Of Reformation Touching Church-Discipline in England*, in *The Works of John Milton*, ed. Frank Allen Patterson et al., 18 vols. (New York, 1931–38), III, 1. Where possible, references to Milton's prose are from Hughes; otherwise, as here, the Columbia edition of the *Works* is cited as CM, with volume and page number.

16. *Christian Doctrine*, I, 28 (CM, XVI, 198).

17. *Christian Doctrine*, I, 1 and 4 (Hughes, pp. 903a, 916b, 930b).

18. *The Reason of Church-government urg'd against Prelaty*, II. 2 (Hughes, p. 673b).

19. The phrasing of the King James is ambiguous—as is the Greek: *telos gar*

nomou Christos. Paul seems to suggest here (as elsewhere) that outward observance of the law, *for the sake of* the law is at an end, for Christ is now the *end* of the law. (*Telos* implies both conclusion and purpose.) Thus, the Jerusalem Bible interprets: "the law has come to an end with Christ." The New English Bible agrees but provides an alternative reading: "Christ is the end of the law as a way of righteousness for everyone who has faith."

20. On Milton's doctrine of Christian liberty, see Arthur E. Barker, "Structural and Doctrinal Pattern in Milton's Later Poems," in *Essays in English Literature from the Renaissance to the Victorian Age Presented to A. S. P. Woodhouse,* ed. Millar MacLure and F. W. Watt (Toronto, 1964) , pp. 169–94.

21. *Christian Doctrine,* I, 27 (Hughes, p. 1007a). Cf. 2 Corinthians iii, 3: "not in tables of stone, but in fleshly tables of the heart."

22. Cf. Madsen, *From Shadowy Types to Truth,* p. 82: Milton "creates his own types."

23. *Biographia Literaria,* 2d ed., ed. J. Shawcross, I (Oxford, 1954), p. 202.

24. Ibid.

25. Coleridge, *Biographia,* II, 20.

26. Coleridge, *Table Talk,* 12 May 1830; cited by Shawcross, ed., *Biographia,* II, 270.

27. Coleridge, *Biographia,* II, 209n.

28. Coleridge, *Aids to Reflection,* ed. T. Ashe (London, 1892), p. 136; cited by Shawcross, in *Biographia,* II, 273.

29. *Poetic Diction: A Study in Meaning* (New York, 1964), p. 143.

30. See Don Cameron Allen, "Milton and the Descent to Light," *JEGP,* LX (1961), 614–30; and Carolyn W. Mayerson, "The Orpheus Image in *Lycidas,*" *PMLA,* LXIV (1949), 189–207.

31. This phrase has not been satisfactorily explained. See A. S. P. Woodhouse and Douglas Bush, *A Variorum Commentary on the Poems of John Milton,* II (New York, 1972), pp. 486–501.

32. Leviticus xii, 6–7: "And when the days of her purifying are fulfilled . . . she shall bring a lamb of the first year for a burnt offering, and a young pigeon, or a turtle dove, for a sin offering."

33. My italics; Milton's "old Law" is Luke's "according to the law of Moses."

34. See Romans iii, 20: "by the deeds of the law there shall no flesh be justified . . . for by the law is the knowledge of sin."

35. *Christian Doctrine,* I, 16 (CM, XVI, 111).

36. *Christian Doctrine,* I, 17 (CM, XV, 345).

37. *Christian Doctrine,* I, 18 (CM, XV, 349).

38. Milton's saint comes "vested all in white": "Those that are arrayed in the white robes, who are they, and whence come they? . . . These are they that come out of great tribulation and they washed their robes and made them white in the blood of the lamb" (Revelation vii, 13–14).

39. *Christian Doctrine,* I, 7 (Hughes, p. 977a).

40. See Arnold Stein, *Heroic Knowledge: An Interpretation of "Paradise Regained" and "Samson Agonistes"* (Minneapolis, 1957), p. 128: "The flesh becomes word. Christ says it, and then becomes it."

41. *Images and Themes in Five Poems by Milton* (Cambridge, Mass., 1957), p. 158.

42. Addison, *Spectator,* no. 273, in *Milton Criticism: Selections from Four Cen-*

turies, ed. James Thorpe (New York, 1950), p. 30; Johnson, "Milton," in *Lives of the Poets*, I (Garden City, 1958), p. 138.

43. *Answerable Style: Essays on "Paradise Lost"* (Seattle, 1967), p. 158.

44. *"Paradise Lost" and Its Critics* (Cambridge, 1947), p. 83.

45. Samuel Johnson, *The Rambler*, no. 140 (20 July 1751); cited by Christopher Ricks, *Milton's Grand Style* (New York, 1963), p. 49.

46. Ricks, *Milton's Grand Style*, p. 49.

47. See Owen Barfield, *Saving the Appearances: A Study in Idolatry* (New York, 1957).

48. Cf. John ii, 18–22: "What sign shewest thou unto us? . . . Jesus answered and said unto them, Destroy this temple, and in three days I will raise it up. Then said the Jews, Forty and Six years was this temple in building, and wilt thou rear it up in three days? But he spake of the temple of his body."

49. *Of Reformation*, I (CM, III, 2).

50. See also Psalm cxxxv, 15–18: "The idols . . . have ears but they hear not. . . . They that make them are like unto them."

MILTON'S ANTIPRELATICAL TRACTS: THE POET SPEAKS IN PROSE

John A. Via

John Milton's tracts of 1641–42—harsh, satiric attacks on the corruption of the English church—are an extension and development
of the major themes and principal imagistic patterns of his academic exercises and early poetry, particularly *Prolusion 6, A Mask,
Lycidas,* and the *Epitaphium Damonis.* The tracts are overwhelm-
ingly negative in their thrust, but largely overlooked are their
significant positive elements. First, biblical apocalyptic imagery
describes the national Christian regeneracy of England; this is a
transfer of the visionary descriptions of apotheosis in the poetry to
the concrete reality of the English historical situation. Second, this
apocalyptic imagery describes individual Englishmen whose responses to God's grace in sum will lead to national regeneracy.
Third, in a careful articulation of his view of the character and
function of the divine Christian poet in his personal statements,
Milton humbly offers himself as the type for the response of others,
as a model for individual regeneracy which leads to national regeneracy. The tracts refine primary Miltonic concerns and show the
intimate relation of his poetry and prose.

I

M ILTON'S ANTIPRELATICAL tracts of 1641–42 are a stark redirec-
tioning of the central concerns of his academic exercises and early
poems. This he acknowledges in the personal passage of *The Reason of
Church-Government*: "I should not chuse this manner of writing wherin
knowing my self inferior to my self, led by the genial power of nature to
another task, I have the use, as I may account it, but of my left hand"
(YP, I, 808).[1] Milton knew what his left hand was doing; the passage
functions with characteristic ironic ambiguity. The left hand carries
out the desires of the same person who directs the right hand, but from
a different angle. The left hand is also the inferior one, the sinister one,

and Milton intends this, too. He does not indicate a dichotomy of endeavor; he does not signify that his labor is any less pertinent and meaningful. Instead, he asserts that his concerns are now pointed in another direction for a different purpose—with the ironic gibe that the direction is sinister because of that with which he must deal. In the academic exercises his major emphasis is on the ethical harmony which is necessary for spiritual regeneracy, the most powerful statement of which is *Prolusion 7*, but these positive patterns are frequently juxtaposed and intertwined with negative patterns of disharmony. This is especially true of the negative imagery of Night in *Prolusion 1*, the severe attack on scholastic philosophy in *Prolusion 3*, the castigation of Error in *Prolusion 4*, and the low humor, pointed scurrility, and biting irony of *Prolusion 6*. This last exercise, in fact, is the clearest prose precedent for the style and tone of the antiprelatical tracts, particularly in its direction to a specific audience, though the circumstances of its composition and delivery are assuredly different from those of the tracts.

In the poems the central concern is regeneracy, the harmonious integration of the natural and spiritual orders: the first beginnings in the academic verses which lead to the masterful integration of the Nativity Ode, the shifting foci on the major themes of regeneracy and poetic function in the poems of the second phase which lead to the accomplishment of *Lycidas*. But there is also the awareness of danger to the regenerative process and the fulfillment of poetic function in the developing stern emphasis on individual discipline and virtue and the accompanying imagistic emphasis on ecclesiastical corruption. This begins in the rigidity of the Lady's insistence on virginity in *A Mask* and the irony of that poem's patterns of degeneracy, moves to the explicit condemnation of prelatical corruption in *Lycidas*, and culminates in the frustration and despair evinced in the *Epitaphium Damonis*. Milton's awareness of the danger of prelatical perversity prompts his emphasis on individual virtue, leads to poetic frustration, and finally dictates the prose attacks of these tracts. He feels that he must help rid England of prelacy to make possible individual and national regeneration, and to make possible the fulfillment of his poetic aspirations. But it is fair to say that the early poems and prose works are generally characterized by their positive harmony and regenerative emphases.

The antiepiscopal pamphlets, however, are more concerned to show, and to attack vigorously, the characteristics and effects of disharmony, degeneracy, and corruption; Milton's response, and subsequently the character of the tracts, is violent. He enters England's religious controversy and engages the supporters of episcopacy in verbal combat. The characterization of episcopacy and the prelates themselves is ugly; they are typed as the essence of totally depraved and debauched humanity, the negative extremity of the Calvinistic doctrine of depravity. Doubtless some Anglican clergymen in Milton's time, as in any era, answered the description, but his picture is so uniform that it allows no exception. The characterization is one-sided because his intention is satirical. Milton directly satirizes, with unrelenting Juvenalian harshness, the episcopal government of the Church of England and those who support it. He ridicules ecclesiastical corruption because it endangers the moral and spiritual health of the individual Christian and of the Commonwealth. There is a large positive movement in the antiprelatical tracts concerning reform and the character of the reformed Church, but the emphasis is general and vague, while the characterization of episcopal corruption is highly particularized and energetic. Milton knows the enemy well, but he is not clear about the form of church government which should replace the episcopacy, except that it be generally "presbyteriall."[2] His vagueness is apparent in the imagery of the tracts; the positive patterns of the early poetry, the visionary depiction of regeneracy, are imperfectly translated to the tracts because Milton is unsure how those glowing conceptions will be realized in the actuality of the English historical situation. The specific characteristics of national regeneracy must be clarified before the imagistic patterns which figure forth that historical regeneracy will have the forceful resonance of the positive poetic manipulations.

Milton justifies the harshness of his satirical attacks. His most significant defenses are grounded in the decorum of the circumstances, the necessity for severity in the face of enormous evil, and the precedents of the Christian faith itself. The preface to *Animadversions* cites Solomon and Christ as authorities for the use of the "grim laughter" of satire; vehemence is required against abounding spiritual corruption:

it will be nothing disagreeing from Christian meeknesse to handle such a one in a rougher accent, and to send home his haughtinesse well bespurted with his owne holy-water. Nor to do thus are we unautoritied either from the morall precept of SALOMON to answer him thereafter that prides him in his folly; nor from the example of Christ, and all his followers in all Ages, who in the refuting of those that resisted sound Doctrine, and by subtile dissimulations corrupted the minds of men, have wrought up their zealous souls into such vehemencies, as nothing could be more killingly spoken. (YP, I, 662–63)

Milton associates his virulence and scurrility with biblical usages. For good purpose our Lord was blunt and harsh: "I beseech ye friends, ere the brick-bats flye, resolve me and your selves, is it blasphemy, or any whit disagreeing from Christian meeknesse, when as Christ himselfe speaking of unsavory traditions, scruples not to name the Dunghill and the Jakes, for me to answer a slovenly wincer of a confutation, that, if he would needs put his foot to such a sweaty service, the odour of his Sock was like to be neither musk, nor benjamin?" (YP, I, 895).[3] Jesus employed the irony of inversion, speaking of the highest truths in common terms: "Doth not Christ himselfe teach the highest things by the similitude *of old bottles and patcht cloaths*? Doth he not illustrate best things by things most evill? his own *comming* to be *as a thiefe in the night,* and the righteous mans *wisdome to that of an unjust Steward?*" (YP, I, 898). Then Milton gives an extended defense of his vehemence, rejecting the precedents of classical rhetorical decorum, and offering the example of Christ, who taught his followers according to the circumstances of the occasion "sometimes by a milde and familiar converse, sometimes with plaine and impartiall home-speaking . . . otherwhiles with bitter and irefull rebukes" (YP, I, 899). He concludes by citing the severity of God himself against Jereboam in I Kings xiv, 10: "*I will cut off from Iereboam him that pisseth against the wall.*" Thus he justifies his severity as satire decorously in keeping with biblical patterns and motivated by the monstrosity of the opposing forces of evil. We may classify his satire as Juvenalian; he sees it as firmly biblical and in the historical context of Christian controversial prose.

In the *Defensio Secunda* Milton remembers his involvement in the episcopal controversy: "I perceived that men were following the true path to liberty" and "I decided, although at that time occupied with certain other matters, to devote to this conflict all my talents and all my active powers" (YP, IV, 622). He traces his participation in the pamphlet warfare, and concludes that he "brought succor to the ministers, who were . . . scarcely able to withstand the eloquence" of the bishops (YP, IV, 623). In the antiprelatical tracts he performs the physician's dual function: the violent rooting out of the disease of prelacy, and the succor of healing to the body of the Commonwealth. The first involves the predominant and harsh imagistic patterns of evil and ugliness representing the perverse ecclesiastics; the second involves the less elaborate and explicit but no less significant patterns of goodness and beauty depicting the regenerate.[4] Both thematic and imagistic directions involve the same motivation and intention: the restoration of liberty and the fulfillment of national regeneracy. He is the physician, but also the poet whose "eloquence" is devoted to the religious cause, and he performs a sanctified ministerial function.

II

Ecclesiastical corruption and its frustration of regeneracy are depicted in the most elaborate patterns of imagery in the tracts. These images are an expansion and intensification of patterns in Milton's early poetry and prose. The precedents for the negative imagery are particularly evident in *Prolusion 6* in his attack on his academic audience. He uses similar patterns—images of bodily disease and function, the denigration of animal association, references to sexual impropriety, and images of food. The vivid flatus image of the exercise closely parallels the olfactory imagery of Hall's socks in *An Apology* (YP, I, 894), while the imagery of the vomiting university and its diseased students, made so by religious corruption, is also related to the scurrility of the same passage. The imagery of syphilitic corruption and the picture of the dissolute youth of the prelates in *Animadversions* (YP, I, 675–77) is an extension of similar patterns in *Prolusion 6*. Finally, the imagery of the liturgy as food and tradition as tainted viands is associated with the elaborate food metaphor of the exercise.[5] But the intensity of Milton's attack is considerably modified by the light-hearted atmosphere of the college vacation exercise and his easy familiarity with an audience composed of his fellow students, tutors, and officials who sanctioned the low humor of his presentation.

The imagistic patterns of the tracts are anticipated in Milton's early poetry in individual images that function ironically and ambiguously, and in several of the poems they are pointedly anticipated in major patterns. The ugly picture of the Catholic procession and the Mass as bacchanal in *In Quintum Novembris* is very close to the image of the Anglican service in the tracts, where a major aspect of its corruption is its relation to Catholic ceremony. In *Of Reformation* Milton describes the Lord's Supper in images almost identical to those in *Novembris*: "that

Feast of love and heavenly-admitted fellowship, the Seale of filiall grace became the Subject of horror, and glouting adoration, pageanted about, like a dreadfull Idol" (YP, I, 523). The Anglican service is presented in images of darkness, gluttony, and sexual excess in *Animadversions*: "Who is there that cannot trace thee now in thy beamy walke through the midst of thy Sanctuary, amidst those golden *candlesticks*, which have long suffer'd a dimnesse amongst us through the violence of those that had seiz'd them, and were more taken with the mention of their gold then of their starry light; teaching the doctrine of *Balaam* to cast a stumbling-block before thy servants, commanding them to eat things sacrifiz'd to Idols, and forcing them to fornication" (YP, I, 705–06). The Pope in *Novembris* is a fornicator, and the mask-disguise of the Satanic figure as a Franciscan friar is paralleled in images of prelatical disguise throughout the tracts: "trim devis'd mummery," "Mimick Bishop," "your old fallacy wee shall soone unmask," "ye Church-maskers," "the finicall goosery of your neat Sermon-actor." [6] But in spite of these imagistic relations, *Novembris* does not have the harshness of the tracts because it more carefully balances the ugliness of Catholic corruption and the beauty of English holiness, and because the conventional character of a poem written about the gunpowder plot blunts the force of the imagery.

At A Vacation Exercise places the decorum of language in opposition to "those new fangled toys, and triming slight / Which takes our late fantasticks with delight." Linguistic corruption is not related to episcopal excess, but in this academic poem Milton's concern for the decorous and harmonious use of language anticipates the imagery of the tracts. In *Of Reformation* he castigates the Fathers and the prelates: "But let the Scriptures be hard; are they more hard, more crabbed, more abstruse then the Fathers? He that cannot understand the sober, plain, and unaffected stile of the Scriptures, will be ten times more puzzl'd with the knotty Africanisms, the pamper'd metafors; the intricat, and involv'd sentences of the Fathers; besides the fantastick, and declamatory flashes; the crosse-jingling periods which cannot but disturb, and come thwart a setl'd devotion worse then the din of bells, and rattles" (YP, I, 568). His gibe in the poem is made in passing, but even if it were not, the frivolous academic occasion would significantly modify its harshness. There is no such modification of the attack in the tracts.

In the final movement of the Nativity Ode Milton pictures the retreat of the pagan gods before the harmony of the Incarnation. The

patterns are biblical and classical in character, but they function ironically to point to ecclesiastical and liturgical corruption. The passage
quoted above from *Animadversions* and related to the imagery of *In
Quintum Novembris* bears a similar relation to the Nativity Ode. The
dimness of prelatical "golden *candlesticks*," the sacrifices to idols, and
the sexual excesses which Milton associates with episcopacy are similar
to the picture of pagan worship in the Nativity Ode. And as the darkness
of the poem is overcome by the brilliant light and resonant harmony of
the Incarnation, so the *Animadversions* passage is immediately balanced
by Milton's invocation to God: "Come therefore O thou that hast the
seven starres in thy right hand" (YP, I, 706).

Arcades depicts the movement of the Arcadian shepherds from the
darkness of unregeneracy to the brilliance of regeneracy symbolized by
the Countess.[7] Their journey is a religious quest through the dangers of
the wood of the world under the guidance of the Genius, who at once
is the wise servant of God and a representative of the religious function
of the poet-singer. In *The Reason of Church-Government*, Milton pictures the discipline and order of the angelic hierarchies and the host of
the redeemed in heaven, and then returns to the experiential present:
"how much lesse can we believe that God would leave his fraile and
feeble, though not lesse beloved Church here below to the perpetuall
stumble of conjecture and disturbance in this our darke voyage without
the card and compasse of Discipline. . . . if it be at all the worke of man,
it must be of such a one as is a true knower of himselfe, and himselfe in
whom contemplation and practice, wit, prudence, fortitude, and eloquence must be rarely met" (YP, I, 752–53). The voyage is the religious
quest of the whole Church and its individual members, and it has its
guide, "the card and compasse of Discipline," the nautical navigation
aid which is provided by men of learning, wisdom, virtue, and eloquence—regenerate guides of the Church, the nation, and the individual
like the Genius of *Arcades*. The Countess is the personification of heavenly wisdom and virtue, and her wisdom is underscored by biblical
allusions to Solomon. So in *The Reason of Church-Government*:

For if there were no opposition where were the triall of an unfained goodnesse
and magnanimity? vertue that wavers is not vertue, but vice revolted from
itselfe, and after a while returning. The actions of just and pious men do not
darken in their middle course; but *Solomon* tels us they are as the shining
light, that shineth more and more unto the perfet day. But if we shall suffer

the trifling doubts and jealousies of future sects to overcloud the faire beginnings of purpos't reformation, let us rather fear that another proverb of
the same Wiseman be not upraided to us, that the way of the wicked is as
darknesse, they stumble at they know not what. (YP, I, 795)

The historical movement of the English Church is a regenerative process, a trial of wisdom and virtue, and it is pictured in terms of light. Its
wood of danger is "the dark, the bushie, the tangled Forrest" (YP, I,
569) of ecclesiastical corruption. In *Of Reformation* this is apparent:
"after so many darke Ages, wherein the huge overshadowing traine of
Error had almost swept all the Starres out of the Firmament of the
Church; how the bright and blissfull *Reformation* (by Divine Power)
strook through the black and settled Night of *Ignorance* and *Antichris-
tian Tyranny*" (YP, I, 524).

III

The most explicit interpenetration of the patterns of poetry and
prose is seen in the relation of the tracts to *A Mask*. Arthur Barker has
clearly indicated the relation:

Episcopacy assumed in his eyes the lineaments of Comus; it was the public
manifestation of the perversions of carnal sensuality against which he had
striven in favour of high seriousness. The reformed discipline of the Puritan
church similarly assumed the aspect of the virgin Lady, possessed of transcendent spiritual powers. Its triumph over episcopacy corresponded to the triumph
of chastity over lust. . . . Milton's contrast between the degeneration of religion
which has resulted from the forces animating the bishops and its purification
as designed by the Puritans exactly parallels the Elder Brother's contrast between the imbruting of the spirit by lust and the spiritualizing of the body by
virtue.[8]

The Reason of Church-Government draws the distinction which Barker
indicates.[9] The Old Covenant of Law is superseded by the New Covenant of Grace, Milton says, alluding at several points to the Pauline
characterization of the Law as weak and beggarly and grounded in the
flesh (Galatians iv). Episcopacy, in citing the Law as basis for its organization and ceremony, is likewise grounded in the flesh. Its ministry consists of "carnall things," "nests it selfe in worldly honours," and "runnes
back againe to the old pompe and glory of the flesh." Religion must be
"pure, spirituall, simple, and lowly, as the Gospel most truly is." The
relation to *A Mask* is apparent.

A stronger characterization appears in *Of Reformation*, where Milton personifies the Church as a woman, the episcopal prostitute and the Presbyterian virgin. The prelates "thought the plaine and homespun verity of *Christs* Gospell unfit any longer to hold their Lordships acquaintance, unlesse the poore thred-bare Matron were put into better clothes; her chast and modest vaile surrounded with celestiall beames they overlai'd with wanton *tresses,* and in a flaring tire bespecckl'd her with all the gaudy allurements of a Whore" (YP, I, 557). The corrupt prelates themselves are "mis-shapen and enormous," but they "blanch and varnish" their deformities. They are "a Tyrannical crew and Corporation of Impostors, that have blinded and abus'd the World." They have changed "a moderate and exemplary House, for a mis-govern'd and haughty *Palace.*" They exhibit a "universall rottennes, and gangrene in the whole *Function.*"[10] These inversions of spiritual functions exactly parallel the corruption of Comus and his crew in their orgiastic perversion of religious ceremony, and Comus' transvaluation of spiritual and natural goods in his temptation of the Lady.

The Attendant Spirit describes the imbruting of the human spirit by lust: "And they, so perfect is their misery, / Not once perceive their foul disfigurement, / But boast themselves more comely then before / And all their friends, and native home forget / To roule with pleasure in a sensual stie" (CM, I, 87–88). The Elder Brother's picture is uglier:

> but when lust
> By unchaste looks, loose gestures, and foul talk,
> But most by leud and lavish act of sin,
> Lets in defilement to the inward parts,
> The soul grows clotted by contagion,
> Imbodies, and imbrutes, till she quite loose
> The divine property of her first being.
> Such are those thick and gloomy shadows damp
> Oft seen in Charnel vaults, and Sepulchers
> Lingering, and sitting by a new made grave,
> As loath to leave the Body that it lov'd,
> And link't it self by carnal sensuality
> To a degenerate and degraded state.   (CM, I, 102)

The prelates similarly imbrute, as the opening movement of *Of Reformation* makes apparent; there Milton refers to the prelates' "new-vomited Paganisme of sensuall Idolatry." They "make *God* earthly, and fleshly, because they could not make themselves *heavenly,* and *Spiri-*

tuall." He goes on vividly to condemn Anglican liturgy and liturgical garments.[11] In *An Apology* he condemns the clergy in the words of Isaiah as *"dumbe and greedy dogs"* who have made beasts of the laity through their avarice, and says: "So little care they of beasts to make them men, that by their sorcerous doctrine of formalities they take the way to transforme them out of Christian men into *Iudaizing* beasts" (YP, I, 932). He emphasizes the corruption and degeneracy of the episcopacy: blindness, vomit, impurity, sensuality, deformity. It is associated with the inadequacy and carnality of the Old Covenant of the Law and the emptiness and idolatry of paganism. And its ugliness is worse because it pretends spirituality, as Comus pretends to participate in the heavenly harmony and celebrates in perverse religious rites.

As the regenerate Lady recognizes Comus' language as "visor'd falsehood" and "false rules pranckt in reasons garb," so Milton in *Animadversions* castigates the language of the prelates:

Setting aside the odde coinage of your phrase, which no mintmaister of language would allow for sterling, that a thing should be taxt for no other then holy, and ancient, let it be suppos'd the substance of them may savour of something holy, or ancient, this is but the matter; the forme, and the end of the thing may yet render it either superstitious, fruitlesse, or impious, and so, worthy to be rejected. The Garments of a Strumpet are often the same materially, that cloath a chast Matron, and yet ignominious for her to weare, the substance of the tempters words to our Saviour were holy, but his drift nothing lesse. (YP, I, 686)

The metaphors of the passage are mixed—base metal and clothing both bespeak language—but the point is clear, and the force of Milton's indictment is intensified by the association of prelacy with the Satanic temptation of Christ and the application of the Church-Whore metaphor to language.[12]

Other imagistic patterns in the tracts are anticipated in *A Mask*. The herb *haemony*, provided by the "Shepherd Lad" who is much like Jesus, signifies experiential knowledge and allows the Attendant Spirit and then the brothers to perceive Comus' evil. The *asperges* of Sabrina, signifying the grace of God, totally frees the Lady from evil's power. In *Of Reformation* the eyesalve of regeneration removes the film of degeneracy, overcoming darkness with light (YP, I, 566).[13] Comus mesmerizes the Lady with magic dust, which prevents her from seeing his perversity and signifies the earthiness of the imbruting which he hopes to effect;

later the dust of degeneracy meets the water of God's grace to become the mud of perverse response. So in *Of Reformation* the prelates, when "they feel themselvs strook in the transparent streams of divine Truth, they would plunge, and tumble, and thinke to ly hid in the foul weeds, and muddy waters, where no plummet can reach the bottome" (YP, I, 569).[14] In both passages regeneration is pictured as clear water and degeneracy as mud, and the patterns are tangentially related to the ages of the Church as Milton describes them in *Animadversions*: "the gold of those Apostolick Successors that you boast of, as your *Constantinian* silver, together with the iron, the brasse, and the clay of those muddy and strawy ages that follow" (YP, I, 700–01).

Reformed church discipline is personified as a woman: "And certainly discipline is not only the removall of disorder, but if any visible shape can be given to divine things, the very visible shape and image of vertue, whereby she is not only seene in the regular gestures and motions of her heavenly paces as she walkes, but also makes the harmony of her voice audible to mortall eares" (YP, I, 751–52). She is very close to the Lady of *A Mask*, whose rhythmic, regenerate steps are recognized as the "different pace, / Of som chast footing" by Comus, whose own rhythm is "the tread / Of hatefull steps." Her song is like the beautiful song of the Lady which, in its regenerate goodness, blends with the heavenly harmony. The Lady's movement through the dark wood to the glittering falseness of Comus' palace and out again to the harmonious brilliance of Ludlow Castle is an experiential pattern close to that of *Arcades*. Thus the passages of *The Reason of Church-Government* discussed in relation to *Arcades*—the imagery of the hard journey—are equally related to *A Mask*, the Attendant Spirit, Sabrina, and the Lady sharing the signification of the Genius of the Wood and the Arcadians.[15]

A Mask anticipates poetically what the antiprelatical tracts picture in severe satiric prose. Image and theme interpenetrate, but the poem is not severe because it is concerned to depict the process of regeneration and the significance of regenerate response in experience, not to attack ecclesiastical corruption. Certainly there are harsh patterns in *A Mask*, but they are balanced by the positive imagery of regeneracy: brilliant light, harmonious sound, and smooth, rhythmic movement. *A Mask* is a poetic whole with positive intentions; the tracts are not balanced because the particularization of negative patterns tends to obscure the larger and more general positive movements.

IV

The imagery of the second movement of *Lycidas* relates to the imagery of the tracts as pointedly but not as extensively as that of *A Mask*. After Hippotades blames Lycidas' unfulfilled life and early death on the corruption of ecclesiastical institutions, in the image of the Church as "that fatal and perfidious Bark / Built in th' eclipse, and rigg'd with curses dark," the Apostle Peter appears, bearing the golden and iron keys of judgment, to castigate the corrupt clergy:

> How well could I have spar'd for thee, young swain,
> Anow of such as for their bellies sake,
> Creep and intrude, and climb into the fold?
> Of other care they little reck'ning make,
> Then how to scramble at the shearers feast,
> And shove away the worthy bidden guest;
> Blind mouthes! that scarce themselves know how to hold
> A Sheep-hook, or have learn'd ought els the least
> That to the faithfull Herdmans art belongs!
> What recks it them? What need they? They are sped;
> And when they list, their lean and flashy songs
> Grate on their scrannel Pipes of wretched straw,
> The hungry Sheep look up, and are not fed,
> But swoln with wind, and the rank mist they draw,
> Rot inwardly, and foul contagion spread:
> Besides what the grim Woolf with privy paw
> Daily devours apace, and nothing sed,
> But that two-handed engine at the door
> Stands ready to smite once, and smite no more.   (CM, I, 80–81)

The central metaphor is biblical, the minister as pastor, the shepherd of his congregational flock, the human counterpart of Christ, who described himself as "the good shepherd: the good shepherd giveth his life for the sheep. But he that is an hireling, and not the shepherd, whose own the sheep are not, seeth the wolf coming, and leaveth the sheep, and fleeth: and the wolf catcheth them, and scattereth the sheep" (John x, 11–12). In *Of Reformation* the prelates are "lank" and "shallow" (YP, I, 569), and throughout the tracts they are described in inverted pastoral imagery.

Incidental images parallel the usages of *Lycidas*. In the poem Saint Peter is the "Pilot of the *Galilean* lake" because of his fisherman's occupation and the previous image of the Church as "Bark," of which he is the first leader. In *Animadversions* Milton contrasts the regenerate devotion of Simon Peter as a fisher of men with the degenerate corruption of Simon Magus, the sorcerer who sought to buy the gift of the Holy Spirit: "If we fishing with *Simon* the Apostle can catch nothing; see what you can catch with *Simon Magus*; for all his hooks, & fishing implements he bequeath'd among you" (YP, I, 710).[16] The true fisherman is the regenerate minister; the perverted magician is the greedy prelate. In *The Reason of Church-Government* faith is imaged as a "floting vessell" and the struggle for reform as "the vain hope of our founder'd ships" (YP, I, 794, 799). But central to the imagery of the tracts are pastoral patterns closely related to those of *Lycidas*. Milton invokes God's blessing in *Of Reformation*: "looke upon this thy poore and almost spent, and expiring *Church*, leave her not thus a prey to these importunate *Wolves*, that wait and thinke long till they devoure thy tender *Flock*, these wilde Boares that have broke into thy *Vineyard*, and left the print of thir polluting hoofs on the Soules of thy Servants" (YP, I, 614). The prelates are *"Wolves"* here as they are in *Lycidas*, and they are "wilde Boares" who trample the *"Vineyard"* of the regenerate who are seeking to grow in grace.[17] In *An Apology* the prelates are similarly depicted:

The Apostles ever labour'd to perswade the Christian flock that they *were call'd in Christ to all perfectnesse of spirituall knowledge, and full assurance of understanding in the mystery of God.* But the non-resident and plurality-gaping Prelats the gulphs and whirle pools of benefices, but the dry pits of all sound doctrine, that they may the better preach what they list to their sheep, are still possessing them that they are sheepe indeed, without judgement, without understanding. . . . No marvell if the people turne beasts, when their Teachers themselves as *Isaiah* calls them, *Are dumbe and greedy dogs that can never have anough, ignorant, blind, and cannot understand, who while they all look their own way every one for his gaine from his quarter,* how many parts of the land are fed with windy ceremonies instead of sincere milke; and while one Prelat enjoyes the nourishment and right of twenty Ministers, how many waste places are left as darke as *Galile of the Gentiles, sitting in the region and shadow of death;* without preaching Minister, without light. (YP, I, 931–32)

Milton turns the metaphor against the prelates; they pervertedly interpret it on the literal level, treating their congregational flocks as dumb beasts without regenerate understanding. The sheep in *Lycidas* "are not fed, / But swoln with wind," and the flock of *An Apology* is "fed with windy ceremonies." The Isaiah citation denigrates the prelates in its animal imagery, and the allusion is more forceful because of the full biblical passage: "His watchmen are blind: they are all ignorant, they are all dumb dogs, they cannot bark; sleeping, lying down, loving to slumber. Yea, they are greedy dogs which can never have enough, and they are shepherds that cannot understand; they all look to their own way, every one for his gain, from his quarter" (Isaiah lvi, 10–11). The prelates imbrute men; they feed their sheep with the wind of empty words; they fleece them through their avarice and gluttony; they lead them away from the light of regenerate understanding to the darkness of ignorance. In *Animadversions* Milton admonishes the English clergy: "Open your eyes to the light of grace, a better guide then Nature. Look upon the meane condition of *Christ*, and his *Apostles*, without that accessory strength you take such paines to raise from the light of Nature, and Policie" (YP, I, 702). This underscores a major distinction of the antiprelatical tracts and indicates a fundamental imagistic pattern. The reformers of the English Church have the "light of grace"—they are regenerate; those who corrupt the Church are without the light of grace and have in their perversity put out even the light of Nature—they are unregenerate. The dark eclipse of *Lycidas* is overcome by the brilliance of heavenly apotheosis; the corruption considered in the tracts is not so effectively balanced, but when it is, it is by the "light of grace."

The gustatory patterns of *Lycidas* anticipate patterns which occur throughout the tracts. There the evil shepherds creep into the fold "for their bellies sake." In *Of Reformation* Milton warns against men who "beg so devoutly for the pride, and gluttony of their owne backs, and bellies," men "whose mouths cannot open without the strong breath, and loud stench of avarice, Simony, and Sacrilege." He pictures them "warming their Palace Kitchins, and from thence their unctuous, and epicurean paunches, with the almes of the blind, the lame, the impotent, the aged, the orfan, the widow" (YP, I, 610–11). This passage is informed by biblical usages like Philippians iii, 18–19, "the enemies of the cross of Christ . . . whose God is their belly." It shares the scurrility of *Prolusion 6* in its images of the prelates' rank breath; it is indicative of a major pattern which encompasses the imagery of food in *Prolusion 6*, and such references in this tract as the harsh image of cooled prelatical zeal as a porridge "that gives a Vomit to GOD himselfe" (YP, I, 537).

Animal images which denigrate episcopacy have already been discussed in relation to pastoral patterns, but they are significant in their own right. In *Lycidas* the corrupt ecclesiastics are presented only as ravenous wolves, but in the tracts they are diminished in a variety of animal associations. They are "Ferrets and Moushunts" who slither through ancient texts to find obscure support for their institutions. They are "a continuall *Hydra* of mischiefe, and molestation, the forge of discord and Rebellion." They are the "rude oxen" who pull the Church "mounted upon the Prelaticall Cart."[18] They are the supporters of corrupt tradition which is "the perpetuall cankerworme to eat out Gods Commandements." They are "Vulturs" of wealth who "creepe into the Church indiscernably."[19] In similar patterns the prelates are pictured as criminals who debase Christian virtues which "must lie prostitute to sordid Fees, and not passe to and fro between our Saviour that of free grace redeem'd us . . . without the truccage of perishing Coine, and the Butcherly execution of Tormentors, Rooks, and Rakeshames sold to lucre." The episcopate is "to our purses, and goods a wastfull band of robbers."[20]

Natural imagery in *Lycidas* indicates the unregenerate understanding of the persona who cannot come to terms with the fact of death. He expresses it in the picture of "the gadding Vine o'regrown," "the Canker to the Rose," the "Taint-worm," and the killing "Frost." After gaining some regenerate insight through the assurance of the Phoebus figure and the assertions of the Apostle Peter, his perception of nature changes and is illustrated in the harmonious beauty of the flower passage (132–64). Attacking the episcopal argument that the prelacy is necessary to prevent schism, Milton employs similar imagistic patterns in *The Reason of Church-Government*. He indicates that prelacy brings a "num and chil stupidity of soul" in its attempt to prevent schism. He continues:

The Winter might as well vaunt it selfe against the Spring, I destroy all noysome and rank weeds, I keepe downe all pestilent vapours. Yes and all wholesome herbs, and all fresh dews, by your violent & hidebound frost; but when the gentle west winds shall open the fruitfull bosome of the earth thus overgirded by your imprisonment, then the flowers put forth and spring, and then the Sunne shall scatter the mists, and the manuring hand of the Tiller shall root up all that burdens the soile without thank to your bondage. (YP, I, 785)

Episcopacy does prevent schism—and freedom and vitality. It is the degeneracy of winter which would prevent the regeneracy of spring, imagery strikingly similar to the natural imagery of *Lycidas*. The Son-Sunne will come and God the Tiller will not allow corruption to triumph.

The negative emphasis of the imagistic and thematic patterns in

Lycidas thus anticipates the intensification of the patterns in the tracts, but, like *A Mask, Lycidas* does not have the harshness of the prose. The second movement of the poem damns ecclesiastical corruption, but its intensity is immediately modified by the poem's other concern: the consolation of heavenly fulfillment for the regenerate pictured in the apocalyptic imagery of apotheosis. This emphasis is present in the tracts, but not with such fullness.

The *Epitaphium Damonis* is the pivotal point of Milton's early literary efforts, the last poem before he turns to the tracts; in it he speaks of the despair of poetic paralysis and diagnoses the cause of the frustration of his hopes for national regeneracy and poetic accomplishment, even while he positively states his poetic plans. He says, "you, my Pan's pipe, will hang, far away . . . on an aged pine, utterly forgot by me, or else, transmuted, you will, with the aid of native Muses, sound forth a truly British strain" (CM, I, 313). His aspiration is to move from the lesser mode of classical pastoral poetry to the higher modes of native epic and, pictured in Manso's two cups, divine poetry. The image also relates to the shepherd-persona's pastoral song in *Lycidas,* which is raised to a "higher mood" before his "Oat proceeds." In the opening paragraph of *Of Prelatical Episcopacy* he describes the prelacy as "the broken reed of *tradition*" (YP, I, 624). He indicates a new direction for the religious life of the nation: the broken reed of episcopacy must be exchanged for the new strains of reformed church government solidly grounded on the "*Divine* authority" of Scripture, the new harmony that will be measured by the "Reed" of the evangelist in Revelation xi, 1–2 (YP, I, 760–61).

In the *Epitaphium Damonis* the new song of divine poetry, and the new song of individual and national regeneration, are frustrated by the "wolf" who sees Milton first and strikes him dumb, by the "hungry wolves" who endanger the fold, and by the cattle, wolves, and asses who feel nothing for others and think only of themselves. The prelatical wolves frustrate Milton poetically and the nation religiously; but at the same time there is a countermovement in the poem's conclusion. Like *Lycidas,* Damon is apotheosized in the light and harmony of the virgins around the throne of God in the apocalyptic vision of Revelation, the positive light and harmony balancing the negative frustration of ecclesiastical corruption. This apocalyptic emphasis is apparent in its gradual exfoliation in the poetry—in *Elegia 3, In Obitum Praesulis Eliensis, On the Death of a Fair Infant, Winchester, At A Solemn Musick,* and *On Time*—but nowhere more forcefully present than in *Lycidas* and the *Epitaphium Damonis.* It is the ground for the positive thematic and imagistic movements of the tracts.

V

The visionary consolation of the final fulfillment of individual regeneracy pictured in the biblical apocalyptic imagery of the closing movements of *Lycidas* and *Damonis* represents the full resonance of patterns seen throughout the early poems; it significantly informs the positive movements of the antiprelatical tracts. In the poems the imagery is apocalyptic and visionary. While its significance is directed to present experience, the full brilliance and harmony of the apotheosis remains the hope of the living and the possession of those lifted to eternity. The Bishop of Winchester in *Elegia 3* stands among the heavenly choirs, a "radiance as of the stars" gleaming "in his shining face." The Felton figure in *Eliensis* is borne through "the ranks of the wandering stars" to the "shining portals of Olympus." The child of *Fair Infant* returns to "the golden-winged hoast," having taught us in her presence and by the example of her innocence to live regeneratively.[21] The Marchioness of Winchester returns to "blazing Majesty and Light" and we are left to weep "tears of perfect moan." The apotheosis of *On Time* will occur in the "then" of "long Eternity" when we "all this Earthy grosness quit," while the apocalyptic vision of *At A Solemn Musick* is the final hope of those who on earth are attuned to heaven "till God ere long / To his celestial consort us unite." The regenerate poet-personae of *L'Allegro, Il Penseroso,* and *Lycidas* perceive the final apocalyptic fulfillment, but must live presently with hope; the old man of the companion poems will eventually be apotheosized; the Lycidas figure goes to heavenly glory, while his poet-friend remains to face the trial of "fresh Woods, and Pastures new." And in *Damonis* we are left with the hope only; the poetically and religiously paralyzed persona cannot translate the hope of final fulfillment into regeneratively involved action.

In the antiprelatical tracts Milton attempts to transfer the poetic vision of the apotheosis of the regenerate man to the reforming historical situation of England. The visionary consolation of *Lycidas* and *Damonis* is transmuted to the compensation of regenerate reform in the present time. The hopeful and confident expectation of reformation, of individual regeneracy leading to national regeneracy, brings the apotheosis into the historical and living present. And as the theme of regenerative fulfillment is translated into history, so the apocalyptic imagery which it involves is applied to the contemporary situation.

This is apparent at the conclusion of *Of Reformation*, as Milton describes an England historically reformed by God's grace and depicts the positive response of men:

Then amidst the *Hymns*, and *Halleluiahs* of *Saints* some one may perhaps bee heard offering at high *strains* in new and lofty *Measures* to sing and celebrate thy *divine Mercies*, and *marvelous Judgements* in this Land throughout all AGES; whereby this great and Warlike Nation instructed and inur'd to the fervent and continuall practice of *Truth* and *Righteousnesse*, and casting farre from her the *rags* of her old *vices* may presse on hard to that *high* and *happy* emulation to be found the *soberest, wisest*, and *most Christian People* at that day when thou the Eternall and shortly-expected King shalt open the Clouds to judge the severall Kingdomes of the World, and distributing *Nationall Honours* and *Rewards* to Religious and just *Common-wealths*, shalt put an end to all Earthly *Tyrannies*, proclaiming thy universal and milde *Monarchy* through Heaven and Earth. Where they undoubtedly that by their *Labours, Counsels*, and *Prayers* have been earnest for the *Common good* of *Religion* and their *Countrey*, shall receive, above the inferiour *Orders* of the *Blessed*, the *Regall* addition of *Principalities, Legions*, and *Thrones* into their glorious Titles, and in supereminence of *beatifick Vision* progressing the *datelesse* and *irrevoluble* Circle of *Eternity* shall clasp inseparable Hands with *joy*, and *blisse* in over measure for ever. (YP, I, 616)

The passage is fraught with imagery made familiar in the early poems. The musical harmony is characteristic: the "joyous sounds" of *Elegia 3*, the "undisturbed Song of pure concent" in *At A Solemn Musick*, the "unexpressive nuptial Song" of *Lycidas*, the joyous song of Damon. The "Eternall and shortly-expected King" is the Christ of the Nativity Ode, *The Passion*, and *Upon the Circumcision*. The angels are present in virtually all of the poetic visions, but here the regenerate of England are placed above the "inferiour *Orders* of the *Blessed*." The vital movement of the English saints is characteristic, paralleling the movement of the shepherds toward regeneracy in *Arcades* and the triumphant motion of the Lady through the wood of evil in *A Mask* to the harmonious dance at Ludlow Castle. To the cluster of apocalyptic imagery brought down to the historical present, Milton adds the mathematical perfection of the "Circle of *Eternity*." This passage at the close of *Of Reformation* evinces another significant relation to the poems. It occurs at the end of an extended movement which begins with the picture of the prelates as wolves and boars, and moves through an historical picture of the operation of God's grace in England.[22] The negative animal imagery is related to the pastoral patterns of *Lycidas*, which significantly inform the negative imagery of the tracts, but so also do imagistic patterns in the historical sequence. Milton refers to the "proud Ship-wracks of the *Spanish* Armado" and the "Navall ruines that have larded our Seas," images reminiscent of the "fatal and perfidious Bark" of *Lycidas*. As Lycidas triumphs over the shipwreck of faith in heavenly apotheosis, so the English saints triumph in time over dangers to their faith, the shipwreck of faith (1 Timothy i, 18–19) which the Spanish Armada signifies, being shipwrecked itself through the power of the beginning English reformation. The English saints stand as a bulwark against spiritual "*Tyrannies*," as the "guarded Mount" of *Lycidas* shields England from the spiritual perversity of the Continent.

Again, in the *Animadversions*, Milton sets forth in prayer the glory of regenerate England:

O perfect, and accomplish thy glorious acts; for men may leave their works unfinisht, but thou art a God, thy nature is perfection; shouldst thou bring us thus far onward from *Egypt* to destroy us in this Wildernesse though wee deserve; yet thy great name would suffer in the rejoycing of thine enemies, and the deluded hope of all thy servants. When thou hast settl'd peace in the Church, and righteous judgement in the Kingdome, then shall all thy Saints addresse their voyces of joy, and triumph to thee, standing on the shoare of that red Sea into which our enemies had almost driven us. And he that now for haste snatches up a plain ungarnish't present as a thanke-offering to thee, which could not bee deferr'd in regard of thy so many late deliverances wrought for us one upon another, may then perhaps take up a Harp, and sing thee an elaborate Song to Generations. . . . Come forth out of thy Royall Chambers, O Prince of all the Kings of the earth, put on the visible roabes of thy imperiall Majesty, take up that unlimited Scepter which thy Almighty Father hath bequeath'd thee; for now the voice of thy Bride calls thee, and all creatures sigh to bee renew'd. (YP, I, 706–07)

The apocalyptic imagery of Christ's Second Coming describes the historical regeneration of England; indeed, the two events merge. The poetic and visionary is made historic and immediate as, figurally, the regeneration of England participates in the divine salvation of Israel in its passage through the Red Sea and the Wilderness, the redemption of Christ's sacrificial act, and the ultimate fulfillment of goodness on the

Day of Judgment. The apocalyptic imagery of brilliant light, musical harmony, and positive vitality continues. The passage bears close comparison to the Nativity Ode in the detail of its imagery. Milton is present, too, as the one who may "take up a Harp."

The zeal of the regenerate is apocalyptic in *An Apology for Smectymnuus*:

then Zeale whose substance is ethereal, arming in compleat diamond ascends his fiery Chariot drawn with two blazing Meteors figur'd like beasts, but of a higher breed then any the Zodiack yeilds, resembling two of those four which *Ezechiel* and S. *John* saw, the one visag'd like a Lion to expresse power, high autority and indignation, the other of count'nance like a man to cast derision and scorne upon perverse and fraudulent seducers; with these the invincible warriour Zeale shaking loosely the slack reins drives over the heads of Scarlet Prelats, and such as are insolent to maintaine traditions, brusing their stiffe necks under his flaming wheels. (YP, I, 900)

The reformers of England are two of the four beasts of Ezekiel i and Revelation iv. They destroy episcopal corruption which is pictured as the whore of Babylon from Revelation xvii—and all this in patterns of energetic movement and brilliant luminosity directly from the poems, particularly *At A Solemn Musick*. This is the proper response to God's grace, the response of total and zealous commitment.

These patterns in the tracts show Milton's intention experientially and historically to apply the visionary and apocalyptic imagistic patterns of the early poems, and they indicate the presence in the tracts of a large, but not carefully articulated, movement of positive character.

VI

While the apocalyptic passages aim to describe the historical reformation of the English nation, they also indicate that the movement of England to regeneracy is being achieved as the sum of hundreds of thousands of individual responses to God's grace: "the *Hymns*, and *Halleluiahs* of *Saints*" are the musically harmonious sign of the regeneration of those individual Christians; the flaming, purified, and purifying zeal of total commitment must reside in the redeemed individual. This is a positive reversal of the negative imagistic and thematic movements of the tracts, which depict the frustration of the regenerative response by episcopal corruption. Thus a second positive movement involves imagery which pictures the character of the response demanded from the thousands whose personal regeneracy is the basis for national regeneracy, and this imagistic direction is anticipated in and informed by the patterns of the poetry.

A major theme in the poetry is regeneracy. The figures of *Elegia 3* and *Eliensis* achieve heavenly fulfillment because they are regenerate. *Elegia 4* pictures the faithful Christian minister as the shepherd who cares for his congregational flock. The resonant harmony of the Nativity Ode rests in its theme of the Incarnation, which is the ground of man's redemption, the historical event which integrates the divine and human realms. *L'Allegro* and *Il Penseroso* show the life of regenerate involvement which leads to the prophetic wisdom of old age and is based on the religious experience of youth.[23] *Arcades* depicts the movement of a questing group of shepherds from ethically informed paganism to involvement in the process of Christian regeneration, while *A Mask* pictures the successful trial of the Lady's regeneracy. *On Time* and *At A Solemn Musick* describe the brilliant harmony of the redeemed. *Lycidas*, *Mansus*, and the *Epitaphium Damonis* all are involved with regenerate individuals. The theme is pointedly central to the poetry; it is not so obvious in the tracts, but it is significantly present.

The individual response is grounded in the reasonable and conscious acceptance of the truths of the Christian faith revealed in the Scriptures, as Milton indicates in the *Animadversions*:

For certainly, every rule, and instrument of necessary knowledge that God hath given us, ought to be so in proportion as may bee weilded and manag'd by the life of man without penning him up from the duties of humane society, and such a rule and instrument of knowledge perfectly is the holy Bible. . . . Wee shall adhere close to the Scriptures of God which hee hath left us as the just and adequate measure of truth, fitted, and proportion'd to the diligent study, memory, and use of every faithfull man, whose every part consenting and making up the harmonious *Symmetry* of compleat instruction, is able to set out to us a perfect man of God or *Bishop* throughly furnish't to all the good works of his charge. (YP, I, 699–700)

National regeneration in the apocalyptic movements is imaged as the mathematical perfection of the "Circle of *Eternity*"; here the basis for national regeneracy is individual response to the "harmonious *Symmetry* of compleat instruction" which the Scriptures afford. Mathematical figures unite the two imagistic movements, and they draw into relation individual response and the process of national regeneration. The presbyterial organizations of the faithful are described as the encompassing cubes of the "parochiall Consistory," the "little Synod," and the "generall assembly," and Milton asserts that these "smaller squares in battell unite in one great cube, the main phalanx, an embleme of truth and stedfastnesse" (YP, I, 789) against the prelatical pyramid which "aspires and sharpens to ambition, not to perfection, or unity" (YP, I, 790). In the eulogistic digression on the Long Parliament in *An Apology* the assembly is depicted as "one globe of brightnesse," an image doubly emphasizing regeneracy in terms of light and geometrical perfection; of that more will be said in a moment.

The individual Christian layman is capable, dignified, and worthy; Milton compares the laymen of England to the humble followers of Jesus during His earthly ministry: "hence is it that a man shall commonly find more savoury knowledge in one Lay-man, then in a dozen of Cathedrall *Prelates,* as we read in our Saviours time that the common people had a reverent esteeme of him, and held him a great prophet whilst the gowned *Rabbies,* the incomparable, and invincible Doctors were of opinion that hee was a friend of *Beelzebub*" (YP, I, 690). The layman possesses dignity because of his creation in the image of God and because of God's grace manifested in the Incarnation, Crucifixion, and Resurrection of Christ, which are the price of his redemption: "But he that holds himself in reverence and due esteem, both for the dignity of Gods image upon him, and for the price of his redemption, which he thinks is visibly markt upon his forehead, accounts himselfe both a fit person to do the noblest and godliest deeds, and much better worth then to deject and defile, with such a debasement and such a pollution as sin is, himselfe so highly ransom'd and enobl'd to a new friendship and filiall relation with God" (YP, I, 842). Many Englishmen have responded to God's grace. In *Of Reformation* Milton speaks of the faithful who have fled England and ecclesiastical corruption for religious freedom, a passage reminiscent of the picture of Thomas Young in *Elegia 4*: "Next what numbers of faithfull, and freeborn Englishmen, and good Christians have bin constrain'd to forsake their dearest home, their friends, and kindred, whom nothing but the wide Ocean, and the savage deserts of *America* could hide and shelter from the fury of the Bishops" (YP, I, 585). He praises the "Magistrates, and great numbers of sober, and considerable men" who presented the Root and Branch Petition, regenerate men scorned by the prelates because they had a trade "as *Christ himselfe* and Saint *Paul* had" (YP, I, 676–77). We are reminded of the persona of *Lycidas*, who tended "the homely slighted Shepherds trade"; the Genius of *Arcades*, who was in "helpful service" to the Countess of wisdom and virtue, the Countess symbolic of England itself; the Attendant Spirit of *A Mask*, who "to the service of this house belongs" in his pastoral function of guiding the maiden lady, as the regenerate of England now defend the "chast and modest" maiden who is the English Church; and the faithful shepherds Thyrsis and Damon in the *Epitaphium Damonis*. The character of the regenerate response in history is the same as the character of the regenerate response of the figures of the poetry.

Particularly representative of positive regenerate response are the faithful Christian ministers and magistrates. In pastoral patterns like those of the poetry, but in the prose of the *Animadversions*, the minister is the good shepherd and faithful gardener who nurses his flock and tends his growing plants: "a Church-mans jurisdiction is no more but to watch over his flock in season, and out of season. . . . But true Evangelicall jurisdiction or discipline, is no more, as was said, then for a Minister to see to the thriving and prospering of that which he hath planted" (YP, I, 716). The minister makes "a kind of creation like to Gods, by infusing his spirit and likenesse into them, to their salvation, as God did into him; arising to what climat so ever he turne him, like that Sun of righteousnesse that sent him, with healing in his wings, and new light to break in upon the chill and gloomy hearts of his hearers, raising out of darksome barrennesse a delicious, and fragrant Spring of saving knowledge, and good workes" (YP, I, 721).

In *The Reason of Church-Government* Milton indicates the separate functions of the minister and the magistrate in medical imagery consistent with the positive apocalyptic imagery of the tracts and reminiscent of the healing function of the Shepherd Lad of *A Mask*, the dead Diodati of the *Epitaphium Damonis*, the live Diodati of *Letter 8*, and the figure of Young as physician in *Elegia 4* (YP, I, 835–48). The magistrate as civil official is the physician who gives the medicine of punishment to the disease of men's evil acts in society. The minister as spiritual guardian is the physician who treats the disease of ignorance with "the daily Manna of incorruptible doctrine" and the diseases of malice and evil with the medicine of admonition and reproof. He is aided by the deacons of the Church, his nurses. The separate but equally important functions properly performed make possible for the individual Christian a life of liberty in the service of God which is "perfect freedom," the restored and healthy freedom of regeneration.

One of the best sustained passages of positive emphasis in the tracts is Milton's eulogy of the Long Parliament in *An Apology*; it points to the imminent possibility of national regeneration and involves many of the clusters of imagery which we have seen. He characterizes the digression in a typical musical image: he will "after this harsh discord" of attack on his prelatical opponent "touch upon a smoother string" (YP, I, 922); at the end he wonders "how to break off suddenly into those jarring notes, which this Confuter hath set," but is confident that he can do it "without breach of harmony" (YP, I, 928). The discord of his attack is appropriate for the unregenerate character of his opponent; the harmony of his praise is appropriate for the regenerate Parliament; and even his discord is harmonious because it is a purified use which points to harmony by inversion.

The members of Parliament are characterized by their goodness and virtue, which have been lifted to spiritual dimension "with the helpe of divine grace"; they are characterized by their love for the Christian faith and "native liberty." Their faith has been tried and proven in the universities, "which were intended to be the seed plots of piety and the Liberall Arts, but were become the nurseries of superstition, and empty speculation" (YP, I, 923); they are the good plants among the rank weeds; they have fought their way through the overgrown garden. They bring into the immediate historical situation the visionary poetic function of the orator-rhetor-poet of the Prolusions, particularly *Prolusion 7*; the pastoral figure of the Christian minister in *Elegia 4*; the heaven-sent child of *Fair Infant*; the consecrated poet of the Nativity Ode, *Elegia 6*, the Italian sonnets, Sonnets 1 and 7, and *Ad Patrem*; the regeneratively involved persona of *L'Allegro* and *Il Penseroso*; the Genius leading the Arcadians to the Countess in *Arcades*; the Attendant Spirit guiding the children through the wood of *A Mask*. Most emphatically they fulfill the function of the poet-shepherd-priest of *Lycidas*, and represent the restoration of garden care disrupted in the *Epitaphium Damonis*. They are, historically, the agents of God for the regeneration of men.

The Parliament which they compose is "one globe of brightnesse and efficacy" which counters the "dazl'd resistance of tyranny," and this image, emphasizing their regeneracy in patterns of brilliant light and mathematical perfection, is the most significant image in the antiprelatical tracts. It brings to the historical present the visionary, apocalyptic emphases of the poems: the "Globe of circular light" which presages the descent of Truth, Mercy, and Justice in the Nativity Ode; the "blazing Majesty and Light" of the apotheosis of the Marchioness in *Winchester*; the "radiant state she spreds, / In circle around her shining throne" of the Countess in *Arcades*; the "bright head encircled by a radiant crown" of Damon. These poetic patterns are translated into historical reality to characterize the active, regenerative function of the members of the Long Parliament. The "one globe of brightnesse and efficacy" coalesces with other patterns in the tracts to form a significant complex of positive imagery which pictures regeneracy. In the *Animadversions* Milton contrasts the "light of grace" which the regenerate possess with the perverted "light of Nature" which illumines the prelates (YP, I, 702), indicating that the Scriptures alone afford "the harmonious *Symmetry* of compleat instruction" (YP, I, 700). In *Of Reformation* England clasps "the *datelesse* and *irrevoluble* Circle of *Eternity*" (YP, I, 616). The joys of the regenerate are depicted in *The Reason of Church-Government*: "our happinesse may orbe it selfe into a thousand vagancies of glory and delight" (YP, I, 752). These mathematical images coalesce, too, with a view of the church militant as a cubic phalanx in *Church-Government* (YP, I, 789–90), the final perfection of the apocalyptic circle and globe becoming the strength of the classical military formation. Through the action of the Long Parliament, the vision can become historical reality; these patterns of luminosity and mathematical perfection function to affirm that.

Finally, Milton pictures God as the servant of Parliament: "Therefore the more they seeke to humble themselves, the more does God by manifest signes and testimonies visibly honour their proceedings; and sets them as the mediators of this his cov'nant which he offers us to renew." He dissolves "their difficulties when they are thought inexplicable, cutting out wayes for them where no passage could be seene. . . . God himselfe condescends, and workes with his owne hands to fulfill the requests of men; which I leave with them as the greatest praise that can belong to humane nature" (YP, I, 927–28). This hyperbolic praise intensifies the imagery of the Shepherd Lad who is Christ in *A Mask*, and the biblically informed imagery of the description of Manso in *Mansus*. Milton's hopes for the Long Parliament will soon be dashed, but for the moment he sees it as God's instrument for the redemption and regeneration of the nation, the political and spiritual instrument which will aid the thousands in their responses, bringing to history the vision of the apocalypse.

Like the apocalyptic passages and the emphasis on the response of the thousands, the autobiographical statements in *The Reason of Church-Government* and *An Apology* modulate the harshness of the satirical movements and provide a positive counterbalance; their function is related to the concerns of Milton's most significant poetic efforts. Certainly the passages are his defense against the criticisms of his opponents, but, like the ironic juxtaposition of poetic movements in *Winchester, On Time,* and *At A Solemn Musick,* the positive thematic and imagistic patterns of the personal passages are juxtaposed with the satiric harshness of his attacks on prelacy—the positiveness of regenerate response, the negativity of degeneracy and corruption.

A central concern of the major poetic efforts is to picture the positive response of the individual to the regeneration made possible by God's grace and to depict the individual actively involved in the process: the Nativity Ode describes the Incarnation event, the historical entry of God's grace into the world; *L'Allegro* and *Il Penseroso* picture the range of regenerative human involvement; *Arcades* and *A Mask* figure forth individual participation in the process; *Lycidas* shows the experiential involvement of the poet-priest and the ultimate fulfillment which grace affords. The antiprelatical tracts move away from the concern with individual regeneracy of the early poetic considerations to emphasize the horror of national degeneracy as embodied in the episcopacy, and inversely, the possibility of national regeneration. It is this shift from individual regeneracy to national degeneracy, which can become national regeneracy, that is the key to the integral function of the personal passages. As the tracts make clear in their severity, the national regeneration of England cannot be effected through the corrupt episcopacy, or indeed through any institution which does not respect the dignity and liberty of the individual Christian. And as the tracts indicate in their positive movements, national regeneration can be achieved only as the sum of hundreds of thousands of individual responses to God's grace. The personal passages of *The Reason of Church-Government* and *An*

Apology function to show the foundation of national regeneracy—they are the model for individual response and involvement. Hopefully with proper humility because he has the biblical example of the Apostle Paul as precedent, Milton himself is the model. He speaks, hopefully with convincing force, out of his own experience.

The second book of *The Reason of Church-Government* opens with Milton's personal statement.[24] He justifies his involvement in the controversy on the basis of his responsibility to use his gifts in God's service, and pictures the involvement in commercial terms. His regenerate knowledge is a product "which God hath sent him into this world to trade with," and "his alloted parcels" are "pretious truths of such an orient lustre as no diamond can equall." In contrast the prelates are "great Marchants" who market "the fals glitter of their deceitfull wares" and "abuse the people, like poor Indians with beads and glasses." He compares his task with the similar responsibilities of the Hebrew prophets and John the Evangelist. He must use "those few talents which God at that present" has given him or suffer terrible pangs of conscience, because the Church is a cornered prey "at the foot of her insulting enemies."[25] To be silent would violate the "ease and leasure" for reflection and study which was made possible for him "out of the sweat of other men," and would doubly damn one who had "the diligence, the parts, the language of a man, if a vain subject were to be adorn'd or beautifi'd," but was "domb as a beast" when God's cause was to be pleaded.[26] He reasserts that "neither envy nor gall hath enterd me upon this controversy, but the enforcement of conscience only," and in the continued justification utilizes typical imagery: his lack of experience as his "green yeers," an image similar to the vegetation metaphor of Sonnet 7, as is the reference to his current involvement as writing "thus out of mine own season, when I have neither yet compleated to my minde the full circle of my private studies."

Tracing his academic preparation he indicates his hopes for literary achievement, quietly claiming divine inspiration: "an inward prompting which now grew daily upon me, that by labour and intent study (which I take to be my portion in this life) joyn'd with the strong propensity of nature, I might perhaps leave something so written to aftertimes, as they should not willingly let it die" (YP, I, 810). He states his intention "to be an interpreter & relater of the best and sagest things among mine own Citizens throughout this Iland in the mother dialect. That what the

greatest and choycest wits of *Athens, Rome,* or modern *Italy,* and those
Hebrews of old did for their country, I in my proportion with this over
and above of being a Christian, might doe for mine" (YP, I, 811–12). He
indicates his aspirations in the "Epick form" and his intent to go beyond
the classical poets to the "pattern of a Christian *Heroe*" as exemplified
in the Book of Job; his aspirations in "Dramatick constitutions" which
are "doctrinal and exemplary to a Nation" when biblically modified to
a "divine pastoral Drama" like the Song of Solomon or a "majestick
image of a high and stately Tragedy" like the Book of Revelation; and
his desire to write odes and hymns like the songs "throughout the law
and prophets." In each instance he states the classical example and
counters it with a biblical example, and then he states the fivefold function of the regenerate poet:

These abilities, wheresoever they be found, are the inspired guift of God rarely
bestow'd, but yet to some (though most abuse) in every Nation: and are of
power beside the office of a pulpit, to imbreed and cherish in a great people the
seeds of vertu, and publick civility, to allay the perturbations of the mind, and
set the affections in right tune, to celebrate in glorious and lofty Hymns the
throne and equipage of Gods Almightinesse, and what he works, and what he
suffers to be wrought with high providence in his Church, to sing the victorious
agonies of Martyrs and Saints, the deeds and triumphs of just and pious Nations
doing valiantly through faith against the enemies of Christ, to deplore the general relapses of Kingdoms and States from justice and Gods true worship. (YP,
I, 816–17)

The poet is a divine agent like the minister, and through his poetry
inculcates virtue in the epic, purges the passions in the tragedy to restore
harmony, praises God and the works of his servants in odes and hymns,
and castigates evil in the nation and the Church.[27] Later he says that
Truth may be spoken "not only in Pulpits," that public assemblies,
theaters, and pulpits may serve the same purpose.

Again Milton affirms his devotion to poetry:

Neither doe I think it shame to covnant with any knowing reader, that for some
few yeers yet I may go on trust with him toward the payment of what I am now
indebted, as being a work not to be rays'd from the heat of youth, or the vapours
of wine, like that which flows at wast from the pen of some vulgar Amorist, or
the trencher fury of a riming parasite, nor to be obtain'd by the invocation of
Dame Memory and her Siren daughters, but by devout prayer to that eternall
Spirit who can enrich with all utterance and knowledge, and sends out his
Seraphim with the hallow'd fire of his Altar to touch and purify the lips of

whom he pleases: to this must be added industrious and select reading, steddy observation, insight into all seemly and generous arts and affaires, till which in some measure be compast, at mine own peril and cost I refuse not to sustain this expectation from as many as are not loath to hazard so much credulity upon the best pledges that I can give them. (YP, I, 820–21)

The passage is fraught with typical patterns and has ironic bearing. Milton covenants to fulfill the poetic aspirations which he has expressed, and thereby justifies his controversial prose as a temporary occupation necessary before his poetic plans can be effected. He promises divine poetry, made possible through the rigid discipline of study, and the moral life which brings the purification by fire of Isaiah vi, 6, an image central to the Nativity Ode. This discipline will lead his poetic accomplishments beyond the "heat of youth" and "vapours of wine" of *Elegiae 1* and *6* and beyond the simply ethical bearing of poetry inspired by "Dame Memory and her Siren daughters." The Muses are the daughters of Memory, and Milton calls them the Platonic Sirens; they are responsible for the harmony of poetry, and they are given classical ethical dimension by the compact metaphor. But this classical ethical harmony, signifying the natural order, must be purified and lifted to spiritual dimension by the operation of God's grace, and that is Milton's point.

The personal passage closes with a hyperbolic description of his decision not to enter the ministry; he cannot "subscribe slave" and has been "Church-outed by the Prelats." He has already taken the required oath twice, upon receipt of his two degrees at Cambridge, but the statement does not have to be explained in terms of perversity or of academic formality as opposed to serious vocational commitment. The simple fact is that the personal passage is a hyperbolic expression in a satirical tract given to one-sided overstatement. A pure spirit "Church-outed" is a more powerful image than that of a young man who decided for many reasons to be a poet-priest instead of a clerical one.

The conception of the poetic function which Milton delineates here in terms of his own experience is analogous to the conception of reformation apparent in the apocalyptic passages and the conception of individual responses described in the positive terms of mathematical, medical, pastoral, and apocalyptic imagery. His is a particularized instance of the kind of response demanded from the thousands whose regenerate characters will lead to national regeneracy. The poet is the type, the model, for the harmonious, resonant, luminous response to

God's grace; he is also the type for the poet, now writing prose with his left hand, who through that medium is attempting to induce in the English historical situation a regenerate response equivalent to that induced through the aesthetic and visionary manipulations of the poetry.

The character of the response is indicated in the range of poetic imagery which culminates in the "hallow'd fire" of Isaiah vi, 6, a prominent image in the integrating vision of the Nativity Ode. The range includes the "heat of youth" and "vapours of wine" which stand for the classical character of Milton's early elegiac poetry; it moves to the ethical classicism of poetry inspired by "Dame Memory and her Siren daughters"; it includes the specifically religious poems inspired by God and sanctified by the purifying touch of "hallow'd fire." It includes the epic, the drama, the odes, and the hymns, and it requires the process of involved toil in learning which is unified with virtue. The poet's response is characterized by the integration of the natural and spiritual dimensions, which involve the classical and Christian directions. The fire does not burn away the natural; it touches and purifies it, and integrates it with the spiritual. And so the response of the thousands, and through them the response of the nation, should be characterized: by toil in learning joined with virtue, by the use of natural goods and powers sanctified by the integrating operation of God's grace. When this is accomplished, on the basis of the model which Milton provides, the "left-handed" poet of the controversial prose will again sing the strains of divine poetry, as the apocalyptic passages indicate: "some one may perhaps bee heard offering at high *strains* in new and lofty *Measures* to sing and celebrate" (YP, I, 616); "And he that now for haste snatches up a plain ungarnish't present as a thanke-offering to thee, which could not bee deferr'd in regard of thy so many late deliverances wrought for us one upon another, may then perhaps take up a Harp, and sing thee an elaborate Song to Generations" (YP, I, 706). This is elaborated in the extended personal statement in *An Apology*.[28]

Milton opens with an animal characterization of his opponent, the author of *A Modest Confutation*: he is a serpent who sucks the poison of his works not from Milton's *Animadversions* which he attacks, but from his own venom. He accuses Milton of being vomited out of Cambridge "after an inordinat and riotous youth spent at *the Vniversity*." Against the accusation Milton asserts the "more then ordinary favour and re-

spect which I found above any of my equals at the hands of those curte-
ous and learned men, the Fellowes of that Colledge wherein I spent
some yeares," and then turns the vomit image back on its author. Cambridge and Oxford are diseased matrons who vomit the good and retain
the vile, becoming sicker in the disease of episcopacy, which will soon be
purged by the "strong physick" of reformation (YP, I, 884–85). Milton
is vomited out, and is but one particular regenerate man; the members
of the Long Parliament, analogously, fought their way through the rank
weeds of the universities to become healthy, vibrant, sturdy plants.

He answers his opponent's accusation that he spends his afternoons
and evenings in playhouses and brothels and his mornings he knows not
where, by affirming simply that in the morning he is home, "up, and
stirring," involved in "devotion," reading "good Authors." He is "with
usefull and generous labours preserving the bodies health, and hardi-
nesse; to render lightsome, cleare, and not lumpish obedience to the
minde, to the cause of religion, and our Countries liberty" (YP, I, 885–
86). Milton uses a forceful biblical image in defense of his evening activity: "Your intelligence, unfaithfull Spie of Canaan? he gives in his
evidence, that *there he hath trac't me.*" His opponent is the whore-
monger, not Milton. He counters the playhouse remark by picturing
ministerial students at Cambridge as "Buffoons, and Bawds; prostituting
the shame of that ministery which either they had, or were nigh having,
to the eyes of Courtiers and Court-Ladies, with their Groomes and
Mademoisellaes." He effectively turns his opponent's arguments back
on him, but the masterstroke is the sardonic irony and humor of his
final comment:

So if my name and outward demeanour be not evident anough to defend me, I
must make tryall, if the discovery of my inmost thoughts can. Wherein of two
purposes both honest, and both sincere, the one perhaps I shall not misse; although I faile to gaine beliefe with others of being such as my perpetuall
thoughts shall heere disclose me, I may yet not faile of successe in perswading
some, to be such really themselves, as they cannot believe me to be more then
what I fain. (YP, I, 889)

Milton's account of his studies is the most familiar segment of the
statement in *An Apology*, but the positive significance and ironic force
of it have never been sufficiently indicated. He traces the phases of his
literary education, in each instance associating the literature with its
attitudes toward women. He studied "the smooth Elegiack Poets," like

Ovid, but when he "found those authors any where speaking unworthy things of themselves; or unchaste of those names which before they had extoll'd, this effect it wrought with me, from that time forward their art I still applauded, but the men I deplor'd." He studied the idealized love tradition of Dante and Petrarch, "who never write but honour of them to whom they devote their verse, displaying sublime and pure thoughts, without transgression." He moves from them to Christian chivalric romance, of which Spenser and Tasso are the most obvious examples, and again emphasizes womanhood: the obligation of the knight to defend "the honour and chastity of Virgin or Matron," the importance of the "noble vertue chastity," and the fact that every man should "secure and protect the weaknesse of any attempted chastity." But he acknowledges that some chivalric authors have missed the mark, and asserts that what others have found "the fuell of wantonnesse and loose living" was never such to him. He turns to philosophy, "chiefly to the divine volumes of *Plato*, and his equall *Xenophon*. Where if I should tell ye what I learnt, of chastity and love, I meane that which is truly so, whose charming cup is only vertue which she bears in her hand to those who are worthy. The rest are cheated with a thick intoxicating potion which a certaine Sorceresse the abuser of loves name carries about; and how the first and chiefest office of love, begins and ends in the soule, producing those happy twins of her divine generation knowledge and vertue" (YP, I, 891–92). Again, in images similar to those of *A Mask*, attention is centered on the significance of chastity and love, and expanded to knowledge and virtue, in patterns Platonically informed. Finally, Milton reaches the significant point that he has not been "negligently train'd in the precepts of Christian Religion." Again he centers on the relationship between man and woman; he affirms that "if unchastity in a woman whom Saint *Paul* termes the glory of man, be such a scandall and dishonour, then certainly in a man who is both the image and glory of God, it must, though commonly not so thought, be much more deflouring and dishonourable." He refers to "that place expressing such high rewards of ever accompanying the Lambe, with those celestiall songs to others inapprehensible, but not to those who were not defil'd with women, which doubtlesse meanes fornication: For mariage must not be call'd a defilement" (YP, I, 892–93). The vital significance of the virtue of the individual Christian is pictured in the particular virtue of chastity, and the allusion to the virgins around the throne of God in Revelation xiv, 1–5 continues the use of the pattern of heavenly apotheosis in *At A Solemn Musick, Lycidas, Mansus,* and the *Epitaphium Damonis.* This is an important modification of Milton's rigidity. *A Mask* involves the harshness of virginity which tends to separate the orders of nature and grace instead of integrating them; here Milton moves to the sounder ground of chastity, the symbol of total virtue which involves the integration of the natural and spiritual in allowing the fulfillment of natural sexual desires within the context of divinely ordained marriage. This pulls him back from the polarizing tendencies of *Lycidas, Mansus,* and *Damonis,* which emphasize virginal purity in the face of ecclesiastical corruption endangering regeneration and poetic fulfillment. It points him toward harmony, restores his balance, and clarifies the association of sexual purity with each phase of his educational and poetic experience: that association functions decorously and ironically in relation to his opponent's accusations of sexual wantonness, but it does much more.

This personal statement functions in the same way as the passage in *The Reason of Church-Government,* but with more meaningful particularity. Milton as poet remains the type for individual regenerate response; he remains the type for the poet, whose manipulations are translated from the integrating resonance of poetry to the vehicle of controversial prose. But the character of the response is more carefully articulated. Essentially Milton's tracing of his literary and philosophical studies is a characterization of his early poetry, and its thematic and imagistic range indicates the character of individual, and national, regenerative response.

His first poetic direction is the sensuous natural verse of "the smooth Elegiack Poets" and is seen in its rarefied form in early Latin poems like *Elegiae 1, 3,* and *5.* He indicates that when he found them speaking unchastely he deplored them, but he significantly indicates, too, that "their art I still applauded." He repudiates the men but not their modes, and the natural imagery of the classical elegiac poets is a major imagistic aspect of Milton's poetry. The stream of classical pastoral flows into the stream of biblical pastoral, and is lifted to new dimensions, and it is a major aspect of the most accomplished verses of Milton's early poetry. Much of the imagery of *Fair Infant* is out of the pastoral; the Nativity Ode fuses classical and biblical pastoral patterns to become the poetic representation of the integration of the natural and spiritual orders which is the full meaning of its Incarnation theme.

The process of regeneration in *Arcades* involves the guidance of the Arcadian pastoral figures by the Genius-shepherd; *A Mask* involves the pastoral progress of the Lady through the wood of danger under the watchful eyes of the Attendant Spirit–guardian angel–shepherd. The personae of *Lycidas* and *Damonis*, and the apotheosized figures whom they address, are shepherds of classical and Christian character. All of these pastoral figures have classical and biblical associations, and hence are the poetic equivalents of the regenerate figures of the antiprelatical tracts: the ministers, the magistrates, the tradesmen, the members of Parliament, all of whom perform pastoral functions.

The second poetic direction is the idealized love tradition illustrated through Dante and Petrarch, the "renowners of *Beatrice* and *Laura*." Explicit representations of the influence on Milton's poetic development are the Italian sonnets, which Milton ironically turns to his own uses, but its most significant utilization, again, is in the major early poems, where, like the pastoral elements, it is infused with Christian significance. The Countess of *Arcades* at once signifies Christian wisdom and virtue and regenerate England, a matron used as an imagistic vehicle. The Lady of *A Mask* is involved in the process of regeneration. Jane Paulet and Rachel (a figure from the Bible and Dante) reach the ultimate fulfillment of Christian apotheosis. The heroic ladies of the antiprelatical tracts are included in the thousands of the regenerate and exemplified in the pure Presbyterial virgin. And in the background of all the figures is the biblical image of the Church as the Bride of Christ in the Song of Solomon and the Book of Revelation.

Allegorical Christian romance, like the major works of Spenser and Tasso, is the third poetic direction. The allegorical dimensions of *Arcades* and *A Mask* most vividly involve this aspect of Milton's handling, but its influence is felt also in the allegorical figures and personifications of the Prolusions. Both the prose and poetry evince the influence of the "divine volumes of *Plato*," as do the specifically Platonic elements of *De Idea Platonica* and *A Mask* and the studious involvement of the persona in *Il Penseroso*.

In his catalogue Milton finally reaches the significance of the "precepts of Christian Religion," carefully indicating that they are "last of all not in time, but as perfection is last," and this indication throws into sharp relief the bearing of his catalogue of influences. It is a hierarchy which moves from the natural to the ethical to the spiritual, imagistically from the sensuous to the apocalyptic. But it does not separate the natural and the spiritual, the orders of nature and grace, because at each level the particular poetic vehicle and the imagistic patterns which it involves are informed by the themes and imagery of the Christian faith which is mentioned last; here, too, is the other significance of Milton's conception of chastity. The peculiar Christian bearing of the virtue is made apparent in the apocalyptic patterns of the passage on the Christian faith; chastity is the vehicle for the expression of total Christian regenerate virtue at each of the other hierarchical levels. It operates, however, to lift each of them to the equal horizontal plane of Christian importance, to sanctify them and make them effective instruments for the expression of Christian truth.

Milton is articulating more carefully here his conception of the character and function of the divine Christian poet than he has previously in the essentially ethical emphases of *Prolusion 7* and the ethical and religious revelations of the poems. The divine poet responds to God's grace with the prolonged toil of learning which leads to knowledge and wisdom, learning inseparable from virtue; he puts that knowledge and wisdom to regenerate use through the medium of his poetry. He is, through his verse and in his life, the prophet who calls men to respond to God's grace. His poetry pictures the integration of nature and grace which is the reality of his regenerate experience. Milton's conception of the poet here illustrates the totally integrated response to experience and the transference of that response to his poetic. The integration of nature and grace in the poem illustrates the integration in the life of the poet: he is "true Poem." And as true poem he is at once the type for his own response in the manipulations of the controversial prose, and the type for the response of the individuals who are the thousands, whose sum of responses will lead to the regeneration of the nation, making historical the visions of the poems: the truly regenerate man as Poem leads to the true poems of the Church and the nation, an harmonious symmetry, a globe of brightness.

VIII

Milton's antiprelatical tracts grow out of concerns which gradually become apparent in the thematic and imagistic patterns of his early poetry. The poems substantially set forth the positive themes of regeneracy, the regenerate function of the poet-priest, and the religious bear-

ing of poetry. The prose is substantially a harsh satirical attack on the
perversity of episcopacy as an institution and the corruption of the prelates as individuals. The poems are concerned with the positive harmony
of regeneracy; the tracts are concerned with the negative disharmony
of unregeneracy which endangers individual regeneration, and which
frustrates the fulfillment of poetic aspirations. But the concern of the
tracts is visible in the poetry and is consistent with its directions: as the
extension of thematic and imagistic patterns present in the poetry; by
inversion and positive manipulation as the continuation of Milton's
deep concern for regeneracy. This consistency is initially apparent in
Milton's justification of the tone and style of the tracts. He defends their
decorum on the basis of similar usages by Jesus and by God himself;
harshness is necessary in the face of all-pervading and all-corrupting evil.

The satirical forcefulness and hyperbole of the imagery are the
one-sided extension of previous patterns in his poetry and prose. The
overwhelming imagery of bodily disease and function, animal degradation, sexual perversion, and gluttony is anticipated in the patterns of
the Prolusions, particularly *Prolusion 6*, though the hilarity of that
early academic exercise is obviously different from the seriousness of
the tracts.[29] The ugly imagery of religious ceremonial emptiness is seen
in the picture of the Roman Mass in *In Quintum Novembris*. The light-
hearted characterization of arid linguistic usage in *At A Vacation Exercise* portends the picture of prelatical verbosity and the twisted use of
words and their meanings. The subtle ironic imagery of ceremonial corruption in the third movement of the Nativity Ode, like the more obvi-
out patterns of *Novembris*, anticipates the harsh pictures of the tracts.
The poems of Milton's second phase, after the Nativity Ode, more directly bear on the prose. The imagery of light and darkness, the significance of the religious quest, and the picture of the dangerous wood of
the world in *Arcades* are patterns which are prominent in the prose. *A
Mask* pointedly anticipates the pamphlets: the figures of Comus and the
Lady virtually correspond to the pictures of the corrupt Church and its
prelates and the reformed Church and its ministers; the patterns of
carnality and spirituality, animal imagery, musical harmony and disharmony, and the movement through the wood are remarkably similar
to aspects of the prose, even with some particularity. The picture of
ecclesiastical corruption in the second movement of *Lycidas* is expanded,

intensified, and reinforced in the tracts, but is essentially the same in its biblical pastoral character.

While these things evince the relation of the themes and imagery of the poetry and prose, a major thematic concern clearly demonstrates the prose as a vital extension of the poetry. In *A Mask* Milton conceives the total virtue of the Lady in the particular virtue of virginity, a stark virtue which tends to separate the natural and spiritual orders because of its rejection of the natural; that virtue is set against the carnal corruption of Comus, who is very much like the prelates of the tracts. In *Lycidas* the reality of the world's evil is depicted in the prelatical corruption of the second movement, which is the source of the religious and poetic frustration of the shepherd-poet-priest whose apotheosis as a virgin is the fulfillment of those things frustrated on earth. The virtual polarization in the *Epitaphium Damonis*, the virginal apotheosis of Damon set against the carnal corruption of the wolves who endanger regeneration and poetic fulfillment, is the bridge to the antiprelatical tracts. Milton's growing awareness of the danger of ecclesiastical corruption leads to the despair and poetic paralysis of *Damonis*, and then to the tracts, which are his attempt to purge that which threatens individual and national regeneracy and poetic accomplishment. But in the attack we witness the beginning adjustment of Milton's balance in the substitution of the more comprehensive virtue of chastity for the restrictiveness of virginity. As he attacks prelacy to purge the nation, he moves closer again to the integrating wholeness of the Nativity Ode vision; the particular vehicle of chastity points to a virtue which can comprehend the natural and spiritual orders. This is the balance he always seeks; he does not find it completely in the antiprelatical tracts. It will come only in the later prose and the major poetry.

Milton's theme is ecclesiastical corruption; his purpose is to demolish episcopacy. But the other intention is to point to national regeneration, and this is the function of the positive movements of the tracts. Three distinct patterns reveal this intention. The first is the translation of the apocalyptic movements of the early poetry to the prose—the attempt to transmute the apotheoses of poems like *Elegia 3, Winchester, On Time, Lycidas, Mansus,* and the *Epitaphium Damonis* to the English historical situation, to make experiential the vision of regenerative fulfillment. This pattern particularly involves the positive imagistic elements of light, musical harmony, and energetic movement so clearly evinced in the early poetry.

A second positive emphasis involves the characterization of the individual responses which in sum will lead to national regeneration, and it is anticipated in the early poems. The historical responses of the Englishmen are the same as the visionary responses of the heroes and heroines of the early poetry: the pastors apotheosized in *Elegia 3* and *Eliensis*, the faithful minister of *Elegia 4*, the seekers and the pastoral Genius of *Arcades*, the guardian Spirit and the Lady of *A Mask*, the pastoral figures of *Lycidas*, *Mansus*, and *Damonis*. The responses are initially described in terms of mathematical perfection; the regenerate are characterized as the humble followers of Christ, their dignity and worth grounded in their redemption in Christ the Son and in their creation in the image of God. They are the tradesmen who fulfill their several obligations, as do the poetic figures. They include the ministers who fulfill the biblical pastoral functions of keeping the flock and tending the delicate plants of their congregations, and the magistrates and ministers who, as physicians, attend the ills of their charges. Finally, they are the members of the Long Parliament, so wholesomely regenerate that God himself is their servant.

The third positive movement of the tracts involves the emphases of the personal passages. Here Milton, having generally characterized national regeneration apocalyptically, and the regeneration of the thousands in broad patterns, provides himself, the poet, as a type for individual regenerative response. This is an extension of the major concern with poetry and the poet which the early poems evince. In the account of his own literary development from the natural themes and imagery of elegiac poetry, through the idealized love conventions of romantic poetry and the chivalric romance, to divine subjects sanctified by the "hallow'd fire" of God's angel, he illustrates the range of regenerative response. This hierarchy is horizontalized by the presence of the particular Christian virtue of chastity at each level, chastity signifying total Christian virtue. The subjects, themes, and imagery are all raised to Christian significance and given Christian bearing: the natural and the spiritual are integrated, as they are in the poetic vision of the Nativity Ode. Milton at once overcomes his own paralysis in the *Epitaphium Damonis* by finding in chastity the vehicle for the expression of total Christian virtue, and provides, in the totally integrating response, which signifies the reality of human regenerative response, a pattern for the thousands to follow—a pattern leading to national regeneration. These three positive emphases set in relief the inversion patterns of the predominant movements of the tracts: the ugliness of evil which ironically implies the beauty of holiness.

Thus the antiprelatical tracts are the extension and culmination of the thematic and imagistic emphases of the early poetic and prose endeavors. They at once show Milton's desperation in the severity of their satirical attacks, and his confidence in their positive emphases, and they point to the beginning restoration of his integrated vision. They savagely attack prelatical corruption, because it hinders the process of regeneration and cripples poetic accomplishment. And they are closer to the poems than we have realized. The left hand performs the same task as the right, but the direction of the effort is different. They are largely negative in their tone and bearing because Milton cannot yet translate effectively the visionary emphases of the poetry to the immediate situation. This is the concern of his future endeavors in poetry and prose. And he succeeds.

University of Kentucky

NOTES

1. All prose citations are from *The Complete Prose Works of John Milton*, ed. Don M. Wolfe et al. (New Haven, 1953–71), cited as YP (Yale Prose) with volume and page. Poetry is from *The Works of John Milton*, ed. F. A. Patterson et al., 18 vols. (New York, 1931–38), cited as CM (Columbia Milton).

2. See Arthur E. Barker, *Milton and the Puritan Dilemma* (London, 1942), pp. 19–59.

3. In Luke xiv, 34–35 Jesus says that salt without savor (man) is fit for the dunghill; in Matthew xv, 17 and Mark vii, 15–23 he speaks of man's evil as excrement, though Protestant translations do not make this as explicit as the Douay use of the word *privy*.

4. The tracts have been examined by Thomas Kranidas in *The Fierce Equation: A Study of Milton's Decorum* (The Hague, 1965). The section dealing with the tracts originally appeared as " 'Decorum' and the Style of Milton's Antiprelatical Tracts," *SP*, LXII (1965), 176–87. Kranidas is enlightening in two significant ways: his perceptive discussion of Milton's patterns of inversion (he calls it "a classic Miltonic procedure, 'knowing good by evil' "), and his careful attention to the imagistic and thematic patterns of the pamphlets. In one respect, however, I think he is misleading. He asserts that all imagistic patterns in the tracts point to the resonant harmony of the *inner* and *outer* man: the inner, his soul and intellect; the outer, his body, actions,

and involvements. This harmony is expressed through the central image of the body as metaphor for order: the healthy body signifies harmony and unity; the diseased body signifies discord and disunity. For Kranidas there is the unity of the regenerate man and the disunity of the unregenerate man. These distinctions are required by the dichotomy of inner and outer. I affirm that the dichotomy is false, that both regenerate Christian and unregenerate prelate possess unity, and that that is Milton's point. The inner man and the outer man, the body and the soul, cannot be separated. They are unities. The antiprelatical tracts picture unity in negative patterns of perverse harmony and in positive patterns of regenerate harmony. Patterns picturing the unity of evil predominate and are grounded in the imagery of evil in the early poems, which they elaborate, intensify, and particularize. But patterns of harmony and regenerate unity are significantly present. Kranidas substantially overlooks these patterns.

5. See YP, I, 639, 678, and 681–82.

6. The citations are to YP, I, 728, 778, 789, 828, and 935.

7. See J. M. Wallace, "Milton's *Arcades*," *JEGP*, LVIII (1959), 627–36; reprinted in *Milton: Modern Essays in Criticism*, ed. Arthur E. Barker (New York, 1965), pp. 77–87.

8. Barker, *Puritan Dilemma*, pp. 15–16.

9. See YP, I, 765–66.

10. All citations are to YP, I, 537–38.

11. See the entire passage, YP, I, 519–22.

12. Later in the same tract he pictures the prelates' use of language in terms of physical violence (YP, I, 707–09). Throughout the tracts language is conventionally imaged in the metaphor of clothing.

13. Later in the same tract Milton speaks of the "quick-sighted *Protestants* eye clear'd in great part from the mist of Superstition" (YP, I, 592).

14. In *Elegia 1* Milton associates the intellectual sterility of Cambridge with the clogged banks of the river Cam.

15. See discussion above at close of section II.

16. The informing biblical passages are Mark i, 16–18, Jesus' call to Simon and Andrew "to become fishers of men," and Acts viii, 5–25, the account of Simon the magician. It is significant that the Greek of verse 20 displays a harshness which most translations do not relate. The King James reading of Peter's rebuke is "Thy money perish with thee"; J. B. Phillips translates it: "To hell with you and your money." In a footnote he observes: "These words are exactly what the Greek means. It is a pity that their real meaning is obscured by modern slang usage" (*The Young Church in Action: A Translation of The Acts of the Apostles* [New York, 1955], p. 22). This might also have served Milton as a justification for his severity.

17. The images of the wolf are informed by biblical passages like Matthew vii, 15: "Beware of false prophets, which come to you in sheep's clothing, but inwardly they are ravening wolves." See also Luke x, 3 and Acts xx, 29. The boar image of the prose passage alludes to Matthew vii, 6: "Give not that which is holy unto the dogs, neither cast ye your pearls before swine, lest they trample them under their feet, and turn again and rend you." The wolf, of course, is a conventional image for Roman Catholic corruption.

18. This image is related to the ironic function of the animal imagery in the *Epitaphium Damonis* 94–111.

19. The preceding citations are to YP, I, 569, 603, 755, 779, and 947.

20. Citations are to YP, I, 591 and 603.

21. See Hugh N. Maclean, "Milton's *Fair Infant*," *ELH*, XXIV (1957), 296–305; reprinted in *Modern Essays in Criticism*, ed. Barker, pp. 21–30.

22. See comments on *Lycidas* and the *Epitaphium Damonis* in section IV above.

23. See John Via, "The Rhythm of Regenerate Experience: *L'Allegro* and *Il Penseroso*," *Renaissance Papers 1969*, pp. 47–55.

24. The passage appears in YP, I, 801–23.

25. Milton alludes to the parable of the talents in Matthew xxv, 14–30, as he does early in the passage in the phrase "entrusted gifts," and as he does in the poetry, particularly Sonnets 7 and 19, and in Letter 5.

26. See the similar emphasis of *Ad Patrem*, where he thanks his father for allowing him the leisure of study.

27. See YP, I, 816, n. 109.

28. YP, I, 882–93.

29. For a characterization of these types of imagery, see Kester Svendsen, *Milton and Science* (Cambridge, 1956), pp. 174–210; and Kranidas, *The Fierce Equation*, pp. 51–71.

MILTON'S BLANK VERSE SONNETS

Lee M. Johnson

At critical points in their destinies, characters in Milton's last three poems often speak in blank verse sonnets to pledge their acceptance of one another, of themselves, or of divine purposes. These blank verse units of fourteen lines, which display structural proportions similar to those of Milton's rhymed sonnets, generally recall and extend the traditional function of the form as a love poem. In *Paradise Lost*, they often accompany the resolutions of characters to embody gestures of reconciliation. They are a way of revealing the spiritual identities of both speakers in *Paradise Regained* and of epitomizing Christ's assent to his mission. To signify acceptance of divine ways, they point to the farewell speeches of Samson and the chorus. Milton's blank verse sonnets appear throughout the major poems and always in the conclusions of narrative or dramatic actions, where they help him impart a final, Christian perspective and form to the larger forms and structural patterns he inherits from classical epic and dramatic traditions.

MILTON CHARACTERISTICALLY mastered traditional poetic forms by extending and improving their range until they could be quite different from their originals. His treatments of the sonnet and the canzone, his two favorite rhymed forms, are cases in point. In both, he learned how best to counterpoint his syntax against their rhyming patterns and introduced other irregularities to enhance the decorum of his matter and manner. This is the difference between his early, textbook canzone in Italian, appended to Sonnet 3, and the irregular canzoni of *Lycidas*, which steadily become more regular throughout each section of the poem and drop their unrhymed and short lines to complement the increasing strength of his thought. It is the difference between his earlier and later sonnets in English, which reveal the development of a more versatile, complex, yet more unified form.

Milton's experimentation with the sonnet and the canzone does not cease but continues throughout the three blank verse poems of his maturity. It should be recalled that between the canzoni of *Lycidas* and the blank verse of *Paradise Lost* Milton's original poems in English are largely confined to sonnets. It has long been commonplace to point out that these sonnets prefigure the style of the blank verse. They also point to the form of some blank verse paragraphs. In 1836, Henry Crabb Robinson recorded Wordsworth's discovery of a blank verse sonnet: "the fine fourteen lines of Milton's *PL*," which Wordsworth termed "a perfect sonnet without rhyme."[1] Extending Wordsworth's observation, I shall discuss how fourteen-line, blank verse units function like sonnets to clarify the moral purport and total structural designs of Milton's last three poems.

There are approximately two dozen fourteen-line units in *Paradise Lost,* nearly a dozen in *Paradise Regained,* and roughly a half dozen in *Samson Agonistes.*[2] Admittedly, there is an element of subjective judgment involved in determining their numbers and in calling them blank verse sonnets. These passages, however, generally display by themselves the structural characteristics of Milton's rhymed sonnets and nearly always appear predictably in their contexts at points of resolution in the destinies of the characters who speak them. By themselves, such passages are all sufficiently self-contained units, like sonnets in a sequence, so that they may be removed from their contexts without suffering an unwarranted loss of sense. This is particularly evident for sonnets which appear as separate verse paragraphs. Most others appear prominently at either the beginnings or ends of their paragraphs. As sonnets, they all have turns of thought or changes in syntax analogous to the characteristic two- and three-part divisions of Milton's rhymed sonnets. Because of the frequent counterpoint between his phrasing and the ends of lines, a distinct shift of emphasis may not always appear precisely at the end of the eighth line, the point at which the octave turns into the sestet, and most blank verse sonnets are in this respect similar to rhymed sonnets like "When I consider how my light is spent," "On the Late Massacre in Piedmont," and "Methought I saw my late espoused Saint." For the blank verse sonnets which I shall cite, octaves and sestets will be set off in braces. Milton's rhymed sonnets also tend to exhibit an extraordinarily heavy concentration of balances, antitheses, parallels, and repetitions of words and phrases, all of which reflect the repetitions of the Petrarchan rhyming pattern. His blank verse sonnets likewise display this tendency, usually to a much more pronounced extent than does the normal run of his blank verse.

Milton's blank verse sonnets in their contexts perform a major role in his definition of the Christian hero. In *Paradise Regained,* they mark the identities of their speakers and summarize the principal stages in the debate on the natures of the private and public life. Their main purpose in *Paradise Lost* and *Samson Agonistes* is to Christianize classical heroism, conventions, and thought. They become a way in which form can aid and justify Milton's acquisition and transcendence of classical literature for his Christian humanism; a way, in other words, of pouring fine, old wine into new skins to render it serviceable, for the sonnet has its origin as a form not in classical but in Christian literature. In *Paradise Lost* and *Samson Agonistes,* sonnets usually accompany a character's crucial decision and in the epic are almost always spoken by characters rather than appearing as portions of the narrative proper. In both the epic and drama, characters usually speak them as pledges of their love and reconciliation to God, to another character, or to a condition of existence. The traditional use of the sonnet as a love poem becomes highly effective when Adam and Eve, for example, speak in blank verse sonnets to reverse their defiance of one another or of God. The resolution of a character's history normally appears near the end of an episode or with the conclusion of a series of actions, and sonnets at these points have an apocalyptic significance. In this way, a Christian form also has the last word over classical forms of presentation.

To illustrate how the sonnet helps in transforming a classical into a Christian epic, it should be noted that all books of *Paradise Lost* contain sonnets except Book II, and Book VI has only one, which appears at its conclusion. Books II and VI are stylistically the most classical and least Christian in their presentations of characters and events. With the lone exception at the end of Book VI, Christian forms like the sonnet and the canzone do not appear in their verse paragraphs. This is not surprising, for Books II and VI largely concern the exploits of Satan and his followers in hell and during the war in heaven, where they conduct their debates and adventures in the manner of classical epic heroes. Their heroics fall precipitously on the third day of battle in Book VI. The Son's victory over the rebel angels has its culminating description in a narrative sonnet, which concludes a larger verse paragraph, and the figurative purpose of the form as a mark of Christian heroism becomes quite evident:

> Yet half his strength he put not forth, but check'd
> His Thunder in mid Volie, for he meant
> Not to destroy, but root them out of Heav'n:
> The overthrown he rais'd, and as a Heard
> Of Goats or timerous flock together throngd
> Drove them before him Thunder-struck, pursu'd
> With terrors and with furies to the bounds
> And Chrystall wall of Heav'n, which op'ning wide,
> Rowld inward, and a spacious Gap disclos'd
> Into the wastful Deep; the monstrous sight
> Strook them with horror backward, but far worse
> Urg'd them behind; headlong themselvs they threw
> Down from the verge of Heav'n, Eternal wrauth
> Burnt after them to the bottomless pit.   (VI, 853–66)[3]

Milton's employment of the sonnet as a Christian form bears good fruit here as a tribute to the Son, the victorious warrior. The apocalyptic function of the form is also clear, as the rebel angels could find cause to admit. Although the fourteen lines of this sonnet are one long sentence, a division between octave and sestet is preserved. The octave concerns the Son's actions on the field of heaven. With the words "rowld inward" the sestet begins and shifts its view to "the wastful Deep" of Chaos and the fall of the devils through Chaos downwards to hell.

Sonnets in *Paradise Lost* not only give form to events of significant moral or thematic purport but also help define and Christianize the total epic structures of the poem. These structures and narrative patterns are part of Milton's inheritance of classical epic designs and establish the balances and symmetry of narrative sequences. *Paradise Lost*, like the *Iliad*, the *Odyssey*, and the *Aeneid*, is an epic of thirds and has a concentric pattern; like the *Aeneid*, in particular, it also has a double-panel structure.[4] As an epic of thirds, Books I–IV, V–VIII, and IX–XII of

Paradise Lost form groups, in which, among other similarities, a departure from Eden concludes each group. In the double-panel structure, the epic consists of two contrasting halves, in which Books I through VI are paired with VII through XII. The concentric or resonating structure of the epic derives from pairs made up of Books I and XII, II and XI, III and X, IV and IX, V and VIII, and VI and VII. The sonnets in *Paradise Lost* help bind these epic structures together and impart a Christian perspective to them.

Michael's sonnet of farewell to Adam at the end of Book XII illustrates the role of sonnets in the design of the epic (XII, 574–87), for it interlinks the poem's beginning, middle, and end in a grand perspective. In the last advice an angel gives Adam, Michael speaks of various modes of knowledge, of the importance of charity, and of the possibility of realizing an inner paradise. According to the epic structure of thirds, by which Books XII, VIII, and IV are interlinked, Michael's sonnet on the mount of speculation not only relates to the final words an angel gives Adam before the Fall, the sonnet with which Raphael concludes his visit to Eden (VIII, 630–43), but also contrasts with Satan's sonnet of self-knowledge on Mount Niphates (IV, 79–92). In the double-panel structure of the epic, Books XII and VI are paired. Michael's principal charge is to remove Adam and Eve from Eden, a mission which is similar to the Son's action, which was cited earlier, in the narrative sonnet at the end of Book VI, when he roots out the rebel angels from heaven (VI, 853–66). Books XII and I are matched in the concentric structure of the epic. In his farewell sonnet, Michael states that Adam may embody an inner paradise to replace and transcend the Eden he must lose. This prospect prepares Adam for life in the fallen world below Eden and projects circumstances which may be compared with Satan's in Book I, when he utters a sonnet of farewell to heaven and greeting to hell (I, 242–55).

The immediate context of Michael's sonnet is Adam's final speech in the epic. Having learned of the coming of Christ, mankind's redemption, judgment, and the final, second Eden, Adam concludes, "that to obey is best" (XII, 561) and that he must now "acknowledge my Redeemer ever blest" (573). Michael then gives his parting words, a thirty-two line verse paragraph, of which the first fourteen lines comprise a single sentence of advice:

To whom thus also th' Angel last repli'd:
This having learnt, thou hast attained the summe
Of wisdom; hope no higher, though all the Starrs
Thou knewst by name, and all th' ethereal Powers,
All secrets of the deep, all Natures works,
Or works of God in Heav'n, Air, Earth, or Sea,
And all the riches of this World enjoydst,
And all the rule, one Empire; onely add
Deeds to thy knowledge answerable, add Faith,
Add Vertue, Patience, Temperance, add Love,
By name to come call'd Charitie, the soul
Of all the rest: then wilt thou not be loath
To leave this Paradise, but shalt possess
A Paradise within thee, happier farr.   (XII, 574–87)

The behavior of the language in the passage just cited, compacted of parallel phrases, is of a kind found in the most complex of sonnets. Its thought and its syntax turn near the end of the eighth line, and repeated phrases in lines one through eight are skilfully counterbalanced by the significant repetitions in lines nine through fourteen. The octave is concerned with the limits of both worldly knowledge and power, while the sestet elaborates those aspects of conduct which lead to wisdom and to hope. This same pattern characterizes those of Milton's rhymed sonnets in which earthly thoughts and heavenly thoughts are contrasted.

In its form, Michael's advice becomes a pledge, a love sonnet of divine solicitude for mankind. Because it heralds a great change in Adam's circumstances, it also has an apocalyptic function. Its matter, finally, concerns the nature of Christ's love, "by name to come call'd Charitie," and how an emulation of that love shall make a holy garden of the soul. The combined effect of Michael's thought and form of expression imparts a strong note of compassion to the final advice an angel gives Adam after the Fall.

As part of the epic structure of thirds, Michael's sonnet should be compared with Raphael's concluding remarks to Adam at the end of Book VIII. In completing his visit to Eden, Raphael speaks a passage of twenty-six lines, the last fourteen of which are a sonnet. The form of his remarks, like Michael's, is a divine love sonnet and therefore epitomizes heavenly concern for man:

> But I can now no more; the parting Sun
> Beyond the Earths green Cape and verdant Isles
> *Hesperean* sets, my Signal to depart.
> Be strong, live happie, and love, but first of all
> Him whom to love is to obey, and keep
> His great command; take heed least Passion sway
> Thy Judgement to do aught, which else free Will
> Would not admit; thine and of all thy Sons
> The weal or woe in thee is plac't; beware.
> I in thy persevering shall rejoyce,
> And all the Blest: stand fast; to stand or fall
> Free in thine own Arbitrement it lies.
> Perfet within, no outward aid require;
> And all temptation to transgress repel. (VIII, 630–43)

Raphael's advice centers on Adam's capacity to be "perfet within." This closely parallels Michael's thought: that Adam can choose to find "a Paradise within," a thought which suggests how fortunate the Fall may be in enabling mankind to regain perfection. Michael's remarks develop from a context which shows that love, not *scientia*, is the true path to wisdom, and Raphael places greater emphasis on Adam's will, the ability of his reason to choose among alternative courses. In the parallel thoughts of the octave and sestet, Raphael carefully balances "free Will" in the octave, which is extended to strengthen the urgency of his remarks, with the concept of inner perfection. Michael, by contrast, directs his final comments to the immediate issue of Adam's expulsion from Eden, thereby preparing mankind for life on "the subjected Plaine" (XII, 640). The shift of emphasis between the two angelic speeches, which point to the same end, perfectly matches Adam's situations before and after the Fall.

In many ways, Adam's fortunes at the end of Book XII are analogous to Satan's unfortunate fall and loss of heaven in Book I, a comparison which is called for in the concentric structure of the epic. Just as Adam must face less attractive surroundings, Satan in Book I confronts his new environment for the first time. Unlike Adam, who is offered a happier, inner paradise through Christ's love, Satan asserts the heretical thought that he himself is author, disposer, and recipient of heaven or hell, as he wishes. He already shows the self-tormenting pattern of thought that leads in Book IV to "the Hell within" (IV, 20), a phrase which, in the epic structure of thirds, should be contrasted with Michael's phrase, the "Paradise within," of Book XII. It is in a self-supporting state of mind, which marks his alienation from God, that Satan reconciles himself to the new conditions of his existence:

> Is this the Region, this the Soil, the Clime,
> Said then the lost Arch Angel, this the seat
> That we must change for Heav'n, this mournful gloom
> For that celestial light? Be it so, since hee
> Who now is Sovran can dispose and bid
> What shall be right: fardest from him is best
> Whom reason hath equald, force hath made supream
> Above his equals. Farewel happy Fields
> Where Joy for ever dwells: Hail horrours, hail
> Infernal world, and thou profoundest Hell
> Receive thy new Possessor: One who brings
> A mind not to be chang'd by Place or Time.
> The mind is its own place, and in it self
> Can make a Heav'n of Hell, a Hell of Heav'n.
> What matter where, if I be still the same,
> And what I should be, all but less then hee
> Whom Thunder hath made greater? Here at least
> We shall be free; th' Almighty hath not built
> Here for his envy, will not drive us hence:
> Here we may reign secure, and in my choyce
> To reign is worth ambition though in Hell:
> Better to reign in Hell, then serve in Heav'n.
> But wherefore let we then our faithful friends,
> Th' associates and copartners of our loss
> Lye thus astonisht on th' oblivious Pool,
> And call them not to share with us their part
> In this unhappy Mansion, or once more
> With rallied Arms to try what may be yet
> Regained in Heav'n, or what more lost in Hell?   (I, 242–70)

It is worth noting how Milton constructs this verse paragraph by using a sonnet as its base. The first fourteen lines of the paragraph constitute Satan's sonnet, his acceptance of hell. The sestet ends with the deceptively profound, ringing lines, "the mind is its own place, and in it self / Can make a Heav'n of Hell, a Hell of Heav'n." Placed at the end of the sonnet, these lines are the culmination of Satan's heroic but inconsistent thought and, at the same time, ironically reveal God's ultimate punishment of him: that Satan may deceive himself into thinking his mind to be its own unsupported place, cut off from all heavenly interference, but that the greater his heroic posture becomes, the more God undermines him, throwing him into more profound depths of hellish self-deception. The final line, "Can make a Heav'n of Hell, a Hell of Heav'n," is the crowning irony and is slightly altered and repeated as a linking line, almost a refrain, to end the second and third parts of the paragraph, as Satan goes on to consider himself and then his "associates and copartners." The construction of the sonnet sets the pattern for the entire paragraph. The sonnet consists of a question and two answers, the second part of the paragraph is a question and answer, the third a question only. The rising proportion of questions to answers counters the cumulative strength of the linking lines, which return at successively shorter intervals. The refrain, based on "heaven" and "hell," starts as a powerful assertion but dwindles into the conclusion of a question, thereby undercutting drastically the bravura of Satan's rhetoric and turning the heroic surface of his utterance upon itself.

The development of Satan's thought in his sonnet of reconciliation to hell, which superficially appears impressive, actually recoils back upon itself to degrade and diminish the force of his arguments. This is the characteristic pattern of his thought. Its descending pattern in the sonnet informs the whole of the verse paragraph. It is the rhetorical structure of all his major speeches and mirrors in miniature the constant degradation of his character throughout the epic.

Satan's declining fortunes are evident in every book in which he appears, and sonnets play a significant role in the presentation of his decline. Sonnets usually occur at the conclusions of books to help signify the resolutions of characters' destinies. Milton's placement of sonnets argues that he considered the form to be an important means of embodying these high points of resolution in the narrative. Hence, the Son, Michael, Raphael, and, as we shall discover, Adam and Eve speak in sonnets at the ends of books as pledges of their love for one another or as marks of their highest stature. The reverse is true for Satan. He speaks in sonnets near the beginnings of Books I and IV, when his heroic character and rhetoric are at their most impressive, but sonnets never appear at the ends of books, where they would elevate him. Near the beginning of Book I, his sonnet of reconciliation to hell, which has just been considered, is also an expression of hatred for God, thereby showing how Satan inverts the form's traditional use as a love poem. At the beginning of Book IV, Satan's stature is lower than it was in Book I, but he again employs sonnets on Mount Niphates in his address to the sun. But the power of the sonnet as a form for the expression of love begins to gain control over the diminished devil. The first begins his speech (IV, 32–45). Although he has "no friendly voice" in the octave, he weakens in the sestet, saying of God, "he deserved no such return." Satan's resolve weakens even further when he comes closest to rapport with God in the second sonnet, which begins, "O then at last relent: is there no place / Left for Repentance, none for Pardon left?" (IV, 79–92). He is weakest in the sestet of this sonnet, for he falls into self-pity and reveals his true character: "onely Supream / In miserie. . . ." Satan rejects the thought of his attempted sonnets of reconciliation with God and recovers his hatred in the rest of his speech. He does not speak a sonnet again in the remaining books of the epic. Sonnets thus measure his character, which is always strongest at the beginnings of books, but even in themselves embody and prefigure his imminent failures. The ultimate thematic interest of his sonnets is in their relationship through the epic structures to the sonnets of other characters, which, unlike Satan's, are not examples of failures but of love and of triumph over evil.

To return to the overarching parallel between Satan's speech of reconciliation to hell in Book I and Michael's parting advice to Adam in Book XII, it should be pointed out that Michael's last words after his sonnet, unlike Satan's, do not suffer from rhetorical deflation. After the sonnet on charity and the inner paradise, Michael must lead Adam down the mount of speculation and remove Adam and Eve from Eden. Whereas the structure of the entire verse paragraph erodes the bold rhetoric of Satan's boasts of victory in defeat, the stern purport of Michael's instructions yields to expectations of hope, which occupy the larger portion of his final remarks:

> Let us descend now therefore from this top
> Of Speculation; for the hour precise
> Exacts our parting hence; and see the Guards,
> By mee encampt on yonder Hill, expect
> Thir motion, at whose Front a flaming Sword,
> In signal of remove, waves fiercely round;
> We may no longer stay: go, waken *Eve*;

Her also I with gentle Dreams have calm'd
Portending good, and all her spirits compos'd
To meek submission: thou at season fit
Let her with thee partake what thou hast heard,
Chiefly what may concern her Faith to know,
The great deliverance by her Seed to come
(For by the Womans Seed) on all Mankind.
That ye may live, which will be many dayes,
Both in one Faith unanimous though sad,
With cause for evils past, yet much more cheer'd
With meditation on the happie end. (XII, 588–605)

This passage is organized like a canzone; that is to say, it has two parts, which resemble a *fronte* and *sirima*, and they are joined by a *chiave*, or linking line. The first part of the passage, which is threatening but short, concerns the descent from the mount and the need to remove Adam and Eve from Eden. The second, longer, and more hopeful part concerns Eve. The two parts are interlinked by the line, "We may no longer stay: go, waken *Eve*," which joins together the lines on Adam's descent with those on Eve. In contrast to the run-on lines and phrases which precede and follow it, the linking line is syntactically distinct within semicolons and reinstates the metrical norm. This line comes as close as blank verse can to imitating the function of a *chiave*, or key line, in a canzone.[5]

The entire verse paragraph of Michael's concluding speech is thus comprised of this canzone-style passage and the sonnet at its head. Milton develops each form with such grace and skill that the blank verse canzone is not anticlimactic to the sonnet. All in all, Michael's final instructions and advice are an excellent illustration of how Milton recalls the characteristics of his two favorite rhymed forms to create a resonant coda of heavenly compassion and solicitude for mankind.

Sympathetic readers of Books XI and XII, which are traditionally slighted for their want of dramatic action or imaginative scope, usually sense that these books gather and surpass reverberations of themes and situations from the whole of the epic to heat their dusky lines with the fires of portentous meanings and events until they become incandescent.[6] Michael's sonnet to Adam in Book XII is just such a passage. By way of the various epic structures of which it is part, it increases its scope at the top of the mount of speculation and is, as we have observed, one of the best vantage points from which to view the poem in its entirety. Its immediate impact within Books XI and XII relates to the sonnets spoken by Adam and Eve. Near the conclusion of Book XI, a despondent Adam is finally shown a vision of God's love after the Flood, and he is moved to utter a sonnet of love and praise for his creator, thereby reconciling himself to his past and to the future. He continues to speak in sonnet-like passages throughout Book XII and is matched by Michael's sonnet of final advice. Then, in the last speech of the epic, Eve speaks a sonnet of love to Adam. These three final sonnets act as pledges of Adam's obedient love for God, God's assured love for mankind, and Eve's love for Adam. They comprise a trinity of thought and form which goes far to redeem the value of the last two books and to establish a clearer perspective on the rest of the epic.

The ways in which Adam in Book XI responds to Michael's presentation of visions from the mount of speculation are central to the increasingly elevated tone of the book. His education is a sort of catechism, in which he asks all the questions. As Michael first unfolds the future of mankind, Adam asks short, increasingly despondent questions about Cain, Abel, and death. When scenes of hedonistic society appear, Adam mistakenly shows approval and, when shown the carnage of war, relapses into despairing questions. The visions reach their culminating point with the Flood. Adam becomes more voluble at this sight, admits he has misinterpreted what he has seen, and asks whether mankind must now perish.

Michael tells Adam of Noah, "the one just Man alive" (XI, 818), through whom mankind is to be regenerated. The example of Noah transforms Adam's despondency into joy, for Noah is the faithful servant of God who redeems Adam for his disobedience. In the double-panel structure of the epic, which pairs Books XI and V, Noah is the mortal counterpart of Abdiel, "among the faithless, faithful only hee" (V, 897), the loyal angel whom Raphael at the end of Book V counseled Adam to emulate.

The vision of the Flood and the example of Noah provide a conjunction of apocalypticism and love, the two aspects which most often inform sonnets in the epic. This is the high point of Adam's regeneration, and with his final lines in Book XI, a separate verse paragraph, he speaks a sonnet, which reveals that he is now beginning to understand the nature of divine grace and that he must rejoice in it:

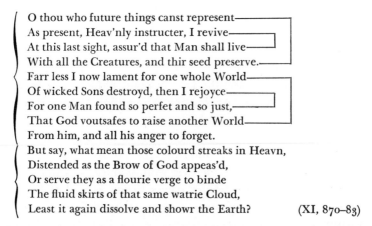

O thou who future things canst represent———
As present, Heav'nly instructer, I revive———
At this last sight, assur'd that Man shall live———
With all the Creatures, and thir seed preserve.———
Farr less I now lament for one whole World———
Of wicked Sons destroyd, then I rejoyce———
For one Man found so perfet and so just,———
That God voutsafes to raise another World———
From him, and all his anger to forget.
But say, what mean those colourd streaks in Heavn,
Distended as the Brow of God appeas'd,
Or serve they as a flourie verge to binde
The fluid skirts of that same watrie Cloud,
Least it again dissolve and showr the Earth?   (XI, 870–83)

The ninth line of the sonnet, which both extends the octave and
explains the image of the rainbow in the sestet, illuminates the nature
of divine grace. The words which end the first eight lines suggest strongly
the rhyming pattern of the Petrarchan octave, which normally encloses
the syntax, and its running over into the ninth line is therefore all the
more surprising. But this is precisely the nature of divine grace, which
overflows, runs on, and abounds. At this point in his regeneration, Adam
understands God's grace best in the image of the rainbow, but by the
end of Book XII his understanding, in accordance with the change in
Michael's mode of narration, will have moved from an image to articulate discourse with the lines that begin, "O goodness infinite, goodness
immense" (XII, 469).

Adam's sonnet of love and reconciliation at the end of Book XI
sets the pattern for the form of his responses to Michael's narration in
Book XII. He no longer speaks in short questions and answers but in
sonnetlike units of fifteen and sixteen lines, which we are to view as
pledges of his renewed trust in life and in the life-giver. By moving from
indignation to satisfaction to overwhelming joy, Adam's remarks in the
last book help to shape its increasing elevation of mood. After Michael
describes the folly and fate of Babylon, Adam expresses fifteen lines of
patriarchal indignation towards mankind: ten lines are statement, the
last five a question, thereby echoing loosely the rhetorical pattern of
Adam's sonnet in Book XI (XII, 64–78). Michael's narration of God's
covenant with the Israelites elicits another fifteen-line response of sonnetlike proportions (XII, 270–84), in which Adam is relieved to see his

faults overcome again. His joy is unbounded when Michael tells of Christ, the Last Judgment, and how the earth "shall all be Paradise" (XII, 464). Adam then speaks the famous sixteen-line paragraph, which begins, "O goodness infinite, goodness immense" (XII, 469). Its first ten lines praise God's grace, the last six ponder the fate of mankind after Christ's Resurrection. Again, one senses that Adam's remarks would have been a perfect sonnet but that in the octave the form could not contain his joy over divine grace. The eighth line ends, "that much more good thereof shall spring," and runs on, "To God more glory, more good will to Men / From God, and over wrauth grace shall abound" (476–78).

The inception of Adam's regeneration, as well as his Fall, traces back to Eve. It is her moving speech to Adam in Book X that marks the turning point in their relationship after the Fall. By reconciling himself to Eve, he can go on to reconciliation with God. Towards the conclusion of Book X, however, Adam and Eve are continuing their bitter condemnations of one another. Their arguments become increasingly despondent and acrimonious, culminating in Adam's vicious rejection of Eve. This creates their greatest domestic crisis. Completely distraught, Eve falls at his feet and pleads for a restoration of love:

> Forsake me not thus, *Adam*, witness Heav'n
> What love sincere, and reverence in my heart
> I beare thee, and unweeting have offended,
> Unhappilie deceav'd; thy suppliant
> I beg, and clasp thy knees; bereave me not,
> Whereon I live, thy gentle looks, thy aid,
> Thy counsel in this uttermost distress,
> My onely strength and stay: forlorn of thee,
> Whither shall I betake me, where subsist?
> While yet we live, scarse one short hour perhaps,
> Between us two let there be peace, both joyning,
> As joyn'd in injuries, one enmitie
> Against a Foe by doom express assign'd us,
> That cruel Serpent: On me exercise not
> Thy hatred for this miserie befall'n,
> On me already lost, mee then thy self
> More miserable; both have sin'd, but thou
> Against God onely, I against God and thee,
> And to the place of judgement will return,
> There with my cries importune Heaven, that all
> The sentence from thy head remov'd may light
> On me, sole cause to thee of all this woe,
> Mee mee onely just object of his ire.   (X, 914–36)

The final sentence of her petition, in which she requests peace and determines her conduct to atone for the Fall, is a love sonnet. She makes her strongest appeal in the sestet, accepting responsibility for her part in the Fall, and offers to ransom herself for Adam to spare him from judgment. This sea change in her behavior is worthy of Christ. In the concentric structure of the epic, for that matter, Eve's language and conduct here in Book X are strikingly similar to the Son's in Book III, when he offers to ransom himself for mankind: "Behold mee then, mee for him, life for life / I offer, on mee let thine anger fall" (III, 236–37). Eve's sonnet also may be compared through the double-panel structure of the poem to Satan's sonnet in Book IV, which begins, "O then at last relent: is there no place / Left for Repentance, none for Pardon left?" (IV, 79–80). Although Satan's attempt at reconciliation fails, Eve's does not. Her petition eradicates Adam's anger, and their regeneration, which soon moves God to send Michael to them, begins at this point.

While Michael revives and educates Adam with visions in Book XI and narration in Book XII, thereby making his advice more and more internal until it ends with the "Paradise within," he imparts all his instructions intuitively through dreams to the sleeping Eve. Through the epic structure of thirds, these restorative dreams in Book XII contrast sharply to a similar situation near the end of Book IV, when Satan as a toad sits at Eve's ear to send her dreams designed to discompose her spirits. Adam returns from the mount of speculation, goes to Eve, finds her awake, and she greets him, saying,

> Whence thou returnst, & whither wentst, I know;———
> For God is also in sleep, and Dreams advise,
> Which he hath sent propitious, some great good
> Presaging, since with sorrow and hearts distress
> Wearied I fell asleep: but now lead on;
> In mee is no delay; with thee to goe,———
> Is to stay here; without thee here to stay,
> Is to go hence unwilling; thou to mee
> Art all things under Heav'n, all places thou,
> Who for my wilful crime art banisht hence.
> This further consolation yet secure
> I carry hence; though all by mee is lost,
> Such favour I unworthie am voutsaft,
> By mee the Promis'd Seed shall all restore.   (XII, 610–23)

This separate verse paragraph, the last speech by a character in the epic, marks the final stage of Eve's regeneration. The divisions in this sonnet are blurred, particularly in the last six lines. Syntactically, the sonnet breaks at the end of line ten, but the phrases—"all things," "all places," "all by mee," and "all restore"—define the true sestet. This points to the salient feature of the entire sonnet: repetitions of words ("all," "hence," "sleep," and the pronouns), internal rhyming ("delay"–"stay"), and a rhyme ("know"–"goe"), all of which preclude easy separation of the piece into distinct parts and result, instead, in a unified paragraph of considerable musical effect. It is as difficult to divide Eve's sonnet as it is now to divide her from Adam. The musicality of her utterance may be, in fact, Milton's way of indicating that she is now in harmony with heaven.

Eve not only pledges her love to Adam in this sonnet but also recapitulates the substance of Michael's remarks in Books XI and XII. In the first four and a half lines, Eve reveals that she knows where Adam has been and that he has apprehended revelations of divine grace. In the middle of her sonnet, she expresses her intuitive understanding of the inner paradise by way of her love for Adam. The inner paradise is based on love, not place, and she will share that love with Adam whether or not they reside in an external paradise like Eden. Her intuitive knowledge of "the Promis'd Seed" in the last four lines is an immaculate conception of a new Eve and an annunciation of the Word as idea and is the best example in the poem of the way in which heavenly communication transcends rational discourse. One might also speculate that it is as if her lines on "the Promis'd Seed" are born of Michael's earlier aside, the parenthetical phrase, "(For by the Womans Seed)," which appears at the end of his last speech (601)—a phrase which is strangely independent of the syntax of his lines and could be viewed as floating free to be implanted in Eve's mind. This would then be another example of the striking ways in which Milton sometimes suspends his syntax. The unique syntactical independence of Michael's parenthetical remark remains a bothersome exception in the syntax of the poem, however, and I cannot find a better explanation for its occurrence than the one I have suggested. Eve's sonnet in general, its last four lines in particular, and especially the rhyme ("know"–"goe"), which encapsulates the thought of the entire paragraph, results from her temporary, superrational mode of perception, one which approximates angelic intuition, the intuitive reason, that Raphael in his speech on the scale of creation suggests may be granted to Adam and Eve if they remain obedient (V, 491–505). Perhaps no stronger evidence than Eve's sonnet could be cited to show Milton's embodiment of the fortunate fall within the epic.

The reconciliation of Adam to Eve is matched by a new accord between Satan and Sin, which also begins in Book X. As Satan returns to hell from his triumphs in Eden, he beholds a marvelous bridge, which is celebrated in Sin's word of greeting, a love sonnet to her husband and sire:

> O Parent, these are thy magnific deeds,
> Thy Trophies, which thou view'st as not thine own,
> Thou art thir Author and prime Architect:
> For I no sooner in my Heart divin'd,
> My Heart, which by a secret harmonie──────────
> Still moves with thine, joyn'd in connexion sweet,
> That thou on Earth hadst prosper'd, which thy looks
> Now also evidence, but straight I felt
> Though distant from thee Worlds between, yet felt
> That I must after thee with this thy Son;
> Such fatal consequence unites us three:──────────
> Hell could no longer hold us in her bounds,
> Nor this unvoyageable Gulf obscure
> Detain from following thy illustrious track. (X, 354–67)

Much has been written about how Satan, Sin, and Death form a parody of the superior heavenly Trinity. This seems to be true of the infernal trinity in Book II, where their stature is heightened through their classical epic presentation. In Book X, however, Satan is relatively domesticated and harmonized with his family, a fact which Sin indicates in the rhyme of "secret harmonie" with "unites us three." Sin's sonnet of greeting and love, moreover, is rather a parody of Eve's sonnets of reconciliation than of any aspect of the Trinity. In Book X, Satan, Sin, and Death become, to my mind, a parody of the superior, earthly, yet spiritual trinity which is developing among Adam, Eve, and the historical Christ. This readjusted view of the infernal trinity is also in keeping with Satan's descent in the scale of creation between Books II and X. The hierarchical descent of Satan, Sin, and Death throughout the poem is partly accomplished by the change in proportions from blank verse which recalls classical conventions to verse based on Christian forms like the sonnet, a change which mirrors the basic shift in the epic from a classical to a Christian concept of heroism. By the end of the epic, the place of conflict between good and evil is no longer in the cosmic expanses of heaven and hell or on the favored ground of Eden, but all that has transpired will be replayed on the modest field of earth. Satan will be rebuffed by a smaller Abdiel in Noah, Sin will fail to taint Mary, and, finally, first Satan, then Death, will grapple with Christ as divine man but both will lose. This narrower view of Satan, Sin, and Death at the end of *Paradise Lost* is called for, in sum, by the gathering human grandeur and Christlike conduct of Adam and Eve before their expulsion from paradise.

Groups of threes are characteristic of the epic. Besides the heavenly, infernal, and earthly trinities, it should be observed that the sonnets of the poem are also best viewed in threes. For example, Satan is assigned three sonnets, which appear in Books I and IV; as counterbalance, there are three sonnets by heavenly figures: the Son's (VI), Raphael's (VIII), and Michael's (XII). Through the characters in Books XI and XII, there are sonnets by Michael, Adam, and Eve. This pattern of threes generally holds true for the other sonnets in the epic, most of which I shall not discuss here. What might be recalled, however, is that threefold patterns are characteristic of Milton's works throughout his life. The twenty-seven stanzas of the hymn *On the Morning of Christ's Nativity*, for example, are comprised of three main sections, which, in turn, consist of stanzas arranged in threes. Or, one should remember that *Lycidas*, also, is built on three sections.

The clearest illustration of a triad in *Paradise Lost* is Uriel's summary of the creation in a triple sonnet, which appropriately appears at the end of Book III (III, 694–735). This is his speech to Satan, who is disguised as a stripling cherub. In his first sonnet, Uriel tells Satan that to extol the works of God, the uncreated creator and first mover, does not merit blame but praise (694–707). Uriel then speaks in his second sonnet of God's "second bidding" and tells in the octave of the ordering of matter and in the sestet of the fifth element, the spirit (708–21). His third sonnet is an account of the earth, sun, and the moon, whose "countenance triform" also helps to grace the earth and paradise with light (722–35). Milton's ordering of words matches the order of sonnets: the first sonnet is on the first cause; the second concerns the dualities of matter and spirit and their movements in God's first two biddings at creation; in the third, three heavenly bodies—earth, sun, and moon—appear, and the three aspects of the moon are celebrated. Above all, though, Uriel's triple sonnet is an expression of love for the perfection of God's creations. It may be compared for comic purposes to Eve's less sublime sonnet of admiration for the speaking serpent in Book IX, another expression of wonder for an aspect of creation (IX, 553–66).

Several sonnets in *Paradise Lost*, finally, reveal Milton's use of the form not so much as a vehicle for love but for the voicing of public attitudes, a function which is of utmost significance later in *Paradise Regained*. By public function, I mean to recall the distinction one makes when indicating the private or public import of Milton's rhymed sonnets—a distinction which recurs with Wordsworth's Miltonic sonnets. This type of passage appears in the epic when Raphael in Book V prepares to make public and rehearse the great events of the war in heaven (V, 563–76). It appears again a bit later when God the Father issues a call to arms to the Son in preparation for the battle (V, 719–32). In both these sonnets, the enormity of major events receives a treatment reminiscent of Milton's earlier public sonnets on the Puritan struggle for liberty.

Milton's experimentation with the public sonnet yields its greatest achievements in *Paradise Regained*, a work which I shall now survey briefly. Milton develops the temptation in the wilderness around Christ's emergence from private into public life. The frequency of blank verse sonnets in this work is greater than that found in the other last poems, and its sonnets are employed to reflect its grand theme: spiritual identity in private and public ideals.

Satan reveals himself by using the public sonnet for its most degraded function, that of flattery. Christ's sonnets, by contrast, are public expressions of the highest order and epitomize his spiritual identity. Disguised as an old swain in Book I, Satan's first words of greeting to Christ are a sonnet of fawning admiration (I, 321–34). Then, unmasked, he tries to tempt and educate Christ in the ways of the world and utters another flattering sonnet (I, 383–96), only to be countered with Christ's sonnet of denunciation (I, 407–20), the public stance of which conveys Christ's knowledge of heavenly history and of Satan's role in those events.

Christ's views on worldly kingdoms and on the nature of wealth attain their strongest expression in the thematic summary which concludes Book II. His resolution of private and public values is a textbook sonnet; rhymes clarify the thought and structure of the octave and sestet, the regularity of which reenforces the firmness of his position:

But to guide Nations in the way of truth
By saving Doctrine, and from errour lead
To know, and knowing worship God aright,
Is yet more Kingly, this attracts the Soul,
Governs the inner man, the nobler part,
That other o're the body only reigns,
And oft by force, which to a generous mind
So reigning can be no sincere delight.
Besides to give a Kingdom hath been thought
Greater and nobler done, and to lay down
Far more magnanimous, then to assume.
Riches are needless then, both for themselves,
And for thy reason why they should be sought,
To gain a Scepter, oftest better miss't.   (II, 473–86)

Immediately thereafter in the first speech of Book III, a troubled Satan speaks another sonnet of flattery, in which he pretends to be greatly impressed by Christ's views on kingship and riches (III, 7–20). He continues, however, to tempt Christ throughout the book with offers of kingly power and glory. His inability to comprehend Christ's resolution of the private and public life into a state of true kingship continues to deepen until Christ dismisses all arguments at the end of Book III with perhaps the most effective speech in the poem. It is a long verse paragraph (III, 387–440), in which his thoughts on biblical history become increasingly more extensive—moving successively from units of seven, nine, eleven, and thirteen to fourteen lines (a sonnet)—to create a strong rhetorical crescendo. Book III, then, ends in much the same way as Book II: Christ has the last words and gives them added strength by concluding with a sonnet.

Frustrated and angry, Satan in Book IV abandons his arguments and resorts to actions. He reveals his true identity by turning from sonnets of flattery to one of hatred and fury. He begins his final speech to Christ before the storm with a sonnet, in which he says, "What dost thou in this World? the Wilderness / For thee is fittest place" (IV, 368–81). After this, *Paradise Regained* shifts from its planes of verbal debate to the physical threats afforded by Satan through the storm and through himself on the question of Christ's identity. With this, the issue of public and private ideals is gone, as are the sonnets, which appeared to such good purpose in the debates.

Sonnets as pledges of love, reconciliation, and apocalyptic events return with *Samson Agonistes*, and Milton's experimentation with them is extended to its furthest limits. They also become a way of reminding us that, although the sources of the play are the Old Testament and Greek tragedy, the work is informed with a Christian viewpoint. They are few in number and are spoken by Manoa, Samson, and the chorus. Manoa has two particularly striking sonnets, in which he shows his affection for his son and attempts to reconcile Samson to God (502–15; 1490–1503), which is also a separate verse paragraph). In reviewing his disastrous marriage, Samson concludes a verse paragraph with fourteen lines of self-criticism, which turn the sonnet as a vehicle for love poetry against itself in a complaint (406–19).

But the drama, like *Paradise Lost*, has its most serious and important sonnets at the end. Samson's last speech of farewell shows acceptance of his identity and love for his people. It is also echoed in fourteen lines of irregular lengths by the chorus:

> *Sam.* Brethren farewel, your company along
> I will not wish, lest it perhaps offend them
> To see me girt with Friends; and how the sight
> Of me as of a common Enemy,
> So dreaded once, may now exasperate them
> I know not. Lords are Lordliest in thir wine;
> And the well-feasted Priest then soonest fir'd
> With zeal, if aught Religion seem concern'd:
> No less the people on thir Holy-days
> Impetuous, insolent, unquenchable;
> Happ'n what may, of me expect to hear
> Nothing dishonourable, impure, unworthy
> Our God, our Law, my Nation, or my self,
> The last of me or no I cannot warrant.
>   *Chor.* Go, and the Holy One
> Of *Israel* be thy guide
> To what may serve his glory best, & spread his name
> Great among the Heathen round:
> Send thee the Angel of thy Birth, to stand
> Fast by thy side, who from thy Fathers field
> Rode up in flames after his message told
> Of thy conception, and be now a shield
> Of fire; that Spirit that first rusht on thee
> In the camp of *Dan*
> Be efficacious in thee now at need.
> For never was from Heaven imparted
> Measure of strength so great to mortal seed,
> As in thy wond'rous actions hath been seen. (1413–40)

The form of the chorus's reply is based on Samson's sonnet of farewell. The octave of Samson's sonnet concerns his physical and spiritual
guides. He declines the assistance of his friends to lead him to the feast
and scorns the presumption of "the well-feasted Priest" to provide religious guidance. In their first eight lines, the chorus defers its guidance
to "the Holy One / Of *Israel*" and draws an implicit, grim comparison
between the spirit of holy fire in Samson and the wine that puts fire
into the heathen priests. In the sestet, Samson speaks of his mission in
relation to the insolent populace, and the chorus recalls in their last six
lines a past illustration of Samson's strength, which they hope shall
revive for the present occasion. The chorus's sonnet (its first) is auda-
cious, imperfect, and thus suited to their characteristically faulty perceptions; but as a sonnet, the speech foreshadows a capacity for clearer
thoughts.

If one be willing to take the freedoms and variations of Milton's
choric writing in stride, as is Louis Martz, the final fourteen lines of the
drama should also strike one as a sonnet.[7] They rhyme as two alternating
quatrains plus a Petrarchan sestet and display proportions characteristic
of Milton's earlier, rhymed sonnets:

> *Chor.* All is best, though we oft doubt,
> What th' unsearchable dispose
> Of highest wisdom brings about,
> And ever best found in the close.
> Oft he seems to hide his face,
> But unexpectedly returns
> And to his faithful Champion hath in place
> Bore witness gloriously; whence *Gaza* mourns
> And all that band them to resist
> His uncontroulable intent,
> His servants he with new acquist
> Of true experience from this great event
> With peace and consolation hath dismist,
> And calm of mind all passion spent.   (1745–58)

In thought and in form the clearest of the chorus's statements, the
passage shares the functions of sonnets in *Paradise Lost*: its moral purport of reconciliation to the ways of God's love in apocalyptic circumstances. Its thought is modeled also on that of classical drama; specifically, it recalls the choric hymns which conclude several Euripidean
tragedies. Like the sonnets in *Paradise Lost*, however, it Christianizes

classical materials with its form, which originates not in the classical but in the Christian era. Like the sonnets of Michael, Adam, and Eve at the end of the epic, it concludes its poem so that a Christian emphasis may predominate, informing the thought and structure of the entire work.

Milton's blank verse sonnets serve a variety of speculations about the general characteristics of his last works. The existence of blank verse sonnets, in general, perhaps helps to clarify why Milton's verse paragraphs never begin nor end in the middle of lines. Because the sonnet is a fixed form, its most harmonious appearance in blank verse would necessitate the construction of paragraphs which should also be complete stanzas. What may even be allowed, furthermore, is that the employment of fixed forms like the sonnet and of a general stanzaic approach in verse paragraphs is a mnemonic aid, which benefits both the reader and the poet, and makes a virtue of necessity for a blind poet, who desires to create the clearest, most polished, memorable work possible but is unable to see on paper, for the purposes of revision, anything he has composed.

What should be suggested, finally, is that Milton's experimentation with the sonnet in blank verse deserves to be called nothing if not brilliant. Measured against the standards of rhymed sonnets, Milton's blank verse sonnets in and of themselves are among the most effective and sophisticated examples of the form's range and capabilities in our literary history. Isolated from the books of *Paradise Lost*, moreover, they comprise one of the most remarkable and ambitious sonnet sequences ever written. From the point of view of an epic or dramatic poet, the sonnets are not any less impressive. At first glance, there is something totally incongruous and comically disproportionate about the appearance of sonnets in the significant perspectives and actions of his major poems. Yet, in Milton's hands, these sonnets convey some of the most searching language of the poems, raising themselves above their contexts, and, in *Paradise Lost* and *Samson Agonistes*, welding together the thought and structures of each to help assimilate and surpass through the scope of their art the materials and traditions on which the poems are based. The sonnet, in short, a form which Milton borrowed from the Italians and in many respects bettered, became, in turn, one of the primary resources he could utilize in his contest with the ancients for supremacy in epic and dramatic poetry.

The University of British Columbia

NOTES

1. *Henry Crabb Robinson on Books and Their Writers*, ed. Edith J. Morley, II (London, 1938), p. 484. A fine example of Wordsworth's own employment of blank verse sonnets is the Wanderer's effusion on the visionary powers of early youth (*The Excursion*, IV, 109–22). The passage combines a Miltonic treatment of blindness with the Wordsworthian theme of sublime perceptions in childhood. A discussion of Wordsworth's extensive use of blank verse sonnets, blank verse couplets, and blank verse Spenserian stanzas may be found in the "Appendix" of my *Wordsworth and the Sonnet*, to be published in late 1973 by *Anglistica*.

2. Two passages in *Comus* (358–71 and 417–30), also, are clearly fourteen-line units, which suggest that Milton may have modeled parts of his earlier blank verse on rhymed forms. (There are three, if one includes the fourteen lines of stichomythia between Comus and the Lady.)

A complete table of blank verse sonnets would be less helpful than my estimates, for a compilation might appear misleadingly definitive and would also be virtually meaningless as description. There are a very few fourteen-line units, moreover, which are not strong in isolation. Lines 37–50 of Milton's invocation to light in Book III, for example, which begin, "then feed on thoughts," initiate a fourteen-line unit, divide into a standard octave and sestet, and use fricatives and dental and glottal stops as cut-off sounds at the ends of lines and phrases to refer to the poet's blindness in exactly the same manner as do the rhymes in the sonnet, "When I consider how my light is spent." Yet, these lines are so thoroughly integrated into their surrounding context that it would seem unfair to treat them as a separate unit.

3. The text of *Paradise Lost* cited throughout is Frank Allen Patterson, ed., *The Student's Milton* (New York, 1930), which preserves the punctuation and paragraphing of the early editions. Subsequent citations will be given in the text.

4. My comments on blank verse sonnets should clarify how all three narrative patterns work together in *Paradise Lost*. Arthur Barker discusses *Paradise Lost* and the *Aeneid* as epics of thirds: "Structural Pattern in *Paradise Lost*," *PQ*, XXVIII (1949), 17–30. J. R. Watson alludes to the resonating pattern in "Divine Providence and the Structure of *Paradise Lost*," *Essays in Criticism*, XIV (1964), 148–55. John T. Shawcross mentions the double-panel and concentric patterns, which he terms *contrasting* and *comparative* forms, in "The Style and Genre of *Paradise Lost*," *New Essays on Paradise Lost*, ed. Thomas Kranidas (Berkeley, 1969), pp. 21–22. Although his earlier essay, "The Balanced Structure of *Paradise Lost*," *SP*, LXII (1965), 696–718, is chiefly on the ten-book, 1667 edition, Shawcross's remarks help to confirm the existence of *contrasting* and *comparative* patterns in the twelve-book, 1674 epic.

The most detailed analyses of epic narrative patterns are on the poems of Homer and Vergil. For Homer, see especially Cedric H. Whitman's chapter, "Geometric Structure of the *Iliad*," in his book *Homer and the Homeric Tradition* (Cambridge, Mass., 1958), pp. 249–84; also, George E. Duckworth's lucid discussions of the double-panel and tripartite patterns of the *Iliad*, the *Odyssey*, and the *Aeneid* in *Structural Patterns and Proportions in Vergil's Poems* (Ann Arbor, 1962). Besides Duckworth's book on Vergil, there is Brooks Otis's excellent piece, *Virgil: A Study in Civilized Poetry* (Oxford, 1963), which demonstrates how double-panel and concentric patterns work in the *Aeneid*.

5. For a discussion of the canzone and Milton's use of the form in *Lycidas* and in some choruses of *Samson Agonistes*, see F. T. Prince's pioneering work, *The Italian Element in Milton's Verse* (Oxford, 1954).

6. I am not indebted to specific passages in the following works, but they pre-eminently give impetus and relate to my general assessment of Books XI and XII: F. T. Prince's article, "On the Last Two Books of *Paradise Lost*," *Essays and Studies*, XI (1958), 38–52; B. A. Wright's book, *Milton's "Paradise Lost"* (London, 1962); Joseph H. Summers's excellent chapter, "The Final Vision," in *The Muse's Method: An Introduction to "Paradise Lost"* (London, 1962), pp. 186–224; and, most recently, Stanley Eugene Fish's essay, "Discovery as Form in *Paradise Lost*," *New Essays on "Paradise Lost*," ed. Kranidas, pp. 1–14.

7. "Chorus and Character in *Samson Agonistes*," in *Milton Studies*, I (Pittsburgh, 1969), p. 133, where he refers to the "sonnet-style" rhyming of these final lines; I am also indebted to his extensive comments on the chorus's faulty perceptions.

FLOWER, FRUIT, AND SEED: A READING OF *PARADISE LOST*

Kathleen M. Swaim

Milton's predominantly floral prelapsarian cosmos employs imagery relating flowers to character, place, and theme (especially Eve = Eden = flowers). The poem's action and poetry hinge on changes in the meaning of *fruit* (especially in Book IX); *seed* and the anticipation of harvest dominate the final books. The postlapsarian cosmos employs metaphor, offering time, history, and human transmutation and fallen potentiality as paradoxical fruit. Diabolical effects center on storms and insects, apparently malign processes by which flowers give way to fruit. Eve is *deflowered* (IX, 901) to become fruitful. The fall marks the initiation into paradox, metaphor, and potentiality. Prelapsarian praise shifts to postlapsarian prayer. Metaphor's imaginative leap linking apparently disparate realms of experience replaces imagery's wholeness and coherence. Edenic imagery is characteristically lovely, sensuous, physical; postlapsarian metaphor requires interpretation through faith and the reader's greater creative energy. Psychological Imagination corresponds to theological Grace; Christ is the agency of both, teaching Adam and us to read the language of mystery, paradox, and metaphor through faith. Milton's poetry like his fiction shifts from floral to fruitful, from paradise without to paradise within, from innocence to experience, from praise to prayer, from discursive to intuitive apprehension.

I N HIS masterly deployment of vegetative imagery in *Paradise Lost,* Milton deserves far more praise and attention than he receives from the usual recognitions of Eden as a magnificently floral paradise or the eating of a piece of fruit as the crux of the narrative. This essay will explore the patterned imagery of vegetation throughout *Paradise Lost,* beginning with the relationship of flowers to character, place, and theme, in particular the poetic equations of Eve=Eden=flowers. The design

includes the miniature reenactment of the whole central action of the
poem within a single image briefly glimpsed—as in "From his slack hand
the Garland wreath'd for *Eve* / Down dropp'd, and all the faded Roses
shed" (IX, 892–93), an image that encompasses human weakening and
the loss of beauty, innocence, immutable paradise, and perfect loving
within the fading of roses and the dropping of petals—and ranges to include a rendering of the whole prelapsarian cosmos as flowers and the
whole postlapsarian scheme of time and history as fruit.[1] Man's prelapsarian relationship to deity is rendered florally as praise; the postlapsarian relationship fruitfully as prayer. Diabolical effects on the human,
the moral, and the vegetative appear as storms and insects. The epic's
action and poetry hinge on changes in the meaning of *fruit*, and the
future promise of the final books lies in *seed*. Vegetative imagery progressively calls attention to and celebrates the *felix culpa* paradox, a shift
in idea that requires and incorporates a shift in the reader's poetic re-
sponsiveness from right reading of imagery to right reading of metaphor.

Flowers are the fairest or choicest part of a plant, beautiful, color-
ful, ornamental, sweet-smelling, delicate, and feminine. Like Eden itself,
they appeal to the eye, the nose, and the touch, and are fixed in space.
In generalized form flowers regularly describe the world of Adam and
Eve as lovely, fresh, and innocent. Eden is a "flow'ry lap" (IV, 254), with
"Flow'rs of all hue" (256), "Flow'rs worthy of Paradise which . . . Nature
boon / Pour'd forth profuse" (241–43). The rose is definitively without
thorn. Adam and Eve's domestic arrangements, the place itself and the
items of furniture, are emphatically floral. "The Silvan Lodge" or
"blissful Bower," likened to "*Pomona's* Arbor" (V, 377–78), encompasses
a roof of "inwoven shade" of laurel and myrtle with walls of acanthus
and other odorous shrubs. As for room divisions,

> each beauteous flow'r,
> *Iris* all hues, Roses, and Jessamin
> Rear'd high thir flourisht heads between, and wrought
> Mosaic.   (IV, 697–700)[2]

And of the floor we read:

> Underfoot the Violet,
> Crocus, and Hyacinth with rich inlay
> Broider'd the ground, more color'd than with stone
> Of costliest Emblem.   (IV, 700–03)

As the couple eat, they "recline / On the soft downy Bank damaskt with flow'rs" (IV, 333–34).[3] When Adam and Eve entertain Raphael, their table is "Rais'd of grassy turf" and has "mossy seats" around it (V, 391–92). The bedroom is wonderfully floral. The bed itself is decked "With Flowers, Garlands, and sweet-smelling Herbs" (IV, 709). Another evocative bedroom description uses flowers to convey the timelessness of Eden and the perfection of their love. Adam and Eve

> lull'd by Nightingales imbracing slept,
> And on thir naked limbs the flow'ry roof
> Show'r'd Roses, which the Morn repair'd.   (IV, 771–73)

Even immediately after the fall, "Pansies, and Violets, and Asphodel, / And Hyacinth" provide the couch of love (IX, 1039–41). Flowers define the Edenic setting, partly as a matter of narrative necessity, more importantly as tone and atmosphere.

Flowers give Eden its unique quality, describing a sensuous physical world of wonderful beauty and freshness, but offering also a number of abstract ideas. The first consciousness of the first parents is offered in terms of flowers to emphasize their innocence (IV, 451; VIII, 253–54 and 286–87). Flowers convey the concept of Edenic time, both as they are invoked to describe the measurement of the passing of time—Eve overhears the end of the conversation between Adam and Raphael "at shut of Ev'ning Flow'rs" (IX, 278)—and as they repeatedly signal the combination of "Eternal Spring" (IV, 268) and "all *Autumn* pil'd" (V, 394), the simultaneous fruit and flower outside the process of seasonal, postlapsarian time. Here "Spring / Perpetual smil'd on Earth with vernant Flow'rs" (X, 678–79). The verb *smile* repeatedly describes the flowery earth, and when we recall that smiles are one of the ways in which the deity impresses His image upon His human creatures the joyousness of Edenic creation and the parallels of plant and character become clearer.

The scent of flowers receives particular emphasis throughout the descriptions of Eden and establishes two dimensions of the poem's world. The uniquely delicious air of paradise is appropriate to Eden's sensuous perfection. The scents are "soft delicious" (II, 400), "buxom" (II, 842; V, 270), of healing balm (II, 402, 842–43; IV, 159), pure and inspiring (IV, 153–55), and linked with music (IV, 264–66).[4] Eden's "odorous sweets" (IV, 166) convey the process of worship as well as a physical description of place. As recorded at the opening of the ex-

tended hymn of morning praise in Book IX, like Adam and Eve and the
rest of creation, the flowers praise God as they begin a new day:

> Now whenas sacred Light began to dawn
> In *Eden* on the humid Flow'rs, that breath'd
> Thir morning incense, when all things that breathe,
> From th' Earth's great Altar send up silent praise
> To the Creator, and his Nostrils fill
> With grateful Smell.   (192–97)

In an image that should remind us of Homeric and other classical approaches to the deity by way of incense and the nourishing odors that
rise in rituals of sacrificially cooked flesh, the scents of flowers celebrate
the day, the light, and the deity through the ascent of their most ethereal
essence. Their worship offers the deity the richest expression of their
essential sensuous nature, as unfallen humans offer God their fullest
self-expression and praise through love, work, and such reasoning as is
possible without moral choice. When fallen, human worship (reflecting
altered self-consciousness, now self-knowledge) takes the form of prayer
(the "first Fruits" of "implanted Grace" in XI, 22–23) rather than praise,
a paradoxical enrichment of the relationship between God and man examined more fully below.

It is the function of the Creator and His creations to multiply the
Good. This may occur as that celebration of Other that is witnessed
through praise or it may occur as the creation of order through labor or
love. Before the fall Adam and Eve are described as created for "delight
to Reason join'd" (IX, 243), but afterward as "to nobler end / Holy and
pure, conformity divine" (XI, 605–06). Within the Edenic setting their
task is "sweet Gard'ning labor" (IV, 328) or in the words of Genesis, to
dress the garden and keep it; within the scheme of time their function is
to "Multiply a Race of Worshippers / Holy and Just" (VII, 630–31).
The former supplies the poem's flower imagery, the latter its metaphors
of fruit. Adam and Eve's Edenic labor consists of winding woodbine
around arbors, or directing ivy where to climb, or finding what to re-
dress in a spring of roses intermixed with myrtle (IX, 215–19). Adam
speaks of "our delightful task / To prune these growing Plants, and tend
these Flow'rs" (IV, 437–38) and "our pleasant labor, to reform / Yon
flow'ry Arbors, yonder Alleys green" (625–26). Work is by definition the
imposition of order, and thus the multiplication of the Good; work
distinguishes man from animal; it "declares his Dignity, / And the re-

gard of Heav'n on all his ways" (619–20). In their capacity for work, for reasoned order, for good, Adam and Eve share their maker's image.[5] Before the fall, flowers serve to define that work as sensuous, exquisite, delightful—in contrast to the sweaty Adam's painful tillage of a land cursed with thorns and thistles afterwards.

Adam and Eve's days are scheduled around morning praise, daily garden work, evening praise, and loving restful nights. The categories of work, praise, and love all find expression through the flower imagery of the poem, and the three are combined in a rich extended metaphor on work in Book V:

> On to thir morning's rural work they haste
> Among sweet dews and flow'rs; where any row
> Of Fruit-trees overwoody reach'd too far
> Thir pamper'd boughs, and needed hands to check
> Fruitless imbraces: or they led the Vine
> To wed her Elm; she spous'd about him twines
> Her marriageable arms, and with her brings
> Her dow'r th' adopted Clusters, to adorn
> His barren leaves.   (211–19)

The diction, vegetation, and human situation here show the honeymoon quality of first love, rendered appropriately through floral imagery. The passage is lovely and traditional, but strictly speaking the image is botanically unsound.[6] Wedding and fertility diction is valid only as a metaphor for human love, process, and fruitfulness. Fruit and metaphor are postlapsarian categories. Critics have regularly observed that the similes or explicit comparisons in *Paradise Lost* interrelate prelapsarian and postlapsarian dimensions; it has not I think been noticed before that the implicit comparisons of metaphor in the poem are also dependent on the postlapsarian. The lines just cited invite a distinction between *fruit* as image and *fruit* as metaphor, a distinction fully elaborated in the final third of the poem. *Fruit* as image (or prelapsarian fruit) encompasses the edibles supplied by the Edenic orchard, rendered with the wonderful sensuousness, harmony, and joy of the present passage; *fruit* as metaphor requires interpretation in relation to human and fallen possibilities, fruitfulness through love, process, and time. Images in the poem are often richly resonant of layered meaning, as when Satan curses the sun in IV, 32–39, and we read *sun* as God, Christ (Son), light, life, order, time, and the like, but in the poem's images the abstract ideas are contained in the visible, whereas metaphor calls for an imaginative leap that links apparently disparate realms of experience. Prelapsarian work is expressed through love and floral imagery. After the fall, work comes to include the sweat of the delving Adam's brow and love to include the pains of Eve's childbearing—richer, more "fruitful" processes despite apparent change for the worse, through the addition of the dimensions of pain, sorrow, and guilt.

Edenic imagery attaches to both Adam and Eve, but flowers are especially associated with Eve. When first described, Eve's hair is likened to a vine curling its tendrils (IV, 306), and later, "Veil'd in a Cloud of Fragrance," she glows with the thick roses bushing round her (IX, 425–27). The clearest indication of the special relationship between Eve and the flowers of Eden is seen when she retires from the abstruse conversation of her husband and Raphael to her gardening:

> To visit how they prosper'd, bud and bloom,
> Her Nursery; they at her coming sprung
> And toucht by her fair tendance gladlier grew.   (VIII, 44–47)

Gladlier tells us much about Eve, Eden, innocent life and joy. As with *fruitless* in the preceding passage, Milton's pun on *nursery* here anticipates and calls attention to Eve's more important, proper, and fated "nursery," the seed of her fruitful womb. When Eden has been lost, Eve's lamentation for the failure of her special relationship with the flowers offers additional insight into the vegetative imagery and the themes of the poem. She cries:

> O flow'rs,
> That never will in other Climate grow,
> My early visitation, and my last
> At Ev'n, which I bred up with tender hand
> From the first op'ning bud, and gave ye Names,
> Who now shall rear ye to the Sun, or rank
> Your Tribes, and water from th' ambrosial Fount? (XI, 273–79)

That Eve should have been the one to name the flowers in Eden is a matter of special importance in the allegorical scheme of the poem. This addition to the Biblical story defines Eve's nature and education and role in contrast to her husband's. As in Genesis, Adam is made to name the animal creation in *Paradise Lost* (VIII, 342–54), a process that includes his understanding of "Thir language and thir ways" (373), and thus signals his proper education and knowledge, as the fact that he knows them to be in "low subjection" to himself (345) signals his self-knowledge, a self-knowledge that God confirms (438–40). Raphael calls flattering attention to Adam's naming of the birds (VI, 73–76) and of the insects (VII, 493). And in VIII, 272 f. we see that Adam "readily could name / Whate'er I saw," including the lights of heaven and the varying terrains of earth. In his initial conversation with deity upon his creation, Adam asks by what name to approach the deity, who "Surpassest far my naming" (359), but receives no explicit answer, a signal of his intellectual inability to comprehend the Incomprehensible One. Eve's role is to name and comprehend the flowers and provide the *nursery* by which flowers become fruit, metaphorically the nursery of the fruit of human love. Adam's comprehension is a function of reasoning, Eve's of loving.[7]

The special association of Eve with flowers is heightened as Eve's person and province are likened to Pomona, the Roman goddess of flowers and fruit (V, 378–79; IX, 394); Flora, goddess of flowers and spring (V, 16); a wood nymph (V, 381; IX, 386), Oread and Dryad (IX, 387); and a harvest queen (IX, 842). The two dimensions of flowers and fruit may be seen in the paired comparisons with Proserpina and Ceres: the latter occurs in IX, 395–96, with emphasis on the unrealized fruitful potentiality of the goddess of grain—"*Ceres* in her Prime, / Yet Virgin of *Proserpina* from *Jove*"; the former in IV, 268–72, with emphasis on floral beauty.[8] This simile, perhaps the best known passage in *Paradise Lost*, establishes the identification of Eve with flowers and supplies the terms of the next stage of the argument, those processes apparently malign by which flowers give way to fruitfulness; Milton distinguishes Eden from

> that fair field
> Of *Enna*, where *Proserpin* gath'ring flow'rs
> Herself a fairer Flow'r by gloomy *Dis*
> Was gather'd, which cost *Ceres* all that pain
> To seek her through the world.

The simile begins in negation, but we quickly see inside Proserpina's story the analogue of Eve's in which Enna parallels Eden, Proserpina Eve, Dis Satan, and Ceres—by suggestion and medieval tradition—Christ. Proserpina and flowers and Eve are "gathered" by the underworld agents of hell and death and time. Ceres differs from the other terms in this sequence and must be read metaphorically; as elsewhere in the

poem when postlapsarian and Christian applicability emerge, a special
kind of imaginative energy is evoked in the reader. The annual process
of the shift from flowers to fruit mirrors also the spiritualizing process
of physical beauty giving way to productive nourishment within a
scheme of seasons and time. The fruitful agency or potentiality is described in terms of loss, pain, process, and the world, as well as—paradoxically—salvation. Paradox, like metaphor, comes with the fall.

Another explicit identification of Eve with flowers, and another of
the most familiar passages in the poem, occurs as Satan makes his fated
approach to Eve on the morning of the fall. As earth is a mixed realm,
with labor and rest, day and night, and later good and evil, so the potentiality of Satan resides among the sweetest emblems of earthly life;
Satan in "ambush hid among sweet Flow'rs and Shades" (IX, 408;
ambush may contain a pun on *bush*). In a passage which again invokes
the flower-among-flowers trope to describe Eve, we read:

> *Eve* separate he spies,
> Veil'd in a Cloud of Fragrance, where she stood,
> Half spi'd, so thick the Roses bushing round
> About her glow'd, oft stooping to support
> Each Flow'r of slender stalk, whose head though gay
> Carnation, Purple, Azure, or speckt with Gold,
> Hung drooping unsustain'd, them she upstays
> Gently with Myrtle band, mindless the while,
> Herself, though fairest unsupported Flow'r,
> From her best prop so far, and storm so nigh.   (IX, 424–33)[9]

The flowers express the essential nature of Eve and provide a total environment of atmosphere and action for her, with emphasis on her loveliness, frailty, and limitations. The poetic equations that emerge here are:
Eve = flowers, "fairest unsupported" and "of tender stalk"; Adam =
prop = reason; myrtle band = their marriage; and Satan = storm.

A storm is a violent disruption of nature's order that interposes between earth and sun, as Satan is a violent disrupter of moral innocence
seeking to separate men from God. The effect of storms on flowers is a
violent bombardment of fructifying rain, an attack that scatters petals
and seems to destroy harmony and design. But the blossoms of fruit trees
or even of roses in the processes of nature and time must be scattered to
make way for the coming fruit and harvest, the "Flow'rs and thir Fruit"
of V, 482. The larger scheme of *Paradise Lost*, including what Geoffrey
Hartmann calls Milton's counterplot,[10] emerges in the necessity that

flowers give way to fruitfulness; in the divine plan, which Milton repeatedly calls our attention to in the background of the action of
the poem, Satan's apparent destruction of innocent beauty—the cross-
fertilizing effect of evil—actually creates a new kind of order and possibility, dynamic rather than static, an order not merely externally
lovely and happy, but potentially the paradise within replete with joy.

Throughout *Paradise Lost* storms are measured against the sun, the
visible cosmic form of divine light, to clarify the moral scheme and the
conditions affecting human fruitfulness. On several occasions Raphael
images the relationship between God and man in the relationship of the
sun and earth. The first recalls the floral incense discussed above:

> The Sun that light imparts to all, receives
> From all his alimental recompense
> In humid exhalations, and at Even
> Sups with the Ocean.   (V, 423-26)

Later Raphael uses the same image to explain potentiality and anticipates the productiveness of man's fruitful worship:

> the Earth
> Though, in comparison of Heav'n, so small,
> Nor glistering, may of solid good contain
> More plenty than the Sun that barren shines,
> Whose virtue on itself works no effect,
> But in the fruitful Earth; there first receiv'd
> His beams, unactive else, thir vigor find.   (VIII, 91-97)

The importance of rain, the mildest form of storms, to divine processes,
especially to multiplying the Good, is clarified in anticipation of fallen
possibilities; the sun's "spots thou seest / As Clouds, and Clouds may
rain, and Rain produce / Fruits in her soft'n'd Soil" (VIII, 145-47). The
psychological alternative to softened soil is of course stoniness of the
heart.

That God = sun in His relationship to men and life on earth needs
little comment, but it is instructive to note how insistently Satan and
the other devils are aligned with disruptive weather and with such
cosmic phenomena as earthquakes, especially in similes. The decision
for Satan's embassy to earth concludes thus:

> As when from mountain tops the dusky clouds
> Ascending, while the North wind sleeps, o'erspread
> Heav'n's cheerful face, the low'ring Element
> Scowls o'er the dark'n'd lantskip Snow, or show'r;

> If chance the radiant Sun with farewell sweet
> Extend his ev'ning beam, the fields revive,
> The birds thir notes renew, and bleating herds
> Attest thir joy, that hill and valley rings.   (II, 488–95)

Such weather imagery supplies the cosmic dimension to the figure of Satan and the concept of evil, and such temporary cosmic-temporal aberration is witnessed against the larger vision of divine good in the pervasive spiritual optimism of the poem as a whole. The largely described and sensuously realized experiences of hell, chaos, and the limbo of fools as stormy establish more fully the chaotic, wasteful, and destructive alternative to divinely ordered, "sunny," experience. The dynamic potentiality of the human and moral condition allows barrenness as well as fruitfulness, destruction as well as creation. Upon the fall, although God, the source of all weather, is shown in a detailed creation of disruptive weather (X, 651–704), the process of Adam's repentance assures him that the God who clothes the first couple will also teach them how to survive the rigors of changing and excessive weather in their moral and physical frailty (X, 1062–81). Michael's catechism in Books XI and XII teaches the same lesson through images from history rather than from the cosmos. When Adam and Eve sing praises to night, the sun's absence, as well as to day (IV, 724), they anticipate their own postlapsarian experience with the fruitfulness of evil within the larger divine scheme. In terms of weather, God's promise to men is imaged in the rainbow, "a flow'ry Verge" (XI, 881) that parallels and places Satanic storming.

The implications of the equation of Satan with storms are invoked in the wonderfully alliterative line in which Milton describes Eve's fallen condition as "Defac't, deflow'r'd, and now to Death devote" (IX, 901). As a storm might *deface* floral beauty, so the *deflowering* attacks innocence and particularly virginity, but the "Virgin Majesty of Eve" (IX, 270) must be sacrificed that the race of mankind may come about. Like Edenic paradise, a static world beyond time and change, the state of being a "Virgin Mother," as Eve is described in XII, 379, cannot be other than temporary—or for her descendants caught in the dynamic of experience cannot be other than a conception based on imagination and faith. Eve is flowerlike in her loveliness and also in her moral and sexual innocence, but her deflowering and fruitfulness are essential to human history:

> Whence Hail to thee,
> *Eve* rightly call'd, Mother of all Mankind,
> Mother of all things living, since by thee
> Man is to live, and all things live for Man.   (XI, 158–61)

Several insect similes in Book I have vegetative dimensions that convey the same moral judgment and vision of divine order as the storm imagery. The first, emphasizing their number, likens the fallen to

> a pitchy cloud
> Of *Locusts*, warping on the Eastern Wind,
> That o'er the Realm of impious *Pharaoh* hung
> Like Night, and darken'd all the Land of *Nile*.   (340–43)

The periodic destructiveness of locusts to vegetation is an ominous and persistent threat—in XII, 186 they "leave nothing green"—but when it is recalled that *this* plague on wicked Egypt is a divine effort on behalf of the chosen people (Exodus x, 12–15), we find consolation in divine power, order, and even wrath.[11] It is a nice artistic touch that in the final book of the poem Michael should explicate this image from the first book when instructing Adam to read experience imaginatively and metaphorically. The bee simile (I, 761 f.), calling attention to the number, energy, and bustle of the fallen, transforms the insect imagery to a clarification of the proper relationship between flowers and insects. The bees "among fresh dews and flowers / Fly to and fro" performing what they believe are "Thir State affairs" of gathering and usurping sweetness—in V, 24–25, "the Bee / Sits on the Bloom extracting liquid sweet"— but they in fact function to propagate the flowers' fertility and fruition.[12] These and similar comparisons throughout the poem make clear the rich range of vegetative imagery in the service of the theme of divine paradox by giving additional forms to the conditions affecting vegetation.

Fruit is the reiterated vegetative term of Book IX and the hinge of the poem's action and themes. An earlier image schooled us to distinguish between fruit as image and fruit as metaphor. As image, Edenic fruit is "compliant" (IV, 332), "amiable" (250), and "still hanging incorruptible" (IX, 622), "delectable both to behold and taste" (VII, 539), entirely delicious and various (IV, 422–23; VII, 542), gleaned from all seasons and all space (V, 337–43), and "savoury . . . to please / True appetite" (V, 304–05). Like the flowers of Eden this fruit is especially remarkable for its smell. The psychological and poetic energies of the poem turn from innocence to experience and from image to metaphor upon the eating of the fruit of the tree of the knowledge of good and evil that Adam and Eve are enjoined not to touch or taste lest they die. During and after the moment of the fall, the adjectives qualifying it are frequently ominous: *foretasted* (IX, 929), *fair enticing* (996), *false* (1011), *fallacious* (1046), *fatal* (X, 4), *defended* (186), and *stolen* (XI, 125). In longer phrases it is *sacred fruit forbidden* (IX, 904), *bad fruit of knowledge* (1073), *that false fruit that promis'd clearer sight* (XI, 413), and as the universe is turned athwart *that tasted fruit* is likened to a *Thyestean Banquet* (X, 687–88). Metaphorically, the potential fruit prepared for by the deflowering of Eve is different, greater, more spiritual and more real, certainly more human than the Edenic piece of fruit. It is history and Christianity. Poetically viewed, it is *all* "the Fruit / Of that Forbidden Tree, whose mortal taste / Brought Death into the World, and all our woe" (I, 1–3). This includes all humanity as well as the rich harvest of the first fruits of prayer and good deeds that the final books of the poem offer to our vision. The analogy and distinction between Edenic and postlapsarian fruit are made most explicit in Raphael's praise of Eve's housewifery:

> Hail Mother of Mankind, whose fruitful Womb
> Shall fill the World more numerous with thy Sons
> Than with these various fruits the Trees of God
> Have heap'd this Table.   (V, 388–91)

Even in descriptive images, Edenic fruits are sometimes equated with abstractions: with obedience and faith in VIII, 325, and, when Adam and Eve are first glimpsed in III, 65–69, with "immortal fruits of joy and love, / Uninterrupted joy, unrivall'd love." But after the fall and with the alteration of the physical and spiritual universes, fruits become metaphorically transformed from physical to spiritual as the paradise itself must be within the souls of men.

In *Paradise Lost* as in Genesis, vegetation is created on the third day and is thus inferior to the animals created on the fifth and sixth days possessing life and motion, and to man created on the sixth day possessing life, motion, and reason, the image of God impressed. The order of creation of vegetation moves from smaller and lower to greater and higher forms: grass, herbs, flowers, vines, grain, shrubs, bushes, and trees, especially fruit trees. In an extended definition of the hierarchical

order implicit in vegetation in *Paradise Lost*, Raphael uses vegetation
to offer Adam an explanation of the process by which body works up to
spirit:

> So from the root
> Springs lighter the green stalk, from thence the leaves
> More aery, last the bright consummate flow'r
> Spirits odorous breathes: flow'rs and thir fruit
> Man's nourishment, by gradual scale sublim'd
> To vital spirits aspire, to animal,
> To intellectual, give both life and sense,
> Fancy and understanding, whence the Soul
> Reason receives, and reason is her being,
> Discursive, or Intuitive; discourse
> Is oftest yours, the latter most is ours,
> Differing but in degree, of kind the same.   (V, 479–90)

The design implicit here governs the materials of the present essay and
outlines the stages of its argument: the flowers are *last, bright, consummate, odorous,* and in their sensuous way spiritous. "Thir fruit" (and
Thir supplies the crucial relationship) is "man's nourishment," useful
rather than decorative, *sublim'd* to serve human potentialities and aspiration, transmutable into reason and faith. Transmutation, process,
and potentiality define the meaning of the fall.

Creatures throughout *Paradise Lost* are what they eat and what they
can transmute literal foods into. Adam and Eve confirm their innocence
in partaking of innocent Edenic fruits. They ratify and image their disobedience, mortality, and fallaciousness in eating the forbidden apple:
Eve "knew not eating Death" (IX, 792). Genesis iii clarifies postlapsarian
eating of "the herb of the field" (18): "Cursed is the ground for thy sake;
in sorrow shalt thou eat of it all the days of thy life" (17)—a confirmation
of sorrow and mortality—and again "In the sweat of thy face shalt thou
eat bread, till thou return unto the ground" (19)—a confirmation of toil
and pain. That the very brief account in Genesis devotes such emphasis
to postlapsarian eating signals its importance. We see the equivalence
of diet and essence also with the angels who "Quaff immortality and
joy" (V, 638), with Death that will feed on the mortality in herbs, fruits,
flowers, and men, and with the serpent condemned to eat dust (XI, 78),
most graphically in the diabolical grove of dust and ashes (X, 565–66),
that false fruit that will "aggravate / Thir penance" (X, 549–50) and
confirm barrenness. God is, of course, "our Nourisher" (V, 398). Milton

is careful to place the only two mentions of *apple* in the poem in the mouth of Satan, and such a confirmed Latinist as Cromwell's secretary surely intended our familiarity with *malum* as both *evil* (noun) and *apple* and our application of that equation. In this as in his imaginative capacities, Satan is a mere literalist. The changes in human diet signal the shift from a static to a dynamic condition as they mirror the poetic initiation out of image and into metaphor, out of simple surfaces and into the complexity and ambiguity that spark imagination and faith. The eating of the forbidden fruit inaugurates the dynamic and paradoxical human condition. Human diet emphasizes transmutation, that is, potentiality in a framework of change and the derived energy that *can* multiply the Good. As Raphael explains, creatures of spirit and reason in dealing with the things of earth *can* transform matter to spirit. Adam and Eve's first choice makes them choosers, and choice, like trial in the words of *Areopagitica*, is what purifies us and must be by what is contrary (Hughes, p. 728). Change allows choice and metaphor.

In a postlapsarian scheme fruits signal work and love, the latter especially as mankind. After the fall Adam comforts Eve with the prospect of the human race, the anticipated performers of golden good deeds, as "Fruit of thy Womb" (X, 1053); especially as a counter to her argument for the suicide or willful barrenness that would cut the first parents off from hope (X, 1043, 1053). Such fruitfulness will be attained within the terms of Eve's punishment for disobedience, pains of childbearing (X, 194–95). Michael likens those who will die of old age to "ripe fruit" that will "drop / Into thy Mother's lap, or be with ease / Gather'd, not harshly pluckt, for death mature" (XI, 535–37). As the process of floral praise becomes fruitful prayer, so too do the human processes of work and love develop. And we may recall the words of Saint Ambrose, which Lovejoy notes as a possible source for portions of Milton's conception of *felix culpa*, that "sin is more fruitful than innocence."[13] Deeds, especially good deeds, as fruit is a traditional image used by Milton in several earlier connections. In the anticipation of the New Jerusalem of Book III we hear of "Golden days, / Fruitful of golden deeds" (337), and in a complementary abstraction Limbo contains those who on earth harvested "the Fruits / Of painful Superstition and blind Zeal" (451–52). The promise of the poem's finale is of that New Jerusalem, "founded in righteousness and peace and love" in which men will "bring forth Fruits Joy and eternal Bliss" (XII, 550–51). Adam and Eve are enjoined to "Be fruitful and multiply" in Genesis and Book VII; after the fall, when the garden and vegetation have become internalized and spiritualized, such fruitfulness is fully realized in their offspring and metaphorically transformed into an inward emphasis upon prayer (and the faith and relationship prayer ratifies) and in outward relationships into good deeds among men.

In the most important metaphorical transformation of fruit, the first fruits of human prayer are couched in an elaborated vegetation metaphor. Christ says:

> See Father, what first fruits on Earth are sprung
> From thy implanted Grace in Man, these Sighs
> And Prayers, which in this Golden Censer, mixt
> With Incense, I thy Priest before thee bring,
> Fruits of more pleasing savor from thy seed
> Sown with contrition in his heart, than those
> Which his own hand manuring all the Trees
> Of Paradise could have produc't, ere fall'n
> From innocence.   (XI, 22–30)

The Son goes on to ask that all men's deeds be *ingrafted* on him (135). Earlier Christ appeared as of "Virgin Seed," the "second root" of Adam, enjoying "Godlike Fruition," the salvation of those who live in him "transplanted" (III, 284–307). The inward spiritual dimension of fruition emerges in contrasting the failure of Cain's sacrifice of unculled first fruits (XI, 433–43) with Abel's offering, performed with all due rites, evoking a redemptive response from the deity: "His Off'ring soon propitious Fire from Heav'n / Consum'd with nimble glance, and grateful steam" (441–42). When we recall that flowers send forth their incense in response to distant emanations of the divine light of the sun, we can see the difference the fall has made in the enriching transformation of the process of worship from praise to prayer. Flowers properly may send their innocent odors upward, but fruits must nourish men, be digested and transmuted into spiritual energy. Adam and Eve and the rest of the unfallen universe behold God's works with "ceaseless praise" (IV, 679). Within Eden, man's "Sanctity of Reason" supplies him with self-knowledge and the government of animals and makes him

> Magnanimous to correspond with Heav'n,
> But grateful to acknowledge whence his good
> Descends, thither with heart and voice and eyes

> Directed in Devotion, to adore
> And worship God Supreme who made him chief
> Of all his works.   (VII, 508–16)

Such adoration signals praise, but the fallen equivalent, prayer, is defined by a much richer self-knowledge, which includes a recognition of fallen unworthiness and gratitude and a dependence upon the wronged deity acknowledged through fallen but rightly directed reason. The first prayers are narrated in the final passages of Book X, twice repeated for emphasis with a significant shift in point of view:

> they forthwith to the place
> Repairing where he judg'd them prostrate fell
> Before him reverent, and both confess'd
> Humbly thir faults, and pardon begg'd, with tears
> Watering the ground and with thir sighs the Air
> Frequenting, sent from hearts contrite, in sign
> Of sorrow unfeign'd, and humiliation meek.
> (1097–1104 and similarly 1086–92)

As much of Book X adumbrates preprayer despair,[14] so the first several hundred lines of Book XI are taken up with explorations of the concept and process of prayer. We learn that Adam and Eve are inspired by "Prevenient Grace descending" (3) from on high that makes their prayer "wing'd for Heav'n" (7). Christ, "thir great Intercessor" (19), clothes their dimensionless prayers with incense fuming at the golden altar and woos from the deity "the smell of peace toward Mankind" (17–19, 38). Divine motions in man make sorrow, repentance, and contrition possible (90–91) and remove "the stony from thir hearts" (3–4). The effects are that they find "Strength added from above, new hope to spring / Out of despair, joy, but with fear yet linkt" (137–39). Milton's fullest description of prayer occurs in lines 141–58 (qualified in 307–14). Patience and submission "to the hand of Heav'n . . . However chast'ning" (372–73) attend its processes. The relationship between man and deity thus becomes transformed and enriched through the fall, more difficult and challenging, rarer in history, more complex in the motions of fuller mutual participation. With the fall of their reason and the loss of their innocence and with the introduction of disruptions that make the created world delusive, dangerous, and stormy, Adam and Eve become initiated into the dynamic tension of paradox when they leave behind the serenity of paradise, a matter of both intellection and style. The richest paradoxes of the poem center on the felicitous good that results from the descent into sin and on Christ's double nature.

Seed is the form the vegetation imagery takes in the final portions of *Paradise Lost*, a term of potentiality for growth, especially in Christ. Of the thirty mentions of *seed* in the poem, twenty-six occur in the final three books. Attention is repeatedly called to Christ as seed, the seed of Adam and Eve, and the children of Israel as Abraham's seed. In the mysterious terms of the judgment of the serpent and Adam and Eve, we find emphasized that "Her Seed shall bruise thy head, thou bruise his heel" (X, 181, echoed in 498–99, 1031–32; XII, 147–51, 155, 232–35, 325–27). Seed brings the vegetation imagery of the poem and its themes and promise emphatically into the scheme of time, including the past or Old Testament time reviewed historically throughout Books XI and XII, and the future or the culmination of New Testament time anticipated as the New Jerusalem, and the present or that metaphorical and transitional segment of time in which we live and Christ is operative. In this present, each just man may live fruitfully in his outward relations and may in his inward relations live spiritually in the blossoming and burgeoning of that paradise he creates within himself.

Harvest or the anticipation of harvest is the idea we are left with at the culmination of *Paradise Lost*. If we learn with Adam the spiritual and paradoxical lesson of the final pages, we too may triumph in the harvest of knowledge, deeds, faith, virtue, patience, temperance, and love (XII, 581–84):

> Henceforth I learn [says Adam], that to obey is best,
> And love with fear the only God, to walk
> As in his presence, ever to observe
> His providence, and on him sole depend,
> Merciful over all his works, with good
> Still overcoming evil, and by small
> Accomplishing great things, by things deem'd weak
> Subverting worldly strong, and worldly wise
> By simply meek; that suffering for Truth's sake
> Is fortitude to highest victory,
> And to the faithful Death the Gate of Life;
> Taught this by his example whom I now
> Acknowledge my Redeemer ever blest.   (XII, 561–73)

The fruitfulness of the new Eden will more than match the abundance of the old Eden, now "the Haunt of Seals and Orcs, and Sea-mews' clang"

(XI, 835), when place has become metaphorical and space internalized. After time has been completed, "the Earth / Shall all be paradise, far happier place / Than this of *Eden*, and far happier days" (XII, 463–65). Eve had complained that the vegetation in Eden "under our labor grows, / Luxurious by restraint" (IX, 208–09) and in a day or so becomes "wanton growth . . . Tending to wild" (211–12). The fruit of Eden is "in such abundance"

> As leaves a greater store of Fruit untoucht,
> Still hanging incorruptible, till men
> Grow up to thir provision, and more hands
> Help to disburden Nature of her Birth.   (IX, 620–24)[15]

Adam assures Eve that there is no danger to their state in God's abundance, and when we are metaphorically released from the merely material garden we rejoice in the fullness of the promise of fruitful opportunities and spiritual nourishment. The confined world of Edenic imagery subject to Old Testament law gives way to the open-ended dispensation of grace, imagination, and faith.

   A final comment on the adumbration of the themes of *Paradise Lost* through the vegetative imagery seems called for, and this is a matter of style. I have referred to Adam and Eve's initiation into paradox. In the artistic movement of the poem we witness the difference between imagery and metaphor, paradise without and paradise within. Carefully controlled imagery within a limited, albeit very rich, frame of reference predominates in prelapsarian time, the world of flowers and the nonmetaphorical uses of fruit we have been examining. Within this scheme language can be used multivalently and provocatively, as in puns on *nursery, fruitless*, and other vegetative terms.[16] Adam's capacity for naming and thus comprehending the natures of the things named shows the right reading of imagery. Eden and its floral loveliness and innocence of personality are imaged through physical description and appeals to the senses of smell, touch, and vision, but the paradise within is offered in symbolic terms, requiring interpretation through faith. Poetically the intellectual functioning of imagination effects its own new dispensation; imagination corresponds to and answers to the theological functioning of Grace. Christ speaks "in mysterious terms" (X, 173) and "more to know / Concerned not Man" (170–71), an oracle to be verified in Christ (182–83). Satan is confined to a literal understanding of language, as in his recounting of the curse to his fellows (494–501), but even an as-yet-uncomforted Adam is supplied with sufficient imagination and faith to read supraliterally (1030–36). In offering comfort and further instruction (XII, 375 f.) Michael teaches Adam to read *seed* as "thy great deliverer" (149) and promises that divine methods and ends will be more plainly revealed to him (XII, 150–51). Part of this lesson seems to lie in the "types and shadows" of XII, 232–33, for the direct voice of God to fallen men is "dreadful" (236), requiring the translation and interpretation of Christ the Mediator (240). Men in history must be "disciplin'd / From shadowy Types to Truth, from Flesh to Spirit" (303–04), and from law to grace and faith (304–06). This is a language of mystery and Christianity and the paradox that attends such mystery in mortal apprehension—for example, the crucified Christ nailing his enemies to the imaginatively transformed cross (413–19) or the exchange of bruises so often repeated in the final books—a language "not but by the Spirit understood" (514). In such a thoroughgoing concern for Adam's instruction in language and literature, Milton is rendering the sense of the early pages of Saint Thomas Aquinas's *Summa Theologica*, especially I.i. 10, "Whether in Holy Scripture a Word May Have Several Senses." Initiation into metaphor includes initiation into allegory or extended metaphor. A different kind of poetry and a different quality of reading energy operate in response to, for example, "the Garland wreath'd for *Eve*" dropping from Adam's "slack hand" (IX, 892–93), than in response to this sample of Michael's instruction:

> And therefore shall not *Moses*, though of God
> Highly belov'd, being but the Minister
> Of Law, his people into *Canaan* lead;
> But *Joshua* whom the Gentiles *Jesus* call,
> His Name and Office bearing, who shall quell
> The Adversary Serpent, and bring back
> Through the world's wilderness long wander'd man
> Safe to eternal Paradise of rest.   (XII, 307–14)

Following Aquinas, Augustine, and the medieval tradition, we must here apply ourselves allegorically, morally, and anagogically as well as literally. Beginning with the symbolic expression through which Christ passes judgment in Book X, language might be described as *defaced* and *deflowered*. What some readers of *Paradise Lost* lament as the "fallen style" of Books XI and XII reflects a certain defacement, or loss of sur-

face beauty. But in reading the poetry as well as in its imagery, the deflowering serves fruitfulness. To put the matter theologically, instead of
looking at the Edenic scene, readers are now asked for Christian *witness*;
secularly, again for *Grace* read *imagination*. The artistic distinction
recalls Raphael's comments on discursive and intuitive reasoning. The
elimination of the simplified surfaces of language, like the *felix culpa*
paradox, makes possible a much richer poetic fruitfulness and spiritual
harvest. The difference in the two poetic modes is like the difference
noted above between praise before the fall and prayer after the fall and
made possible by it. One's fuller participation with deity and with poetry
results, and his apprehension partakes, or can sometimes and increasingly partake, of the quality of angelic intuitive or total reasoning and
of Christian/imaginative vision, rather than the limited discursive reasoning and sensuous pleasure that were his in the merely terrestrial
Eden.

University of Massachusetts, Amherst

NOTES

1. All Milton quotations are from the edition by Merritt Y. Hughes, *John Milton:
Complete Poems and Major Prose* (New York, 1957).

2. In a footnote, ibid., p. 294, Hughes points out that *flourisht* here carries the
meaning of "flower-laden, or adorned with flowers"; see also Christopher Ricks on
flower and *flourish* in *Milton's Grand Style* (Oxford, 1963), p. 55.

3. It is perhaps not going too far to see in the artful phrase "damaskt with
flow'rs" a suggestion of upholstery, as *mosaic, inlay / Broider'd*, and *costliest emblem*
suggest other textures. See *Lycidas* 139, 146, and 148 for similar descriptions.

4. Eve's love song, "Sweet is the breath of morn" (IV, 641–56), is particularly rich
in this kind of description. For additional commentary on Edenic odors see John R.
Knott, Jr., "Symbolic Landscape in *Paradise Lost*," in *Milton Studies*, II (Pittsburgh,
1970), p. 41; Thomas Greene, *The Descent from Heaven: A Study in Epic Continuity*
(New Haven, 1963), pp. 401–02; and Frank Kermode, "Adam Unparadised," in *The
Living Milton: Essays by Various Hands*, ed. Frank Kermode (London, 1960), pp.
107–09.

5. In the tradition so ably traced in A. Bartlett Giamatti's *Earthly Paradise and
the Renaissance Epic* (Princeton, 1966), the provision for work in Milton's paradisiacal
garden protects our first parents from the spiritual dangers of delusiveness and idleness that define such gardens as Spenser's Bower of Bliss.

6. Milton's image is dependent on the wedding of elms to vines in Vergil's
Georgics I, 2, and II, 221, and similar images elsewhere. Giamatti discusses the elm-
vine trope in *Earthly Paradise*, pp. 323–24. On IX, 214–17, see also Joseph Summers's
The Muse's Method: An Introduction to "Paradise Lost" (London, 1962), p. 84.

7. The special link between Eve and vegetation suggests yet another dimension. The relationship between Adam and Eve is to some extent ambiguous, for we are told that they are one (IX, 957–59, 966–67), that they are equals (VIII, 383, 450–51), yet more often and more emphatically that Adam is Eve's superior (e.g., VIII, 558 f.). Without pushing the analogy too far it seems valid to suggest that unfallen Eve corresponds allegorically to what Dante calls the vegetable soul, as unfallen Adam does to the animal soul, and that, when fallen, the first couple correspond to *un'alma sola* (Dante, *Purgatorio*, XXV). Such a composite relationship explains the mathematics of calling Eve's fall plus Adam's fall *the* (or a single) fall, and is further clarified by Milton in *De Doctrina*, I, 7: "For spirit being the more excellent substance, virtually and essentially contains within itself the inferior one, as the spiritual and rational faculty contains the corporeal, that is, the sentient and vegetative faculty" (the Columbia *Works of John Milton,* ed. Frank Allen Patterson et al., 18 vols. [New York, 1931–1938], XV, 25). Such a scheme offers additional insight into the process of matter working up to spirit in V, 479–90, and V, 409–26, and into the relationship of Adam and Eve and the import of their fall. On Adam and Eve as androgyne see Edgar Wind, *Pagan Mysteries in the Renaissance,* rev. ed. (New York, 1968), pp. 212–14.

8. Giamatti traces the flower-among-flowers trope in *Earthly Paradise,* pp. 47–48, and analyzes comparisons with Pomona (pp. 327–28), Ceres (p. 328), and Circe (pp. 329–30). For him the Enna simile "casts a shadow on Eve's fate rather than her character" (p. 319), and he finds an echo of Proserpina in *deflowered* of IX, 901 (p. 343). Wayne Shumaker examines the empathetic relationship of Eve and the flowers in *Unpremeditated Verse: Feeling and Perception in "Paradise Lost"* (Princeton, 1967), p. 187.

9. Hughes has amended the textual *bushing* in line 426 to the less interesting *blushing* in *Paradise Lost: A New Edition* (New York, 1962).

10. "Milton's Counterplot," *ELH*, XXV (March 1958), 1–12. Hartmann too finds the counterplot most richly emergent in the similes of the poem.

11. See John T. Shawcross, "*Paradise Lost* and the Theme of Exodus," in *Milton Studies*, II (Pittsburgh 1970), pp. 10–11, and notes 4 and 13, and Revelation ix, 3–11. Shawcross notes the *hortus conclusus* or enclosed garden of the Song of Songs as a womb symbol for the promised seed and the Exodus generally as a birth metaphor (p. 22), and he calls *Paradise Lost* itself "the fruit of the union of poet and Spirit" (p. 23).

12. That Milton misunderstood the economy of bees in his description of their creation in Book VII—lauding the "Female Bee that feeds her Husband Drone / Deliciously" (490–91)—does not affect the justness of this image. A moral judgment on the fallen angels via vegetative imagery occurs also in the "Autumnal Leaves" simile of I, 302–04; this wasted, fallen, cumbrous vegetable matter was once "the Flow'r of Heav'n" which "thus drooping" the divine forces may tread upon (316, 327–28, and see Hughes's notes pp. 219 and 358). The "scattered sedge" equivalent in lines 304–11 recalls the Exodus context. Beelzebub is judged and placed outside the vegetative scheme in being the lord of flies.

13. Arthur O. Lovejoy, "Milton and the Paradox of the Fortunate Fall," *ELH*, IV (September 1937), 172.

14. So says Kermode in "Adam Unparadised," p. 98. He argues that the theme of *Paradise Lost* is "the power of joy and its loss" (p. 101).

15. *Birth* is *bearth* in early editions.

16. Notable puns on *fruit* and *fruitless* occur also in V, 215 and IX, 615–16, 648, 1101, and 1188. There are a number of puns and metaphors involving *plant, trans-*

plant, rose, withered, ripe, drooping, and the like, especially *root* (II, 382–83; VI, 855; IX, 645; and X, 299). At the creation God "sow'd with Stars the Heav'n thick as a field" by "transplanting" light (VII, 358, 360). Leslie Brisman, in "Serpent Error: *Paradise Lost* X, 216–18," in *Milton Studies,* II, comments on the "mysterious language" introduced by Christ's curse (pp. 29–30 and note 4) and on "the way the pun works in *Paradise Lost,* establishing a sense of community between poet and reader, who are bound together in the knowledge they share of another realm of meaning," that is, both fallen and unfallen nature (p. 28). For further commentary on Milton's punning, see Brisman's footnote 3, p. 34. Davis P. Harding, in *The Club of Hercules: Studies in the Classical Background of "Paradise Lost,"* Illinois Studies in Language and Literature, L (Urbana, 1962), p. 113, traces the conflict between the concrete style of hell and evil and the abstract style of heaven through the action of the poem, and similarly Greene, *Descent from Heaven,* pp. 383–85. In *Earthly Paradise,* Giamatti speaks of "the movement inward from phenomenon to figure, object to metaphor . . . here completed as the greatest of former realities, the garden, is now an image in the mind of man" (p. 349).

VIRGA IESSE: ANALOGY, TYPOLOGY, AND ANAGOGY IN A MILTONIC SIMILE

Jonathan Goldberg

The analogy of the tree that Raphael uses in Milton's *Paradise Lost* (V, 469–503) has generally been understood as a cosmic tree suggesting the Great Chain of Being. However, this interpretation needs to be modified to account for the temporal aspects of the image of the tree's growth. Once viewed as a spatial analogy for a temporal process, the tree can be said to function not only as an analogy but as a typological metaphor. In this context, it is most reminiscent of the Old Testament *figura* of the rod of Jesse. By considering the vertical, horizontal and circular motions described by Raphael, the image can be associated both with the Neoplatonic universe as well as the Christian drama of salvation. Within the imagery of *Paradise Lost*, this image reflects and relates to the "Forbidden Tree" and its fruit reunderstood as Christ upon the cross, Christ as creative Word and re-creative food in the Eucharist. Its revelation of Christ as cosmic and historical image is not, however, the entire meaning of Raphael's image; ultimately, the image is constructed from the eternal vantage point, and its motion and circularity fix a still point of eternity from which all is seen.

IN A POEM as complex as *Paradise Lost*, critics will differ about the location of a poetic center; such differences, however, are ultimately reconcilable in Milton's attempt to represent time and space from the perspective of eternity, "His own works and their works at once to view" (III, 59).[1] In his re-creation of sacred time and space, Milton constructs his poem in imitation of what Mircea Eliade calls the sacred, the recognition that "the cosmos in its entirety can become a hierophany."[2] This principle of cosmic sacredness, and the analogy implicit between the poet's act of creation and the divine act, is itself the overt subject of Milton's poem at times. One of these passages, Raphael's lesson in cosmology to Adam, Merritt Hughes calls "a kind of microcosm of his whole poem" (p. 194). Crucial to Raphael's revelation of the "one first matter" (472) is the analogy drawn between the universe and a tree. The entire passage is worth citing; as a microcosm of *Paradise Lost*, it bears attention.

> O *Adam*, one Almighty is, from whom
> All things proceed, and up to him return,
> If not deprav'd from good, created all
> Such to perfection, one first matter all,
> Indu'd with various forms, various degrees
> Of substance, and in things that live, of life;
> But more refin'd, more spiritous, and pure,
> As nearer to him plac't or nearer tending
> Each in thir several active Spheres assign'd,
> Till body up to spirit work, in bounds
> Proportion'd to each kind. So from the root
> Springs lighter the green stalk, from thence the leaves
> More aery, last the bright consummate flow'r
> Spirits odorous breathes: flow'rs and thir fruit
> Man's nourishment, by gradual scale sublim'd
> To vital spirits aspire, to animal,
> To intellectual, give both life and sense,
> Fancy and understanding, whence the Soul
> Reason receives, and reason is her being,
> Discursive, or Intuitive; discourse
> Is oftest yours, the latter most is ours,
> Differing but in degree, of kind the same.
> Wonder not then, what God for you saw good
> If I refuse not, but convert, as you,
> To proper substance; time may come when men
> With Angels may participate, and find
> No inconvenient Diet, nor too light Fare:
> And from these corporal nutriments perhaps
> Your bodies may at last turn all to spirit,
> Improv'd by tract of time, and wing'd ascend
> Ethereal, as wee, or may at choice
> Here or in Heav'nly Paradises dwell;
> If ye be found obedient, and retain
> Unalterably firm his love entire
> Whose progeny you are.   (V, 469–503)

Milton's revitalization of a Plotinian conception of matter for an explicitly Christian cosmology has, of course, received much comment, and it is not my intention to cover this familiar, if somewhat trouble-some, territory.[3] Not so vexing, the analogy of the tree, critical consensus suggests, is a somewhat traditional image for the cosmic great chain.[4] The "gradual scale" of the tree answers the "bounds Proportion'd" of the chain, and both sets of terms, especially the former, through its Latin origins, suggest a hierarchical cosmos. The image appears to function purely analogically, and a set of one-to-one correspondences seems possi-ble if not explicitly provided by Raphael's language. The increase of light from root to stalk to leaves to flower and fruit mirrors the cosmic levels rising from substance to spirit, and the corresponding strata within man himself, the microcosm. Such analogical equations seem likely in a poet who believes in differences of degree and not of kind, for in order to construct an analogy there must be a substantial link between terms; here "one first matter" serves to join the vegetative image and an organic cosmos.

But, in addition to such a nodus, there must also be gradations, and, as we have seen, degree appears in the analogy Raphael constructs. Since analogies describe vertical relationships between parallel horizontal planes (relationships between tenor and vehicle), the horizontal planes must have sufficient integrity at each level. In other words, an analogy can only be constructed if participation in the link (the "first matter") does not blur distinctions between the planes of reference. Cursory examination seems to indicate that Milton maintains such decorum in Raphael's analogy. The emphatic presence of hierarchical vocabulary should assure the integrity of each plane of reference. Yet this impression of stratified space tends to lose clarity when the terms of the analogy are more closely viewed. When we recall that Raphael's explanation at-tempts an answer to Adam's question "yet what compare?" (467), we can see that as Milton constructs his analogy he is aware of difficulties within the bounds and normative limits of analogy, although the prob-lem is not the one Adam imagines, of no proportion between the infinite and the finite. Since the image presented here is cosmological, poetic dif-ficulties are indicative of Milton's redefinition of a Platonic cosmology.

The problem is crystallized in a typically Miltonic "or" (at l. 476) that immediately sets up an equation between hierarchical stratification and a process of movement through hierarchical levels.[5] Raphael's simile is embedded in a discussion that begins with reference to the Neopla-tonic rhythm of *emanatio–conversio–remeatio*, and the greater purity of those things highest on the chain of being is not so much (or not entirely the result of) having been placed closer to God, as their having aspired to that place.[6] Thus Raphael can state that the levels of matter in the created universe are "more spiritous, and pure, / As nearer to him plac't or nearer tending" (475–76). And, in conjunction with the strictly hierarchical language that we noted above, Milton adds terms that stress the possibility of *conversio* and return: *sublim'd* (483), *aspire* (484), *convert* (492), *turn* (497). These last two verbs, in fact, translate the middle term in the Neoplatonic triad, and appropriately so, since Raphael means to show Adam not merely the one matter in all things, but how that fact conditions the possibility of Adam's return to the source of his being.

Thus, at the very least, Milton turns the chain of being into a Jacob's ladder, and Raphael's descent of the ladder to participate in Adam's more corporeal existence points to the possibility that Adam may ascend the ladder "if ye be found obedient" (501).[7] As in Herbert's "Sunday," straight lines become circular, and hierarchical gradations become part of the great "variety" of Milton's cosmological vision.[8] Milton's "or" permits him to entertain two views of the cosmos, one traditionally medieval in its hierarchical outlook, the other closer in viewpoint to Pico's redefinition of man's place in the cosmic scheme:

Nec certam sedem, nec propriam faciem, nec munus ullum peculiare tibi dedimus, o Adam, ut quam sedem, quam faciem, quae munera tute optaveris, ea, pro voto, pro tua sententia, habeas et possideas. Definita ceteris natura intra praescriptas a nobis leges coercetur. Tu, nullis angustiis coercitus, pro tuo arbitro, in cuius man te posui, tibi illam praefinies. Medium te mundi posui, ut circumspiceres inde commodius quicquid est in mundo. Nec te caelestem neque terrenum, neque mortalem neque immortalem fecimus, ut tui ipsius quasi arbitrarius honorariusque plastes et fictor, in quam malueris tute formam effingas. Poteris in inferiora quae sunt bruta degenerare; poteris in superiora quae sunt divina ex tui animi sententia regenerari.

Neither a fixed abode nor a form that is thine alone nor any function peculiar to thyself have we given thee, Adam, to the end that according to thy longing and according to thy judgment thou mayest have and possess what abode, what form, and what functions thou thyself shalt desire. The nature of all other beings is limited and constrained within the bounds of laws prescribed by Us. Thou, constrained by no limits, in accordance with thine own free will, in whose hand We have placed thee, shalt ordain for thyself the limits of thy nature. We have set thee at the world's center that thou mayest from thence more easily observe whatever is in the world. We have made thee neither of heaven nor of earth, neither mortal nor immortal, so that with freedom of choice and with honor, as though the maker and molder of thyself, thou mayest fashion thyself in whatever shape thou shalt prefer. Thou shalt have the power to degenerate into the lower forms of life, which are brutish. Thou shalt have the power, out of thy soul's judgment, to be reborn into the higher forms, which are divine.[9]

Milton's Adam, unlike Pico's, has a place in the cosmos; but he shares with Pico's man the possibility of movement, to fall to the level of the bestial or to rise to the angelic level. Pico, of course, does not impose the Miltonic limitation of obedience upon his Adam; yet the heavily charged vocabulary of the final words of the passage from *De hominis dignitate* suggests an alliance of free will with rationality (e.g., *animi sententia*) very close to Milton's idea of obedience. Even obedience, hierarchical and limiting as it sounds, is not finally a principle of forced constraint in Milton, but a self-willed self-limitation. Milton nowhere desires the outward imposition that would fix Adam immovably at one level of the cosmos.

If we return to Raphael's simile of the tree, we can see that it is descriptive both of the stratifications of hierarchical levels and of the possibility of movement from one level to another. In functioning simultaneously these two ways, the image takes on a degree of complexity that presses hard on the limits of analogy. For the levels of the cosmos, which we first imagined as fixed and distinct, can now be seen to move, and not simply at their own level. That is to say, implicit in the analogy as first stated was the idea that each horizontal level could be visualized as moving around a fixed point in the center, in which case the parallel planes of the analogy would move simultaneously, thus preserving the correspondences between them. An analogy between moving planes falls well within the normative hierarchical scheme.[10] Milton introduces a further movement, which, instead of maintaining motion at a single level of the cosmos (horizontal motion), allows for the possibility of vertical motion. To complicate matters even further, no principle of simultaneity is described with respect to these vertical movements, since the tree's growth does not seem linked to the possibility of man's growth (ascent), which depends on his obedience. Thus, at once, we have four different kinds of motion which are being compared: the movement around a central point on a single plane (the "active Spheres assign'd," 477); the Neoplatonic cosmic movement of the *circuitus spiritualis*; the natural growth of the tree; the possibility of man's ascent (its reflection in Raphael's descent constitutes a mirror for man's ultimate freedom of movement). The reconciliation of these various motions passes beyond the limits of hierarchical analogy, just as Milton's cosmology represents a shift from the so-called Elizabethan world picture.

In making the comparison, Milton introduces one further point of reference, and through it clarifies much that seems almost irreconcilable. For into the complex spatial circulations that he presents, Milton adds references to time and, therefore, alludes to God's concern for human history. The process of ascent that, in the analogy of the tree, seems simply natural growth, is linked to the possibility of Adam's ascent through the common factor of time. If we look closely at the image of the tree's growth, we may note some emphasis on the temporality of its ascent: from root to stalk to leaves to flower and fruit is a process in which the flower is "last" (481) and "consummate," and the sequence of verbs stresses a process in time to this final fruition. Further, the fruit of the tree, rather than the end of time, is, at once, consummation and re-creation, for nourished by the fruit, man begins his ascent to the level of angelic intelligence. Vital to Raphael's discourse is the insisted upon "time may come" (493) stressed in the final lines of his speech. Raphael's analogy is thus not only cosmological and spatial but also historical, and the movement of ascent that he describes in the Neoplatonic rhythms of love (cf. l. 502) he equates with the other manifestation of God's love for man, re-creative history.

In seeing creation as analogous to re-creation, a familiar idea in *Paradise Lost,* Milton combines in Raphael's speech the two strongest frames of intellectual reference in the poem. For embedded into his Neoplatonic cosmology is a strictly Christian view of history.[11] Neoplatonic return to the One and the Christian return to Eden "or . . . Heav-'nly Paradises" (l. 500; in the new heaven and earth there will no longer be distinctions between earthly and heavenly paradise for all will be one) are equated so that history itself *is* the growth of Milton's tree. History is transcendence. Raphael's description of vertical movements (ascent and descent), and the vertical equations between horizontal planes, are necessarily in movement themselves; but what keeps the various movements in relationship to each other (if not in the neat one-to-one relationship of analogy) is the process of history, which, as it goes forward, moves upward as well (or, more accurately, moves to join "upward" with "downward").

Thus, the union of the cosmos through "one first matter" is reduplicated in history, the movement of time from shadows to truth. Unifying the terms of Raphael's image is the typological sense of history as a process of revelation; as the tree grows and becomes lighter it comes closer to the source of light, comes closer to being the light itself. And what is true of the tree will be true of man in time if he remains obedient, and even after he falls (the paradox of the *felix culpa* unknown to Raphael but not to Milton or his readers). The growth of the tree may be indicative of a natural process in time but only because, as Abdiel says, "God and Nature bid the same" (VI, 176). Thus, the book of nature may provide a moral emblem for a historical process at once natural and supernatural. In its participation in the one matter that vitalizes the entire universe, the tree can point as well to the source of being manifest throughout the "tract of time" (498).[12] To summarize, Milton's tree not only reflects Neoplatonic cosmology, but Christian history as well.[13]

In Christian iconography, a tree like Milton's is the *virga Iesse:* "And there shall come forth a rod out of the stem of Jesse, and a Branch shall grow out of his roots" (Isaiah xi, 1).[14] The progression from root to stem to branch (or flower) Milton recapitulates in his image. This image, popular in Christian art since the eleventh century, of the genealogical tree rising from the sleeping Jesse and flourishing in Christ presents in a vertical image the movement of Christian history. As Emile Male notes, interpretation of the prophecy remains unchanged from the time of Saint Jerome: the rod signifies Mary; the flower, Christ.[15] While we might not expect Milton to follow this allegorical interpretation, it is certainly not surprising to find, in a poem dealing with a tree and its fruit, that the image of the cosmological tree has a place in an imagerial scheme of the poet's. The pattern begins with the first line of *Paradise Lost:* "Of Man's First Disobedience, and the Fruit," where, once we read "Fruit" to mean "result," we perceive Christ figured in an initial pun that announces the subject of the poem and its essential paradox, the *felix culpa*.[16] The pun has the full support of the typological tradition, and is the crux of the almost unbearable wit of Herbert's Christ: "Man stole the fruit, but I must climbe the tree."[17] Milton, of course, is not a witty poet, and instead of the painful condensation that Herbert practices, he creates the metaphorical pattern over the full range of *Paradise Lost.* Thus, to follow the significant terms of Milton's image through the entire poem can reveal the kind of meanings involved in Raphael's discourse.

We have seen that Raphael's tree is part of a *circuitus spiritualis.* The tree growing in time also nourishes man; and, by eating this fruit, man may "aspire." We may note here, then, that, on the one hand, the tree reduplicates the "Forbidden Tree," while, on the other hand, it seems, too, to anticipate the fruit that is Christ. To fully understand the metaphor that Milton makes we need to recall Raphael's later equation (VII, 126): "Knowledge is as food," and recognize the difference between the "fallacious Fruit" (IX, 1046) "greedily . . . ingorg'd" (IX, 791) and the true food that feeds the mind.[18] Such food is the Word.

Again, we can see how Neoplatonic cosmology meets Christian history in the image, for the creative seeds, the *logoi spermatikoi,* identifiable with Milton's "one first matter" are the true food for man.[19] Just as the earth brings forth fruit from the "Seed [that] is in herself" (VII, 312), so man can be fruitful by cultivating his garden within, feeding himself on words, the product of reason:

> sweeter thy discourse is to my ear
> Than Fruits of Palm-tree pleasantest to thirst
> And hunger both, from labor, at the hour
> Of sweet repast; they satiate, and soon fill,
> Though pleasant, but thy words with Grace Divine
> Imbu'd, bring to thir sweetness no satiety.   (VIII, 211–16)

For Adam and Eve are the sires of the "chosen Seed" and Eve's "fruitful Womb / Shall fill the World more numerous with thy Sons / Than with these various fruits the Trees of God / Have heap'd this Table" (V, 388–91). But if, through the fall and the eating of the "fatal Fruit" (X, 4), man has become "mortal food" (XI, 54), Eve's womb still bears the seed of the redemptive fruit for all mankind:

> though all by mee is lost,
> Such favor I unworthy am voutsaf't,
> By mee the Promis'd Seed shall all restore.   (XII, 621–23)

As Adam, in Michael's company, puzzles over the "mysterious terms" (X, 173) of human history, the angel teaches him this metaphorical pattern; for the mystery is couched in the language of Raphael's image. Adam learns the meaning of the seed and sees the flower at the top of Raphael's tree. The unfolding of the terms of the prophecy is history itself, and the tree grows before Adam's eyes until he recognizes the fulfillment of the pattern of Christian history in "The Woman's seed, obscurely then foretold, / Now amplier known thy Saviour and thy Lord" (XII, 543–44) who will destroy and re-create the world "To bring forth fruits Joy and eternal Bliss" (XII, 551). Raphael's tree of time grows to such fruits and provides like food for man if he is to aspire.

In Raphael's image of history as a tree Christ is implicit as the root and the flower, as the creative principle and the re-creative force. A significant parallel can be drawn again to the rod of Jesse when we recognize one major iconographic variation. The tree growing from the sleeping progenitor sometimes rises from Jesse's head; at other times, from his genital region.[20] Thus, one representation emphasizes the generation of the Word, the other, the *semen mulieris*. One version stresses the *logoi;* the other, the *spermatikoi*.[21] The union of "head" and seed Milton makes explicit in God's forecast of Christian history early in *Paradise Lost*:[22]

> And be thyself Man among men on Earth,
> Made flesh, when time shall be, of Virgin seed,
> By wondrous birth: Be thou in *Adam's* room
> The Head of all mankind, though *Adam's* Son.
> As in him perish all men, so in thee
> As from a second root shall all be restor'd,
> As many as are restor'd, without thee none.   (III, 283–89)

This seed, planted in Adam and Eve, almost immediately after the fall begins to bear fruit:

> See Father, what first fruits on Earth are sprung
> From thy implanted Grace in Man, these Sighs
> And Prayers, which in this Golden Censer, mixt
> With Incense, I thy Priest before thee bring,
> Fruits of more pleasing savor from thy seed
> Sown with contrition in his heart, than those
> Which his own hand manuring all the Trees
> Of Paradise could have produc't, ere fall'n
> From innocence.   (XI, 22–30)

For the tree of history grows from and into Christ, "the root and the offspring of David" (Rev. xxii, 16); significantly, in *Paradise Regained,* when Christ describes his kingdom, he invokes the image of the rod of Jesse:

> Know therefore when my season comes to sit
> On *David's* Throne, it shall be like a tree
> Spreading and overshadowing all the Earth.　　(IV, 146–48)

Raphael's image finds a context in the specific Biblical event that Milton makes the subject of his poem, and in the imagerial pattern he develops through his reading of Christian history.[23] Milton's imagery reflects his historical concern, and the decorum we were seeking in analyzing Raphael's simile of the tree can be found not in the traditional species of analogy connected with the unmoving hierarchies of the great chain but in the movement of history to its atonement with Christ. Christian history, in its progression from shadows to truth, ascends to the light, and the growth of the tree to its full flourishing provides an analogy for the processive revelation of Christ in history, the lesson Michael teaches Adam as he unfolds the seed growing secretly to full maturity. Traditional typology of the seed, fruit, and tree is woven into the historical narrative of Milton's poem so that the images themselves come to function figurally, come to have a specific historical meaning, and yet, to refer to the transcendent pattern within history. Cosmologically, this pattern is captured in the "one first matter" of Raphael's discourse; but we can, without distorting Milton's complex views, recognize that in Raphael's simile this one matter is Christ himself, the creative word and re-creative seed.

Since time continuously reveals Christ, the forward horizontal axis bears witness to a constant vertical factor. Further, since the forward motion of Christian history is simultaneously a movement of return, a horizontal metaphor for history could not be adequate.[24] These two criteria influence the choice of Raphael's image, for instead of the usual horizontal line, Milton substitutes a vertical axis on which he traces circular movement. The return to Eden is also a return to the source of being, a closing up of the *circuitus spiritualis*, and the forward movement of history is the growing manifestation of its ascending and retrogressive action. History grows to consummation, as the tree grows to its flower, but such a metaphor is only in part naturalistic. For the natural movement of history, the movement of cause and effect, is subordinate to the movement from figures to fulfillment, the repetition of the exemplary archetype.[25] Granting Christ as both root and fruit of Raphael's tree, the process of growth, significantly registered in images of light and in a temporal scheme, is the revelation of Christ. Thus, hierarchical positioning is only provisional, not the final consummation of history, and not the only destiny of man. The difficulty in constructing analogies, to which Adam refers before Raphael speaks, and to which Milton refers repeatedly in the course of *Paradise Lost*, is inherent in the nature of Christian history. For, metaphorically speaking, history moves towards the ultimate identity of tenor and vehicle. As it moves it maintains at once the paradoxical duality of Raphael's image, at once referring to the present state of things and to the final state. This duality reflects the nature of Christian history, of course, and the complex equations it develops at the spiritual level between historically concrete and real, literal events, persons and images. The duality that the "or" of Raphael's discourse establishes as the conceptual context for the image of the tree is then the true reflection of the duality of history itself. Looked at from one angle, Raphael's image functions analogically. Taking both motion and place into account, the image functions typologically. Finally, viewed from the perspective of God, the image functions anagogically.

Raphael's discourse begins by mentioning "return," ends with an "at last" and develops an image that comes to fulfillment in the consummate flower. The discourse begins by establishing the Almighty "is" and ends by referring to "his love entire." Thus, within the circlings of Raphael's own discourse rests the still penetrating "is" to which he continually returns, which history itself makes increasingly manifest, and which will be "at last" all in all. Raphael's attempt to translate intuitive knowledge into discourse is itself an analogy for the process of Christian history as well as an indication of Milton's artistic stance in *Paradise Lost*; for Milton attempts, as I noted in beginning this study, to see events from the divine perspective.[26] He invites his reader to understand the imagery of *Paradise Lost* in its immediate context, in its historical perspective, and from a perspective outside history. The ability of the reader to do this rests in the very subject of Raphael's discourse, and in Raphael's ability to participate in human fare and discourse. Raphael's actions on earth make real the metaphor that knowledge is food, and the knowledge he feeds Adam in return for Adam's "corporal nutriments" includes not only Adam's present state and obedience but the history that will flow from his disobedience. At the close of *Paradise Lost*, Michael reveals to Adam the newly planted paradise that grows within him; and it is there that Raphael's tree can grow. The poet, in his nightly inspiration, nurtures that seed within himself, and from it *Paradise Lost* grows. Although he is "cut off" (III, 47), new eyes grow within; unpremeditated his verse grows like Raphael's tree to reveal the consummation of time in eternity. In so doing, it passes beyond analogy (the argument from similitude) and typology (similitude and identity) to anagogy (identity).[27]

Temple University

NOTES

1. All citations from *John Milton: Complete Poems and Major Prose*, ed. Merritt Y. Hughes (New York, 1957).

2. *The Sacred and the Profane* (New York, 1959), p. 12.

3. A good guide in these matters is Michael F. Maloney, "Plato and Plotinus in Milton's Cosmogony," *PQ*, XL (1961), 34–43.

4. C. A. Patrides, *Milton and the Christian Tradition* (Oxford, 1966), pp. 59–68, presents a representative attitude and cites typical medieval texts.

5. Cf. Walter Clyde Curry, *Milton's Ontology, Cosmogony and Physics* (Lexington, Ky., 1957), p. 170, who briefly notes the problem.

6. For the presence of the Neoplatonic pattern of emanation and return in Milton's poetry, cf. Jon S. Lawry, *The Shadow of Heaven: Matter and Stance in Milton's Poetry* (Ithaca, N.Y., 1968), pp. 1–20, et passim. The *circuitus spiritualis* is the focus of Edgar Wind's *Pagan Mysteries in the Renaissance* (New York, 1968).

7. Cf. Lawry, *Shadow of Heaven*, p. 195; George Wesley Whiting, *Milton and This Pendant World* (New York, 1958), pp. 59–87, esp. pp. 78–83. On the ladder of Jacob and the rod of Jesse see Arthur Watson, *The Early Iconography of the Tree of Jesse* (London, 1934), p. 7 and pp. 49–52.

8. Cf. Joseph H. Summers, *The Muse's Method: An Introduction to "Paradise Lost"* (New York, 1962), pp. 71–86.

9. *De hominis dignitate*, ed. Eugenio Garin (Florence, 1942), pp. 104–06. Translation by Elizabeth L. Forbes in *The Renaissance Philosophy of Man*, ed. Ernst Cassirer, Paul O. Kristeller, and John H. Randall, Jr. (Chicago, 1948), pp. 224–25.

10. Such analogies are described at great length in E. M. W. Tillyard's *The Elizabethan World Picture* (London, 1943).

11. Renaissance Neoplatonists were, of course, Christian, and the combination of Neoplatonic cosmology with Christian history can be found in their writing; see, e.g., Pico's *Heptaplus*, a seminal work in this respect.

12. The image of the tree is found in the *Timaeus* and, to some extent, Milton's image shares common sources with Marvell's inverted tree; cf. A. B. Chambers "'I was but an inverted tree': Notes toward the History of an Idea," *Studies in the Renaissance*, VIII (1961), 291–99.

13. For a lucid statement of this theory of history, see Erich Auerbach's "Figura,"

trans. Ralph Manheim in *Scenes From the Drama of European Literature* (New York, 1959), esp. pp. 58–60. Extensive application of figuralism to Milton is made in William G. Madsen, *From Shadowy Types to Truth: Studies in Milton's Symbolism* (New Haven, 1968).

14. The word translated as "Branch" in the King James version is rendered as "Flower" in the Vulgate ("Et egredietur virga de radice Iesse, et flos de radice eius ascendat."); in Hebrew, the word means "Nazarene." Although too large a subject to pursue here, Milton surely had this passage in mind in writing *Samson Agonistes*.

15. *The Gothic Image*, trans. Dora Nussey (New York, 1958), pp. 165–66. Cf., Eve as flower in *PL*, IX, 432, and as type of Mary, e.g., V, 385–87; X, 183. The currency of the image in the Renaissance is documented by Russell A. Fraser, *Shakespeare's Poetics* (London, 1962), pp. 34–39.

16. I owe this reading to Professor Edward W. Tayler, who proposed it in his graduate Milton course at Columbia University in 1965.

17. "The Sacrifice," l. 202, *The Works of George Herbert*, ed. F. E. Hutchinson (Oxford, 1941). For the liturgical tradition cf. Rosemond Tuve, *A Reading of George Herbert* (Chicago, 1965), pp. 81–86. Isabel G. MacCaffrey briefly touches on the typology of the tree in "The Theme of *Paradise Lost*, Book III," in *New Essays on "Paradise Lost*," ed. Thomas Kranidas (Berkeley, 1969), p. 75.

18. Such distinctions are even more fully the focus in *Paradise Regained*; cf. Lee Sheridan Cox, "Food-Word Imagery in *Paradise Regained*," *ELH*, XXVIII (1961), 225–43.

19. Associated with Augustinian exemplarism by Curry, *Milton's Ontology*, pp. 180–82. For an elegant exploration of this Plotinian concept, see William Nelson, *The Poetry of Edmund Spenser* (New York, 1963), pp. 210–22.

20. For illustrations, see Watson, *The Early Iconography of the Tree of Jesse*; for the tree growing from the head, see plates VI, VIII, XVI, XIX, XXXI; from the genitals, see plates VII, IX, XI, XIV, XV, XVII, XVIII, XX, XXIII, XXVI. The most notable representation is the Chartres west window (Plate XXVI). Both types are at times displaced: the tree may grow from Jesse's hand placed over his genitals (Plate XXII), or from his stomach. Nonetheless, two basic types of representation may be identified as the basic pattern.

21. Male notes (*The Gothic Image*, p. 165) a possible Eastern origin for the motif. An analogy can be drawn with the lingam, an emblem of Shiva. The myth of the origin of the lingam, as reported in Heinrich Zimmer, *Myths and Symbols in Indian Art and Civilization* (New York, 1946), pp. 128 ff., suggests more than passing similarity to the role of Christ in history. Amanda K. Coomaraswamy notes parallels with the birth of Brahma from the lotus in "The Tree of Jesse and Indian Parallels or Sources," *Art Bulletin*, XI (1929), 216–20. On the lingam-tree topos as a psychological configuration see C. G. Jung, *Four Archetypes* (Princeton, 1970), pp. 40–44. For a more extended discussion of the tree as a psychological symbol see Jung, "The Philosophical Tree," in *Collected Works of C. G. Jung*, XIII (New York, 1967), pp. 251–349, esp. 304–07, 311–15, 332–33, 337–38. Cf. Erich Neumann, *The Great Mother*, trans. Ralph Manheim (New York, 1955), pp. 244–56.

22. Milton capitalizes on this metaphor in *Samson Agonistes*; see, e.g., ll. 119, 192, 197, 535, 727, 1024, 1636, 1639.

23. On the rod of Jesse as a *figura* of the cross see Watson, *The Early Iconography of the Tree of Jesse*, pp. 52–54.

24. Cf. Northrop Frye, *The Return of Eden* (Toronto, 1965).

25. Cf. Norman O. Brown, *Love's Body* (New York, 1966), p. 209: "Events are related to other events not by causality but by analogy and correspondence. In the archetype is exemplary causality."

26. Such a view is implicit in the kind of metaphorical treatment the poem has recently received; cf. Jackson I. Cope, *The Metaphoric Structure of "Paradise Lost"* (Baltimore, 1962); Albert R. Cirillo, "Noon-Midnight and the Temporal Structure of *Paradise Lost*," *ELH*, XXIV (1962), 372–95; Rosalie L. Colie, "Time and Eternity: Paradox and Structure in *Paradise Lost*," *Journal of the Warburg and Courtauld Institute*, XXIII (1960), 127–38.

27. For anagogy as a kind of metaphor see Northrop Frye, *Anatomy of Criticism* (Princeton, 1959), pp. 115–28, 141–46. A recent study of *Paradise Lost* working from this perspective is Leland Ryken, *The Apocalyptic Vision in "Paradise Lost"* (Ithaca, N.Y., 1970).

PARADISES LOST AND FOUND: THE MEANING AND FUNCTION OF THE "PARADISE WITHIN" IN *PARADISE LOST*

Thomas H. Blackburn

Michael, in Book XII of John Milton's *Paradise Lost,* promises Adam that the woeful consequences of his Fall may be mitigated by the achievement of a "Paradise within." This inner paradise differs both from the irrecoverably lost paradise of Eden and from the "perfect glorification" of the faithful in an actual eternal paradise at the end of the world. The paradise promised Adam and his progeny in this world is that "imperfect glorification" characterized in *Christian Doctrine* Bk. II, ch. 25, as "the state wherein . . . we are filled with a consciousness of present grace and excellency, as well as with an expectation of future glory, inasmuch that our blessedness is in a manner already begun." To partake of this blessedness one must participate in the divine vision of time as a single moment. For Adam, Michael in the last two books of *Paradise Lost* makes possible such participation. Through style and structure the epic as a whole encompasses in a single poetic unity both the temporal reality of the loss occasioned by the Fall and the eternal actuality of God's glorification of the faithful. It thus not only embodies the poet's participation in the eternal vision, but also allows a reader to share in it, and thereby discern the possible paradise within himself.

IN THE cosmic vision of Christian history which informs Milton's *Paradise Lost,* man begins and ends his earthly life in a paradise. Newly created, he inhabits for a time the primal paradise in Eden; if he be judged among the faithful at the world's last day, he will enter into "One Kingdom, Joy and Union without end."[1] In the interim between the first and final states of bliss, his prime experience will be the woe and suffering which is the consequence of his Fall. Michael, however, promises Adam that this experience may be mitigated by the achievement of a "Paradise within" (XII, 586–87). In terms of the history of mankind as a whole these three paradises structure a beginning, middle, and end which is dramatized particularly in the action which Adam and Eve as individuals undergo. The relationship of the three paradises, however, may not be immediately apparent to a reader of the poem; the assertion that the paradise within will be "happier far" than the paradise of Eden would seem to cause special difficulties in terms of the logic of the poem, and a special effort may be needed to understand just what that paradise consists of. Ultimately, I shall argue that for the reader of *Paradise Lost* the entire epic is to stand as both an image of the paradise within and a means toward the achievement of it by the individual. This large argument begins more modestly with an exploration of the relationships among the paradises described or alluded to in the epic, then proceeds to a definition of the "paradise within," and finally to an attempt to describe the importance of that conception to an understanding of the structure and meaning of *Paradise Lost* as a whole.

The central problem in the relationship among paradises arises in Michael's prophetic history of the fallen world in Books XI and XII. Near the end of this history Michael recounts to Adam Christ's incarnation, resurrection, and second coming. That Adam and Eve may depart from the Garden "though sorrowing, yet in peace," he explicates thus the fulfillment in Christ of God's "Cov'nant in the woman's seed renew'd." Christ will come again

> When this world's dissolution shall be ripe,
> With glory and power to judge both quick and dead,
> To judge the unfaithful dead, but to reward
> His faithful and receive them into bliss,
> Whether in Heav'n or Earth, for then the Earth
> Shall all be Paradise, far happier place
> Than this of *Eden*, and far happier days.   (XII, 458–65)

For the time being, however, man must endure life in a world "to good malignant, to bad men benign" (XII, 538). But the promise of apocalyptic redemption is not all Michael can offer Adam for his present comfort. After Adam reverently summarizes the lessons to be learned from the divine plan revealed to him for man's future, the angel offers one further point of instruction and one further promise:

only add
Deeds to thy knowledge answerable, add Faith,
Add Virtue, Patience, Temperance, add Love,
By name to come call'd Charity, the soul
Of all the rest: then wilt thou not be loath
To leave this Paradise, but shalt possess
A Paradise within thee, happier far.   (XII, 581–87)

Many readers of *Paradise Lost* have found these two promises of
paradise, with their suggestions of a happiness greater than that to be
found in the unfallen bliss of Eden, sufficient reason to suppose that the
ultimate justification of God's ways to men lies in the higher fulfillment
which is, as it were, the final cause of the Fall.[2] In these readings, Adam's
response to Michael's first prophecy of Christ's kingdom assumes central
importance. Having foretold happier days, Michael paused, and Adam

Replete with joy and wonder thus replied.
    O goodness infinite, goodness immense!
That all this good of evil shall produce,
And evil turn to good; more wonderful
Than that which by creation first brought forth
Light out of darkness! Full of doubt I stand,
Whether I should repent me now of sin
By mee done and occasion'd, or rejoice
Much more, that much more good thereof shall spring,
To God more glory, more good will to Men
From God, and over wrath grace shall abound.   (XIII, 468–78)

Passing over the doubt with which Adam's joy is tinged, and much of
the sober analysis in Adam's later speech before the promise of a paradise within, allows the conclusion that despite the miseries he must endure, man has gained by the Fall more than he has lost. The Fall becomes a necessary event in a growth from childish innocence to moral
maturity, or among readers more theologically inclined, the providential occasion for a manifestation of God's love, mercy, and power on a
scale which dwarfs the wonders of creation and makes pale the bliss of
Eden.

Despite the energy and erudition which have been devoted to the
elaboration of readings of the final books of *Paradise Lost* on the lines
suggested above, those readings still seem unsatisfactory. Too often one
senses special pleading designed to save the epic (or damn it) in terms of
philosophical or religious systems which may be more the reader's than

the poem's or the poet's. The most ingenious of these interpretations seek to show that Milton either consciously or unconsciously betrayed orthodox views of the Fall in the service of his private and contrary human convictions or in the grip of some attractive heresy.[3] One may argue against such interpretations by pointing to signposts throughout the poem, from the initial emphasis on "all our woe" and the tragic invocation to Book IX, to the relentless episodes of death and disaster in Michael's history and the bittersweet balance of the closing lines of the epic. One essential part of the argument would be a demonstration that Milton conceived of Adam and Eve before the Fall as mature moral beings actually involved in choices no less real than man faces after he has fallen into sin (an argument I have proposed elsewhere[4]). The problem, however, can be most directly confronted by a study of the relation between the paradises promised the fallen Adam by Michael and those which our first parents enjoyed, whether in actuality or in prospect, while they still preserved their innocence.

In the direct narrative time-scheme of the epic both the happy paradises to which Michael alludes are yet to be realized in the future. The immediate fact is that Adam and Eve have lost forever the primal paradise they once enjoyed. Disobeying God's command has brought to a premature end that harmony in which they lived, untainted but not untested. A *premature* end it was because the terrestrial paradise itself was destined to end eventually even if man had not sinned. The end of that state—perfect in its own degree, yet, as Raphael discloses, bounded in a hierarchical position below the highest—was in fact foretold by God at the moment when his resolve to create the world is revealed. Adam learned of this as Raphael reports to him God's words to the Son after Satan and his rebellious cohorts have been expelled from heaven:

> I can repair
> That detriment, if such it be to lose
> Self-lost, and in a moment will create
> Another World, out of one man a Race
> Of men innumerable, there to dwell,
> Not here, till by degrees of merit rais'd
> They open to themselves at length the way
> Up hither, under long obedience tri'd,
> And Earth be chang'd to Heav'n, and Heav'n to Earth,
> One Kingdom, Joy and Union without end.   (VII, 152–61)

Adam (and the reader) thus learns that the earthly paradise is not eternal, nor is it the highest state to which many may attain; his ultimate destiny is eternal union with God and the angels. Earlier, at the end of his lecture on the essential unity of all the hierarchies of creation, Raphael had foretold to Adam and Eve the possibility of this destiny:

> time may come when men
> With Angels may participate, and find
> No inconvenient Diet, nor too light Fare:
> And from these corporal nutriments perhaps
> Your bodies may at last turn all to spirit,
> Improv'd by tract of time, and wing'd ascend
> Ethereal, as wee, or may at choice
> Here or in Heav'nly Paradises dwell;
> If ye be found obedient, and retain
> Unalterably firm his love entire
> Whose progeny you are.   (V, 493–503)

In terms adjusted to the occasion and to his audience, Raphael interprets for Adam and Eve the decree he later reveals as from God. In so doing he asserts that obedience to God's will is not only the condition under which man will be preserved from death in the bliss of the Garden, but also the condition which if fulfilled will win him ascent to a state "more refin'd, more spiritous, and pure," in closer union with the Almighty.

Neither God nor Raphael offers any specific timetable for, nor any explicit details of, the vaguely Neoplatonic process of sublimation through which man is to pass into eternal bliss (though it is clear that it is a process devoid of the pain and suffering which accompanies the passage of the fallen from mortality to immortality). Michael, speaking later to the fallen Adam, does suggest, however, what life might have been like for an "innumerable race" of men dwelling still in innocence had Adam not transgressed:

> All th' Earth he gave thee to possess and rule,
> No despicable gift; surmise not then
> His presence to these narrow bounds confin'd
> Of Paradise or *Eden*: this had been
> Perhaps thy Capital Seat, from whence had spread
> All generations, and had hither come
> From all the ends of th' Earth, to celebrate
> And reverence thee thir great Progenitor.   (XI, 339–46)

Free from the woeful vicissitudes which sin brings to the world, preserved from death by obedience to God's sole command, and yet still
moral and free in will by virtue of that command, man could have lived
in perfect harmony until "improved by tract of time" he should "wing'd
ascend / Ethereal." Having proved their merit by perfect obedience,
rather than by the agonizing struggle against an actualized evil that
such proof would require in the aftermath of the Fall, Adam and his
offspring would then be welcomed into a higher state. While man remains unfallen, earthly paradise may indeed be "the shadow of heaven,"
but as Milton makes clear in another context, there are important differences between shadowy types and truth.[5] Paradise in Eden is as near
to heaven as an earthly state may be, but it still is not heaven. In comparison with the eventual heavenly state—eternal and immutable as
God defines it, "One Kingdom, Joy and Union without end"—even
primal earthly bliss is inferior. Raphael does not dwell on this difference in degree, for he is concerned with teaching Adam to value and
preserve the happiness he now possesses, but the order is nonetheless
explicit in his speeches. Eden may serve as a place of trial or instruction
for a heavenly destiny, as the law and the prophets served as shadowy
types of Christ and his redemptive covenant, but man's highest and
happiest fate must be participation in the immutable immortality of
heaven.[6]

Man himself, perfect though he may be for the state in which he is
placed before the Fall, is not created angelic. He is "perfect, not immutable." Had he not fallen, his earthly perfection would have been
transmuted into angelic perfection, but only then would the possibility
of a change for the worse cease to exist. Milton's conception of the inferior status of the created world vis-à-vis eternity is reiterated in *The
Christian Doctrine* as he speaks of God's decree concerning creation:

It is not imaginable that God should have been wholly occupied from eternity
in decreeing that which was to be created in a period of six days, and which,
after having been governed in diverse manners for a few thousand years, was
finally to be received into an immutable state with himself, or to be rejected
from his presence for all eternity.[7]

Since the primary plot of his epic centers on the loss of original earthly
perfection, Milton focusses on the splendor and dignity of that perfection and does not emphasize this inferiority to heaven until some compensation must be found for its loss. As J. Martin Evans shows, and the

passages I have cited demonstrate, however, Milton's view is essentially
that expressed by Saint Augustine in his exegesis of the Fall:

[Augustine] rejected out of hand the belief that Adam was already angelic,
asserting with Theophilus that he was destined to achieve this dignity only if
he preserved his innocence: "He [God] gave him free will, so as still to guide
him by his command and to deter him by the threat of death; and he placed
him in the happiness of Paradise, in a life of security, as it were, whence, provided he preserved his innocence, he was to rise to better things." His conception of Adam's immortality, too, was virtually identical with that of the Greek
apologists. Distinguishing between the states of "posse non mori" and "non
posse mori," he wrote: "So too it was an inferior form of immortality—but immortality it was—by which man was able to avoid death: though the immortality
of the life to come is of a higher order, one in which it is impossible for man to
die." It was this conditional status which distinguished Adam so clearly from
the celestial orders.[8]

Throughout his life on earth, unfallen man is defined by his conditional
status; Adam and Eve could fall at any time before their final ascent to
the angelic ranks. From their state in which it was possible for them not
to die, they might pass not into an eternity where they could not die, but
into a world of sin in which it would be impossible for them to avoid
death. That Adam and Eve did fall does not change the fact that by obey-
ing God they could have passed from a high, yet mutable, paradise to a
still higher and happier paradise in eternity. In their choice to fall, however, they did deny forever the possibility of a choice not to fall and thus
cut themselves off forever from that route to heavenly bliss of which
Raphael tells.

After the Fall, God, through Michael, conveys to Adam and Eve the
prospect of a new conditional status which would once again make possible for man choices which could result in his welcome into heavenly
bliss. Through Christ's redemptive sacrifice the possibility is restored
that the faithful may enter into eternal life, though death remains at
least a physical fact for the duration of the world. As Adam is taught by
Michael to see, death may become paradoxically the "Gate of Life" and
the suffering of sinful man the means to highest victory. This victory
over death and sin, however, is no higher than that which could have
been achieved without suffering by a steadfast resistance to temptation
by unfallen men. Michael's postlapsarian promises must be read in the
context of the hints of future glory which Raphael puts forth earlier in
Eden. Both angels foresee for Adam the same ultimate paradise, decreed

by God for the faithful from the beginning of the world. Both assert that heaven and earth will then become indistinguishably one and that men may then dwell anywhere therein. There is no question of the vision of one angel presenting a happier future than the other; the visions are the same and both present "far happier place and happier days" than those of prelapsarian Eden. The crucial difference is not in the place, but in the process by which man may reach that place. Because Adam and Eve broke faith with God, the gentle metamorphosis implied by Raphael's figure of sublimation can no longer he looked forward to; God's justice must be satisfied, though his mercy will finally triumph (cf. "Die hee or Justice must" [III, 210]). Made impure by sin, man and his world may only pass into the eternal paradise by new tests of obedient faith and through the purgation of suffering, death and fire. The differences in language between Raphael's vision and Michael's clearly reflect the change from gentle ascent to apocalypse and judgment. Most of Milton's images of the end of the sinful world of time come from Revelation, but in Raphael's discourse they are shorn of those elements germane only to the purification and dissolution of a sinful world. In Michael's speeches after the Fall we hear the accents of apocalypse—judgment, fire, and finally, renewal:

> Seed-time and Harvest, Heat and hoary Frost,
> Shall hold thir course, till fire purge all things new,
> Both Heav'n and Earth, wherein the just shall dwell. (XI, 895–97)

> [Christ will come] to dissolve
> *Satan* with his perverted World, then raise
> From the conflagrant mass, purg'd and refin'd
> New Heav'ns, new Earth, Ages of endless date.   (XII, 546–49)

This is also the language of God's prophetic summary in Book III of the end of fallen man's earthly history:

> The World shall burn, and from her ashes spring
> New Heav'n and Earth, wherein the just shall dwell,
> And after all thir tribulations long
> See golden days.   (334–37)

Had man heeded God's command he would simply have found "at length" that earth and heaven had been made one with neither tribulation, nor death, nor conflagration required to intervene to satisfy justice, to prepare him for judgment, and to accomplish his purgation and renewal.

In the contrast between Adam's response to Raphael's preview of apotheosis and his later reply to Michael's counsel for fallen man the difference made by the Fall in the conditions under which the faithful are to achieve their heavenly destiny is also manifest. To Raphael, Adam replies,

> O favorable Spirit, propitious guest,
> Well hast thou taught the way that might direct
> Our knowledge, and the scale of Nature set
> From centre to circumference, wherein
> In contemplation of created things
> By steps we may ascend to God.   (V, 507–12)

He also asserts, in response to Raphael's analysis of the duty of obedience, that "we never shall forget to love / Our maker and obey him whose command / Single, is yet so just" (V, 550–52). There is no talk of suffering or worldly difficulty as the price of love and obedience; Adam and Eve never consider the obedience required of them by God other than "this one, this easy charge," or "one easy prohibition" (IV, 421, 433). In their world of innocence everything else may be freely enjoyed without guilt. Adam's summary of the lesson learned from Michael's visit, on the other hand, clearly reflects the consequences of sin's entry into the world of men:

> Henceforth I learn, that to obey is best,
> And love with fear the only God, to walk
> As in his presence, ever to observe
> His providence, and on him sole depend,
> Merciful over all his works, with good
> Still overcoming evil, and by small
> Accomplishing great things, by things deem'd weak
> Subverting worldy strong, and worldly wise
> By simply meek; that suffering for Truth's sake
> Is fortitude to highest victory,
> And to the faithful Death the Gate of Life;   (XII, 561–71)

In this speech, fear, suffering, death, and the sense of a divorce between man's experience in this world and his merit in terms of eternity define the tragic difference between man's existence in innocence and his life in the aftermath of the Fall.

Despite the irreducible difference between the life of man before and after the Fall, the destiny decreed for the faithful remains at all times the same. Whether man manifests his faith in a refusal to fall or in a postlapsarian struggle with multiple evils, highest victory in heaven may be his—a state happier far not only than fallen life on earth but also than the earthly paradise itself. That God's decree saving all those who will believe in Him remains immutable despite the Fall is testimony to both His justice and His mercy. Whatever trials the fallen faithful may undergo, through Christ's sacrifice and their own steadfastness they may be restored to a condition in which that happier life promised even before the Fall may be theirs as well. More difficult to deal with is the promise proclaimed by Michael that the fallen may achieve a "paradise within" which will itself be happier far and which will comfort and sustain them even during the ages of suffering that must pass until the New Jerusalem actually becomes their native city. We must now turn to the question of the nature and definition of this inner paradise; how may it be happier than the innocence of Eden, or make Adam happier in the possession of it than he was in the Garden, and how is it related to the eternal paradise decreed for all the faithful at the end of time?

Michael tells Adam very little about the "paradise within" beyond injunctions about how he may seek to possess it. It is clear, both from Michael's reference to departure from the "paradise of Eden" and from the qualifying "within," that the comfort Adam is to find will require facing the loss of paradise as a place. We should remember, however, as Roy Daniells points out, that man's original paradise in Milton's poem was no less a condition of the mind and spirit than a place of comfort for the body.[9] Man's inner harmony was there in perfect accord with a natural setting which embodied and reflected the harmony of all creation. We may also remember, on the other hand, that Milton elsewhere in *Paradise Lost* presents an inner reality which persists even in the face of contrary external actualities. Satan embodies for us the initial discovery that in certain ways the mind may become "its own place." To his cost he finds that it cannot make a heaven of hell, nor a hell of heaven, but it can keep hell burning within him even while he is physically in the midst of all the delights of paradise.[10] Michael's proposal to Adam involves a conception which has an ironic symmetry with Satan's state of mind: as a kind of equal but opposite mirror of Satan's ubiquitous inner hell, Michael suggests that Adam's "mind" may become a paradise for him, even in the midst of the hellish external world to which his sin has led. Though man has lost the original and innocent harmony of his outer existence, he may apparently recover something of the inner condition of his innocence. To discover more about this recovery we must turn to certain concepts outlined in *The Christian Doctrine.*

That heavenly and earthly paradise which is the final destination of the faithful, both before and after the Fall, may be identified with the state of "Perfect Glorification which is affected in eternity" defined in the thirty-third chapter of the first book of *The Christian Doctrine.* The "fulfillment and consummation" of this glory will "commence from the period of Christ's coming to judgment and the resurrection of the dead" when the just shall be welcomed into "new Heaven and new Earth" and God shall be "all in all" (vol. 16, pp. 337–38, et passim). Speaking of this glorification in an earlier chapter, Milton notes that "its perfection is not attainable in the present life," but in their own lifetime the faithful may achieve an "imperfect glorification" (I, xxxiii; vol. 16, p. 337). This state, reflecting in its title a use of "imperfect" in its Latin root sense, that is, incomplete or unfinished rather than in some way defective, is defined thus:

Imperfect glorification is that state wherein, being justified and adopted by God the Father, we are filled with a consciousness of present grace and excellency, as well as with an expectation of future glory, inasmuch that our blessedness is in a manner already begun. (I, xxv; vol. 16, p. 63)

As perfect glorification is identical with the eternal paradise of *Paradise Lost,* so imperfect glorification may be identified with the "paradise within." Were it not for the references to justification and adoption, this state might also be connected with that of Adam and Eve before the Fall as they frequently demonstrate consciousness of their present grace and are taught by Raphael to expect an even greater future glory. Milton, in *The Christian Doctrine,* however, is addressing himself to fallen man.

The most critical part of the above definition for our present purposes is the assertion that in imperfect glorification fallen man's "blessedness is in a manner already begun." Chronological paradox is involved here: though man in the present life may not actually attain completed blessedness, he may yet in some manner possess it. An important clue to this apparent paradox may be found in the *Christian Doctrine* description of the processes and events which make imperfect glorification possible for fallen man.

In the justification and adoption of fallen man by God the Father the central act is the satisfaction of divine justice by Christ's sacrifice. Decreed by God in his foreknowledge, this satisfaction was freely offered even in the moment of judgment on Man's fall:

Even before man had, properly speaking, confessed his guilt, that is, before he had avowed it ingenuously and in the spirit of repentance, God nevertheless, in pronouncing the punishment of the serpent, previously to passing sentence on man, promised that he would raise up from the seed of the woman one who should bruise the serpent's head, Gen. iii. 15, and thus anticipated the condemnation of mankind by a gratuitous redemption. (I, xiv; vol. 15, p. 253)

In *Paradise Lost* the condemnation of man is similarly anticipated. In the structure of the epic the scenes in heaven where God decrees the ultimate triumph of his mercy and the Son volunteers to satisfy justice are placed in Book III, six books before the Fall itself is dramatized. When God's promise of redemption in the woman's seed is revealed, albeit cryptically, in Book X, the anticipatory order between it and the curse on man is maintained, and this revelation comes well in advance of the eventual "ingenuous avowal" of guilt by Adam and Eve in lines 1086–92. In the first four lines of Book XI we also learn that Adam and Eve's avowal of guilt and desire to repent has been fostered by "Prevenient Grace" which had "remov'd / The stony from thir hearts." The "gratuitous redemption" of mankind as it is effected by Christ in his sacerdotal and mediatorial offices is in fact prior in cause, if not in time, to all of the steps which man may take toward regaining to know God aright. Prior in cause, if not in time, because, as Milton asserts in the *Christian Doctrine* and expresses in the structure of *Paradise Lost*, Christ's mission for the deliverance of man is performed "from the foundation of the world" (I, xv; vol. 15, p. 293). Even those who lived before the incarnation of Christ or since then have not had Christ revealed to them may be "saved by faith in God alone," yet their salvation is nonetheless "through the sole merit of Christ, inasmuch as he was given and slain from the beginning of the world" (I, xx; vol. 15, p. 393). In an earlier chapter of the *Christian Doctrine*, Milton defines Christ's sacerdotal function as "that whereby he once offered himself to God the Father as a sacrifice for sinners, and still continues to make intercession for us" (I, xv; vol. 15, p. 291). He then glosses "once offered" in a way which illuminates not only the eternal nature of Christ's sacrifice, but also the nature of the blessedness enjoyed by those who are imperfectly glorified: "once offered: *virtually* and as regarded the efficacy of his sacrifice, from the foundation of the world, as above stated; *actually* in the fullness of time, and that once for all" (I, xv; vol. 15, p. 239; italics mine).

The difference between "virtual" and "actual" in this context points to a difference between an understanding rooted in the eternal and achronological perspective of God, and one based in the time-bound perceptions of what Jon S. Lawry has called "lateral human history."[11] In the eternal vision which beholds past, present, and future in a single glance, Christ's sacrifice and the saving effects thereof always exist and always have existed regardless of the earthly particulars of time and place associated with his incarnation, crucifixion, and resurrection. The actual, historical coming of Christ is no less real therefore, and belief in its actuality no less necessary for men who live in an age in which that coming is revealed, but a vision limited to the historical fact would be blind to a vital part of the significance of the incarnation and of God's plan for his world. In the unregenerate, purely temporal view of history, as Milton asserts in speaking of the necessity for belief in resurrection, "the righteous would be of all men most miserable, and the wicked, who have a better portion *in this life,* most happy" (*CD*, I, xxiii; vol. 16, p. 351; cf. *PL*, XII, 537–40). Restriction of the vision of rewards and punishments to the period of this life, as does limitation of Christ's meaning and presence to his one historical appearance, leaves no hope of happiness in a "paradise within" for the faithful. (It would also make nonsense of the claim, expressed by Milton at length in *Paradise Regained*, that in his first coming Christ "regained" paradise for mankind.) The bare fact about the world, from a temporal point of view, is that it goes on "under its own weight groaning," rife with all the woes that Michael so fully prophesies for Adam and his progeny in *Paradise Lost*.

Those regenerated by God through Christ, however, in their faith may partake of a vision which transcends the limitations of the actual to find reality in the "virtual." This sense of transcending time, of possessing as real that which has not yet been actualized in the historical succession of events, is central to Milton's conception of faith and its effects. Glossing in the *Christian Doctrine* his definition of "saving faith," he quotes Hebrews xi, 1, and then explicates one step further: "Faith is the substance of things hoped for, the evidence of things not seen, where by substance is understood as certain a persuasion of things hoped for, *as if they were not only existing, but actually present*" (I, xx; vol. 15, p. 395, italics mine). From this faith arises "hope, that is, a most assured expectation through faith *of those future things which are already ours in Christ"* (I, xx; vol. 15, p. 407, italics mine). Though the righteous, until their final delivery at Christ's second coming, may *actually* endure death, suffering, and misery as the fruit of sin in Adam and themselves, through faith they may *virtually* enjoy that kingdom which is to be theirs in "the fulness of time" and thus enjoy happiness in the midst of temporal adversity. This virtual possession of an eternal kingdom defines the "manner" in which, for the faithful fallen, "blessedness" may be "already begun," and is also the key to the nature of the paradise within of *Paradise Lost.*

Not all of the fallen, however, accept the proffered grace and enjoy the fruits of redemption. God "invites fallen man to a knowledge of the way in which he is to be propitiated and worshipped," but man may choose whether or not he will believe in God's grace and act accordingly: "believers, through his gratuitous kindness, are called to salvation, and such as refuse to believe are left without excuse" (I, xvii; vol. 15, p. 345). In the renovation of the natural faculties perverted in the Fall, man may be led to "seek the knowledge of God," and "for the time, at least, undergo an alteration for the better," but this process alone cannot make salvation sure (I, xvii; vol. 15, p. 353). "Supernatural renovation" must also take place, which will serve not only "to restore man more completely than before to the use of his natural faculties, as regards his power to form right judgments and exercise free will, but to create afresh, as it were, the *inward* man, and infuse from above new and supernatural faculties into the *minds* of the renovated" (I, xviii; vol. 15, p. 367, italics mine). Believers are thus "regenerated by God in his own image in the faculties of the mind"—re-created, as it were, as the old man of sin is destroyed and they enter into a new life defined thus in the *Christian Doctrine*:

The primary functions of the new life are comprehension of spiritual things and love of holiness. And as the power of exercising those functions was weakened and in a manner destroyed by the spiritual death, so is the understanding restored in great part to its primitive clearness, and the will to its primitive liberty, by the new spiritual life in Christ. (*CD* I, xxi; vol. 16, p. 5)

In this new spiritual life man is given what amounts to a second chance to make again the crucial choices which mean for him the difference between heaven and hell. If he uses these restored powers in love and obedience of God his temporal reward will be "imperfect glorification" or the "paradise within" and his eternal destiny "perfect glorification."

From the end of Book X to the end of Book XII of *Paradise Lost* we follow with Adam as he undergoes both natural and supernatural renovation. Softened by God's grace and instructed by Michael, Adam progresses from the confusion and anguish of his first fallen moments to a clearer understanding of his situation and to a sense of renewed powers of choice as he is made aware of God's plan for the world. This progression may be most clearly seen in the growth of his understanding of the meaning and implications of the curse on the serpent. From an initial ignorance of any but the most literal meaning, and the despair that leads Eve and him to contemplate ending all human life in their own, Adam moves to a vague sense of a more promising significance in the curse and gains some hope for the future. Led by Michael from "shadowy Types to Truth," by the end of Book XII he has attained to a full comprehension of God's "cov'nant in the woman's seed renew'd"; as a result his grief is turned to joy. That joy is then tempered to fresh expressions of love and obedience to God and to knowledge which, when accompanied by acts which manifest his faith, may win for him a "paradise within." As the epic ends, however, we are returned from the joyous "virtual" realities of the spiritual life to the actualities of history; Adam and Eve (and with them all men) are still at the beginning of the test of their regenerated powers. As are all such promises emanating from God, Michael's promise to Adam of a "paradise within," no less than that of eternal life, is an "if-then" proposition. "If" Adam adds "deeds to [his] knowledge answerable," if he perseveres in faith, love and obedience, "then" he will find "blessedness" begun for him "in a manner" in this life, and life everlasting in the world to come. It is no coincidence that the conditions which will bring about the greatest possible happiness for the fallen are the same as those which would have preserved Eden for the unfallen: the end of both periods of trial is the same and God's decrees, though conditional, are immutable.

The blessedness possible in this life for fallen man must, nonetheless, be not only "imperfect" with respect to that in eternity, but also to that in the primal paradise. No power in man's possession could restore to his world the Garden free from death, pain, and suffering, or restore the perfect harmony which there existed between his state within and his state without. How, then, given this clear loss, can the "paradise within" be happier than the paradise of Eden? The answer, as John

Diekhoff suggests, is partly to be found in the specific terms of the comparison as it is made in *Paradise Lost* (but not in quite the same way as he analyzes them).[12] If one simply compares the "paradise within" with the harmony of inner and outer paradises which Adam and Eve enjoyed in Eden before the Fall, the greater happiness is clearly that of innocence unmarred by sin's consequences. On the other hand, if we remember that the "paradise within" (or "imperfect glorification") involves virtual possession of eternal life in heavenly paradises and suppose that the comparison is with the terrestrial paradise per se (that is, not with that paradise in its aspect as a "shadow of heaven" or virtual eternal paradise in its own right), then, since the "ages of endless date" in "new Heav'n and new Earth" are a higher state than *any* earthly bliss, the comparison makes sense. Milton carefully keeps Michael's comparison in terms of the local paradise which Adam and Eve have declared themselves loath to leave, referring only to the place and avoiding any of the images or allusions which earlier expressed the numinous unity of physical and spiritual perfections which gave the place meaning before the Fall. Even if we do not at this point recall the fatal dissolution of that unity which followed the Fall, we are still offered a comparison which pits an actual but lower kind of perfection against one which though virtual is of a higher order.

Just as Milton, in Raphael's instruction of Adam, emphasized the glories of Eden rather than its relative imperfection compared to the immutable eternity of heaven, so Michael at the end of his discourse, concerned to comfort man now fallen from that original glory, selects the point of comparison which emphasizes hope rather than loss. Man, at least the faithful among men, will be happier than was possible in Eden, but that is still not to say, as Dennis Burden reminds us, that because "Adam is, as a result of his atonement, better off than he was in Paradise," he is therefore "better off than he would have been had he stayed obedient."[13] Until the end of time the righteous and faithful man among the fallen will perforce find the world in which he lives inimical to him and suffering and death the rule of his temporal existence. In such a world faith and obedience require struggle and suffering, but we should remember that eternal life in heaven could have been achieved without sacrificing happiness on earth. There is no intrinsic superiority in the "race" to be run "not without dust and heat" over the trials of choice between good and evil which man faced before the Fall, and would have continued to face until, tested by time, he deathlessly entered into immutable eternity. Allen H. Gilbert errs when he supposes that Milton expressed the belief that "the wisdom of human experience and the excellence gained through suffering" are better than the virtue of Adam and Eve unfallen.[14] It is true, as Gilbert says, that eternal bliss "is to be possessed only by those who are faithful in the struggle against evil," but he does not perceive that Adam and Eve in the Garden possess an opportunity for that exercise of faith no less than man does in the fallen world.[15] Their struggle involved neither pain nor suffering, but the acceptance of those evils as a condition of the struggle is necessary and commendable only because in a fallen world the price of avoiding them is no less than withdrawal from the race or capitulation to the enemy. Though Adam and Eve are to be cheered by "meditation on the happy end" which Michael has revealed to them they are yet at the beginning of the agonizing race of the world, and their "faith unanimous" is to be "sad / With cause for evils past" (XII, 603–04). Providence is to be their guide in the world to which they are now exiled from a paradise barred them by "dreadful faces" and "fiery arms." The reality of loss in the present is seen in the "natural tears they dropped," and the "wandering steps and slow" with which they begin their journey through history (XII, 644–49).

In balance with this sense of loss must be placed the possibility of the paradise within which can mitigate, though not obliterate, its effects. Possession of this inner paradise depends on a perception of the history of the world *sub specie aeternitatis*. While the world continues to exist, "under her own weight groaning," that step out of time can only be taken by participating in the perspective of omniscient divinity. God, from his "prospect high / Wherein past, present, future he beholds" (III, 77–78), views all time as one spatiotemporal moment. In this moment evil is perpetually and instantaneously turned to good, transmuted by God's prescient decree not only in its very moment of manifestation but from the beginning of time. Evil, from the perspective of eternity, simply has no duration of existence. Man, however, must live out his life in a world in which his sin has given duration to evil. The difference between these two perspectives is very like that to which Raphael points when he characterizes intuitive reason as the angelic mode opposed to man's discursive reasoning, or that noted in his account of creation when he asserts that "Immediate are the acts of God, more swift / Than time or motion, but to human ears / Cannot without process of speech be told" (VII, 176–78). Though man, through instruction accommodated to his capacity such as that which Michael offers, may approach the perspective of eternity and by faith find comfort in it, he cannot withdraw his actual person from the confines of time nor in this life recover for himself the union of inner righteousness with outer happiness which was his primal paradise.

In *Paradise Lost*, before the Fall, Raphael supplies the history which places man's earthly paradise in eternal perspective. After the Fall Michael, in what is relatively speaking a moment of time, delineates another such perspective for Adam, placing the new circumstances resulting from sin back in the framework of beginning and end determined by eternal providence, thus permitting him to see the world of fallen history *sub specie aeternitatis* even when he is yet to embark on his voyage through it. In the epic as a whole the narrator both claims and creates a point of view which subsumes time in eternity. Not only by his invocations, but also by the *in medias res* beginning, the numerous proleptic similes and allusions, and the structural placement of God's conditionally foreordained decrees at a point in the epic where the actions to which they pertain are yet part of the narrative future, Milton provides for the reader participation in a model of the divine vision of time as a single moment.[16] Yet we remain constantly and forcibly aware of the tragic drama which is being played out in time, and the central fact of this drama remains man's irredeemable loss of his original paradise. Both the temporal reality of the loss in man's Fall and the eternal actuality of God's providential glorification of the faithful are thus simultaneous and indivisible expressions of the poem. Without denying the particular reality of "all our woe," the epic in its structure embodies a universal perspective which constitutes the vision necessary to a "paradise within," and which not only reflects the poet's achievement of that perspective, but also makes it possible for a reader to share in it. Read aright, the epic should provide for its readers an experience tantamount to the discovery of the possible paradise within themselves.

Louis Martz seems to have sensed something of this aspect of *Paradise Lost* as he writes, "the poem is an action of thoughts within a central, controlling intelligence that moves with inward eyes toward a recovery of Paradise."[17] That the theme of *Paradise Lost* is as much the recovery of paradise as its loss is undoubtedly true, but I believe Martz has misplaced the focus of that "inward eye." As I have suggested, the recovery of paradise is the ultimate concern of the entire poem from the point of view of poet and reader; to focus on Milton's marvelous imaginative achievement in the portraying of a primal terrestrial paradise, however, is to hit on the one paradisiacal state which can never be recovered.[18] As Michael says in Book XI, "God attributes to place / No sanctity, if none be thither brought," and the loss of any sanctity in the original garden is confirmed at the flood when, pushed from its place and with all its verdure spoiled, it becomes an "island, salt and bare" (XI, 829–37). To that garden, or to the state of perfect harmony between inner and outer environments in an earthly setting, man may never return. The garden, within the poem, may still provide a shadowy type which will express to the reader some aspects of the eternal paradise for which he may yet hope, but it cannot be confused with that paradise. What man may recover is that same prospect of a heavenly destiny which was promised the unfallen Adam and Eve. He may also recover some of the inner peace that was his in Eden, that is, the "paradise within," an inward vision of the eternal reality of good enjoyed even in the midst of the preponderant temporal actuality of evil. In the recovery of this inner peace, faith in the eternal paradise to come is a vital factor, but the recovery involved here is one of a conditional destiny momentarily forfeited, rather than of a place once actually enjoyed. The paradise within is rooted not in atavistic memory but in apocalyptic faith.[19]

In unparalleled measure *Paradise Lost* embodies an attempt to render the divine vision in poetic art which may touch and teach men directly, by the means which make "our sage and serious poet Spenser a better teacher than Scotus or Aquinas."[20] The reader of philosophy or theology (or of *The Christian Doctrine*) may learn what the divine vision is, but the reader of *Paradise Lost* may experience that vision, and perhaps even learn what it would feel like to believe in it. Even if we do not take as definitive of Milton's view of the aim of poetry his question in *Reason of Church Government* whether the plays of Sophocles or Euripides "shall be found more doctrinal and exemplary to a nation" than works in some other genre, it is clear that he always felt that his art had some connection with the divine vision and might move others to see and heed it.[21] In perceiving the interrelations of form, structure, and expression which make the epic an embodiment of an eternal unity, one experiences the vision which is the knowledge of God, of his justice and

mercy. *Paradise Lost* thus would seem to accomplish what for Milton
was the end of all learning:

The end then of learning is to repair the ruins of our first parents by regaining
to know God aright, and out of that knowledge to love him, to imitate him, to
be like him, as we may the nearest by possessing our souls of true virtue, which
being united to the heavenly grace of faith, makes up the highest perfection.[22]

The close parallels between the language of this passage and the instructions given Adam by Michael for the attainment of a paradise
within confirm the idea that *Paradise Lost* as a whole may stand in the
same relation to a reader as Michael's prophetic history does to Adam.
As bard and priest in *Paradise Lost*, Milton, in a poetic vision which
comprehends past, present, and future within the unity of a single epic
action, takes us beyond the limits of man's discursive reason to the limits of art at which the inexpressible finds expression. Only in such art
could the paradoxes of time and eternity, central not only to Milton's
idea of faith but to much of human experience, find adequate expression.

Swarthmore College

NOTES

1. *Paradise Lost*, VIII, 162. All quotations from *Paradise Lost* are from Merritt Y.
Hughes, ed., *John Milton: Complete Poems and Major Prose* (New York, 1957). Subse-
quent references will be by book and line in the text. For the clearest recent account
of the relation between Milton's poetry and providential Christian historiography, see
French Fogle's introduction to his edition of *The History of Britain* in *Complete
Prose Works of John Milton*, ed. Don M. Wolfe et al. (New Haven, 1953–), V, xxiii–xiv.

2. For arguments on this point, see: A. O. Lovejoy, "Milton and the Paradox of
the Fortunate Fall," *ELH*, IV (1937), 161–79; C. A. Patrides, "Adam's 'Happy Fault'
and XVIIth. Century Apologetics," *Franciscan Studies*, XXIII (1963), 238–43; Allan H.
Gilbert, "The Problem of Evil in *Paradise Lost*," *JEGP*, XXII (1923), 186; Leon Howard, "The Invention of Milton's Argument: A Study of the Logic of God's Ways to
Man," *Huntington Library Quarterly*, IX (1946), 149–73.

3. See especially Millicent Bell, "The Fallacy of the Fall in *Paradise Lost*,"
PMLA, LXVIII (1933), 863; E. M. W. Tillyard, "The Crisis of *Paradise Lost*," in his
Studies in Milton (London, 1951), p. 11; A. J. A. Waldock, "*Paradise Lost*" and Its
Critics (Cambridge, 1947).

4. "'Uncloister'd Virtue': Adam and Eve in Milton's Paradise," *Milton Studies*,
III (Pittsburgh, 1971), pp. 119–37.

5. The difference is made most clear in Michael's speech in XII, 300–07.

6. This ultimate heavenly state is described by God in III, 333–41. It is also the
state referred to by the angelic choir in *Paradise Regained*, II, 616–17.

7. All quotations from *The Christian Doctrine* are from *The Works of John Milton*, ed., Frank Allen Patterson, 18 vols. (New York, 1931–1940). To facilitate reference, citations will be identified in the text by book and chapter as well as by volume and page in the *Works*. The quotation noted here is from I, vii; XV, pp. 3–5.

8. *"Paradise Lost" and the Genesis Tradition* (Oxford, 1968), pp. 93–94.

9. "A Happy Rural Seat," in *"Paradise Lost": A Tercentenary Tribute*, ed. Balachandra Rajan (Toronto, 1969), p. 15.

10. See I, 254–55; IV, 18–23; IX, 467–68.

11. *Earth the Shadow of Heaven* (Ithaca, 1968), p. 155.

12. *Milton's "Paradise Lost": A Commentary on the Argument* (New York, 1940), p. 130.

13. *The Logical Epic: A Study of the Argument of "Paradise Lost"* (London, 1967), p. 36.

14. "The Problem of Evil in *Paradise Lost*," *JEGP*, XXII (1923), p. 186.

15. Ibid., p. 188.

16. It is not my intention here to embark on a full-scale analysis of the structure of *Paradise Lost*. Many points which would support my generalizations may be found in the works of such scholars and critics as Jackson Cope, Ann D. Ferry, Isabel Mac-Caffrey, and Christopher Ricks.

17. *The Paradise Within* (New Haven, 1964), p. 106.

18. Martz's identification of the recovered paradise with that image of original innocence found in the middle books of *Paradise Lost* is summarized in the conception of the epic as "a picture with a dark border but a bright center" (ibid., p. 140).

19. Michael Fixler in his essay "The Apocalypse Within *Paradise Lost*," in *New Essays on Milton*, ed. Thomas Kranidas (Berkeley, 1969), in fact argues that the entire structure of the epic may be modeled on the apocalyptic pattern of Revelation: see especially pp. 133–35.

20. *Areopagitica*, ed. Hughes, *Complete Poems and Major Prose*, pp. 728–29.

21. See especially, *Reason of Church Government*, ibid., p. 652, and pp. 669–70.

22. *Of Education*, ibid., p. 630.

SELF AND LANGUAGE IN THE FALL

Jun Harada

Paradise Lost provides for the reader a built-in reading device
which, through saving him from a single uncritical reading of the
epic, stimulates his self-knowledge as an ignorant sinner. This is
fully observed in the function of the form of soliloquy uttered first
by Eve and echoed by Adam at the Fall, the traditionally defined
epic crisis in the poem. By beguiling the speaker into a selfhood
which is nothing but a Satanic appetence, the form of soliloquy betrays itself as the form of self-tempting. Only the reader can fully
understand what is taking place in the speaker's mind. As for
Adam's fall the need of soliloquy is more crucial because of his conscious self-temptation from the start. The reader witnesses that
Edenic language deteriorates into fallen language that is enacted
by, and acts on, the speaker who is falling. The once harmonious
dialogue ceases to make the couple happy but drives them to face
the shame of their nakedness and set them in enmity against each
other. The fate of the honest language of their quarrel illustrates
Milton's critical attitude toward the contemporary problem of the
so-called improvement of the language for the secularistic sake of
utility.

PARADISE LOST is the kind of epic that is structurally designed to
prevent the reader from getting a one-dimensional literal reading
of statements uttered by characters of the poem. The mechanism of soliloquy, for example, functions to make the reader realize the internal
relationship between the form of talking to one's self and the speaker's
state of self-enclosure, which is one of the peculiarities of fallen beings.
Thus the adoption of this medium itself reveals the real character and
motive of the speaker. It is the reader who looks into this relationship
and realizes the intractability of the fallen speaker's nature which the
reader finds within himself. His awareness of affinity with fallen charac-

ters renders him able to rediscover his own degenerated self. In *Paradise Lost* the reader is always encountering the archetypally heightened image of himself. The reading of *Paradise Lost* is an act of self-exposure and a way to self-knowledge.

The Fall scene of *Paradise Lost* invites the reader to view the process of the original human couple's secularization from a theocentric being of integrity into a naked self of confusion. This pilgrimage enables the reader to face the origin of his own feelings of sorrow and emptiness. This paper traces the Miltonic genealogy of the naked self of fallen men originally produced within the persons of Adam and Eve. The discussion proceeds on the level of the reader's consciousness of his fallen self, which is found inherently guilty in the anthropocentric process of degeneration of his first parents.[1] In the course of the discussion special attention will be paid to the form of speeches which become corrupt, degenerating to the reader's level, *pari passu* the degradation of Adam and Eve's own natures from the monolithic integrity of Paradise to secretive fraud and open antagonism. Following the example of the epic, which begins *in medias res*, the criticism starts with the scene of Eve's imminent crisis in order that, standing *ab intra*, we may command the entire view of the Fall scene.

Eve is now seen about to resolve to eat the fruit to acquire sapience after hearing the Tempter's "persuasive words, impregn'd / With Reason, to her seeming, and with Truth" (IX, 737–38).[2] Besides, she is presented as hungry: it is towards noon and an eager appetite is raised in her by "the smell / So savory of that Fruit" which entices her to "touch or taste" and solicits "her longing eye" (740–43). In this way the reader finds her besieged not only with that Satanic desire towards sapience which is essentially alien to her but also with her own physical appetite which mobilizes all her sensory organs—visual, olfactory, tactual, gustative, and auditory. She is attacked most fatally through the auditory organ which enables the Tempter to win "Into her heart too easy entrance" (734).[3] This suggests that there is no serious resistance against the serpent on the part of Eve. Rather, as the narrator's words "too easy entrance" indicate, she seems to be willing to succumb to the enemy through her own desire. Thus the Miltonic notion of the inseparability of sapience and appetite works strategically on her to carry out the Fall from within her.[4] The fruit appears to her only an object that satisfies her appetence for both knowledge and food at once. At this time, however, another picture of Eve is introduced. It should be noted that she does not eat the fruit as quickly as her appetite would drive her to but "yet first / Pausing a while, thus to herself she mus'd" (743–44). Her attention is drawn inwards to look into the self that is going to eat the fruit which she knows all too well is forbidden. "Pausing a while" indicates a lapse of time in which she prepares herself to rationalize the evil appetite against her better knowledge.[5] And thus she utters to herself: "Great are thy Virtues, doubtless, best of Fruits" (745). She is apparently addressing the fruit, but in reality, as the narrator clearly points out, she is musing to herself. The soliloquy that she chose as a form of behavior at this moment of crisis is the problem on which centers Eve's initiation of the Fall.

In *Paradise Lost* soliloquy is a theatrically heightened expression uttered only by fallen characters who are bound to be consciously aware of their inescapable situations.[6] Its importance lies in the closed form in which one pursues oneself, never finding a higher intelligence outside oneself.[7] The real issue of soliloquy is not noticed by the self-absorbed speaker himself but understood by the reader, who is situated in a position to overhear the speaker talking to himself. When Eve listened to the Tempter's oration (679–732), she was still reasonable enough about God to say "God so commanded, and left that Command / Sole Daughter of his voice" (652–53) and she emphatically stated, "the rest, we live / Law to ourselves, our Reason is our Law" (653–54). This indicates two things: one, that she knew rightly the quality of God's commandment as something above "our Reason," and the other, that her using the plural of the first person throughout suggests that she was still conscious of coexistence with Adam. She does not say that "my Reason is my Law." Adam did know that their oneness was the only bulwark effective against the Tempter, telling her "If such affront I labour to avert / From thee alone, which on us both at once / The Enemy, though bold, will hardly dare" (302–04). But when the real crisis comes to Eve, she chooses not to listen to "our Reason," but to hear the self. And Eve's self is now, as the reader knows, nothing but a naked appetite waked. And her soliloquy is characterized by the fact that its content is all an imitation of the Tempter's: eulogy of the fruit, and the injustice of God as the forbidder.[8] The reader knows that through this demonic act through which she identifies herself with Satan Eve is able to "unspell" herself from God and that she is cutting off her true being, that of the image of God. In this way soliloquy functions to suppress her true knowledge of God and Adam in order to satisfy what pleases her appetite for both sapience and food. It may be said that soliloquy is the form of "Verlorensein in sich selbst" and thus functions to relieve her of the burden of consciousness of a higher being and to leave her to do what an alienated self pleases.[9] To the reader her every verbal effort is a locus of libido within her which is transformed through the channel of soliloquy (776–79) into the self-justified conduct of the concupiscent fruit-eating.

In this vehicle of soliloquy Eve sees the fruit as justifiably satisfactory for her present need, since, according to her, it is "Fair to the Eye, inviting to the Taste, / Of virtue to make wise" (777–78). Thus it becomes the object of idolatry through the inner process of soliloquy, which functions to sublimate the speaker's Satanic chaos of desire into a seemingly logical, divine order. This is the origin of fetishism, which apparently gratifies the need of "both Body and Mind" but really ruins both of them. In this sense it might be said that the choice of soliloquy is a ritualistic act of her *engagement* to the devil by her willing self which must, as the reader knows well, have heard Adam's repeated warnings: "within himself / The danger lies, yet lies within his power" (348–49), and also must have overheard Raphael's story to Adam of Abdiel who flatly exposed the reality of the fallen by saying to Satan: "Thyself not free, but to thy self enthrall'd" (VI, 181). And now the reader learns that soliloquy works the same effect upon the one who is driven to adopt it by the enthralled Tempter, for in fact by making the fruit divine Eve is worshipping her own Satanic self. Thus soliloquy functions as the medium through which the cosmological scale of Satan's evil is internalized in the person of Eve to become for the first time an indigenous vice of mankind. This naturalization process of sin is completed when she appears unruly: "So saying, her rash hand in evil hour / Forth reaching to the Fruit, she pluck'd, she eat" (780–81). This means also the completion of her separation from her true self. In the preceding scene she was motivated "by a strange desire" to part with Adam and used plausible Areopagitican reasoning (322–41). That speech must be understood to be a foreshadowing of the real break to come. As she was urged on by a strange desire to argue with Adam for the sake of the physical separation, so now she is driven by a conscious desire for the object to make a specious argument for being spiritually separated from God. This is the process of alienation and individuation carried out through the form of soliloquy. Left to the full play of her appetitive self, she is so impatient that she cannot wait to finish the speech: "So saying . . . she pluck'd, she eat," and her despicable state of being is described: "Greedily she ingorg'd without restraint" (791).[10] These gestures are combined to make up a beastly voracious image of Eve, who should, in her own mind, have become a "Goddess humane" (732). Only the reader can enjoy the irony of this *peripeteia* which does not entail recognition on the part of the subject herself.

At this moment Nature "Sighing through all her Works gave signs of woe" (783). Even Earth feels the wound of Eve's ruin. Her microcosmic significance affects the cosmological order of the universe. Irony lies in the fact that Eve's fulfillment of desire results in the total loss of fruitful Nature. Only the reader is aware of this implication that the very time of realization of appetite is really the moment of her destruction and of her total estrangement from Nature.[11] It is a pity that again she cannot participate in the *anagnorisis* of this grave reversal of Nature as well as her fortune. In this way the narrator prepares for the overhearer of the soliloquy to be situated at a place of detachment from which he can understand Eve's whole situation as she unknowingly conducts the disclosure of her self. It does not follow, however, that John Peter's claim *tout comprendre, c'est tout pardonner* is justified in the case of Eve.[12] The reader sees that Satan's fraud did not directly lead her to behave as he asked. She was conscious enough to scrutinize her innermost desire through the medium of soliloquy. In the soliloquy the deceived Eve consciously imitates the self-tempted, self-depraved rhetoric of Satan and thus she is intentionally self-tempted. This must be her responsibility in the Fall.[13] Adam warned Eve: "within himself / The danger lies" (348–49); and God had declared about the Fall: "Whose fault? / Whose but his own?" (III, 96–97).[14]

Eve is, however, stupidly ignorant of this grave situation, and instead "Greedily she ingorg'd without restraint, / And knew not eating Death" (791–92). This kind of euphoria shows that she does not think that her being is at a complete break with Paradise (which only the reader is aware of) but that it still continues in Edenic bliss. The problem is that although she has been entirely lost, she remains to her consciousness a paradisiacal being through the euphoric aftereffect of the soliloquy. She does not suspect the misery of her own loss, which, in turn, aggravates her situation "without restraint." As long as she imagines herself happy, there is no checking the deterioration within her. In Paradise innocence kept man "from knowing ill" (1055) but in the fallen world ignorance—a fallen kind of innocence—blinds man to knowing the reality of his own self. The reader sees that Eve's sense of happiness is Satanic stupid goodness, an infatuation of no hope. Thus worsening her situation pleasingly, she resumes talking to herself: "O Sovran, virtuous, precious of all Trees / In Paradise, of operation blest / To Sapience" (795–97). This shows a more intensified euphoric mythology developed by Eve. Her idolatry of the fruit functions to have her imagine herself wise enough to outrun God's knowledge. She says, "I perhaps am secret; Heav'n is high, / High and remote to see from thence distinct / Each thing on Earth" (811–13). This purely self-made illusion keeps her innocent of the cold reality of the synoptic character of God's vision which the reader has been informed of in Books II and III.[15] In this respect she comes to resemble Satan who at least seems not to have believed God to be omniscient before the rebellion (see V, 682 f.). The tension between the "happy" figure of Eve as she sees herself and the grave concern for her condition on the part of the reader makes him wholly participate in the epic scene.

The thought of secrecy leads her to trifle with another illusion: whether she should share with Adam her power or "rather not / But keep the odds of Knowledge in my power / Without Copartner" (819–21). It is clear to the reader that this haughtiness comes from a complete severance from Adam which she does not yet realize. Then, a flash of doubt comes to her, "what if God have seen, / And Death ensue?" Though mentioning death, she is ignorant of what it is like.[16] The freshest information about it was given her by the Tempter: death is a sublimation from human to divine and it is to be wished (713–15), and accordingly she developed the thought of defying death (760–75) on the belief in Satan's explanation. The Tempter's statement of death is a pagan ideology of man's immortality—metamorphosis of men and gods in the mythological world, and the deification of men practiced in the Roman Empire.[17] In this sense his statement is the Satanic prophecy of human history that is to come into being after this imminent falling of Eve and Adam. And it must be pointed out that the prophecy proves to be true, since our history has almost entirely been the process of *imitatio Satani*. Now a fear of her extinction and of Adam's possible wedding with another Eve occupies her mind (827–30). And this makes her decide to deceive Adam into complicity. Satan resolved to tempt man out of jealousy (IV, 502–75), so she follows the same pattern of the Satanic motive of fraud.[18] As Satan's self-adoration seduced his angelic colleagues into self-destructive revolt, so Eve's self-pursuit leads Adam into destruction. A fallen being can not stand alone, ironically enough, against the fact that he asserts independence from God. The fruit works for Eve as a Faustian drive, a never-ending thirst for something without which her life seems, at least to her, to be nullified. Faustian heroism presupposes miserable dependence on worldly materials. Eating the fruit, she plunges herself into this fatal trap, the hell of Tantalus. Apparently she was free to choose the fruit and to consider outrunning God and Adam, but the real process is that she was driven by a chain reaction of concupiscence. Within this context of necessity jealousy is produced in her: "And *Adam* wedded to another *Eve,* / Shall live with her enjoying, . . . Confirm'd then I resolve, / *Adam* shall share with me" (828–31). However heroic she may sound about love and death, it is clear to the reader that she is most cowardly afraid of a self-produced shadow of another Eve. Behind her proclamation of love her inner voice whispers to the reader that "so dear I love me." The problem is that as long as she talks to herself she imagines herself to be free and wise. Again the form of soliloquy proves to be a fit vehicle of self-beguilement.

Thus successfully deceiving herself, Eve now turns to Adam for temptation and talks about the effects of the fruit: "opener mine Eyes, / Dim erst, dilated Spirits, ampler Heart, / And growing up to Godhead" (875–77). In reality, however, her mind is plunged into a fear of extinction and jealousy. Here for the first time she appears as a conscious liar. It should be noted that she is not talking to herself but to Adam. In the soliloquy it was only the reader who was aware of how degenerate the speaker was. But in the dialogue now not only the reader but also Eve the speaker herself knows how self-corrupted she is. Dialogue is the form whereby the speakers are made self-conscious by hearing and seeing themselves projected upon each other.[19] When she says to Adam, "Which [becoming Godhead] for thee / Chiefly I sought, without thee can despise" (877–78), she must be conscious of her own lying, for before she boasted of keeping "the odds of Knowledge in my power / Without Copartner." Like Satan she wears a mask to cover ruin "with bland words at will" (855).[20] One difference between them is that Satan is an accomplished impostor, while Eve is a novice in evil. In fact, though she assumes "countenance blithe," the reader and Adam as well can easily notice distemper flushing her cheek (887).

Thus addressed by the false Eve, however, Adam is not deceived but immediately understands the truth of the situation: "*Adam,* soon as he heard / The fatal Trespass done by *Eve,* amaz'd, . . . Speechless he stood and pale" (888–94). His amazement and sorrow quickly pass into inward silence. The reader suspects that in this silence there must have been an inner voice talking to him about how to meet the situation. True grief does not take the form of articulate speech, much less a theatrical soliloquy. But when he breaks silence, he utters an over-pitched lamentation using the same vehicle of soliloquy that his predecessor employed. As Eve gave vent to self-temptation in the Fall in the form of soliloquy, so Adam starts falling with the same pattern (see 895). And as, while talking to herself, she addressed the fruit in the second person with her gaze fixed on it, so he addresses her in the second person while talking to himself. Adam's case is, however, more complicated than hers, since it was rather easy for her to fall because she was deceived by the other. But from the beginning he must fall by himself. He has to find a certain rhetorical basis on which he can proceed to a rationalization of his own fall. By proclaiming, "some cursed fraud . . . mee with thee hath ruin'd, for with thee / Certain my resolution is to Die" (904–07), he precludes any possibility of intervention by his "better knowledge." Such a decided exclusion of God's way makes his resolution seem unnaturally quick, as pointed out by many critics. The problem is that he does not depend on an intellectual introspection into the principle of the Edenic life when he must solve the gravest problem in his life which is, as he knows too well, given him by God. He ought to have spoken *up* directly to God, which should have been the most heart-moving dialogue between God and Adam. Instead he spoke *down* to the self of him who chose the breaker of God's decree. At the root of his falling lies a kind of wishful obscurantism which places an irrational element in human love above the principle of the universal order. Adam articulates to himself: "no, no, I *feel* / The Link of Nature draw me: Flesh of Flesh, / Bone of my Bone thou art" (913–15; italics mine). He is appealing to the feeling within him, not listening to a higher intelligence from without. "The Link of Nature" is not a conceptual substance but an instinctive amorphous drive that Adam now feels. As the transitive incomplete verb "feel" indicates, his primary concerns are not the link of Nature itself but his sense of its attracting power. In this sense his rhetorical basis is an uncritical emotionalism. His mentioning of flesh was originally associated with soul. Praising God's creation of Eve, he said, "And they shall be one Flesh, one Heart, one Soul" (VIII, 499). Milton himself in a divorce pamphlet attacked the notion of woman as mere flesh and emphasized the idea of a helpmeet as the foundation of an ideal marriage.[21] As Eve knew rightly the doctrine of "our Reason is our Law," but dismissed it quickly only to give way to appetite, so Adam knew quite well the idea of "one Soul" but now suppresses it consciously in order to be linked with flesh only.

Compared with Adam, however, Eve seems to comprehend better the idea of a whole self. In the preceding argument she said, "what hinders then / To reach, and feed at once both Body and Mind?" and then hearing of Adam's resolution, she exclaims, "[I] gladly of our Union hear thee speak, / One Heart, one Soul in both" (966–67). It is obvious to the reader that her alleged "one Soul" is merely a rhetorical substitute for the oneness of evil concupiscence in Adam and her. But it is worth noticing that the false Eve holds at least the idea of wholeness of self, while Adam is so disturbed that he loses the real self of him who once taught her about the oneness of body and soul. Eve's rhetorical superiority as a tempter must be understood by the fact that she has conceived the Tempter's seed of the fruit. This suggests the fundamental difference between their falls. Eve falls of herself hopefully in order to satisfy her hunger both for wisdom and food at once, which indicates that her fall is originally from a motive to gratify her whole self, as she said, "at once both Body and Mind." On the contrary Adam falls against himself so as not to lose the fallen Eve, who, as he knows well, is no more a rational soul but a being of flesh and appetite, belonging to Satan. She falls up to aspiration, while he falls down to desperation.[22] But what is common to both of them is a staunch loyalty to the kind of self that pleases their inordinate appetites. They are both willing enough, whether deceived or compelled, to be involved in this self. Considered in this way, "what seemed remediless" does not seem remediless to the reader. Adam believes it when, according to Stanley Fish, he "accepts the horizon of his own perspective as final."[23] By circumscribing himself to the self of flesh Adam intentionally narrows the scope of cognition.

So "what seemed remediless" is an illusion fictionalized by his narrowed self that shuts out the possibility of looking beyond his horizon. Again the form of soliloquy helps to accelerate the fall of the speaker.

In the course of falling, Adam's relation with Eve becomes inverted, and the pattern of courtly love takes the place of Edenic love. At the moment of his fall her gesture is like that of the *midons* ("my lady") who deigns to grant grace to the starved lover vassal for the reward of his self-sacrifice: "In recompence . . . from the bough / She gave him of that fair enticing Fruit / With liberal hand" (994–97).[24] The fruit is "fair" to his eyes and "enticing" to his mind—this is exactly what Eve experienced at her fall. Unlike Eve, however, he did not primarily want the fruit itself. He only wished not to lose Eve, the flesh. To them the fruit is their pledge of love. Their love must be kept secret from God, and the reader, as well as Adam, knows it is essentially lust and destruction, which is undoubtedly a feature of courtly love. When Adam says, "to lose thee were to lose myself," he identifies her with a "myself" that is a self of mere concupiscence. He loves "thee" who is substantially "myself." This practice of self-love forms an essential part of courtly love.[25]

Adam's language may sound like Edenic love, since Eve was to him, "Best Image of myself and dearer half" (V, 95). But the paradisiacal love incorporated the coalition of the double images into their original substance. Their oneness in love was possible there, since it participated in the higher perfection of the love of God. It is clear to the reader that in the light of the speech by Adam who is about to fall, the Edenic self as God's image has deteriorated into the Satanic self of flesh. As Edenic innocence degenerates into ignorance, which worked in Eve's fall, so the concept of oneness is deprived of its paradisiacal content and becomes an emptied name which functions as a fatal trap to deceive Adam into a oneness of destruction. The reader sees throughout these episodes the monolithic honest quality of Edenic language changing into the hypocritically ambiguous quality of our fallen language.

This is the reason the dialogue exchanged by Adam and Eve excites the reader to look beneath their apparently harmonious language. For example, responding to his resolution, she praises him highly: "O glorious trial of exceeding Love, / Illustrious evidence, example high!" (961–62). Yes, his love is really "exceeding" and "high" in the sense of excess and hybris. Her ostentatious applause betrays to the reader her flippancy and specious solemnity only supported by the Satanic rhetoric.[26] When she tried to beguile him, she never employed a word about death throughout the thirty-line utterance, but once she hears his fictional no-death speech, God "would be loath / Us to abolish, lest the Adversary / Triumph" (946–48), she becomes bold enough to take advantage of it. The reader hears the words "death" and "die" uttered at the rate of once per four lines in her speech (964–89). Blinding themselves to facing cold reality, they progress smoothly through the dialogue in which they know that they are lying to themselves, to each other, and to God. Thus their dialogue works on them to deliver a fear of death to the winds (989), to make the fruit not pernicious but divine (956), and to reconsolidate the Link of Nature into the bond of human nature (956). In reality, however, this dialogue is the most insecure one they ever engaged in. It must be read in an inverted way; death is never delivered to the wind, the fruit is most pernicious, and "the Bond of Nature" is nothing but the bondage of sin.[27]

Thus presenting the origin and nature of man's fallen self and the resultant use of hypocritical language, the poem comes to the stage where evil concupiscence, their central motive in the Fall, is finally culminated in "amorous play" (1034–45). Combining the *tristitia post coitum* and the fruit's effect of opening their eyes, the narrator makes them conscious of their own depravity which they have been veiling through monologues and a dialogue. But now the mask does not work before the ontological reality: "hee cover'd, but his Robe / Uncover'd more" (1058–59). What matters here is that the fallen Adam's first realization of the truth is connected with his sexual exhaustion (1046 ff.). This is best illustrated in the Samson simile:

> So rose the *Danite* strong
> *Herculean Samson* from the Harlot-lap
> Of *Philistean Dalilah*, and wak'd
> Shorn of his Strength.   (1059–62)

The harlot Dalilah-Eve effeminates the Samson-Adam in amorous play, who wakes only to find himself enslaved to the enemy that is, ironically enough, the very object he loved most. The bond of nature proves not to unite but to disjoin the lovers to be finally inimical to each other: the *Danite* and the *Philistine*. Fallen love deceives the lovers who belie themselves and thus it makes them realize their own vanity.

In this sense the Fruit of Knowledge proves to be a complex symbol

effecting the stirring of appetite, sexual frustration, and the exposure
of misery. It is after all, as Adam was compelled to admit, the "Bad
Fruit of Knowledge" (1073) which ruthlessly uncovers everything only
to shame him. Before the Fall nakedness was so natural an adornment
of the majesty of man that he was not conscious of it.[28] But now the bad
knowledge compels the partaker to feel guilty of his nakedness. In the
course of falling it was possible for Adam and Eve to conceal their
wickedness at least from themselves and from each other in order to be
self-beguiled enough to fall. The pretended innocence is no longer
possible, for as Eve repeatedly emphasizes, the fruit opened their eyes.
And Adam deplores the fact that "our Eyes / Op'n'd we find indeed,
and find we know / Both Good and Evil, Good lost, and Evil got" (1070–
72). He is made to know this truth by seeing the naked parts that are
"most / To shame obnoxious, and unseeming." In this way for the first
time he discovers the reality of his being as evil and unclean. The Fall
is a lapse from happy, innocent consciousness to guilty consciousness of
himself, from angelic blessed reason to a degraded *nosce te ipsum* as an
ignorant sinner. From now on in the history of mankind the act of
concealment of self will after all "uncover more," as Adam and Eve
experienced.

It is ironical that the fallen couple finally choose an asexual monstrous banyan tree (1101–07) to cover their organs of production from
themselves and each other.[29] Significantly the sexless tree refuses to
participate in their surreptitious hypocrisy to conceal the reality of their
own shame. This is the first time Nature betrays man. In the course of
falling they have been alienated, according to Roland M. Frye, from
God, themselves, and each other.[30] Now this time they are obliged to
see themselves alienated from Nature. This is the knowledge of "Evil
got." The banyan tree episode suggests an inseparable connection of
fallen cogitation and *copula carnalis*, both of which concur to satisfy
our concupiscence only to make an internecine struggle against each
other.[31] This is the way the couple are finally led to face the "truth"—
nakedness of their own. However they may try to evade it, it invites
disclosure of self because it originates in their own desires and is brought
to consciousness by the opening of their eyes. The disclosure works on
them to find that their self consists of, according to the narrator, "high
Passions, Anger, Hate / Mistrust, Suspicion, Discord" (1123–24), and
that their understanding and will are "both in subjection now / To

sensual Appetite" (1128–29). Their love turns out to be a mere link of the physical organs—a bondage of shame.

With the discovery of self their speech alters its style from hypocrisy to accusation (1067–98). Their naked language ruthlessly lays bare what the preceding language of deception concealed. The dishonest language, as examined above, secretly aggravated the situation to an irrevocable extreme, while the honest language they employ now provokes enmity to an open quarrel of no end. In the fallen world speech is an act either of deceiving each other or of breeding enmity against each other, and thus it prepares the way for the despair of those engaged in it. The Royal Society of London for Improving Natural Knowledge, whose activity began about the time of Milton's mature works, aimed, according to Thomas Sprat, "to return back to the primitive purity" of language, by rejecting all amplifications, digressions, and swelling of style. This means that the Society advocated an honest language which was intended to deliver "so many things, almost in an equal number of words."[32] Its reformed "close, naked, natural way of speaking" indeed disclosed secrets of nature and man, but, as later history has proved, its alleged mathematical exactness reduced all significance of nature and man to mere physicality, utility, and efficiency, mainly serving that kind of materialism which has continued from the Restoration to the present technological days, with their domination by the secularistic ideology of money fetishism.[33] And there is no denying that the speech of fallen sapience advocated by the Society paved the way for our unstable modern society. It may be said that in the fallen world the disclosed truth heaps upon the discoverer damnation, which Milton renders in the image of the fallen couple's nullifying efforts throughout the Fall scene.

Thus at the close of the book, where the narrator gives the final comment upon the misery of their quarrel, the reader hears it as metaphorically meaningful for the reality of his self and world:

> Thus they in mutual accusation spent
> The Fruitless hours, but neither self-condemning
> And of thir vain contest appear'd no end.   (1187–89)

Paradise Lost is a challenging epic that continuously works to make the reader aware of his guilty self as reflected in the figures of these prototypical characters who degrade self and speech to the extent that we do.

Aichi University of Education, Japan

NOTES

1. It may be said that nowadays the reader of *Paradise Lost* is not likely to fall into a literal reading of the explicit story level, as did the Romantic Satanists and recent Miltonoclasts such as A. J. A. Waldock and John Peter. For my concept of the reader I am indebted to John M. Steadman's two brilliant essays: "Ethos and Dianoia: Character and Rhetoric in *Paradise Lost*," in *Language and Style in Milton*, ed. Roland David Emma and John T. Shawcross (New York, 1967), pp. 233–51; and "Milton's Rhetoric: Satan and the 'Unjust Discourse,'" in *Milton Studies*, I (Pittsburgh, 1969), pp. 67–92; and to Stanley Eugene Fish, *Surprised by Sin: The Reader in "Paradise Lost"* (London, 1967), and the same author, "Discovery as Form in *Paradise Lost*," in *New Essays on "Paradise Lost*," ed. Thomas Kranidas (Berkeley, 1969), pp. 1–14. The difference between Fish's concept of the reader and mine is that to him the reader "falls before the lures of Satanic rhetoric" and thus "diplays . . . the weakness of Adam," while my reader does not participate in this kind of fall because of his awareness of the theatricality of Satanic rhetoric. Fish goes on to say, "Rhetoric is thus simultaneously the sign of the reader's infirmity and the means by which he is brought first to self-knowledge" (*Surprised by Sin*, p. 38). Understanding the necessity for the speaker to use rhetoric, my reader finds the same necessity operating within himself. In this sense my conscious reader does not fall "before the lures of Satanic rhetoric," but with his eyes open identifies himself critically with the Satanic element within him.

2. All references to *Paradise Lost* are to the text of Merritt Y. Hughes, *John Milton: Complete Poems and Major Prose* (New York, 1957).

3. For the significance of the organ of hearing in *Paradise Lost* and contemporary Puritans' writings see William G. Madsen, *From Shadowy Types to Truth: Studies in Milton's Symbolism* (New Haven, 1968), ch. 2: "Eve, whose understanding is more vulnerable than Adam's, is assaulted chiefly through the ear" (p. 163).

4. Roland Hagenbüchle gives an etymological basis for their inseparability: "'Sapience' liegt das lateinische 'sapere' zugründe, was ursprüglich schmecken, kosten und später auch verstehen bedeutet" ("'Sapience' is based on the Latin root of 'sapere' and it originally meant to taste, diet and later it came to signify to understand.") (*Sündenfall und Wahlfreiheit in Milton's "Paradise Lost"* [Berlin, 1967], p. 76). (All translations are mine.) For Milton's comparison of Knowledge to food see *Paradise Lost*, VII, 126–30; *Paradise Regained*, II, 371; and *Samson Agonistes*, 1091 ff.

5. Referring to this line, Dennis H. Burden thinks that Eve is still vaccilating whether "to approve" or "to disapprove of the act" (*The Logical Epic: A Study of the Argument of "Paradise Lost"* [London, 1967], p. 136). The fact is, however, that she is besieged by all the powers within her and is already inclined to approve of the act. The problem here is not the alternative between the two but an effort to actualize evil concupiscence on the part of her consciousness.

6. J. B. Broadbent gives a very important comment on soliloquy in *Paradise Lost*: "The characters of *Paradise Lost* do not soliloquise until they have fallen" (*Some Graver Subject: An Essay on "Paradise Lost"* [New York, 1960], p. 80).

7. According to Hagenbüchle the monologue primarily functions "diesen Prozess der Individualisierung aufzuzeigen und zugleich das Zerwürfnis des Menschen mit sich und dem Schöpfer zum Alusdruck zu bringen" ("to exhibit this process of individualization and at the same time to express man's strife with the Creator") (*Sündenfall*, p. 69). Berta Moritz-Siebech says, "Die Verwendung des Monolog in IX ist darum so bedeutsam, weil Milton damit seine Absicht, die Entscheidungen ins Innere zu verlegen, unmissverständlich zu erkennen gibt" ("The use of monologue in Book IX

is therefore very significant, for with it Milton can quite clearly express his intention to transfer the crisis into the interior.") (*Untersuchungen zu Miltons "Paradise Lost"* [Berlin, 1963], p. 84).

8. Satan's soliloquies are closely examined by Steadman, "Milton's Rhetoric," pp. 80–81.

9. Hagenbüchle says, "Selbstherrliche Vereinzeln ist für Milton ein wesentliches Merkmal des Bösen" ("The self-authorizing separation is to Milton an essential symptom of the evil.") (*Sündenfall*, p. 66).

10. Appetite itself, both physical and spiritual, is good. Adam and Eve enjoyed it in Eden and it is also shared by angels. See Raphael's instruction (IV, 736–75; V, 414–15; VIII, 612–29). Appetite is, according to Milton, turned into evil concupiscence or desire of sinning when "Temperance over Appetite" fails. See *The Christian Doctrine*, in the Columbia *Works of John Milton*, ed. Frank Allen Patterson et al., 18 vols. (New York, 1931–38), XV, 193 (cited hereafter as CM with volume and page number). And also see the simile of books and meats in *Areopagitica* in *Complete Prose Works of John Milton*, ed. Don M. Wolf et al. (New Haven, 1953–), II, 512 (cited hereafter as YP with volume and page number).

11. "Denn im Selbstgesprach zeight sich der Sprechende wie er ist ohne Verhüllung und Verzerrung" ("because in the form of self-talking the character of the speaker becomes evident without any disguise and distortion") (Moritz-Siebech, *Untersuchungen*, p. 84).

12. *A Critique of "Paradise Lost"* (New York, 1960), p. 128. See a good criticism of it in Fish, *Surprised by Sin*, p. 250.

13. Hagenbüchle repeatedly states the role of Satan as "blosser Katalysator" of the human fall (*Sündenfall*, pp. 58–59, 74, 79). For the form of soliloquy as responsibility see Arnold Stein's "Satan's Metamorphoses: The Internal Speech," in *Milton Studies*, I, 97.

14. The Fall comes from within. God told the Son: "They trespass, Authors to themselves in all / Both what they judge and what they choose" (III, 122–23).

15. Even Belial admits, if only tactically, the omniscience of God (II, 189–93); and Milton describes God: "Him [Satan] beholding from his prospect high, / Wherein past, present, future he beholds" (III, 77–78). See also *Christian Doctrine*, CM, p. 57. Isabel G. MacCaffrey gives an interesting comment on the topic in *"Paradise Lost" as "Myth"* (Cambridge, 1959), pp. 53 f.

16. See Steadman, "Ethos and Dianoia," p. 206.

17. Milton attacked the Roman practice of deification of Julius Caesar and Augustus in the *Tenure of Kings and Magistrates*, YP, Il, 204. Also see *Paradise Regained*, II, 81–84.

18. Broadbent (*Some Graver Subject*, p. 260) and Peter (*A Critique of "Paradise Lost,"* p. 128) alike regard jealousy as the motive. Helen Gardner ascribes it to solitude (*A Reading of "Paradise Lost"* [Oxford, 1965], p. 90). See also Roland M. Frye, *God, Man, and Satan* (Princeton, 1960), p. 28.

19. Significantly Eve was first made self-conscious by meeting and talking to Adam at her creation scene (IV, 477 ff.).

20. A. Bartlett Giamatti says, "to be fallen is to assume a mask to cover inner ruin" (*The Earthly Paradise and the Renaissance Epic* [Princeton, 1966], p. 342).

21. "But this reason cannot be sufficient of it self; for why then should he for his wife leave his father and mother, with whom he is farre more flesh and bone of bone, as being made of their substance" (*The Doctrine and Discipline of Divorce*, YP, II, 309).

22. Emblematically Eve is the peacock of Pride and Adam the goat of Incontinence. See Samuel C. Chew, *The Pilgrimage of Life: An Exploration into the Renaissance Mind* (New Haven, 1962), p. 3.

23. Fish, *Surprised by Sin*, p. 264. Critics have managed to propose some measures for their salvation—Fish: Adam should get counsel from higher intelligences (ibid.); Arnold Stein: Eve should deny Adam (*Answerable Style: Essays on "Paradise Lost"* [Minneapolis, 1953], p. 108); Burden: Adam should divorce her (*Logical Epic*, p. 170). Irene Samuel is confident of Eve's redeemability. See *"Paradise Lost:* The Dialogue in Heaven," in *Milton: Modern Essays in Criticism*, ed. Arthur E. Barker (New York, 1965); and C. S. Lewis says, "God might have had other cards in his hand, but Adam never raised the question" (*A Preface to "Paradise Lost"* [London, 1942], p. 127). Interestingly, Irene Samuel suggests a form of the question Adam should have raised: "And yet was 'How can I live without thee?' a helpful question to ask? Might he not instead have asked, What can I do *for* her?" (*"Paradise Lost* as Mimesis," in *Approaches to Paradise Lost: The York Tercentenary Lectures*, ed. C. A. Patrides [London, 1968], p. 28).

24. Balachandra Rajan contrasts Eve's "masculine aggressiveness" with Adam's "dazed and feminine acquiescence" (*"Paradise Lost:* The Web of Responsibility" in *"Paradise Lost": A Tercentenary Tribute*, ed. B. Rajan [Toronto, 1967], p. 132).

25. See Paul Zweig, *The Heresy of Self-Love: A Study of Subversive Individualism* (New York, 1968), part 2.

26. Broadbent gives a good analysis of this part in "Milton's Rhetoric," *MP*, LVI (1959), now included in *Milton: Modern Judgment*, ed. Alan Rudrum (London, 1968), pp. 280–81.

27. According to Rajan, "the forging of the link is the breaking of the chain and the sealing of the bond tears a greater bond to pieces" ("The Web of Responsibility," p. 131). See also interesting criticisms by Jon S. Lawry, *The Shadow of Heaven: Matter and Stance in Milton's Poetry* (New York, 1968), p. 252, and by Helen Gardner, *A Reading of "Paradise Lost,"* p. 90.

28. See IV, 289–90, 713.

29. I must disagree with Kester Svendsen's idea of the fecundity of the banyan tree in this scene. It is surely fecund but this is not Milton's "expression of human generation." See *Milton and Science* (Cambridge, 1956), p. 135. As the allusion shows, the tree multiplies itself by taking root from the twigs bended in the ground, which means that the tree is asexually fecund. It is, as Louis L. Martz points out, essentially "a barren, grotesque, monstrous tree" (*The Paradise Within: Studies in Vaughan, Traherne, and Milton* [New Haven, 1964], p. 134). It seems to be Milton's humorous intent to make the reader watch his original parents finally resort to a sexless tree to cover "those middle parts."

30. See Frye, *God, Man, and Satan*, pp. 59–62.

31. Saint Augustine gives a cogent gloss: "For this holds sway in the whole body, moving the whole man, without and within, with such a mixture of mental emotion and carnal appetite that hence is the highest bodily pleasure of all produced: so that in the very moment of consummation, it overwhelms almost all the light and power of cogitation." *The City of God*, Bk. XIV, chap. XVI (London, 1947), II, 47.

32. Thomas Sprat, *The History of the Royal Society*, 1697, ed. Jackson I. Cope and Harold Whitmore Jones (St. Louis, 1958), p. 113.

33. Ibid.

THE BUOYANT MIND IN MILTON'S EDEN

Dan S. Collins

Milton's depiction of the movement of mind in unfallen man is consistent with the universal ascent of all creation toward its perfect source described by Raphael in Book V of *Paradise Lost*. Although most critics interpret the prelapsarian action of the epic as a series of anticipations of the fall, Milton utilizes Eve's dream and Adam's comments on astronomy and the birth of his own consciousness, his search for a helpmeet, and his first experience of sexual attraction to demonstrate the mind's inherent buoyancy, in each episode rising further toward its angelic perfection by maintaining a willing dependence upon God's sustaining grace and exercising reason to discipline lesser faculties, particularly the imagination. The accessibility of the unfallen mind to material and spiritual evil does not imply inevitable acts of disobedience but instead provides opportunity for achieving self-mastery and participating in the continuing refinement of the divinely instituted order. The eventual reversal of this upward movement of mind occurs only after the intellectual sufficiency of mankind to prosper in Eden has been established. When it finally occurs, the fall (which originates in Adam's unwillingness to discipline his imagination and obey the dictates of his reason) happens abruptly and needlessly at the apex of a spiritual ascent, not gradually at the end of an inexorable descent into the world of matter.

DESPITE THE burden of catalogues, invocations, formal similes and other static or monumental elements, *Paradise Lost* remains basically fluid, its plot movement and characterization at every point governed by two contending currents, one ascending toward spiritual freedom and perfection, the other falling perpetually into the world of fixed limitations, of determined, perishable matter. Although the ascending movement is the more general and inclusive, it is at several points so dominated or obscured by the descending flow that the full

context of certain events is not readily apparent, as, for example, the
psychological immobility governing Satan's early speeches was not apparent to many eighteenth- and nineteenth-century readers of Book I.
For recent critics the scenes in Eden prove to be the most difficult to
place in full perspective, for the imminence of the fall tends to draw all
events toward it and throw a pall of decadence over the alleged perfection of unfallen nature. Acutely sensitive to the many anticipations of
the fall planted by the author in Books IV–VIII, the modern reader
tends to define Edenic man as a potential or even an actual sinner and
sees only irony in Milton's characterization of him as a creature sufficient
to stand.[1]

To A. B. Giamatti a typical descriptive passage (IV, 237–40) reveals
a characteristic "lack of vitality" in Milton's Eden—everything is "slow,"
"aimless," "drooping." "We tend to feel there is too much to no purpose;
that perhaps Nature is soft and to live in it would have a softening,
even corrupting, effect on us."[2] As to Adam and Eve, their innocence
strikes J. B. Broadbent as a perfect balance that becomes less stable:
"the knife edge between man's 'disposition to do good' and his 'liability
to fall,' as Milton puts it in De Doctrina, is sharpened through Books V,
VII, and VIII."[3] Obviously the movement discerned by these critics,
and by scores of others, runs precisely counter to the universal movement described by Raphael at the outset of his dialogues with Adam:

> O *Adam*, one Almighty is, from whom
> All things proceed, and up to him return,
> If not deprav'd from good, created all,
> Such to perfection, one first matter all,
> Indu'd with various forms, various degrees
> Of substance, and in things that live, of life:
> But more refin'd, more spiritous, and pure,
> As nearer to him plac'd or nearer tending
> Each to thir several active Spheres assign'd
> Till body up to spirit work, in bounds
> Proportion'd to each kind.   (V, 469–79)[4]

Although he speaks very generally of "All things" reascending to their
spiritual perfection, Raphael is thinking particularly of the human
body and the concoctions of liver and heart that convert the mixed
elements of food into waste, vital spirits and animal ("intellectual")
spirits. Most of all he is thinking of the activities of the mind as the
culmination of this spiritualizing ascent:

flow'rs and thir fruit
Man's nourishment, by gradual scale sublim'd
To vital spirits aspire, to animal
To intellectual, give both life and sense,
Fancy and understanding, whence the Soul
Reason receives, and reason is her being.   (V, 482–87)

If Raphael is correct in matters affecting the unfallen mind, there should be visible an ascending movement that would enable man to attain spiritual perfection rivaling that of the angels, thus eliminating any suggestion of aimlessness in Eden. Although it might be most visible in the actions of the mental faculties, it would not be mere process but would instead be at all times the expression of less visible causes—divine love and the human will to obey:

And from these corporal nutriments perhaps
Your bodies may at last turn all to spirit,
Improv'd by tract of time, and wing'd ascend
Ethereal, as wee, or may at choice
Here or in Heavenly Paradises dwell,
If ye be found obedient, and retain
Unalterably firm his love entire
Whose progeny you are.   (V, 496–503)

One need not simply deny the possibility of any such affirmative movement of mind by assuming, as does Broadbent, that the psychology available to Milton was inappropriate to the depiction of Edenic perfection since it refers only to the fallen mind.[5] Obviously Milton was well aware that much of the psychological commentary of his day not only suggested that the human mind contained sinful predilections from the moment of its creation but implicated the Creator himself in the fall of his flawed creature. Thus when he has occasion, in *Areopagitica*, to reply to those who "complain of divine providence for suffering Adam to transgress" Milton frames his answer in terms of God's gift of the mental faculties, particularly the incredible tirelessness and infinite range of the fancy, which might appear inimical to the state of perfection: "[The similarity of the material upon which sin and virtue work] justifies the high providence of God, who though he command us temperance, justice, continence, yet pours out before us, even to a profuseness, all desirable things, and gives us minds that can wander beyond all limit and satiety."[6] The two long speeches on the faculties he devises for Adam, in *Paradise Lost*, provide further testimony of his concern with the human mind and the aspersions lodged against it. To a greater extent than has hitherto been realized, the depiction of Eden in Books IV, V, VIII, and IX is intended to disperse allegations of man's inherent mental imperfection and to illustrate the power of his mind to transcend any subversive impulse. The purpose of the present essay is to describe patterns of events devised by the poet to show prelapsarian man not only intellectually sufficient to stand but to rise to his spiritual perfection.

The psychological depreciation of man's mind against which Milton formulated his counterassertion was rooted in Platonic and Neoplatonic theories of the antipathy of body and soul that had evolved, in the theological psychology of the Renaissance, into the principle of the intractability of the senses to the guidance of the mind. Since Milton insisted upon the total unity of flesh and spirit in the creation of each soul, for him the area of alleged incorrigibility was concentrated within the faculties of the soul and concerned the amenableness of the fancy (the convergence of man's animal qualities) to the discipline of the understanding, the godlike faculty. Genesis itself suggests that when God considered the fancy he found it difficult to justify the creation of man. In the time of Noah the Deity had repented his creation of the human species because "the wickedness of man was great in the earth and the imagination of his heart was only evil continually" (Gen. vi, 5). Nor did the destruction of all but a chosen remnant satisfy God that the human imagination had been cleansed; instead he resolved never again to express such complete disappointment in man, since "the imagination of man's heart is evil from his youth" (Gen. viii, 21). If the ways of God were to be justified to men and the perfection of man in Eden portrayed, the human fancy required the first justification.

The properties of fancy best known and most in need of justification in the seventeenth century were the ability to dissemble and the accessibility to evil spirits. Essential though the normal function of the fancy was in presenting sense stimuli in forms meaningful to the judgment, Milton's audience was far more sensitive to the occasional abuse of this function by Fancy herself (to use the conventional personification) or by the good and evil spirits who could command her at will. Even the unique virtues of the fancy—the perpetual wakefulness and the infinite range that could transport her to the stars—seemed somewhat abnormal and contrary to man's proper humility.[8] Although she was linked in these ways to the world of spirits and capable of celestial flight, she was most generally characterized by her "low" qualities, for she was "the reason of brutes," as Burton notes, and obedient to the sensitive appetite.[9] Fancy's ability to disguise the reports of the senses at the behest of the appetites is strikingly described by Milton in the *Reason of Church-Government*:

For truth, I know not how, hath this unhappiness fatal to her, ere she can come to the trial and inspection of the understanding; being to pass through many little wards and limits of the several affections and desires, she cannot shift it, but must put on such colors and attire as those pathetic handmaids of the soul please to lead her in to their queen. And if she find so much favor with them they let her pass in her own likeness; if not, they bring her into the presence habited and colored like a notorious falsehood. And contrary, when any falsehood comes that way, if they like the errand she brings, they are so artful to counterfeit the very shape and visage of truth that the understanding not being able to discern the fucus which these enchantresses with such cunning have laid upon the feature sometimes of truth, sometimes of falsehood interchangeably, sentences for the most part one for the other at the first blush, according to the subtle imposture of these sensual mistresses that keep the ports and passages between her and the object.[10]

In order to vindicate the fancy, Milton needed, first of all, to remove the fear of the faculty as an instrument always available to evil spirits and, second, to minimize the fancy's incorrigible propensity to distract the mind with irrelevant "toys" or to corrupt it with disguised longings and fears of the appetites. For these reasons it was desirable, in the first instance, to depict a state of Edenic security so profound that no assaults of Satan upon the human fancy could disturb it, and this Milton accomplished in the sequence concerning Eve's dream of disobedience. The second vindication required scenes such as the dialogues of Adam and Raphael, in which the separate functions of the faculties could be portrayed and the distraction and sensual infatuations of fancy in a state of excessive security could be anticipated and prevented by the disciplining powers of reason. Much of the action that occurs in Milton's Eden can thus be accounted for as a corrective to the uneasy suspicions that from the moment he was endowed with the faculty of imagination man was ill adapted to a life of perfection. Nevertheless, the response is never apologetic but affirmative, and resembles the ascending responses to disparagement which eventually transport the second Adam, in *Paradise Regained*, to heavenly security.

I

The ascending movement first becomes visible when Satan attempts to reverse it during his first brief contact with humanity. By depicting the fallen angel's futile attempt to reduce the actions of the mind to a physical level where they can be controlled by physical means, Milton is able to demonstrate the physical perfection of the Edenic mind and its complete security from demonic conjuration. When Satan, having temporarily eluded the angelic guard, exerts his demonic sorcery upon the slumbering Eve, Milton clearly indicates—especially by a strong pun on "forge"—that the fallen angel is conducting a purely physical attack upon the mind,

> Assaying by his Devilish art to reach
> The organs of her Fancy, and with them forge
> Illusions as he list, Phantasms and Dreams,
> Or if, inspiring venom, he might taint
> Th' animal spirits that from pure blood arise
> Like gentle breaths, from Rivers pure, thence raise
> At least distemper'd, discontented thoughts,
> Vain hopes, vain aims, inordinate desires
> Blown up with high conceits ingend'ring pride.   (IV, 801–09)

His targets are (1) the understanding, which he hopes to deceive with false images generated within the fancy, and (2) the emotional center (the heart), which he intends to program by altering the chemical balance of the animal spirits, which convey messages of fancy and understanding to the heart. Both assaults are repelled, though by different guardians, and only the attack upon the understanding falls to Adam to explain. Eve's account of her dream of disobedience indicates that her fancy has been strongly stimulated, but unfortunately for Satan, translation of his evil into psychological terms exposes it to the purgative power of reason, which is constantly occupied in imposing order upon the mingled sensations, conjectures, and conceptions within the cell of fancy in a manner analogous to the imposition of order by liver and heart upon the mixed elements of food to bring forth spirit, nutriment, and waste. (Throughout the action in Eden Milton frequently points up this analogy.[11]) Instead of operating as causes, Satan's manipulations of the fancy remain matter upon which efficient cause is exerted —the fodder of reason—and since his forgeries contain no nourishment for the mind he must endure their routine expulsion as the excrement of experience. The perfection of Eden does not imply an absence from the mind of unacceptable concepts; instead it implies a reliability of the mind to expel all thoughts and fancies which do not pertain to man's obedient love of God. Satan's attack upon the organs of fancy fails because the fancy is governed by a faculty which, even in Eden, possesses the power to deny as well as to affirm.

These issues explain the response the poet devises for Adam when he is suddenly obliged to explain his wife's unprecedented dream of disobedience. Assured that no decision of the understanding has occurred to transform mental activity into moral judgment, Adam confines his explanation to the psychological processes, providing, as he does so, the definitions useful to Milton at the outset of his development of the theme of unfallen mentality:

> But know that in the soul
> Are many lesser Faculties that serve
> Reason as chief. Among these Fancy next
> Her office holds, of all external things,
> Which the five watchful senses represent,
> She forms Imaginations, Aery shapes,
> Which Reason joining or disjoining, frames
> All what we affirm or what deny, and call
> Our knowledge or opinion; then retires
> Into her private Cell when Nature rests.
> Oft in her absence mimic Fancy wakes
> To imitate her; but misjoining shapes,
> Wild work produces oft, and most in dreams,
> Ill matching words and deeds long past or late.
> Some such resemblances methinks I find
> Of our last Ev'ning's talk, in this thy dream,
> But with addition strange; yet be not sad.
> Evil into the mind of God or Man
> May come and go, so unapprov'd, and leave
> No spot or blame behind.   (V, 100–19)

Although Adam must soon acquire additional knowledge that will complicate his responsibility in diagnosing the forgeries of the fancy, his correctness at this point in merely affirming the intrinsic security of the mind against psycho-physiological corruption is attested to by God's blessing which shortly descends upon him. Although evil itself—disloyalty to God, for example—might appear as an image in the fancy of angel or man, the understanding remains capable of detecting and expelling it without a trace of shame or regret remaining.[12] Even as he makes this assertion, Adam is using his understanding to expel the image of disobedience from Eve's mind and from his own, with such success that later Eve cannot recall it when the serpent reenacts portions of it in her presence.

At this point Adam is in no position to appreciate as fully as Milton's audience the role of providence in defending the purity of the unfallen mind. As the reader knows, Satan, in addition to stimulating Eve's fancy, had intended to inspire venom into her mind, causing a distemper that could not be instantly cleared by an act of reason. But the angelic guard arrives in time to prevent this second exercise of demonic art, and instead of the "Vain hopes, vain aims, inordinate desires" Satan had striven to implant, Eve experiences only cold horror when she witnesses the performance of the act of disobedience and simple hunger when she sees and smells the forbidden fruit. If this protective act of providence is considered along with Adam's affirmation of the mind's purgative powers, the general point of the episode remains the same: the Edenic mind is sufficiently insulated from physical impurity. Nevertheless, by introducing the threat of a chemical distempering of the mind—so meaningful to readers during the Age of Melancholy—Milton illustrates the constant working of a hidden cause without which the reason cannot function. Furthermore, by keeping knowledge of the threat from the intended victims, Milton generates suspense and interest in the theme which, at this point, he prepares for future elaboration.

But although he intends to confront Adam with a sense of the inadequacy of the mind to resist the appetites of love, Milton does not postpone the subject of the distempering of the mind by diverting it into a subconscious area from which it may later burst onto the surface of the action. Particularly puzzling, in this respect, is Fredson Bowers's reading of the incident as an imperfect clearing away of evil, in which the evil of the dream is purged but the Satanic venom remains in Eve as an infection from which "must flow her later pride that sets her in opposition to Adam." Such an infection would represent only a temporary evasion of reason, ending when "the impostume breaks within her" and the understanding is afforded the opportunity to cast it out and restore the purity of her spirits and her thoughts.[13] However, the concept of a disease gathering to a head and erupting before the restorative of reason can act runs counter to every concept of Edenic perfection and raises many questions about the justice of providence governing the Garden. (The second Adam is not exposed to so devious a temptation, although Satan does assault him with dreams.) Most of all it raises questions about the credibility of the poet, who seems to be taking elaborate pains to assure his readers that all significant thoughts, and many that are not significant, must be promptly brought before the eye of reason. Although he does not quench the theme of mental distemper with a final pronouncement, Milton does give assurance that "all was cleared" when Adam kissed away the tears standing in Eve's eyes. It would seem that the causal elements within the episode have run their course when God accepts the prayers of Adam and Eve and "to thir thoughts / Firm peace recover'd soon and wonted calm" (V, 209–10). Furthermore, the emotional condition that Milton establishes within his characters at this point is incompatible with pride festering within Eve, for the prayers she offers, together with Adam, are spontaneous and emotionally revealing. Both innocence and excitement reign during these prayers, which regularly are offered up in whatever style seems appropriate and on this day lack neither the spontaneous eloquence nor the "holy rapture" that reveal a divine evocation.

Interpreting the dream episode from the point of view of seventeenth-century psychology—that is, from the point of view of the fallen soul—Murray Bundy makes what has long been accepted as the authoritative conclusion: that the dream reveals Eve's vanity and Adam's analysis of it exhibits both an intellectual cocksureness and a fatal uxoriousness. According to this view, Reason, after showing a capacity to recognize the malicious origin of the dream and the reprehensible vanity upon which it worked, closes its eyes to both in one of the first anticipations of the fall.[14] However, the rapturous hymn discredits this interpretion, for it shows God's approval of the preceding act of reason, his willingness to inspire an eloquence of word and song that completely obliterates the Satanic forgeries. The overall movement is upward toward God, not downward toward the fall. The poet is too wise to permit uxoriousness, vanity, and intellectual pride to darken the Edenic mind at this point when he is concerned to demonstrate its security—a security resting firmly upon the protective concern of God and the purgative power of reason.

II

The mission of Raphael to Eden has a purpose directly opposite to that of the dream episode.[15] The security of the Edenic mind having been verified by the repulsion of Satan's conjuration, God next directs Raphael to warn Adam "to beware / He swerve not too secure" (V, 237–38). Sufficient though reason may be to purge the mind, its benefits may be lost by overconfidence, for without careful governance the very pleasures of Eden may become occasions of disobedience. Raphael's concern, then, is not so much with Satan as with a quality of Eden that he observes as he passes through the Garden: "Nature here / Wanton'd as in her prime, and play'd at will / Her Virgin Fancies, pouring forth more sweet, / Wild above Rule or Art, enormous bliss" (V, 294–97)—here fancy is often filled with a pleasing wildness to which understanding or discipline tend to defer. Perhaps it is with the thought of Adam and Eve accepting the pleasing irregularities of material nature as a standard for judgment that the archangel quickly begins his conversation with the assertion that nature should normally ascend toward spiritual perfection; standing firm requires one to rise by the exertions of reason aided by the loving providence of God.[16]

Once Raphael's narratives of rebellion and creation are completed, the remainder of this warning visit is given over to two episodes (Book VIII) presenting tendencies within man to swerve yet at the same time showing the sufficiency of the mind to govern these tendencies. The first demonstrates the need to be always prepared to deal with the morally indifferent ideas which the mind itself generates in great profusion and which sometimes contain the seeds of doubt and discontent. The second demonstrates the obligation of will and reason to recognize and suppress the idealized fictions created by the fancy at the behest of the affections and infused into the will with great strength and persistence. The first of these episodes, dealing with the fancies of science, comprises no significant threat to Adam since the subject is unappealingly abstruse, but in view of Raphael's praise of heavenward-tending thoughts, Adam grimly embarks upon astronomical speculations, thus driving Eve out of earshot despite her ability to understand high thoughts (49–50). When Raphael recognizes these "studious thoughts" as the natural inclination of the fancy to range into the heavens and fill the mind with ideas beyond human comprehension, Adam is overjoyed to learn that he has no responsibility for these uncertain and unrewarding speculations. Most significantly, he sees that it is from within ourselves—not from the stars —that these arid fancies arise. Raphael has left him "clear'd of doubt," "freed from intricacies" and assured that "God hath bid dwell far off all anxious cares . . . unless we ourselves / Seek them with wand'ring thoughts, and notions vain" (179–87).[17]

Now aware that he must not become too secure about his capacity to govern the fancy's impulse to rove endlessly and fill the mind with "fond impertinencies" irrelevant to the experience of daily life (188– 97), Adam enthusiastically returns to earth for his next topic, which is intended to concern his creation but which develops into an analysis of the faculties and the pleasing wildness within the mind which reason must subdue.

Adam's account of his first hours of consciousness (and of unconscious fancy) reveals a providential pattern available to the reader's apprehension but disregarded by Adam, in his excessive security, until awakened to his responsibilities by Raphael. The faculties are tested separately and successively so that Adam should be able to grasp the contribution of sensation, fancy, and reason to any perception and realize the need to interpret every impulse and image in the light of the understanding. In particular he is shown the power of fancy to portray events unavailable to the waking sense, treasurable in their vivid and moving concreteness but often distorted by the affections. Thus in lines 257–87 Adam recalls his first sensations—seeing, standing, smelling, walking, speaking, reclining, and lapsing again into unconsciousness. Even at this level there is a sense of joy and an instinct to seek the creator of the sensory world. In lines 287–309 the fancy is employed to introduce the Creator, as accommodated to the human imagination, and to provide from above a comprehensive view of Eden and its richness unavailable to the waking senses—but also apparent is the predilection of the fancy, when unchecked by judgment, to express unqualified approval at the behest of appetite: "what I saw / Of earth before scarce pleasant seem'd. Each Tree / Load'n with fairest Fruit, that hung to the Eye / Tempting, stirr'd in me sudden appetite / To pluck and eat" (305– 09). Significantly, Adam is wakened and his understanding is activated before any real or imagined employment of God's gifts can occur. The understanding is tested far more extensively (309–451) than the lower faculties, beginning with simple verification of fancied experience and proceeding through intermediate grades of activity to creative thought. It is a formal test, as God confesses at its apparent conclusion, with cues arranged to guide Adam's thought toward the area where his own pleasing wildness is most difficult to subdue—the area of love. The naming of the animals thus turns out to be a preparatory task arranged to impress Adam with his dissimilarity to the paired beasts and set him thinking about a mate for himself. When he responds with a general request, God presses him further to make careful distinctions which define his mate as primarily a companion with whom he may share the pleasures of reason. Only after Eve—Woman—has been conceived by the understanding without any distraction of sense or fancy is the Creator willing to expose Adam's mind to the most potent subrational stimulus, sexual love ("heart's desire"). At this point there is the sense of an ending, as there had been when Adam's doubts about astronomy were cleared, and both intellectual attainment and divine approval are reflected in God's closing speech:

> I, ere thou spak'st
> Knew it not good for Man to be alone,
> And no such companion as then thou saw'st
> Intended thee, for trial only brought,
> To see how thou couldst judge of fit and meet.
> What next I bring shall please thee, be assur'd,
> Thy likeness, thy fit help, thy other self,
> Thy wish, exactly to thy heart's desire.   (444–51)

Despite the sense of accomplishment, however, the mind has merely been readied for the crucial test which now occurs, and Milton maximizes the intensity of the test by subtly comparing the effect of beauty upon the mind to Satan's earlier-averted threat, the inspiration of emotionally disturbing stimulants into the brain. Furthermore, God chooses to introduce this last gift, as he had the Garden itself, to Adam's fancy unchecked by wakened reason.[18] Consequently, when Adam has been overcome with sleep, leaving only the cell of fancy open and the judgment inoperative, he is unable to resist the impulse to respond with uncritical superlatives. Just as the fancied view of the Garden surpassed any earthly beauty he had previously seen, so now the vision of woman exceeds every value he had conceived. Within an instant the bloody rib in the hand of God emerges into a creature

> so lovely fair,
> That what seem'd fair in all the World, seem'd now
> Mean, or in her summ'd up, in her contain'd
> And in her looks, which from that time infus'd
> Sweetness into my heart, unfelt before
> And into all things from her Air inspir'd
> The spirit of love and amorous delight.   (471–77)

Obviously the image will have a lasting effect since it is "infused into the heart" (a phrase with dire connotations used by Raphael to describe Satan's conquest of the drowsy Beelzebub); reason will be severely challenged to make the concept of the rational helpmeet prevail over this image of amorous sweetness.

As Adam sits recounting these mental events to Raphael, it becomes clear that the experience of wooing and winning the flesh-and-blood Eve has not diminished the power of fancy's image in his mind. Although his judgment advises him that the picture is an hyperbolical extension of the truth, the preeminence of the fancied image persists:

> . . . well I understand in the prime end
> Of Nature her th' inferior, in the mind
> And inward Faculties, which most excel,
>
> .   .   .   .
>
> yet when I approach
> Her loveliness, so absolute she seems
> And in herself complete, so well to know
> Her own, that what she wills to do or say,
> Seems wisest, virtuousest, discreetest, best.   (540–51)

The projection of the heart has become a goddess, an idol that the mind inclines to worship (553). But Adam accepts this irregularity as an unimportant eccentricity of nature, noting that he is "in all enjoyments else / Superior and unmov'd, here only weak / Against the charm of Beauty's powerful glance. / Or Nature fail'd in mee, and left some part / Not proof enough such Object to sustain" (531–35).

Clearly Adam has been led into a position in which his excessive security is embarrassingly visible. Whereas he had been troubled by apparent disproportions in Nature's governance of the stars, he is unconcerned by Nature's carelessness in the design of his own mentality. The fancy inspired during the suspension of his judgment exists in striking juxtaposition to the reasoned concept of the helpmeet, yet he willingly tolerates the inconsistency. Although the affirmative quality of reason is operating, the critical function is quiescent. The fanciful image of Eve, like "wanton" Eden, is not in itself reprehensible except insofar as Adam regards its poetic truths literally, bringing it into conflict with reason instead of firmly fitting it into the mind as a complement of the abstractly understood helpmeet. At the point where Eve's beauty, rich enough to inspire fancy's image of a goddess, impels Adam to dismiss the concept of the helpmeet and begin to worship the goddess image, obedience to God becomes impossible. What is needed is not Satan's contempt of fancy's hyperbole ("cease to admire, and all her Plumes / Fall flat and shrink into a trivial toy"[19]) but a sense of control and proportion.

Milton has carefully prepared the way for Raphael's rebuttal, which consists of a flat denial that nature has left any weakness in the mind and an assertion that Adam's judgment retains its potency if permitted to exercise its critical power. Knowing that he is superior to Eve, he must assert his superiority and thus bring under control the poetic image that threatens to rule not only his own mind but Eve's as well. The problem that Raphael discerns is not an impostume gathering in Eve's mind from Satan's infection but a hypertrophy of the fancy acquired in emulation of her husband. The unreal role of goddess is inspired by Adam's deference rather than by Satan's subliminal suggestions. The antidote is a gradually attained discipline which Adam must first apply to himself. The more he bases his actions upon the reasoned concept of his own superiority "The more she will acknowledge thee her Head / And to realities yield all her shows" (574–75). Adam is only "half abashed" at Raphael's comments because he has been only half-reproved: "In loving thou dost well, in passion not." And his response is to affirm those reasonable qualities in his relations with Eve which delight him far more than the appetitive element in love. Furthermore, he asserts that his freedom of choice is unimpaired—he is not foiled by what he feels. Once more he is prepared to resume the ascending movement of mind and appropriately requests Raphael to describe the love of purely spiritual beings. Although the archangel's answer is little more than a quarter as long as Adam's rhapsodic praise of the goddess image, it is nevertheless a fittingly affirmative statement, joyous without the unreasonable superlatives that characterize the utterances of the fancy:

> Easier than Air with Air, if Spirits embrace,
> Total they mix, Union of Pure with Pure
> Desiring; nor restrain'd conveyance need
> As Flesh to mix with Flesh, or Soul with Soul. (VIII, 626–29)

Again reason's sovereignty is affirmed and the note of rapture that preceded Raphael's coming is sounded again as he prepares to depart. Book VIII ends with the strong expectation that Adam will soon be given opportunity to subdue the wild fancy that has suddenly appeared as a rival to reason. If he succeeds, reason will attain new freedom and love will hold greater spiritual delights than it has heretofore.

Obviously nothing accidental has occurred. All the attitudes which critics see as premonitions of fall are systematically implanted by God or evoked as exercises needed to strengthen the mind and free the understanding from the distractions of the disorderly, the exotic, and the fictitious. The normal flow of matter up to spirit requires both the irritants of mind and the expulsive or disciplining reaction by which the mind is purged or balanced. Throughout Books IV, V, and VIII such exercises of mind have produced happiness, rapture, and incentive to exercise more choices each day of eternity. No inevitabilities face Adam and Eve at this moment and there is great likelihood (for all who can suspend foreknowledge) that they will be endlessly victorious, endlessly rising until their spiritual maturity is attained. Already they are less likely to fall than they had been before Eve's dream or Raphael's visit; for Satan the chances of successfully tempting them are depressingly slim.

III

One last step remains to prepare the Edenic mind for its confrontation with the Prince of Darkness: Eve's mind must be stabilized, as Adam's has been, to prevent the swervings that affect the overly secure. Although she has heard portions of Raphael's discourse, she remains hampered, as Adam had been, by the presence within her fancy of a distorted image of her completeness and self-sufficiency, and Adam bears the responsibility to purge her mind of this fiction—and to avoid its reestablishment within his own mind. The lecture on the faculties that had comforted Eve after her dream now requires revision in the light of Satan's invasion of Eden and Adam's warier view of the mind. The

occasion for such a new commentary arises quite naturally on the morning following Raphael's departure when Eve makes a routine request
to work apart from Adam during the morning hours. To his objection
that Satan's presence makes separation hazardous, she cites the confidence in reason's expulsive power that he had expressed earlier. If evil
into the mind of god or man may come and go, so unapproved, and leave
no spot or blame behind, then each unfallen soul, unassisted by aught
but its own reason, is capable of repelling Satan, whose only target is
the mind. It is an affirmative and reverent answer, supported by her reasonable assertion that a loving god would not create man so imperfectly
that he could not resist temptation. But although her argument is sound,
her conception of the confrontation with Satan is colored by her self-
image as a person "absolute and in herself complete," which in this instance prompts timocratic visions of honor:

> [Satan's] foul esteem
> Sticks no dishonor on our front, but turns
> Foul on himself; then wherefore shunn'd or fear'd
> By us? who rather double honor gain
> From his surmise prov'd false, find peace within,
> Favor from Heav'n, our witness from th' event.
> And what is Faith, Love, Virtue unassay'd
> Alone, without exterior help sustain'd?   (IX, 329–36)

Eve's questions call forth Adam's new statement on the faculties, which
for twenty-seven lines affirms both the providence of God and the perfection of his gift of reason yet takes into account the danger of deception or self-deception: "Reason [God] made right, / But bid her well
beware, and still erect, / Lest by some fair appearing good surpris'd /
She dictate false, and misinform the Will / To do what God expressly
hath forbid" (IX, 352–56). Eve's excessive security needs just the antidote that Adam's discourse provides, and her pretensions to honorable
combat call for just the sort of polite depreciation that Adam confers
upon them: "who can know, / Not seeing thee attempted, who attest?"
(IX, 368–69). The high point of his reply, however, is his recognition
that reason operates only as a function of God's providence.[20] Whereas
he had been content to deal with proximate cause in his earlier speech
he now argues from the perspective of ultimate cause. Although one
must remain watchful, he notes, reason can succeed only if the terms of
trial are kept within the competence of the human understanding (not,

for example, requiring a knowledge of astronomy). Trial will come un-sought—in the terms God provides, not our own. To show her constancy to God, Eve need not present herself in the guise of a warrior goddess but rather as an obedient wife accepting her husband's counsel (as she had done after the dream).

Eve's right to enjoy moments of solitude in Eden are beyond ques-tioning, but it is essential that Adam reassert his natural superiority by winning the present debate, and his speech is so cogent and so appropri-ate in every respect that his victory seems assured.[21] The sufficiency of reason to promote man's rise to angelic spirituality is never more ap-parent than at this moment. Nor does Adam falter in the closing sen-tence of his speech, as is frequently asserted; instead he chooses to end with a suggestion "for trial only" that is meant to evoke a reasonable response as had been God's suggestion that he find companionship among the animals.[22] In the present instance Adam, hoping that Eve will discern the tide of providence upon which reason floats, proposes that she may work apart from him, after all, if she will justify the separa-tion on the grounds of vigilance. To avoid being surprised during his hours of routine security, a person may expose himself to evil and thus guarantee that he will be fully alert for the ensuing encounter. Eve's proper reply should be that this is carnal reliance or carnal security, for it eliminates the providential role in determining the conditions of trial and assumes that man is not normally vigilant.[23] By choosing the unrea-sonable alternative she exposes her unreadiness to resist the frauds of Satan and places Adam under a moral imperative to require her close presence. Failure to repudiate the false choice he had presented, par-ticularly when Eve characterizes it as his "last reasoning words," would implicate him in her unreason and carnal security. But duty is hard, for it obligates him to display an even greater severity toward Eve than Ra-phael had shown toward him, and when the moment comes for the at-tractive goddess to become the half-abashed helpmeet his will fails. Obviously he has fallen beneath the spell of the goddess image as he stands speechless, delighting his eye upon Eve's beauties and "Goddess-like desport."

The turn toward self-management, away from providence, thus comes with startling suddenness at the end of a dialogue in which obedi-ence to God's will has been continually asserted. It is a reversal, similar to the Aristotelian reversal in showing characters suddenly dominated

by fate but dissimilar in that nothing has been fated until this moment
when the power of decision is abruptly surrendered by Adam. Throughout his speech Adam had appeared to be a man of reason rather than
of fancy; Eve, too, despite the emotional edge that crept into her utterances, remained obedient and faithful until Adam supplied irrational
words for her approval. With the removal of the providential support,
however, reason and spirit appear to be totally subdued, leaving Adam
and Eve fated to respond to the promptings of their emotions with the
predictability of Pavlov's dogs. Deep irony pervades statements like
Eve's "Reason is our law," and every act brings the human mind downward toward the nadir of Eve's genuflection before the Tree of Knowledge and show of obeisance to the power that had infused "sciental sap"
into its fruit (IX, 835–37). So completely are the minds of Adam and Eve
ruled by fancy that when Eve returns fallen and false Adam addresses
the goddess image, not the real woman, comparing her to the best efforts
of the imagination:

> O fairest of Creation, last and best
> Of all God's works, Creature in whom excell'd
> Whatever can to sight or thought be form'd,
> Holy, divine, good, amiable, or sweet!   (IX, 896–99)

As they share the forbidden fruit, both Adam and Eve experience a
single fancy—a dream that wings are growing to carry them to heaven
(IX, 1009–11)—and this constitutes the chemical distempering sought
originally by Satan in his conjurations but now self-administered by his
intended victims. Upon awakening they find that their inmost powers
of fancy and reason have erred, and their understanding is forever
dimmed:

> Soon as the force of that fallacious Fruit
> That with exhilarating vapor bland
> About thir spirits had play'd, and inmost powers
> Made err, was now exhal'd, and grosser sleep
> Bred of unkindly fumes, with conscious dreams
> Encumber'd, now had left them, up they rose
> As from unrest, and each the other viewing
> Soon found thir Eyes how open'd, and thir minds
> How dark'n'd.   (IX, 1046–54)

Thus ends with great finality one line of development of the theme of
the mind that had begun with Satan's attack upon the animal spirits of

Eve's mind. The buoyancy of mind that maintained a constant movement upward toward spiritual perfection now is lost and must be reestablished by new acts of providence. The fall, when it occurs, comes from a height that has been attained and is painful and impressive because so much is lost. It is, as Milton describes it in *De Doctrina*, a spiritual death—sudden, violent, and destructive of a condition of life. It is not, as many critics would have it, the last fluttering heartbeat of a life wasted to the point of extinction.

University of Massachusetts, Amherst

NOTES

1. Criticism of Milton's Eden has been dominated by the premise that unfallen man is inconceivable. Since this thesis received its ultimate formulation in Millicent Bell's "The Fallacy of the Fall in *Paradise Lost*," *PMLA*, LXVIII (1958), 863–83, there has been dissent, beginning with Dennis Burden, *The Logical Epic: A Study of the Argument of "Paradise Lost"* (Cambridge, Mass., 1967), J. M. Evans, *"Paradise Lost" and the Genesis Tradition* (Oxford, 1968), and Stanley Fish, *Surprised by Sin* (New York, 1969), and culminating in Diane Kelsey McColley, "Free Will and Obedience in the Separation Scene of *Paradise Lost*," *SEL*, XII (1972), 103–20, and Stella P. Revard, "Eve and the Doctrine of Responsibility in *Paradise Lost*," *PMLA*, LXXXVIII (1973), 69–78. My statement of the problem was written too early to benefit from the contributions of McColley and Revard, both of whom find in Milton's Adam and Eve a sufficiency to stand.

2. *The Earthly Paradise and the Renaissance Epic* (Princeton, 1966), p. 303.

3. *Some Graver Subject: An Essay on "Paradise Lost"* (New York, 1960), p. 197.

4. Except where otherwise specified, citations follow the text of Merritt Y. Hughes, *John Milton: Complete Poems and Major Prose* (New York, 1957).

5. Broadbent, *Some Graver Subject*, p. 197.

6. Hughes, *Complete Poems and Major Prose*, p. 733.

7. See, for example, John Davies of Hereford's *Mirum in Modum* (1602), stanzas 30–34, in *Complete Works of John Davies*, ed. A. Grosart, I (New York, 1967), pp. 6–7. See also J. B. Bamborough, *The Little World of Man* (London, 1952), pp. 36–40.

8. As Davies of Hereford points out, fancy can range through hell as easily as through heaven (*Mirum in Modum*, stanza 31), *Complete Works*, I, 8.

9. Robert Burton, *The Anatomy of Melancholy*, ed. Floyd Dell and Paul Jordan-Smith (New York, 1927), I, i, 7, p. 140.

10. Hughes, *Complete Poems and Major Prose*, p. 675.

11. Note, for example, Raphael's comment on the digestion of mental food (VII, 126–30) and Adam's description of conversation as "food of the mind" (IX, 239).

12. Davies of Hereford indicates that the thoughts disapproved by the understanding are consigned to oblivion unless reason approves their retention by the memory. "[Reason] rules *Sans* check, then doomes without appeale, / No second sentence can hirs contradict; / She rules alone the whole *Mindes* common weale, / By

holsome *Heasts*, and *Lawes*, and *Iudgements* strict; / Which to the *Memory* she doth reueale, / Else it *Obliuion* would interdict" (*Complete Works*, I, 8).

13. "Adam, Eve, and the Fall in *Paradise Lost*," *PMLA*, LXXXIV (March 1969), 269.

14. "Eve's Dream and Temptation in *Paradise Lost*," *Research Studies*, State College of Washington, X (Pullman, Wash., 1942), 289.

15. Fish, *Surprised by Sin*, p. 234, endorses Northrop Frye's view that the great events of *Paradise Lost* should be read "as a discontinuous series of crises" in which the most important factor is not the consequences of previous actions (*The Return of Eden* [Toronto, 1965], pp. 102–03). The evidence I am presenting, however, suggests that a pattern emerges even among apparently unrelated events.

16. Evans, *Genesis Tradition*, p. 269.

17. It is difficult to reconcile the sentiments in these lines with Russell E. Smith's claim that throughout the dialogue with Raphael Adam is consumed with an intemperate desire for knowledge, "Adam's Fall," *ELH*, XXV (December 1968), 527–39.

18. Evans, *Genesis Tradition*, pp. 261–65, traces the long history of the legends concerning Adam's dream and notes that Milton rejected most of the legendary material and treated the dream in accordance with his own literary purposes. The passage remains rather pointless, however, until one grasps the contrast between the reasoned and the fanciful pictures of woman that the dream provides.

19. *Paradise Regained*, II, 222–23.

20. "Our light of knowledge will soon grow dimme, if we securely content our selves with that we have, and do not more illuminate our understanding by the light of Gods Word, from which (as the light of the Moone from the Sunne) is was first borrowed" (John Downame, *A Treatise of Security* [London, 1622], p. 57).

21. At this point when the two disputants have fallen into the roles of Reason (Adam) vs. Fancy (Eve), Reason must establish control over Fancy.

22. Bowers, "Adam, Eve, and the Fall," p. 271, presents this reading as an attractive alternative to his present interpretation. He does not note the resemblance of the speech to God's trial of Adam nor does he observe that the issue at this point is unassisted reason vs. reason relying upon providential aid.

23. In *De Doctrina Christiana*, Milton classifies carnal security as a condition opposed to the fear of God, one of the virtues whose exercise is the internal worship of God. The Columbia *Works of John Milton*, ed. Frank Allen Patterson et al., 18 vols. (New York, 1931–38), XVII, 63.

"MY NATIVE ELEMENT":
MILTON'S PARADISE
AND ENGLISH GARDENS

Charlotte F. Otten

Although Milton's Paradise has classical and pastoral antecedents, it contains many native English elements. The herbals, gardening manuals, and "Paradise" gardens of Milton's day feed his epic, making his Garden more real than the "feigned" gardens of mythology. It is Milton's willingness to incorporate in his "delicious Paradise" some of the features of the actual gardens of his day and the practices of contemporary gardeners that makes him able to bridge the gap between the mythical and the real, between Art and Nature. The comparison of eight horticultural features of Milton's Garden with English garden materials (location, pure air, trees, flowers, furnishings, walks and alleys, bower, gardening) brings out the vitality of his Paradise and shows his epic couple participating in a thoroughly human experience.

THAT MILTON's Garden was supposed to excel all other gardens is obvious from Milton's text: his Paradise is better than Enna's "faire field," Daphne's "sweet Grove," the Nyseian Ile, and Mount Amara (IV, 267–85); better than the gardens of Adonis, Alcinous, and Solomon (IX, 439–43). Adam and Eve's Bower of Bliss is to be preferred to that of Pan, Silvanus, and Faunus (IV, 707–08) and the fruit of their Garden to that of India East or West, Pontus's middle shore, the Punic Coast, and Alcinous's garden (V, 339–41). Giamatti observes, "Milton's ostensible task was to make the earthly paradise in Book IV perfect and delightful, and out of allusions to and reminiscences of almost every Biblical, classical, modern, and 'real' garden he could find, he composed his own complete, integrated vision."[1] However, the abundant commentary on Milton's Garden deals only rarely with the "real" garden. By the "real" garden I mean the English gardens of Milton's day, with which he would have been familiar either from observation or from reading about them in the garden manuals and herbals available to him in England.

There has been resistance, however, to the notion of a real garden. Joseph Warton's criticism in 1753 that the fountains, flowers, and trees of Milton's Paradise "are easily feigned, but [have] no relative beauty as pictures of nature, nor any absolute excellence as derived from truth" is echoed by Eliot and Leavis.[2] John R. Knott, arguing for the pastoral rather than the literal garden, suggests that we must "take some things on faith: thornless roses, an unvarying climate, and fruit of 'golden rind.' "[3]

At first glance Milton's Garden appears to be one massive paradisiacal cliché, but a second look uncovers native English materials in the construction of the Garden itself, in the furnishings, gardening tools, the semitechnical horticultural terminology, and the rural practices associated with husbandry. The question, therefore, that I should like to consider is this: If Milton's Garden did not owe everything to its paradisiacal antecedents, what parts of that Garden have their roots in English soil and in English horticulture?

One need not travel so far in Milton's world as Broadbent suggests —to the Pison or the Ganges, to the Persian Gulf of "Golden Sand," or to Morocco or the Bermudas—to find contemporary analogues, sources, and influences for Milton's Garden.[4] England itself contained paradisiacal gardens. The added subtlety is this: that the Englishman's garden was partly modelled on the idea of the Genesis Paradise, and Milton's Genesis Paradise was partly drawn from the English gardens. Although the description in Genesis is admittedly vague, the dream of a Paradise garden like Eden runs strong in English garden literature and is still regarded as an ideal in England today.[5] John Parkinson's *Paradisi in Sole Paradisus Terrestris* is an excellent illustration of the paradisiacal impulse in gardening. On his title page Parkinson pictures not an English rural couple of the seventeenth century but Adam and Eve at work in the Garden: Adam is gathering fruit from a tree while Eve is propping up a drooping flower. Though the book was designed as a practical gardening manual, not as an illustrated commentary on the opening chapters of Genesis, Parkinson cannot begin his book without acknowledging the Source of all successful gardening: "But my purpose is onely to shew you that Paradise was a place (whether you will call it a Garden, or

Orchard, or both, no doubt of some large extent) wherein Adam was first placed to abide; that God was the Planter thereof, hauing furnished it with trees and herbes, as well pleasant to the sight as good for meate, and that hee being to dresse and keep this place, must of necessity know all the things that grew therein, and to what uses they serued, or else his labour about them, and knowledge in them, had been in vaine."[6]

The herbalist John Gerard describes the English gardens (his own herbal garden was famous) as though each little plot is an Hesperian Paradise: "what greater delight is there than to behold the earth apparelled with plants, as with a robe of embroidered worke, set with Orient pearles and garnished with great diuersitie of rare and costly jewels? If this varietie and perfection of colours may affect the eie, it is such in herbs and floures, that no *Apelles*, no *Zeuxis* euer could by any art expresse the like . . . setting forth to vs the inuisible wisdome and admirable workmanship of Almighty God."[7]

Milton, like Parkinson and Gerard, refers to God as the "sovran Planter" (IV, 691; IV, 209–10), and all three draw from Genesis ii, 8 as the authoritative statement on the subject. It must also be noted that, while Milton's description of Paradise has hyperbole in it, often stressing that which rises above the imaginable and that which is unattainable on this stained earth, it is precisely this same hyperbolic diction that Parkinson and Gerard use in describing the actual English gardens of their day. Gerard revels in words like "apparelled with plants," "robe of embroidered worke," "Orient pearles," and "garnished with rare and costly jewels." And it is Milton who sounds like an echo with "broiderd the ground," (IV, 702), "stone / Of costliest Emblem" (IV, 702–03), "wrought / Mosaic" (IV, 699–700), and "Orient Pearle" (V, 2).

Of course the exotic gardens of the East are thick with fragrances exuded by trees, shrubs, and flowers. Solomon's garden of the Canticles boasts mountains of myrrh and hills of frankincense (IV, 6). No less fragrant are the Christian Latin Paradises. Milton's Garden shares in this love of fragrances: the trees drop myrrh (V, 23) and "rich Trees wept odorous Gumms and Balme" (IV, 248); his Eve is "Veild in a Cloud of Fragrance" (IX, 425). Though the concern for fragrance has its Eastern and Christian antecedents, it is also a vital part of the English garden scene. Eleanour Rohde observes: "the gardens of our Elizabethan ancestors were indeed scented gardens. It is perhaps not too much to say that in no other period of our history were the scents of flowers so keenly appreciated."[8] Parkinson's *Paradisi* is like an alabaster box of fragrance: he describes the Damaske Rose as "of the most excellent sweet pleasant sent, far surpassing all other Roses or Flowers."[9] And Gerard says that "if odours or if taste may worke satisfaction, they are both so soueraigne in plants, and so comfortable that no confection of the Apothecaries can equal their excellent vertue."[10] So scientific a man as Francis Bacon cannot extol scents enough in "Of Gardens": "God Almighty first planted a garden and indeed, it is the purest of human pleasures. . . . And because the breath of flowers is far sweeter in the air (where it comes and goes, like the warbling of music) than in the hand, therefore nothing is more fit for that delight, than to know what be the flowers and plants that do best perfume the air."[11] He follows this with a catalogue of fragrances. Knott states that Milton "goes far beyond the customary brief reference to rich odors," but a survey of the ever-popular herbals and gardening manuals shows that references to odors are neither brief nor unusual.[12] What may strike today's reader as "Eastern exotic" or as pastoral would have struck Milton's contemporaries as "English normal." For the Englishman did not think it presumptuous to choose as the title of his gardening manual *The Garden of Eden, or An accurate Description of all Flowers and Fruits now growing in England.*[13]

The Englishman, whether a rural Gervase Markham or a sophisticated William Temple, whether owner of a plat or a park, considered his own little piece of Paradise as his most personal possession. Milton, too, delighted in gardens and was familiar with gardening techniques. In *A Second Defence* he alludes to the subject of gardening, to parterres, to grafting, to "a most delectable walk." And in *Animadversions* he describes horticultural practices in detail.[14] According to John Aubrey, "After dinner he used to walk three or four hours at a time. He always had a garden where he lived."[15] David Masson's description of the "rich, teeming, verdurous flat" of Horton sounds like a chapter out of a gardening manual.[16] Milton's house at Aldersgate Street was situated in a garden; his house in Westminster had a garden which opened into Saint James's Park; and his final house in the Artillery Walk leading to Bunhill Fields in the parish of Saint Giles, Cripplegate, had a "considerable garden in the rear," where Milton was often seen by the villagers.[17] His description of the "happy rural seat" (IV, 247) of Paradise with its "Hill and Dale and Plaine" (IV, 243) springs from his own rural experience. Broadbent finds so much of England in the "happy rural seat" that he considers it "almost laughably the England of Penshurst, Cooper's Hill and Appleton House." [18]

Milton's Paradise also has something of the more lavish English gardens in it. Certain aspects of William Temple's Moor Park resemble Paradise and certain aspects of Milton's Paradise resemble Moor Park. The very knowledgeable Sir William, who had spent the greater part of his life abroad and who had seen most impressive state gardens, found no place on earth to equal the beauty of Moor Park: "It lies on the side of a hill . . . the border of the walk set with standard laurels, and at large distances, which have the beauty of orange trees. . . . The lower garden . . . is all fruit trees ranged about the several quarters of a wilderness which is very shady; the walks here are all green." [19]

To point out the "English" in Milton's Paradise is not at all to deny the presence of the traditional "inszenierende Staffage" ("landscape clichés") in Milton's Garden. As Curtius observes in *European Literature and the Latin Middle Ages*, an idyllic garden has standard furnishings: "From Homer's landscapes later generations took certain motifs which became permanent elements in a long chain of tradition: the place of heart's desire, beautiful with perpetual spring . . . the lovely miniature landscape which combines tree, spring, and grass; the wood with various species of trees; the carpet of flowers." [20] That Milton's Paradise owes something to Homer and Ovid, to Stephanus and Conti, is apparent. His Paradise "assimilates and refines upon the whole European tradition of paradises, gardens, pleasances, fortunate isles, and lands of the blessed as subjects for conventional description." [21] But the presence of the English horticultural elements operates as a modifying interpretive force. The construction of his Paradise is not so different from that of contemporary English gardens. It is Milton's willingness to incorporate in his "delicious Paradise" (IV, 132) some of the features of the actual gardens of his day that makes him able to bridge the gap between the mythical and the real, between the fictional and the historical, even between Art and Nature. Just as his Adam and Eve are not merely epic characters but are real people requiring medication for ocular disturbances (XI, 411–16), so his Adam and Eve must have a recognizably real garden.

Since Adam and Eve are both particular and universal, the universal nature of their Garden cannot be brushed aside. As Lawrence Babb points out in *The Moral Cosmos of "Paradise Lost,"* "Milton represents

Paradise with vivid but general imagery. . . . The poet has assembled generic images of sight, sound, and odor which collectively call up a vision of natural luxuriance and profusion, beautiful beyond anything which we can ever hope to see but which could have been when the world was young."[22] Those generic images, which evoke the beauties of an unspoiled world, are so vivid because they are not apophatic. Milton's universal garden, not the negation of all particular gardens, is the affirmation of the good in all of them. If the image of a completely universal garden were not permeated by particular gardens, it would be inconceivable and unimaginable. Milton's memory of particular gardens, including English "Paradises" of his day, contributes to the vitality and the cataphatic quality of his Paradise. Support for this view can be established by a comparison of the following eight horticultural features of Milton's Garden with contemporary English garden materials.

1. LOCATION

High; enclosed; with a mount: "Crowns with her enclosure green, / As with a rural mound" (IV, 133–34).

A view of the "neather Empire neighbouring round" (IV, 135–45).

Milton's mount has not only mythology in it but contemporary geography. E. M. Clark observes: "it is securely planted upon the summit of a 'rural mount,' corresponding to any Abyssinian amba, which geographers describe as a conical and almost inaccessible sandstone rock or mount rising anywhere from one hundred to three thousand feet above the surrounding plain."[23] But the mount was also an essential feature of an English garden because it provided a view. Bacon's elaborate garden requires a mount in the middle "with three ascents and alleys enough for four to walk abreast . . . and the whole mount to be thirty feet high."[24] And Lawson's *A New Orchard and Garden* gives explicit instructions for the construction of four corner mounts in a small garden.[25] John Evelyn's description of the view at Cliveden surpasses them all: "I went to *Clifden* that stupendious natural Rock, Wood & Prospect of the Duke of Buckinghams. . . . the place alltogether answers the most poetical description that can be made of a solitude, precipice, prospects & whatever can contribute to a thing so very like their imaginations. . . . on the platforme is a circular View to the uttmost verge of the Horison, which with the serpenting of the *Thames* is admirably surprising."[26] Late in the epic it is the Mount of Paradise that

Adam and Michael ascend, "from whose top / The Hemisphere of Earth in cleerest Ken / Stretcht out to amplest reach of prospect lay" (XI, 378–80); and it is the Mount of Paradise that is moved out of its place after the fall (XI, 829–35).

The notion of enclosing a garden did not originate in the Renaissance. Springing from the East and represented in many pictures and expositions of medieval gardens, the enclosing of a garden was as much a practical matter as an aesthetic one. Both Milton's Paradise and the English gardens required protection. An English gardener like Thomas Hill would not have had to go to Abyssinia to understand the need for a barrier. In fact, his small garden called for a double enclosure: "for that Gardens being not well fenced and closed . . . is many ways endamaged, as well by beastes, as by Theues, breaking into it." [27]

As might be expected, Milton chooses natural barriers for his Paradise: a thicket (IV, 136) of undergrowth of shrubs and bushes (IV, 175–76); high trees (IV, 139); a stand of fruit trees inside the barrier for a double enclosure (IV, 147). John Evelyn takes intense delight in a proper barrier: "Is there under *Heaven* a more glorious and refreshing object of the kind, than an impregnable *Hedge* of *one hundred* and *sixty foot* in *length, seven* foot *high*, and *five* in diameter, which I can shew in my poor *Gardens* at any time of the year, glitt'ring with its arm'd and vernish'ed *leaves*? the taller *Standards* at the rudest assaults of the *Weather, Beasts,* or *Hedge-breakers, Et illum nemo impunè lacessit.*"[28]

Ralph Austen chooses tall trees to shelter fruit trees, as Milton does for Paradise. Praising walnut trees specifically for their "exceeding great height, and bigness," Austen insists that the use of trees "that naturally grow great and high" will be very profitable for the protection of fruit trees.[29]

2. Pure Air

Air so pure that it is a source of "vernal delight and joy, able to drive / All sadness but despair" (IV, 155–56).

Of course a proper Paradise must have pure air. The seventeenth century, perhaps as much as the twentieth, understood what smoke and sulphur, what stink and darkness meant. Milton refers to the city as a place "where Houses thick and Sewers annoy the Aire" (IX, 446); and Evelyn describes Londoners of 1661 as "pursu'd and haunted by that infernal smoake." "Sir," he says in the epistolary introduction to his

Fumifugium, "I prepare in this short Discourse, an expedient how this pernicious *Nuisance* may be reformed; and offer at another also, by which the Aer may not only be freed . . . but render not only Your Majesties Palace, but the whole City likewise, one of the sweetest, and most delicious Habitations in the World . . . by improving those Plantations which Your Majesty so laudably affects, in the moyst, depressed and Marshy Grounds about the Town, to the culture and production of such things, as upon every gentle emission through the Aer, should so perfume the adjacent places with their breath; as if, by a certain charm, or innocent *Magick,* they were transferred to that part of *Arabia,* which is therefore styl'd the *Happy,* because it is amongst the Gums and precious spices. . . . And, I am able to enumerate a Catalogue of native *Plants* . . . whose redolent and agreeable emissions would even ravish our senses, as well as perfectly improve and meliorate the Aer about London."[30]

While Evelyn is reporting scientific facts, it is remarkable that Milton's paradisiacal diction coincides at various points with Evelyn's:

> now gentle gales
> Fanning thir odoriferous wings dispense
> Native perfumes, and whisper whence they stole
> Those balmie spoiles. As when to them who sails
> Beyond the *Cape of Hope,* and now are past
> *Mozambic,* off at Sea North-East windes blow
> *Sabean* Odours from the spicie shoare
> Of *Arabie* the blest, with such delay
> Well pleas'd they slack thir course, and many a League
> Cheard with the grateful smell old Ocean smiles.   (IV, 156–65)

It is precisely in the context of pure air that Milton alludes to "*Arabie* the blest," "odoriferous wings," "Native perfumes," and "balmie spoiles." Whether Milton's diction is due to the influence of Diodorus Siculus or of Evelyn is difficult to determine, though the date of Evelyn's work makes it a doubtful influence. If verbal similarity is the test, then it is Evelyn (or perhaps some source, for Evelyn was a great borrower) who influenced Milton. But, more importantly, it is Evelyn describing a state *attainable* in England.[31]

Air so potent as to be able to dispel sadness is more than a piece of standardized Paradise equipment for Milton and his contemporaries. Basing their arguments on physiology, Renaissance physicians and gardeners were convinced that fruit trees are healthful, both physically and psychologically. Ralph Austen is perhaps the most articulate of the writers on the salutary effects of fruit trees:

> But chiefly the *Pleasure this sense* meets with is from the *sweet smelling blossomes* of all the fruit-trees, which from the time of their breaking forth, till their fall, breath out a most precious and pleasant odor; perfuming the ayre throughout all the Orchard. . . .
>
> And besides the *pleasure* of this perfumed ayre, it is also very profitable, and healthfull to the body. Here againe, *Profit and pleasure* meet and imbrace. *An Odores nutriunt*, is a question amongst *Philosophers*: some hold sweet perfumes nourishing, doubtlesse they give a great refreshing to the spirits, and whatsoever delights and cheers the spirits is without controversie very advantagious to the health of the body; for the spirits are the chiefe workers in the body, from which proceed all, or most of the effects wrought in the body, good or bad, according to the temper of the spirits.
>
> *Sweet perfumes* work immediatly upon the spirits for their refreshing. . . . sweet and healthfull Ayres are speciall preservatives to health, and therefore much to be prised.[32]

Eve's awareness of the role that fruit trees play in creating pure air makes her lament, "how shall we breath in other Aire / Less pure, accustomed to immortal Fruits?" (XI, 284–85) This is no idle, irrational babbling on her part; nor is it elliptical speech. If she could have talked with Bentley, Pearce, and Empson, she would have explained to them the relationship of fruit trees to pure air. Empson finds it necessary to view these lines as "something like a pun in the way she is enabled at once to sum up her argument and trail away in the weakness of her appeal; it is a delicate piece of brushwork such as seems blurred until you step back."[33] No piece of brushwork this; Milton has simply endowed Eve with a piece of common knowledge of the seventeenth century: "Now, a *sweet perfumed, fresh, wholsome* Ayre (which is chiefly found in *Gardens of fruit-trees*) is greatly available to the Preservative purpose."[34]

3. TREES

"All Trees of noblest kind for sight, smell, taste" (IV, 217); "fruit burnisht with Golden Rinde" (IV, 249); "fruit of all kindes, in coate, / Rough, or smooth rin'd, or bearded husk, or shell" (V, 341–42); "earthly fruits" (V, 464); "immortal Fruits" (XI, 285).

Milton's choice of trees pleasant to the sight is more than a piece of aestheticism.[35] His contemporary world believed in the health-giving

properties of things pleasant to the sight. Ralph Austen sums up current
arguments for pleasant sights: "Likewise, *the sight* is delighted with
pleasant and delicate *Colours of the Leaves, Blossomes, and Fruits,* That
shew themselves in great variety. . . . especially the *Colour greene* is accounted helpfull to the sight. . . . *Objects of the sight, as comming into
a faire Garden . . . doe delight and exhilarate the spirits much.*"[36] It is
difficult to identify the native English fruit trees in Milton's Paradise.
Since no vegetable life was subject to death in the prelapsarian world,
all "earthly" fruits in Paradise were "immortal"; the false fruit was
"mortal" only in the sense that it "Brought Death into the World" (I,
3). The four specific fruits mentioned by Milton are grape, berry, apple,
and nectarine, though this may be only a reference to all Paradise fruits
which are filled with the traditional nectar. English gardens, able to
compete with the finest of conventional Paradises, contained at least
some of the following: peaches, nectarines, grapes, figs, apricots, pears,
plums, apples (including Golden Pippin).[37] In addition, Milton describes some fruit as having a golden rind and the fruit of the Tree of
Life as "vegetable Gold" (IV, 220). "Vegetable Gold" has provoked
much commentary; it is indeed a "strange phrase . . . attributing life
and growth to a mineral substance."[38] On the other hand, "vegetable
Gold" might not have seemed so strange to Milton's world, for whom
the Golden Pippin was the brightest and best of fruits. Moreover, there
is an account of the banqueting house at Whitehall where "the roof was
wrought with ivy and holly, and from it hung wicker rods garnished
with . . . pomegranates, oranges, pompions, cucumbers, grapes. In true
Elizabethan fashion the fruits were spangled with gold."[39]

4. FLOWERS

Milton chooses flowers "worthy of Paradise" that grow profusely
(IV, 241–43); he expresses a firm dislike for "Beds and curious Knots"
(IV, 242). And, although Eve thinks that the flowers of Eden will never
grow in another climate (XI, 273–74), most of the flowers of Paradise
could be found growing not only in Homer's Greece but also in Milton's
England: iris, jasmine, violet, crocus, hyacinth (IV, 698–701), and thorn-
less roses (IV, 256) of "Carnation, Purple, Azure, or spect with Gold"
(IX, 429).

Milton's flowers are ordinary sun-loving and shade-loving plants

(IV, 244–46). As a matter of fact, the herbals are filled with more flowers than Adam and Eve could have taken care of. Since Parkinson's *Paradisi* describes "the Rose without thornes single and double," it is doubtful that Milton's use of thornless roses "lifts the description into the realm of the miraculous," as Knott contends.[40] The colors of Milton's roses—and many additional colors—can also be found in the herbals, including the gold-specked rose of Paradise.[41]

His aversion to knots, mazes, and labyrinths in Paradise may be related to the Art-Nature dichotomy. He likes prelapsarian "raw." Bacon, too, dislikes "knots, or figures, with divers-coloured earths. . . . You may see as good sights many times in tarts."[42] Perhaps Milton associated mazes and labyrinths with the fantastically intricate gardens of both the ancients and of his contemporaries. Pliny's villa, though comfortable, had more of Art than Nature in it.[43] And the Pratoline Garden of Florence (which Evelyn describes in his *Diary* and which Milton had seen) had pavilions, amphitheaters, fountains, and "an Hercules whose Club yeilds a Showre of Water, which falling into a huge *Concha* has a Naked Woman riding on the back of Dolphins."[44] Milton knew that whether it was a Pratoline labyrinth or an English cottage knot, each required planning, work, and detailed instructions. The illustrations from gardening manuals almost overwhelm the twentieth-century gardener; one can imagine the amount of work required to make the simpler knots like "Cink foyle" or the "Flowre deluce" of *The Covntrie Hovsewifes Garden*.[45] Adam and Eve were busy enough lopping, pruning, propping, without having to keep a knot in shape. Milton's acute sense of verisimilitude comes into play here: he makes his Garden a manageable one for the inhabitants; even so, Eve in typical housewifely fashion complains about having only two hands (IX, 207–12).

Milton's preference for the natural is probably linked to his own rich rural experiences. Although it is true that by the time he came to Chalfont, Saint Giles, he was blind, his memory would have held pictures of the Buckinghamshire meadows, wooded slopes, upland commons, streamsides, forests—all rich in flora. Gerard's visit to Buckinghamshire had uncovered such unusual flowers as the small canterburie bell, elecampane, the garden angelica; and the later studies of George C. Druce, recorded in *The Flora of Buckinghamshire*, describe the beautiful uncultivated flowers of field and stream—columbine, larkspur, yellow water lily, opium poppy, wake robin, and hundreds of others.[46] No poet's eye could have seen these without recording and remembering. Surely one whose "exercise was chiefly walking" would have seen a little of his own Buckinghamshire in the "flours of all hue" (IV, 256) of Paradise.[47]

5. Furnishings

A raised table of "grassie terf" surrounded by "mossie seats" (V, 349–92).

Though at first glance a grassy turf table and mossy seats may seem like primitive dining equipment, these were not foreign to Milton's England. Carey and Fowler suggest that a grassy turf table and mossy seats were used "because the shaping of wood had not yet begun," but long after technology had made tables and seats of wood, marble, and other materials, William Lawson, the Yorkshire gardener, showed a fondness for turf seats planted with camomile, violet, or daisy.[48] Moreover, whether the medieval gardens actually contained raised turf seats or whether these seats were only the projection of the artists' imagination is not certain, but it is a rare picture of a medieval garden that does not have a mossy seat somewhere.

6. Walks and Alleys

"Yonder Allies green, / Our walks at Noon" (IV, 626–27); "echoing Walks between" (IX, 1107); "Satan many a walk travers'd" (IX, 434); "leave . . . these happie Walks" (XI, 269–70).

Essential to the enjoyment of an English garden was a series of walks. The smallest cottage and pond gardens called for walks. Milton, sharing his countrymen's delight in these walks, assigns many English-type alleys to Paradise. So important are these that Adam makes provision in his daily work schedule for keeping the walks clear of branches. The Englishman found the walks practical as well as beautiful: "The commodities of these Alleis and walkes, serue to good purposes, the one is, that the owner may diligently view the prosperitie of his herbes and flowers, the other for the delight and comfort of his wearied mind . . . in the delectable sightes, and fragrant smells of the flowers, by walking up and downe, and about the Garden in them."[49] Milton's primitive sire is not Fenimore Cooper's hero gliding swiftly through the "spicy forest," leaving no perceptible footprint upon the flowers. Even Satan takes the paths. And when it comes time for Adam and Eve to leave Paradise, Adam, like any good Englishman, mourns the loss of the "happie Walks."

7. BOWER (ARBOR)

"Thir blissful Bower; it was a place / Chos'n by the sovran Planter" (IV, 690–91); "as in the dore he sat / Of his coole Bowre" (V, 299–300); "So to the Silvan Lodge / They came, that like *Pomona's* Arbour smil'd" (V, 377–78).

A bower, or an arbor, is a shelter from heat or storm. Milton uses the word *bower* to denote both a completely closed arbor and one partially or fully open at both ends. He refers to "Walks, and Bowers" (VIII, 305), "paths and Bowers" (IX, 244), "Dales and Bowrs" (X, 860); like any competent horticultural architect he provides a door for the living quarters of the occupants. Although prelapsarian Mesopotamia may not have been as hot as the Middle East is today, Adam is quite concerned about heat. Milton stresses the fact that the bower is shady and cool. What is surprising is that his English contemporaries were so addicted to shady arbors in so cool a climate as England's. "All gardens," says Rohde, "seem to have boasted of at least one walk under a 'vaulting or arch herber,' these herbers being constructed either of trellis work covered with vines, or framed of 'pleached' trees—wychelm, hornbeam, whitethorn or limes. In large gardens these herbers or covered galleries were a prominent feature."[50] Bacon, who loathed the knot, loved the decorated "covert alley" with turrets and "coloured glass gilt, for the sun to play upon."[51] Milton's shady arbor, more natural than Bacon's, has artless touches that require no turrets or sun-catchers. Lovely in itself, Milton's blissful bower needs no emblematizing to make it spiritual, as does William Prynne's:

> Gardens are fraught with Arbors, *Trees, whose shade*
> *Cooles and repels Heate, stormes* which would invade,
> And scorch us sore: Christ hath a *shade most sweete*
> *Against all scalding Heates, all stormes we meete.*[52]

What Milton makes clear to his readers is this: the shady arbor contains rather simple flowers that "Broiderd the ground, more colour'd then with stone / Of costliest Emblem" (IV, 697–703).[53] It is used to entertain angelic visitors as well as for love-making; it has no hint of the luxuriousness of classical love bowers or of Spenser's; and because the bower was planted by God Himself, it, like the rest of His creation, was "very good." When I look at Milton's arbor, I do not see, as Broadbent does, that "in the background is Ezekiel's vision of Adam's kingly splendor . . . sardius, topaz, and the diamond . . . as well as the amorously emblematic jewellry of the Song of Solomon."[54] I see in the background Ralph Austen's fruit trees "bespangled, and gorgeously apparelled with greene Leaves"; John Parkinson's Damaske Roses "surpassing all other Roses or Flowers"; and John Gerard's plants "setting forth to vs the inuisible wisdome and admirable workmanship of Almighty God."[55]

8. GARDENING

"After no more toil / Of thir sweet Gardning labour then suffic'd / To recommend coole *Zephyr*, and made ease / More easie" (IV, 327–30); "But with such Gardning Tools as Art yet rude, / Guiltless of fire had formd, or Angels brought" (IX, 391–92).

In a real garden, real people do real work, regardless of whether their place is called Eden or England, though in Paradise work would put no sweat on the brow.[56] Following his Biblical source, Milton has his couple engage in "sweet Gardning labour."[57] As for actual gardening practices in Milton's England, so sophisticated a gentleman as Evelyn not only commends but extols gardening.[58] Even royalty gardened: Charles II was renowned for his planning and gardening of the east front of Hampton Court.[59] The popular writers, in an attempt to raise gardening above the level of "the loose unleter'd Hinds," introduced their garden manuals with a discourse on the dignity of husbandry. Heresbachius, for one, alludes to early illustrious predecessors who worked in gardens: he cites Alcinous and Laertes as men continually occupied with husbandry and concludes with the supreme example, "Christ himself glorieth to be sonne of a Husbandman."[60] As a sidelight on the dignity of gardening, it is interesting to note that the "mistaken gardener" of the Resurrection scenes painted by Renaissance artists is none other than the Lord Himself with a gardening tool in his hand.[61]

Milton's Adam, no less a gardener than Alcinous, Laertes, or Charles II, has all the instincts of a gardener: he rises at dawn and sets up his schedule for the day. He explains to Eve that the arbors and allies need pruning and that unsightly blossoms clutter the walks (IV, 616–32). Husbandry was a subject extremely familiar to both men and women of Milton's day; there were books ranging from Thomas Tusser's *Fiue Hundreth Points of Good Husbandry* (1573) to Gervase Markham's *The English Hovse-wife* (1614).

Since Milton obviously regards gardening as an occupation worthy of the Paradise couple, he reinforces the actuality of their gardening efforts by having them *lop* (IV, 629; IX, 210); *prune* (IV, 438); *prop* (IX 210); *bind* (IX, 210); and do *scant manuring* (IV, 628).[62] It was not his intention to create a garden that served only as a metaphor for spiritual activity; nor, on the other hand, was it Milton's intention to create a dreamlike fantasy made blissful by its perpetual idleness. The lopping, pruning, propping, binding, and manuring of Adam and Eve do not detract from the luster of Paradise, but these activities make them and their Garden credible. So literal is Milton that he uses the semitechnical terminology of agriculture to describe the condition of the fruit trees of Paradise:

> where any row
> Of Fruit-trees overwoodie reachd too farr
> Thir pampered boughes, and needed hands to check
> Fruitless imbraces. (V, 212–15)

Most commentators in glossing *overwoodie* and *pamperd* treat the terms etymologically, and hence fail to get the pomological point.[63] The explanation of these terms appears in *The Solitary or Carthusian Gard'ner*:

I suppose then a Tree to have Five Sorts of Branches . . . : *Wood-Branches, Fruit-Branches, Crumpled-Branches, Branches of False-Wood*, and *Luxuriant Branches*.

1. The *Wood-Branches* are those that form the Shape and Roundness of the Tree, and must be *Prun'd* with Judgment according to the Strength of the Tree, from Four to Twelve Inches long.
2. The *Fruit-Branches* are smaller than the Wood-Branches. . . .
3. The *Crumpled-Branches* are very small Branches, confus'd and intangled together, and that can neither yield wood nor Fruit. . . .
4. The *Branches of False Wood* are those that grow on the Good Branches. . . .
5. The *Luxuriant-Branches* are those that spring out from the large Wood-Branches.[64]

Since, according to the pomology of the time, wood-branches are the backbone of the tree, providing shape and strength, they require careful pruning. Unpruned wood-branches—too long, too full, too thick—are "overwoodie" branches. Moreover, since the luxuriant-branches spring directly from the wood-branches, excessive luxuriancy would damage the tree's productivity, robbing the smaller fruit-branches of air, light, and growth. A "pampered" branch ("overfed") is a luxuriant-branch unpruned. Since fruit grows on neither wood-branches nor on luxuriant-branches, pruning is essential in order to accommodate the smaller fruit-branches. Milton's charming pun on *fruitless* would have been understood by any gardener who knew what failing to pinch back or to prune meant.

The "scant manuring" (IV, 628) that Adam speaks of is directly connected with arboriculture; branches that are overgrown require more than *scant* manuring. Although the term *manure* (noun) occurs in the husbandry manuals as a synonym for *dung*, *manure* also occurs as a verb meaning "to cultivate." In addition, there is a specialized meaning, "to train or to rear a plant" (OED). Clearly it is this latter meaning that clarifies Adam's activities: Adam complains that their *training* and *rearing* is all too scant and that the bushes or trees require lopping to curb "thir wanton growth" (IV, 629). Otherwise the walks will be impassable. Gardening manuals, designed for the novice as well as the experienced gardener, describe tools and the art of pruning. Milton does not scorn to put tools in the hands of his epic pair. Although he does not specify the exact tools of Paradise, a contemporary reader of *Paradise Lost* might have easily pictured any number of tools found in the manuals or in his own toolshed.[65] By means of so simple a device as the use of tools, Milton makes his first parents dynamically human. Participating thoroughly in the human experience, Eve, with a homely parting touch after the Fall, expresses regret for the loss of her gardening activity. Like any gardener taking a vacation, she wonders what will happen to the plants while she is gone. (XI, 277–79). Using English rural activities because they are fit for Paradise, Milton enlivens Paradise with a bit of rural England.

Milton's Paradise is not "a mere fiction of what never was." His two creatures, "wedded to this goodly universe" by their beneficent Creator, enjoyed, through gardening, "a simple produce of the common day."

His use of the herbals and gardening manuals, and of actual gardens, shows the Miltonic blend which never isolates one tradition but draws on all of them, including English native, to feed the epic poem. The poem is richer for it.

Grand Valley State College

NOTES

1. A. Bartlett Giamatti, *The Earthly Paradise and the Renaissance Epic* (Princeton, 1966), p. 300.

2. *Adventurer*, p. 101, in *Eighteenth-Century Critical Essays*, ed. Scott Elledge, II (Ithaca, 1961), p. 713. Cf. T. S. Eliot, "A Note on the Verse of John Milton," *Essays and Studies*, XXI (1936), 32–40, and F. R. Leavis, *Revaluation* (London, 1936), p. 47.

3. "Symbolic Landscape in *Paradise Lost*," *Milton Studies*, II (Pittsburgh, 1970), p. 38.

4. J. B. Broadbent, *Some Graver Subject: An Essay on "Paradise Lost"* (London, 1960), pp. 174–75.

5. See Edward Hyams, *The English Garden* (London, 1964), pp. 205–40.

6. *Paradisi in Sole Paradisus Terrestris* (London, 1629), p. 3.

7. *The Herball or Generall Historie of Plantes*, enlarged and amended by Thomas Johnson (London, 1636), p. 4. The term *embroidered* was frequently used in a semitechnical sense; e.g., Louis Liger d'Auxerre, *The Compleat Florist* (London, 1706), p. 135, uses it so.

8. *Garden-Craft in the Bible and Other Essays* (London, 1927), pp. 123–24.

9. Parkinson, *Paradisi*, p. 413.

10. Gerard, *Herball*, p. 4.

11. "Of Gardens," in *Bacon's Essays*, ed. Richard Whately (Boston, 1871), pp. 443–44.

12. Knott, "Symbolic Landscape," p. 41.

13. This is the title of the second edition of Sir Hugh Plat's *Floraes Paradise*, edited by his kinsman Charles Bellingham (London, 1653).

14. *The Works of John Milton*, ed. Frank Allen Patterson et al., 18 vols. (New York, 1931–1938), VIII, 33; III, 158–59.

15. *Minutes of the Life of Mr John Milton* (1681), in *The Early Lives of Milton*, ed. Helen Darbishire (London, 1931), p. 6.

16. *The Life of John Milton*, I (New York, 1946), pp. 555–56, 562.

17. William Riley Parker, *Milton*, I (Oxford, 1968), pp. 192, 400, 608.

18. Broadbent, *Some Graver Subject*, p. 184.

19. "Gardens of Epicurus," in *Five Miscellaneous Essays by Sir William Temple*, ed. Samuel Holt Monk (Ann Arbor, 1963), pp. 28–29.

20. E. R. Curtius, *European Literature and the Latin Middle Ages* (London, 1953), p. 186.

21. John Carey and Alastair Fowler, *The Poems of Milton* (London, 1968), p. 615.

22. *The Moral Cosmos of "Paradise Lost"* (East Lansing, 1970), p. 139.

23. "Milton's Abyssinian Paradise," *University of Texas Studies in English*, XXIX

(1950), 144–45; Clark cites Allan Gilbert, *A Geographical Dictionary of Milton* (New Haven, 1919), p. 18.

24. Bacon, "Of Gardens," p. 446. See also H. Inigo Triggs, *Garden Craft in Europe* (London, 1913), which refers to the Tudor terraced mount at Rockingham and at Boscobel (p. 205).

25. William Lawson, *A New Orchard and Garden* (London, 1618), p. 12.

26. *The Diary of John Evelyn*, ed. E. S. de Beer, IV (Oxford, 1955), pp. 176–77.

27. *The Profitable Art of Gardening* (London, 1586), p. 7. Enclosures are also described in Hill's *The Gardeners Labyrinth* (London, 1577), pp. 13–16.

28. *Sylva*, 2d ed. (London, 1670), p. 128.

29. *A Treatise of Fruit-Trees* (Oxford, 1657), pp. 116–17.

30. John Evelyn, *Fumifugium* (London, 1661).

31. Carey and Fowler, *Poems of Milton*, p. 618, attribute Milton's diction to the influence of Diodorus: see also G. W. Whiting, *Milton's Literary Milieu* (New York, 1964), pp. 66–67.

32. Austen, *A Treatise of Fruit-Trees*, pp. 37–38.

33. William Empson, *Some Versions of Pastoral* (London, 1950), p. 162.

34. Austen, *A Treatise of Fruit-Trees*, p. 38.

35. I have in progress a more detailed study of myrtle, laurel, and acanthus in Paradise.

36. Austen, *A Treatise of Fruit-Trees*, pp. 36–37; he cites Bacon as his authority.

37. Temple, "Gardens of Epicurus," pp. 24–26.

38. For a lengthy note on the alchemical references, see Carey and Fowler, *Poems of Milton*, p. 623.

39. Rohde, *Garden-Craft in the Bible*, p. 131.

40. Parkinson, *Paradisi*, p. 416; for the emblematic aspect of the flowers of Paradise, see Carey and Fowler, *Poems of Milton*, p. 627. Knott, "Symbolic Landscape," p. 40.

41. Parkinson, *Paradisi*, p. 421.

42. Bacon, "Of Gardens," p. 445.

43. Pliny, *Epistulae*, V. vi. 32–37. For a detailed description of ancient gardens see August F. von Pauly and Georg Wissowa, *Pauly's Real-Encyclopädie der Classischen Altertumswissenschaft* (Stuttgart, 1893–1956), "Gartenbau."

44. Parker, *Milton*, p. 170. Evelyn, *The Diary of John Evelyn*, II, 418–19; Evelyn describes more than sixty royal or private gardens and gives short notices of forty minor ones.

45. William Lawson, *The Covntrie Hovsewifes Garden* (London, 1617), pp. 4–8.

46. Gerard, *Herball*, pp. 449–50, 793, 1000; Iver Heath was rich in flora and frequently visited by herbalists and later botanists. *The Flora of Buckinghamshire* (Arbroath, 1926).

47. Aubrey, *Minutes of the Life*, in Darbishire, *The Early Lives of Milton*, p. 6.

48. Carey and Fowler, *Poems of Milton*, p. 699.

49. Thomas Hill, *The Gardeners Labyrinth*, p. 24.

50. Rohde, *Garden-Craft*, p. 129.

51. Bacon, "Of Gardens," p. 445.

52. "A Christian Paradise," in *Mount-Orgueil* (London, 1641), p. 124.

53. Leonard Meager in *The English Gardener* (London, 1670) gives a list of suitable arbor plants, among them "sweet-bryer, jessamine, roses, piracantas, lawrels" (pp. 248–49).

54. Broadbent, *Some Graver Subject*, p. 180.

55. Austen, *A Treatise of Fruit-Trees*, p. 37; Parkinson, *Paradisi*, p. 413; Gerard, *Herball*, p. 4.

56. Milton's introduction of gardening labors and gardening tools is not a concession to "human standards of orderliness" (Knott, "Symbolic Landscape," p. 45), but is in complete harmony with Milton's conception of the first couple's full humanity.

57. According to *The Book of Jubilees*, the angels "instructed him to do everything that is suitable for tillage," *The Apocrypha and Pseudepigrapha of the Old Testament*, ed. R. H. Charles, II (Oxford, 1913), p. 16. See also Francis Gentil, *The Solitary or Carthusian Gard'ner* (London, 1706), p. i: "The *Culture of Gardens* . . . has always been look'd upon as the First *Art* in the World: Nothing can afford more Pleasure than the pursuit of it."

58. John Evelyn, *Acetaria* (London, 1699); his contributions to English gardening literature include a projected collaboration with Dr. Thomas Browne (letter 28 January 1657–58).

59. Evelyn, *The Diary*, III, 324, n. 4.

60. Heresbachius, *Foure Books of Husbandrie* (London, 1586), pp. 5–6.

61. See Lorenzo di Credi, "Our Lord Appearing to Mary Magdalene," Uffizi Gallery, Florence.

62. A number of the gardening manuals give detailed instructions and illustrations of the art of pruning. See Stephen Blake, *The Compleat Gardeners Practice* (London, 1664); Joseph Blagrave, *The Epitomie of the Art of Husbandry* (London, 1685).

63. Carey and Fowler suggest: "*overwoody* Probably 'excessively bushy'; *pampered* Primarily 'overindulged'; but a secondary play on Fr. *pampre* . . . may be Miltonic. Some authorities regarded the two words as etymologically related" (*Poems of Milton*, p. 687).

64. Gentil, *The Solitary or Carthusian Gard'ner*, p. 69.

65. See d'Auxerre's *The Compleat Florist*, which has ten pages of illustrations of gardening tools, pp. 145–54.

THE STYLE AND STRUCTURE OF MILTON'S *READIE AND EASIE WAY*

Keith W. Stavely

The second edition of *The Readie and Easie Way* was published when all politically conscious Englishmen knew that a restoration was imminent. A recognition of this fact, and its near-tragic implications for Milton's cause, governs the style and structure of the pamphlet. When Milton contemplates the forces leading England to the Restoration, his coordinate, linear style implies that the situation is beyond rational control. When he proposes his ready and easy way, his more structured style generates an image of the politics of pure reason. These two styles alternate throughout the tract and create a pattern of futile but heroic political struggle. Periodically, Milton makes his serenely rational plan more detailed and socially comprehensive, but the intervals between these propositions are filled with denunciations of political reality, insinuations that no republican solutions are feasible at the moment. As this pattern unfolds, suggestions of political fantasy, suggestions that Milton realizes his plan is all too ready and easy, become more and more prominent in the positive or rational sections. The tract concludes with a sentence in which the style of reasoned presentation is gradually replaced by the style of futility. Realism defeats the fulfillment of wishes, but does not quite extinguish political commitment.

I

ABDIEL-LIKE, Milton produced for twenty years assertions as sweeping as this one from *The Second Defence*:

Whence I insist that [the Independents] were also superior both in law and in merit, for nothing is more natural, nothing more just, nothing more useful or more advantageous to the human race than that the lesser obey the greater, not the lesser number the greater number, but the lesser virtue the greater virtue, the lesser wisdom the greater wisdom. Those whose power lies in wisdom, experience, industry, and virtue will, in my opinion, however small their number, be a majority and prove more powerful in balloting everywhere than any mere number, however great.[1]

269

And Milton's audience was usually as unresponsive as Abdiel's was to be. During the early 1640s Milton could believe, with some justification, that his conception of Christian liberty was shared by the great majority of his countrymen. His pamphlets, from *Of Reformation* to *Areopagitica*, reflect some such belief, for his style of both thinking and writing grew more coherent, urbane, and plausibly resonant as the nation's resistance to civil and ecclesiastical absolutism grew stronger and more comprehensive. In *Of Reformation* the argument is simple, if not crude, the tone and syntax invariably communicate a righteous zeal, and Milton confines his social imagination to a prayerful yearning for the literal Christian apocalypse. In *Areopagitica* the arguments are subtle, the tone and syntax flexible, now leisurely, now urgent, and Milton's social imagination builds its apocalyptic expectations on these humane intellectual and stylistic foundations.

Nevertheless, *Areopagitica* remains tinged with fantasy. Who but Milton could have believed that in 1644, Parliament, trying at once to wage a civil war and reorganize the church, would consider the abolition of censorship a key to true reformation?[2] Except for the divorce tracts, which earned him the notoriety of a libertine, anarchist, and atheist, all Milton's early prose writings went unheeded. When it became clear, as it did after the execution of Charles I, that he could no longer consider himself a spokesman for the English people, Milton's political arguments grew increasingly unreal and his prose style increasingly schizophrenic. His predicament is embodied in the simple fact that *Eikon Basilike* was published sixty times in 1649, *Eikonoklastes* only twice.[3] Most Englishmen never accepted a government without a king, which meant, as Hobbes pointed out in commenting on *The Second Defence*, that throughout the 1650s Milton had to defend an oligarchy in order to avoid what he considered to be the majority tyranny of a Restoration.[4] He had to pretend, as in the passage quoted above, that whoever held power at the moment embodied his ideals of right reason, active virtue, and grace. This political predicament was the major reason Milton never celebrated the Commonwealth or Protectorate in a style resembling that of *Areopagitica* in flexibility and imaginative scope. In the positive sections of Milton's later tracts, imaginative vision is replaced by terse expositions of first principles. The polemical sections of these tracts, directed first against the Presbyterians in *The Tenure of Kings and Magistrates*, then against the mass of Englishmen in *Eikono-*

klastes, become increasingly bitter and long-winded, an assertion substantiated by a comparison of the second edition of *Eikonoklastes* with the first.

The passage from *The Second Defence* quoted above is thus either naïve or disingenuous. Du Moulin was right to insist that every English government after 1649 was upheld by the "military excellence" of Cromwell, not by his superior wisdom, virtue, and piety. His death in September 1658 precipitated a futile search for a legitimate civil authority to replace him: Richard Cromwell as Lord Protector, Richard and an elected parliament, the Rump, the Rump deposed and reinstalled. All these magistrates and legislatures were the utterly powerless creatures of the only potent non-Royalist force in England, Cromwell's army. The Restoration became inevitable in February 1660 when General Monck, commanding the troops he had led from Edinburgh to London, exerted pressure on the Rump to readmit the secluded members of the Long Parliament, well known to be Royalists.[5] It will be my contention in this essay that the two opposed tendencies in Milton's later prose writing outlined in the preceding paragraph achieve full rhetorical discipline in *The Readie and Easie Way to Establish a Free Commonwealth*. As I see it, the structure of this tract dramatizes a struggle between pure social reason and the perverse and irrational forces which control the immediate political situation and are insuring the Restoration.[6]

II

The publication dates of *The Readie and Easie Way* are indispensable to a correct understanding of what kind of response Milton expected from his audience. The first edition was probably largely finished before February 21, 1660, and published between February 21 and March 3. At the aforementioned behest of General Monck, the Rump had voted on February 21 to readmit the secluded members of the Long Parliament, most of whom were Presbyterians and Royalists. Milton casually refers to this resolution in the first paragraph of the first edition: "(the Parlament now sitting more full and frequent)." The second edition appeared shortly before the Restoration, in late April 1660, Milton having extensively rewritten his pamphlet in response to the writs for electing a new parliament which the Long Parliament had approved on March 16.[7] As he had done in the Defences and, most recently, in the two antiecclesiastical pamphlets of 1659, Milton continued to address those in power as if they were reason and virtue incarnate, capable of giving a fair and respectful hearing to his republican arguments. But this publication history, with Milton twice revising his pamphlet to bring it up to date, indicates quite clearly that this prose style of uncompromising right reason has become consciously disingenuous, a gesture of disdain for the obvious balance of political forces. Otherwise we must suppose that Milton, while aware of the activities of General Monck and the Long Parliament, somehow managed to be the only man in England innocent of their implications. He thus pretends that the Long Parliament's "sitting more full and frequent" will increase his chances of persuading it, although he well knew that this very fact virtually guaranteed the Restoration. Likewise in the second edition, as we shall see, Milton discusses the Parliament about to be elected in disregard of the crucial fact that it was certain to restore a Stuart king.

We are now in a position to assess the degree of utopianism in Milton's final political proposals. Zera S. Fink has shown that the theory of the mixed state was one of the "chief bases of seventeenth century utopianism." Harrington and others believed a mixed state could be constituted so as to be a "perfectly balanced government, in which the defects of fallen man would be so compensated for that it would last unimpaired and unchanged forever." After tracing the development of Milton's ideas on the mixed state through all his prose works, Fink argues that in the final version of them in *The Readie and Easie Way*, Milton projected an eternally enduring government. This plan was utopian, but unconsciously so, in that Milton aimed at its actual adoption.[8] Barbara Lewalski, denying any utopian implications, emphasizes the rhetorical pragmatism of *The Readie and Easie Way*. Milton did try to get his plan adopted. One point she does not make is that the outline of the proposed government, a legislative body and an executive some of the members of which are to be chosen from among the members of the legislature, is clearly derived from Milton's years of membership on the Council of State, many of the members of which were also members of the various parliaments that came and went between 1649 and 1660. She discusses the changes Milton made for the second edition, by which he sought to attract Harringtonians, Fifth Monarchists, and even Presbyterians into an anti-Royalist coalition.[9] But as I have argued, even Milton must have realized that such maneuvers would

prove futile in April 1660. The correct way to analyze the relative proportions of realism and utopianism in Milton's plan, I believe, is to say
that his realism is founded on a premise that is now willfully utopian,
the premise, namely, that he is addressing a nation still open to the pure
reason of a republican. This rational, and therefore utopian, pragmatism is perhaps most clearly evident in a passage from *A Letter to a
Friend,* written in late 1659, between the Rump's two brief terms in
office:

Being now in Anarchy, without a counselling and governing Power; and the
Army, I suppose, finding themselves insufficient to discharge at once both Mili-
tary and Civil Affairs, the first thing to be found out with all speed, without
which no Commonwealth can subsist, must be a Senate, or General Council of
State, in whom must be the Power, first to preserve the publick Peace, next the
Commerce with Foreign Nations; and lastly, to raise Monies for the Manage-
ment of these Affairs; this must either be the Parliament readmitted to sit, or a
Council of State allow'd of by the Army, since they only now have the Power.
The Terms to be stood on are, Liberty of Conscience to all professing Scripture
to be the Rule of thir Faith and Worship; and the Abjuration of a single
Person. (CM, VI, 104)

The Readie and Easie Way is a confrontation between this kind of
succinct, unadorned reasoning and what constantly interrupts it or
modifies it, polemics against recalcitrant political circumstances, con-
ducted in a style which conveys a recognition of the imminent and
inevitable defeat of the Good Old Cause.

III

According to K. G. Hamilton, a typical Miltonic sentence is "complex, mainly periodic, though with some balanced or loose components,
and with some coordinate elements within the basically subordinate
structure."[10] Consider this example from the autobiographical digression in *The Reason of Church Government*:

But were it the meanest under-service, if God by his Secretary conscience injoyn
it, it were sad for me if I should draw back, for me especially, now when all men
offer their aid to help ease and lighten the difficult labours of the Church, to
whose service by the intentions of my parents and friends I was destin'd of a
child, and in mine own resolutions, till comming to some maturity of yeers and
perceaving what tyranny had invaded the Church, that he who would take
Orders must subscribe slave, and take an oath withall, which unless he took

with a conscience that would retch, he must either strait perjure, or split his faith, I thought it better to preferre a blamelesse silence before the sacred office of speaking bought, and begun with servitude and forswearing. (YP, I, 822–23)

The initial complex suspension ends quietly and soberly, but the sentence is twice prolonged and intensified by what Morris W. Croll has analyzed as devices of the baroque style in prose: an apposition and a "trailing effect," in which a member is linked not to the general idea of the preceding member, but to its last word: "it were sad for me if I should draw back, for me especially, now when . . . the difficult labours of the Church, to whose service by the intentions of my parents. . . ."[11] The trailing clause soon develops into a more emphatic and comprehensive suspension than the initial one, containing within itself a secondary trailing clause, which in turn produces a secondary suspension: "till comming to some maturity . . . and perceaving what tyranny . . . that he who would take Orders . . . take an oath withall, which unlesse he took with a conscience that would retch, he must either . . . I thought it better to preferre. . . ." This interplay between loose and Ciceronian or suspended constructions allows Milton to enlarge the scope of his discussion as much as necessary, here giving him an opportunity to demonstrate the crucial relationship between the intolerable state of public affairs and his private life. It also determines the emotional texture of the sentence. Again and again, Milton's energetic repugnance for the violation of conscience inherent in the established Church is renewed and intensified in the suspended members, then sharply exploded in the main clauses. The entire discussion, and Milton's simultaneous emotional reaction to the issues it raises, is rounded off into a sense of coherence and completion by a periodic return in the final main clause: "I thought it better to preferre a blameless silence before the sacred office of speaking bought, and begun with servitude and forswearing." Thus Milton's posture here and in all his so-called optimistic pamphlets (from *Of Reformation* up to, and in part including, *The Tenure*) is that of a man contending vigorously and unweariedly with the enemies of reason and virtue on as broad a front as possible, confronting, encompassing, and demolishing their sins and errors with the intricacies of his ample syntax. This is a syntax, furthermore, designed to resolve the tension between general principle and particular circumstance, a tension especially strong in the social thought of a figure such as Milton who again and again in his prose expresses his contempt for unexamined habits, customs, and traditions. In spacious and strenuous constructions such as the one I am discussing here, Milton judges flawed particulars by placing them literally within a context of general principle.

E. N. S. Thompson, however, says that the syntax of *The Readie and Easie Way* is for the most part coordinate. The long sentences are not constructed; they are simply strung together.[12] Here, for example, is a typically dense and extended characterization of monarchy:

Whereas a king must be ador'd like a Demigod, with a dissolute and haughtie court about him, of vast expence and luxurie, masks and revels, to the debaushing of our prime gentry both male and female; not in their passetimes only, but in earnest, by the loos imploiments of court service, which will be then thought honorable. There will be a queen also of no less charge; in most likelihood outlandish and a Papist; besides a queen mother such alreadie; together with both thir courts and numerous train: then a royal issue, and ere long severally thir sumptuous courts; to the multiplying of a servile crew, not of servants only, but of nobility and gentry, bred up then to the hopes not of public, but of court offices; to be stewards, chamberlains, ushers, grooms, even of the close-stool; the lower thir minds debas'd with court opinions, contrary to all vertue and reformation, the haughtier will be thir pride and profuseness. (CM, VI, 120)

The major difference between this passage and the one from *The Reason of Church Government* is that Milton here reluctantly acknowledges the accumulating force of the particular circumstances his rhetoric had always sought to confront and transform. A subordinated syntax shaping an abundance of content attempts to encompass and, in a sense, defeat as many opponents and hostile circumstances as possible. But a linear polemic such as this one suggests an infinite proliferation of corrupted social conditions which cannot all be transformed. As soon as one is condemned and disposed of, the republican voice must encounter another and another and another. The connecting links of the passage enhance this effect: "*not* in their passetimes *only, but* in earnest, . . . a queen *also . . . besides* a queen mother such alreadie; *together with* both thir courts . . . *then* a royal issue, *and ere long* severally . . . *to the multiplying of* a servile crew, *not of* servants *only, but of* nobility and gentry, *bred up then* to the hopes *not of* public, *but of* court offices; to be stewards . . . *even* of the close-stool" (my italics). These transitions generate an embarrassment of riches, a feeling that the reformer has been presented with more raw material than he can ultimately cope with. They also generate a sense of the dizzy momentum of events: the advent of Charles II will lead English society straight to the close-stool. Warfaring rhetoric has turned into a wayfaring which can only conclude in a lucid perception that the Restoration will result in the flat contradiction of all true ideals:[13] "the lower thir minds debas'd with court opinions, contrary to all vertue and reformation, the haughtier will be thir pride and profuseness."

My point, then, is that for this tract Milton altered his characteristic syntax so that it reflects a political situation decisively altered in favor of his opponents. Traveling openly through a hostile social landscape, denouncing what cannot be reformed, represent the only self-respecting posture still available to a virtuous citizen. All others may plunge ahead to the close-stool, but the genuine republican will move firmly along his own path, dramatizing the process he witnesses all around him and stating clearly what it means. This syntax and this posture prevail throughout this section of the pamphlet, although the sense of being surrounded by hostile and irresistibly powerful forces emerges most often in passages attacking the nation at large for its counterrevolutionary backsliding. One such passage more or less concludes this particular stretch of polemic:

That a nation should be so valorous and courageous to winn thir liberty in the field, and when they have wonn it, should be so heartless and unwise in thir counsels, as not to know how to use it, value it, what to do with it or with themselves; but after ten or twelve years prosperous warr and contestation with tyrannie, basely and besottedly to run their necks again into the yoke which they have broken, and prostrate all the fruits of thir victorie for naught at the feet of the vanquishd, besides our loss of glorie, and such an example as kings or tyrants never yet had the like to boast of, will be an ignominie if it befall us, that never yet befell any nation possessd of thir libertie; worthie indeed themselves, whatsoever they be, to be for ever slaves: but that part of the nation which consents not with them, as I perswade me of a great number, far worthier then by their means to be brought into the same bondage. (CM, VI, 123)

In this sentence Milton appears to be writing as he does in the passage from *The Reason of Church Government*. He confronts the forces that threaten his cause, broadening the issues and the focus of his indignation through a series of subordinate and interpolated clauses, then explosively releases the accumulated emotional and conceptual energies in the long-delayed predication, "will be an ignominie if it befall us, that never yet befell any nation possessd of thir liberties." The people are conclusively indicted by this procedure. Their errors and failings are seen to exist, again literally, within a larger order, an elaborately constructed and massive edifice of principled judgment. This kind of closed and final amplitude is frequently achieved in Milton's earlier prose, particularly in *Areopagitica,* but Milton will not allow himself or anyone else to pretend that the enemies of reformation and revolution can be so thoroughly crushed in the spring of 1660. This is suggested by the way in which the climactic thrust of the major predication is dissipated by a series of antidemocratic afterthoughts: "worthie indeed themselves, whatsoever they be, to be for ever slaves: but that part of the nation which consents not with them, as I perswade me of a great number, far worthier than by their means to be brought into the same bondage." Coordinate or trailing members appended to such a carefully and elaborately subordinated period as this one demonstrate Milton's recognition that he is as unable to deal conclusively with the masses of sentimental Royalists as he is with the disastrous logic of events or the densely trivial society a restoration will produce.

If the situation is governed, so to speak, by irrationality, perversity, and madness, then the rational way can only be made to appear ready and easy by coolly ignoring the actual situation while making one's proposals. This Milton proceeds to do in the section immediately following the one I have been analyzing.[14] His first detailed presentation of his plan is a more elaborate version of the passage from *A Letter to a Friend* quoted above:

> For the ground and basis of every just and free government (since men have smarted so oft for committing all to one person) is a general councel of ablest men, chosen by the people to consult of public affairs from time to time for the common good. In this Grand Councel must the sovrantie, not transferrd, but delegated only, and as it were deposited, reside; with this caution they must have the forces by sea and land committed to them for preservation of the common peace and libertie; must raise and manage the public revenue, at least with som inspectors deputed for satisfaction of the people, how it is imploid; must make or propose, as more expressly shall be said anon, civil laws; treat of commerce, peace, or warr with forein nations, and for the carrying on som particular affairs with more secrecie and expedition, must elect, as they have alreadie out of thir own number and others, a Councel of State. (CM, VI, 125–26)

Milton leads up to this outline by suggesting with superbly ironic naïveté that the writs which had been proclaimed on March 16 for the election of a "free" (that is, other than the Long) Parliament could serve as the basis for implementing his plan. The new Parliament could simply constitute itself as his perpetual senate. Milton knew perfectly well how the elections would turn out. The new Parliament would be dominated by Cavaliers and Presbyterians and would proceed immediately to bring in the son of Charles I. Disdaining these certainties, Milton imagines the way history would go if men were the least bit reasonable. As he presents it here, that way is certainly ready and easy, for he blandly forgets the hostile and irresistible forces he has just embodied so compellingly in the preceding section. Despite its dominance elsewhere, he simply alludes to the danger of a Restoration in a decorous parenthesis, in the midst of an exposition of first principles. He minutely defines the constitutional status of the "Grand Councel" ("the sovrantie, not transferrd, but delegated only, and as it were deposited") and thus provides a rational solution for one of the primary causes of the tumult and conflict of the previous twenty years. The inverted formal syntax of this discussion of sovereignty initiates a series of parallel clauses, firmly securing the necessary functions of government in good order: "must reside . . . they must have . . . must raise . . . must make or propose . . . treat . . . must elect." The passage has all the balance and poise of a paragraph by Burke, but it denies the characteristically warm emotional appeal of Burke's prose. It projects a state divorced from tradition and existing social structures, founded instead on pure reason. The implication is that only by extracting from its political life all given emotional commitments could England retain in 1660 even the remotest hope that emotion would someday become socially creative rather than disastrous: "For it may be referrd to time, so we be still going on by degrees to perfection." (CM, VI, 132)

IV

Milton embodies the impossibility of this hope for a ready and easy rational way, at least for the foreseeable future, in the organization of the pamphlet, which alternates from beginning to end between sections conveying a sense that events have passed quite beyond republican or rational governance and sections explaining the futile but reasonable plan for stabilizing the revolution. A description of the rational state is superseded by a denunciation of the irrational realities of the political situation, is restated more copiously and fully, and is again superseded.

Near the beginning, Milton makes explicit the recognition of political reality enacted throughout in the style and structure: "If thir absolute determination be to enthrall us, before so long a Lent of Servitude, they may permitt us a little Shroving-time first, wherin to speak freely, and take our leaves of Libertie" (CM, VI, 111). He then proceeds to calm recapitulation of English history since 1641 (CM, VI, 112 ff.), arguing that the actions of Parliament during the 1640s were eminently rational, grounded as they were in the law of nature. Milton is here attempting to depict a political situation fully governed by general principles, but when he comes to the period of negotiations with Charles I in 1647–48, the shape and rhythm of his discourse become less poised and steady, more tangled and difficult, reflecting the nearly unmanageable crisis which developed at that time:

and yet they were not to learn that a greater number might be corrupt within the walls of a Parlament as well as of a citie; whereof in matters of neerest concernment all men will be judges; nor easily permitt, that the odds of voices in thir greatest councel, shall more endanger them by corrupt or credulous votes, then the odds of enemies by open assaults; judging that most voices ought not alwaies to prevail where main matters are in question. (CM, VI, 114–15)

Here is the beginning of the wayfaring, coordinate, or trailing style. Clause is piled upon clause, as though one cannot quite portray this situation as fully governed by the law of nature, cannot quite fashion and absorb it into patterned syntax and the rational order it reflects. Disaster was averted at this point, however, so Milton contemplates from a slight distance the headlong situation which would have resulted had Parliament agreed to the Treaty of Newport:

and the dangers on either side they seriously thus waighd: from the treatie, short fruits of long labours and seaven years warr; securitie for twenty years, if we can hold it; reformation in the church for three years: then put to shift again with our vanquishd maister . . . bishops not totally remov'd . . . thir lands alreadie sold, not to be alienated, but rented . . . delinquents few of many brought to condigne punishment; accessories punishd. (CM, VI, 115)

In imagining what did not happen then but almost certainly will now, Milton employs an extremely loosened version of the coordinate style, simply listing the provisions of the treaty. Signing it, that is, would have meant the abject surrender of reasoned principle to irrational sentiment, custom, and tradition.

This historical summary then concludes with a sketch of the Crom-
wellian period of heroic virtue and right reason:

> Nor were thir actions less both at home and abroad then might become the
> hopes of a glorious rising Commonwealth: nor were the expressions both of
> armie and people, whether in thir publick declarations or several writings other
> then such as testifi'd a spirit in this nation no less noble and well fitted to the
> liberty of a Commonwealth then in the ancient *Greeks* or *Romans*.[15] (CM,
> VI, 116)

This is balanced, shapely, high classic panegyric, far removed from the
dense thicket of menacing circumstances evoked only a few paragraphs
earlier. I would argue, therefore, that Milton subjects his ready and
easy rational plan to the pressures of political reality even before he
explicitly presents it. In keeping with the realistic and pessimistic
import of the tract's structure, its persona tends to make inflated and
exaggerated claims for the cause he espouses, the history in which he
has participated, and the alternative future he is proposing. Since he
has just made the reader experience the dangers and frustrations of actual political life as close to overwhelming, he can lead him adequately
to envision a nobler political order only by ignoring such pressures,
thereby acknowledging them.

The transition from historical survey to what is to be done in the
present situation is handled in a way that sharply juxtaposes the two
political alternatives, the two styles, and the overriding sense of futility
which have already begun to emerge:

> if by our ingratefull backsliding we make these [signal assistances from Heaven]
> fruitless; flying now to regal concessions from his divine condescensions . . .
> making vain and viler then dirt the blood of so many thousand faithfull and
> valiant *English* men, who left us in this libertie, bought with thir lives; losing
> by a strange after game of folly, all the battels we have wonn, . . . treading back
> again with lost labour all our happie steps in the progress of reformation; and
> most pittifully depriving our selves the instant fruition of that free government
> which we have so dearly purchased, a free Commonwealth, not only held by
> wisest men in all ages the noblest, the manliest, the equallest, the justest govern-
> ment, the most agreeable to all due libertie and proportiond qualitie, both
> human, civil, and Christian, most cherishing to vertue and true religion, but
> also . . . planely commended, or rather enjoind by our Saviour himself. (CM,
> VI, 118–19)

The first half of this quotation is another description and denunciation
of the moral and practical consequences of restoring monarchical gov-

ernment, and once again momentum is transmitted from participial to participial, consequence to consequence, until the reader begins to experience the destruction of all principled human aspiration and social organization. The passage then turns on the clause, "and most pittifully depriving our selves the instant fruition of that free government which we have so dearly purchased." The ensuing apposition, "a free Commonwealth," brings the passage to a standstill, or at least it attempts to. The effect is that the speaker tries to erect a dike to hold back the flood, but as he goes on to pile superlative upon superlative, all framed by a "not only . . . but also" construction, his voice acquires the now-familiar rhythm of uncontrolled momentum. Seeking to buttress the republican defenses against catastrophe, he acknowledges one more time the near-omnipotence of the forces responsible for the impending catastrophe.

The remainder of the pamphlet continues this movement back and forth between these two apparent alternatives: the nation's surrender to the logic of political reality or its ready and easy escape into a condition of republican pure reason. The next two sections are the ones analyzed in detail above, the long condemnation of monarchy and popular slavishness, followed by the lucid outline of the free commonwealth government. The latter introduces a defense of the principle of a permanently enduring senate (CM, VI, 126 ff.). Here Milton is debating with the Harringtonians, who favor rotating the members of the legislative body. Since they are one of the few rational groups left in England, this section is characterized by calm argument and examination of the historical evidence. However, the appeal to Harrington and his disciples is before long carried on in the coordinate tones and rhythms of the polemical and pessimistic sections of the tract:

I see not therefor, how we can be advantag'd by successive and transitorie Parlaments; but that they are much likelier continually to unsettle rather then to settle a free government; to breed commotions, changes, novelties and uncertainties; to bring neglect upon present affairs and opportunities, while all minds are suspense with expectation of a new assemblie, and the assemblie for a good space taken up with the new setling of it self. (CM, VI, 127)

However trenchant we may find this as an analysis of the vagaries of elections and of periodically elected legislatures, it clearly derives from an awareness of recent political history and contemporary political loyalties: the people cannot be relied upon to elect genuine republicans. This actual circumstance is the reason imagined circumstances are strung together in the quoted passage in a manner that recalls all the speaker's direct responses to the current situation. As we have seen and will continue to see, Royalist reality invades the world of republican social reason even, and perhaps most tellingly, when the republican persona works most determinedly to shut it out.

The same rhetorical effect emerges from the description of the electoral procedures Milton's plan might reluctantly tolerate. Elections would be designed gradually to refine irrational elements of society out of the active body politic, and the speaker continues on to suppose that a truly reformed citizenry would thereby be nurtured:

> To make the people fittest to chuse, and the chosen fittest to govern, will be to mend our corrupt and faulty education, to teach the people faith not without vertue, temperance, modestie, sobrietie, parsimonie, justice; not to admire wealth or honour; to hate turbulence and ambition; to place every one his privat welfare and happiness in the public peace, libertie, and safetie. (CM, VI, 131–32)

Here again the speaker makes highly inflated claims for his plan, listing the noble qualities that would be instilled in the populace, organizing the passage with a cadenced network of parallel infinitives, rounding the discussion off quite elegantly. And here again the reader is given to understand that this ready and easy balance and harmony amounts to an admission of futility, a concentrated effort temporarily to forget the obvious facts.

Milton summarizes the ostensible impact of this section by claiming that "the way propounded is plane, easie and open before us; . . . I say again, this way lies free and smooth before us" (CM, VI, 133). That these statements mean that the way is ready and easy only in an imaginary world of pure reason is again emphasized in the next section (CM, VI, 134 ff.), in which a relatively calm analysis of monarchy is soon interrupted by urgent and exasperated rhetorical questions: "Can the folly be paralleled? . . . Shall we never grow old anough? . . . Is it such an unspeakable joy to serve, such felicitie to wear a yoke?" (CM, VI, 136). Finally Milton predicts in detail the kind of society his plan would help to create, a society of religious liberty and opportunities for social advancement made possible by representative local governments and courts and a vastly improved school system. This fuller program is set forth in a style of careful and formal reasoning. It begins with an assured definition of first principles: "The whole freedom of man consists either in spiritual or civil libertie" (CM, VI, 141). After adapting to his present purposes the arguments on "spiritual libertie" he had published the year before, Milton presents his ideas on local government and education:

> The other part of our freedom consists in the civil rights and advancements of every person according to his merit: the enjoyment of these never more certain, and the access to these never more open, then in a free Commonwealth. Both which in my opinion may be best and soonest obtained, if every countie in the land were made a kinde of subordinate Commonaltie or Commonwealth, . . . where the nobilitie and chief gentry . . . may build, houses or palaces, befitting thir qualitie, may bear part in the government, make thir own judicial laws, or use these that are, and execute them by thir own elected judicatures and judges without appeal, in all things of civil government between man and man. (CM, VI, 143–44)

> They should have heer also schools and academies at thir own choice, wherin thir children may be bred up in thir own sight to all learning and noble education not in grammar only, but in all liberal arts and exercises. This would soon spread much more knowledge and civilitie, yea religion through all parts of the land, by communicating the natural heat of government and culture more distributively to all extreme parts, which now lie numm and neglected, would soon make the whole nation more industrious, more ingenuous at home, more potent, more honorable abroad. (CM, VI, 145).

Milton proposes no less than to transform the entire landscape of England into an embodiment of pure reason. Despite the superbly cool and collected tone, however, the syntax of these passages is closer to the extended coordination of the polemical sections of the tract than to the intricate and ample hybrids of looseness and suspension which K. G. Hamilton calls typically Miltonic. Here as elsewhere in the tract the speaker makes no attempt to convey the impression that his position is successfully grappling with that of his opponents. The ready and easy amplitude of these sentences suggests instead that a rational republic would beget miniature reproductions of itself as readily and easily as a monarchy generates triviality and degradation. The only difference is that monarchical potency functions in the real England of 1660, republicanism in an imaginary one in which all social forces would be on its side. Also, I must once more emphasize that the cool and collected rational tone moves toward sentimentality, particularly in the latter portion of the passage on a reformed school system. The parallel subjunctives and the rounded conclusion formed by the series of comparatives build into the passage an intimation that though the speaker may think

he is proposing a practicable solution, he is in fact consoling himself
with a private dream of social reason, one which might eventually become a public reality, but not in this place at this time.[16]

v

It is clear that Milton's understanding of the situation in which he
is writing is not such as would lead him to think that his plan might be
accepted and implemented. He exploits the considerable resources of
his prose rhetoric to convey just the opposite reading of current affairs.
Directly in the polemical sections, indirectly in the proposing ones, he
speaks "the last words of our expiring libertie" (CM, VI, 148). This is
most sharply and powerfully true of the concluding section, which begins ironically enough with a false statement: "I have no more to say at
present" (CM, VI, 147). About half of this concluding section is a suspended and massive sentence, too long to quote at this point, which
duplicates the form of one discussed earlier:[17] "But if the people be so
affected . . . whatever new conceit now possesses us" (CM, VI, 147–48).
The analysis made of that previous sentence applies equally well to this
one. The speaker makes a final heroic effort to contain the multitude of
unreformed social conditions within a grand pattern of reason and principle, but, as earlier, he finds it impossible to stop declaiming after the
climactic predication, "our condition is not sound but rotten, both in
religion and all civil prudence." He instead goes on to repeat his condemnations and dark predictions in summary form: "and will bring us
soon, the way we are marching, to those calamities which attend alwaies
and unavoidably on luxurie, all national judgments under forein or
domestic slaverie: so far we shall be from mending our condition by
monarchizing our government, whatever new conceit now possesses us."
Such loose ends dangling from this recollection of Milton's warfaring
prose style indicate that for now, at least, circumstance shall not be overcome. Thus it would be dishonest to end the tract on a positive note.

These then are the words with which Milton takes his leave of
liberty:

But I trust I shall have spoken perswasion to abundance of sensible and ingenuous men: to som perhaps whom God may raise of these stones to become
children of reviving libertie; and may reclaim, though they seem now chusing
them a captain back for *Egypt*, to bethink themselves a little and consider
whether they are rushing; to exhort this torrent also of the people, not to be so

impetuos, but to keep their due channell; and at length recovering and uniting thir better resolutions, now that they see alreadie how open and unbounded the insolence and rage is of our common enemies, to stay these ruinous proceedings; justly and timely fearing to what a precipice of destruction the deluge of this epidemic madness would hurrie us through the general defection of a misguided and abus'd multitude. (CM, VI, 148–49)

This sentence embodies the organization of the entire pamphlet in intensified form. The primary syntax is simple, straightforward, and full of rational hope: "But I trust I shall have spoken perswasion to abundance of sensible and ingenuous men." But the virtually certain defeat of these hopes grows more and more evident in the long chain of dependent clauses added in the second edition, first in a parenthetical qualification, "though they seem now chusing them a captain back for *Egypt*," surrounded by the primary hopeful phrases, which themselves end with the dangerous participial, "rushing." The threatening implications of "rushing" are taken up by "this torrent also of the people, not to be so impetuos," but are restrained by "but to keep thir due channel." The participial clauses begin positively ("recovering and uniting"), are interrupted by a longer, more threatening aside ("now that they see alreadie how open and unbounded the insolence and rage is of our common enemies"), and can only partially recover with a phrase that ends with the words "ruinous proceedings." The final clause begins with brave adverbs, "justly and timely," but their impact is weakened by the governing participial they modify, "fearing," and is overwhelmed by a "deluge" of decisively bleak prepositional phrases: "to what a precipice of destruction the deluge of this epidemic madness would hurrie us through the general defection of a misguided and abus'd multitude."[18]

The struggle enacted in this final sentence, with the voice of reason slowly but surely turning into a voice bravely and honestly recognizing the true balance of political power, is the struggle enacted in the tract at large. My argument should not, however, be taken to mean that *The Readie and Easie Way* tells the story of a developing quietism or political cynicism in its author. Rather, what is most impressive within the stylistic and structural patterns I have outlined is the endurance of the speaker's commitment to a rational and free Commonwealth. Despite his or Milton's forcefully communicated understanding of the immediate futility of republican ideas, he continues to the bitter end to challenge and invite his audience: "But I trust I shall have spoken perswasion to abundance of sensible and ingenuous men." Only covertly through syntactic and structural ironies, after all, does Milton say republican politics have become impossible. As against these ironies, his surface argument comes to mean that he retains some hope for the ultimate social realization of freedom and truth. If not, if we must conclude that Milton ends his twenty years as a political activist by arriving at the political position announced in *Paradise Lost*, that "Tyranny must be" because "inordinate desires / And upstart Passions" will always "catch the Government from Reason" (XII, 85–96), then we must also conclude that he adopts this position only with the utmost reluctance.

Boston University

NOTES

1. Don M. Wolfe et al., ed., *Complete Prose Works of John Milton* (New Haven, 1953–), IV, 636 (cited hereafter as YP).

2. Arthur E. Barker, *Milton and the Puritan Dilemma, 1641–1660* (Toronto, 1942), pp. 78, 88.

3. Francis F. Madan, *A New Bibliography of the "Eikon Basilike" of King Charles the First* (London, 1950), pp. 2–4; summarized in YP, III, 150.

4. See Barker, *Puritan Dilemma*, p. 162.

5. Godfrey Davies provides, in *The Restoration of Charles II, 1658–1660* (San Marino, Calif., 1955), a detailed account of the context in which Milton was writing.

6. For a detailed exposition of matters here summarized, see my doctoral dissertation, "The Evolution of Milton's Prose Rhetoric" (Yale, 1969).

7. See *The Works of John Milton*, ed. Frank Allen Patterson et al., 18 vols. (New York, 1931–38), VI, 358–59, and the textual notes to p. 111 on p. 359 (cited hereafter as CM).

8. "The Development of Milton's Political Thought," *PMLA*, LVII (1942), 708, 734, 736.

9. "Milton: Political Beliefs and Polemical Methods, 1659–60," *PMLA*, LXXIV (1959), 191–202. See especially 196–97.

10. "The Structure of Milton's Prose," in *Language and Style in Milton: A Symposium in Honor of the Tercentenary of "Paradise Lost,"* ed. Ronald D. Emma and John T. Shawcross (New York, 1967), p. 313.

11. Professor Croll's essays, indispensable to the student of seventeenth-century prose style, have been collected by J. Max Patrick, and others, as *Style, Rhetoric, and Rhythm: Essays by Morris W. Croll* (Princeton, 1966). On appositions and trailing clauses, see p. 224.

12. "Milton's Prose Style," *PQ*, XIV (1935), 5.

13. On warfaring and wayfaring, see YP, II, 515n.

14. These structural divisions are not as clear-cut as my discussion may suggest. Brief statements contrasting the republican plan with what is actually happening

appear now and then in the polemical sections: "Wheras in a free Commonwealth, any governor or chief counselor offending, may be remov'd and punishd without the least commotion . . . the happiness of a nation must needs be firmest and certainest in a full and free Councel of thir own electing, where no single person, but reason only swaies" (CM, VI, 121–22). The arrangement of key terms in these sentences suggests the rational stability of the proposed government. In the first sentence "free Commonwealth" stands guard over the potentially tumultuous verbs, "offending . . . remov'd and punishd," until the danger of conflict is ruled out in the final phrase. The second sentence moves in an orderly manner from effect to efficient to final cause: "The happiness of a nation . . . a full and free Councel of thir own electing, . . . where . . . reason only swaies."

15. True to himself to the end, Milton bestows all praise for the right reason upon his own *Defences*. This passage continues as follows: "Nor was the heroic cause unsuccessfully defended to all Christendom against the tongue of a famous and thought invincible adversarie; nor the constancie and fortitude that so nobly vindicated our liberty, our victory at once against two the most prevailing usurpers over mankinde, superstition and tyrannie unpraisd or uncelebrated in a written monument, likely to outlive detraction, as it hath hitherto convinc'd or silenc'd not a few of our detractors, especially in parts abroad."

16. Granting the accuracy of Lewalski's analysis (see above discussion in section I and n. 9), I find it difficult to believe that Milton seriously expected or even hoped that the revisions he made for the second edition would help to fashion a republican coalition. The primary impact of these revisions is to clarify the alternating rhetorical rhythm I have outlined. The two editions may be compared by consulting the textual notes in CM, VI, 359 ff.

17. See above, section III.

18. The phrase, "to som perhaps whom God may raise of these stones to become children of reviving libertie," is no doubt a reference to the words of John the Baptist at Matthew iii, 7–9, and Luke iii, 8: "I say unto you, that God is able of these stones to raise up children of Abraham." Louis L. Martz has pointed out to me that this phrase and the ensuing references to flood waters may also constitute an allusion to *Metamorphoses*, I, 381–415, in which Deucalion and Pyrrha repopulate the world after the Flood by casting stones behind them. Both references suggest, in line with my argument, that Milton does not expect the English political situation to improve without miraculous divine intervention.

MILTON'S *COMUS:*
SKILL, VIRTUE, AND HENRY LAWES

Franklin R. Baruch

In *Comus*, Milton uses the great tradition of the *vir bonus dicendi peritus* ("a good man skilled in speaking") both to pay a masquing compliment to Henry Lawes and to provide central roles for all three Egerton children. He does this by restricting the possession of virtue and both moral and physical skills to the Attendant Spirit and his dramatic extension, Sabrina. The gradations of virtueless skill and unskilled virtue figure forth patterns of both image and meaning, especially when we remember the perceptions and assumptions of the first viewers and readers. As a result, we see Milton fulfilling and using the demands of the masque genre through his complex use of Lawes as both the actual teacher and the dramatic guide of the children. The long dialogue of the brothers has added thematic and dramatic cogency; and the final scene between Comus and the Lady emerges in a new perspective, in which the Lady ultimately becomes Comus' teacher. This blend of masquing lesson, compliment, and decoration continues in the epilogue: here, the supposedly arcane references help to complete the vision of virtue and skill, and thus offer the final gesture to Lawes.

M UCH OF the attention given to Milton's *Comus* has sprung from a concern with the pairings seen as operative in the poem. Virginity and profligacy, natural and religious virtue, celibacy and marriage, order and disorder—the list is an abundant one, with results often richly suggestive.[1] It is perhaps inevitable that this focus in *Comus* scholarship should have come about. By the very nature of the form, one looks for contending or, at least, separated elements to be in union at the close. If that union is not possible, we find one alternative to have lost. Thus, the universe of the masque is one of solutions produced by the viewer's or reader's perception of true relationships. It is a universe, too, in which a chief delight consists in the delicacy and appropriateness of compliment offered to those involved with the piece. In their turn, these courtly gestures and decorations at their best become fused with the intellectual and spiritual levels of the work.

I should like to suggest that *Comus* draws upon two commonplaces of rhetorical, ethical, and religious tradition as it accomplishes these masquing functions. They are a pair of concepts central to the assumptions of the age. The first is that the attainment of both virtue and skill is necessary in order to become a good orator, a good teacher, or, indeed, a good man. The second point Milton uses both to comment upon and complete the first. It is that certain areas of knowledge are the province only of God, though He lends such knowledge to certain beings in order to permit virtue to be tried through temptation. In Milton's masque, these recipients of God's allowance are the divinely good Attendant Spirit and the essentially Satanic Comus.[2]

In this connection, we must notice how the poet restricts the possession of both virtue and the skilled control of nature to the Attendant Spirit and to Sabrina. She, however, is an extension and amplification of his image at the close of the masque. This uniqueness provides a delightful compliment to Henry Lawes within the circumstances of the masque: the musician, who was probably responsible for Milton's commission for the work, played the role of the Attendant Spirit. Thus we have an early example in Milton's career of his linking matter to the power afforded by genre itself. In this way complex purposes are achieved. Later, the poet was to use the might of the pagan epic to sing his Christian song of man's weakness and God's mercy. He was to use the elements of classical tragedy to suggest both the tragic hero and the Hebraeo-Christian exemplum. Here, the process emerges in a slighter shape, but with entertaining effect. The features of the masque are made to compliment Lawes. In addition, Milton uses Lawes's actual and masquing roles as the teacher of the Egerton children in order to provide all three offspring, not just the daughter alone, with thematically and aesthetically important roles.

It is not possible to overestimate the importance of our having a sense of unfolding occasion, in order to see these accomplishments in *Comus*. No other art form is as intricately and specifically concerned with a moment in time, as is the masque with that of its birth and performance. Part of the pleasure was derived from the relationship existing among the masquers, the audience, and the occasion of the production.[3] To be sure, we shall never know the little jokes and understandings that may have been clear to those at Ludlow. On the other hand, we may be certain that *Comus*, like so many masques, derived some of its vitality from the fact that it was in part a family affair. It was thus responsive to those factors commonly surrounding children, their parents, and, in this case, their teacher. We shall miss a great deal of the poem's magic, if we pay intellectual and emotional heed only to the story of the Lady's plight, or focus exclusively on her moral superiority to Comus. We shall similarly lose out if we restrict ourselves to finding the allegorical meanings attached to the instruments of protection and release. And we shall err because, although such matters are in the foreground, Milton's audience and early readers would have been responding to others as well. I suggest that their delight may well have been enhanced by their perception of the compliment to Lawes. Perhaps more important, this pleasure may have grown as the compliment itself was then observed to perform a number of functions both simultaneously and gracefully. It pointed a familiar and appropriate lesson. It focused on the children as children, thus amplifying the qualities of the occasion. It implied good, pertinent things about the Earl himself. Finally, the gesture to Lawes brought the story to a delicate and suggestive close. As both master musician and composer, Lawes could appropriately be made to represent the combination of virtue and skill so familiar to the age. But, as I shall seek to show, this masquing compliment is also pointing to the qualities inherent in the office of Lord President. It is also showing the new incumbent's children to be part of an age-old story of learning and growth. And the masquing compliment does these things while, on another level, the work is carrying forward its tale of virtue against vice.

One of the most convincing reasons for feeling that Milton did have these effects in mind is that some supposed difficulties in the piece vanish when they are examined in this light. In particular, we come to a clearer understanding of the roles played by the brothers. They share with their sister a vital and, under the circumstances of the Ludlow performance, a charming function in the masque. This importance Milton would certainly have wished to give to the male heirs of the Earl. In my opinion, he fulfilled that purpose. For too many readers of Milton's poem, the boys' philosophical discourse, their awkwardness, and their ineffectiveness have been strange, accidental, and unfortunate side effects in what is the story solely of the Lady.[4] Milton was not so careless: if his main story concerns the triumph of virtue over evil, the brothers and their sister are also part of another design. This other framework is structured on the fact that the children's instructor has that role in both the masque and in actual life, and that he is the sole repository of virtue and inclusive skill in the piece. The Egerton offspring are thus pointed out as excellent young ones, but young nevertheless. They are still in need of teaching. And on another level, delightful allegorical figure is given to the intrinsic limitations imposed upon all humans by a hierarchical universe.

In order to recapture something of what would have impinged on the minds of the first viewers and readers of *Comus*, the direct, chronological approach to the text is most helpful. It is the one that permits the factors I have mentioned to emerge in the relationships I believe Milton wished them to have.[5] To this end, we must consider the poem with a special deliberateness. It is a method made necessary because we are no longer in both conscious and unconscious touch with rhetorical, ethical, and religious precepts taken as assumptions by Milton's era. We must for the moment try to join an age in which the figures suggestive of virtue and skill would have been instantly obvious, convincing, and entertaining.

The first section of the poem (lines 1–169) is a process of identification in which the Attendant Spirit and Comus, the allegorical poles of the masque, make known their attributes and their natures. The first of these proclamations is structured so that the Attendant Spirit and his mission emerge from a network of virtue aided by skills. And they are skills both spiritual and physical. Indeed, Milton here focuses on the creature as a link between those two realms of being. It is as if the entire universe is formed so that virtuous, divine power may come naturally to the aid of the virtuous human who is also humanly weak.

Milton actually creates four clusters of statement for Lawes. First (1–17), there is the Attendant Spirit's delineation of the major difference between a pure, serenely untroubled heaven and an impure earth. The passage ends with the main point: there are some humans who seek to join the two realms "by due steps," and his skills are being sent to labor in their behalf. Next (18–42), this universe of "Jove" is extended through the ordered image of the Neptune myth. The emphasis here is on Bridgewater's reflection of a kind of divine rightness. This quality is seen in the Earl's skillful use of "temper'd awe to guide / An old and haughty Nation proud in Arms." It is thus part of a vision, traditional enough at the time, in which royal rule is made part of the workings of the harmoniously moving universe itself. To help celebrate this glory, the Earl's children are moving through that ancient symbol of error, a wood. We note that they are "fair offspring nurs't in Princely lore." It is a nursing that the play itself will continue and perfect. Following this (43–77), the Attendant Spirit sets up the opposing myth, that of the Circe-Bacchus union that produced Comus. There is very special emphasis on the absolute perfection of Comus' performance as the skilled master of physical phenomena. The evil one is a genius at his craft. He even surpasses "his mother at her mighty Art." Furthermore, the efficacy of his crystal glass is demonstrated when we feel the encompassing solidity of the victims' enchantment. We glimpse them as they "roll with pleasure in a sensual sty." It is a kinesthetic pinpointing of nature overturned for evil purposes by an enormous skill. Finally (78–92), the Attendant Spirit's introductory revelations are used to juxtapose Comus' amoral skill and his own. "As now I do" really sums up the situation. The actively virtuous human, limited in ability within the realm of nature, must be given aid in Comus' wood. To help accomplish this task, the Attendant Spirit at once uses his own transformational powers. He changes himself into a shepherd, an opposing allegorical force too obvious to require comment.

The values are swiftly altered in the universe that takes over the stage with the appearance of Comus and his crew. If, as we have seen, the Attendant Spirit's skills are part of the virtuous context of his being, then a polar effect enters with Comus. Indeed, his entire initial passage is based on the idea of how well he operates within the cosmos of his own perverted values. The Attendant Spirit has already described those powers having to do with seduction and enchantment. Now we must pay attention to the stage direction preceding Comus' entrance (between 92 and 93): it reveals the prominence that Milton wishes to give to the insignia of the enchanter's abilities, the charming rod and the glass, and to the evidence supplied by the grotesquely headed victims who accompany him. We must take this care because the energy of Milton's masque depends very strongly on the degree to which the other characters and we, the beholders and readers, are aware of how artful Comus' performance really is. We need, that is, to sense the very polish of his craft. That skill is the cause of the events, as well as the source of much of the decorative contrast demanded by the genre. In terms of our particular interest here, it is one of the poles of skill and moral identity that give generative force to the unfolding of Milton's tale.

But Milton's subtlety is what is so compelling. The invocation to revelry that falls from Comus' lips establishes more than the topsy-turvy value of this very strange new world we see before us. It simultaneously enshrines the consummate art of the leader of the revels as that art celebrates itself (93–144) through inversions of values basic to Milton's era. Perhaps most important is the use of the dance itself. Comus' pulsating, increasingly insistent rhythms suggest how music and dance, the ancient symbols of order and even of God, can with appalling skill be put to the creation of disorder when the musician is evil.[6] The passage ends with "Come, knit hands, and beat the ground, / In a light fantastic round": Milton, I think, wants the response not only of the victims, but of the viewer and reader as well. It is we, finally, who must know the power of the skilled villain now before us. And it is the rhythms that teach us.

With this oblique presentation of Comus' skills accomplished, Milton closes in on them by having them respond directly to the approach of the Lady (145–69). Comus' perfect physical art is now clarified through his own overt reference to it, as well as his almost mustache-twirling delight in its use. In this, his manner imitates that of Edmund and Iago, who, in good Machiavellian fashion, achieve their nearest approach to joy when they are lost in admiration of their own evil; it is, too, a pattern that Milton's own Satan will later follow. On the level of the main allegorical meanings of the masque, Comus obviously thus becomes the false shepherd-teacher-priest. In keeping with the antiphonal demands of the genre, his disguise is also a polar response to the pastoral covering the Attendant Spirit has assumed for worthy purposes. We must, however, see the vitality of the means and acts that Comus uses, and must see them in our special framework. We shall then understand that these deeds are part of Milton's fusion of masquing compliment and appropriate lesson. That is, the poet is figuring forth the need for combined virtue and skill, as well as the precept that both completes and adorns it: the control of nature is reserved to supernatural agencies, both heavenly and infernal.

Masques demanded opposing responses that hinted at hidden meanings. These figurative motions are frequently taking place in *Comus*. Here, we may note the way in which Comus, responding to the antiphonal force of the Lady, goes into hiding, just as the Attendant Spirit had done when the enchanter himself approached. These responsive patterns are of course central to the masquing design. I should like to stress, however, that we are dealing with more than the allegorical differentiation of opposite natures. As the early viewers and readers of the masque most surely did, we need to become progressively aware of the function assigned to the idea of skill itself in the poet's plans. Our perceptions must respond to the way Milton uses the very perfection of performance by the diametrically opposed Attendant Spirit and Comus. Those two arts advance the intellectual and decorative content of the masque, and give a very special sense of occasion to it as well.

Yet another universe of skills and moral identity takes over with the soliloquy and song of the Lady (170–243). It is a world immediately suggested with the phrase "if mine ear be true." We are now on the human level. Skill is now clearly finite. The Lady is surrounded by the dark wood, which represents the normal workings of natural law. We find that here simple physical cause leads to predictable and equally simple physical effect. The Lady, caught in the darkness, is dependent largely on her hearing. Now, this initial presentation of her skills is rather different from the ones we have seen in the Attendant Spirit and Comus. One can almost feel the core of inability that Milton places at the center of the blank verse. He surrounds the Lady and her perceptions with a galaxy of large, threatening images having to do with darkness and entrapment. But her fears are of man on the natural level, and of the dangers posed by nature itself. She knows her limitations, this girl, and they all have to do with threat on the material, natural plane. In particular, this is the area where female youth would be most intensely in peril. Lines 170–209 may be said, I think, to be an incrementally structured vision of alarm. But it is alarm that is quite justified under the circumstances Milton has provided for the Lady's thoughts.

It will be noticed, however, that lines 210–20 are correspondingly and responsively indebted to the idea of skill. When the Lady is speaking of nonphysical contexts of combat, the realm of the spirit, the conclusion is different. It is not a blue-nosed smugness that emerges. Instead, as an antiphonal contrast, we have a sureness born of the fact that her thoughts are now focused on the area of moral conflict. Here her skills are the powerful ones that human virtue can supply. They are skills that include the knowledge of one's final dependence on God's grace to achieve victory over Satan and his representatives. This is, of course, a basic truth of Christianity obviously being used on the primary allegorical levels of the masque. But, for our special interests here, we may note that Milton also transforms the religious truth into the delightful dramatic irony that follows. The Lady is confident that "a glist'ring Guardian, if need were" would be sent. Lawes is thus kept central to Milton's scheme. In him alone virtue and complete skill reside. Without her knowledge, then, the Lady's words announce to all that the teacher has been made available to the student in circumstances that demand a master touch.

And it is to emphasize the gap between the Lady's skills on the natural level and on the spiritual that Milton then returns her (221–43) to the frame of physical darkness. Her corresponding weakness in it leads to the magically evocative power of her song to Echo. In Milton's desire to develop the concept of skill itself, he uses this song to stress his point in an appropriately feminine, mythological frame. He will use Sabrina for a similar reason. The Lady's soliloquy has already indicated her awareness of her limited physical powers. Now Milton reinforces the concept. Painful though it is to ignore the loveliness of the verse, we should focus on what the song really says: Echo has a power that the Lady would like to call upon for help; she needs this help because she is in the realm of nature, a nature that at times physically hides one person from another. Her own human skills in the physical world are normally limited, and she knows it.

Comus' response to the song (244–64) touches significantly on his memory of his mother and her attendants "culling their Potent herbs and baleful drugs." It is a reference that not only puts forward an anticipatory allegorical opposition to haemony: it also shows again in full measure how superbly skillful the evil clan is in their dealings with nature. How easily they move and succeed amid the workings of the physical universe! Simultaneously, the passage serves to introduce the first conversation between Comus and the Lady (265–330). She is completely fooled, as we would expect her to be. Comus' disguise as a shepherd is, after all, a perfect one. It is a further testimonial to his skills in the area of physical being. I believe Milton uses the stychomythia of the scene (277–90) to present an antiphonal response of the differing souls involved in the encounter. Her absolute and innocent truth is repeatedly framed by his lies. And the effect is expanded in lines 291–330. Here, again, his false offering of help and shelter, along with her trust and acceptance, figures forth material skill devoid of virtue, and virtue antiphonally without material skill.

Now we see the Lady's brothers and hear their conversation. It is a dialogue not beside the point and almost madly inappropriate, as has at times been assumed. Instead, it is at the very heart of Milton's expanding configuration for skill and virtue. What the poet does, I think, is to use the brothers' long discussion (331–489) both to clarify the skill-virtue polarization we have seen, and to assign the boys their vital and appealing roles in the masque. Like their sister, they are the victims of a dark, threatening natural world. Like her, too, they can offer no real control over that world. Milton is to use their bravery in this cosmos to touch them with their own compliment: especially under the circumstances of the Ludlow performance, the audience would be willing enough to be delighted by the boys' valor, even if imperfectly supported by learning. But the poet will also use that valor to reinforce one of his principal points: human beings are ultimately dependent in an encounter involving an overthrown natural order.

I am sure Milton used the scene to charm his audience, probably by poking gentle fun at the Egerton boys' qualities of mind or speech. Possibly some particular use was made of their real-life performances as Lawes's pupils. We cannot know with certainty. But we may be more sure that the scene is shaped so that the Elder Brother's words (414–75) afford strong clarification of the qualities that belong to skill and virtue. It seems to me that the principal framework Milton uses here is that of a constantly reverberating world of natural image and material threat. But that world is brought forward in order to be rejected. In the Second Brother's view, of course, all is very unpromising for their sister. He can focus only on the fact that physical, female beauty is singularly subject to physical threat (especially 393–403), even though the Elder Brother, in speaking of Wisdom (375–85), has used the natural bird image, as well as that of the earth itself, to suggest the true power of the mind and soul. In his climactic response, intended both to comfort and to teach, the Elder Brother makes a decisive split between material and spiritual powers. He points to the ultimate strength of the individual soul, which under the pressures of the plot would be calling particularly upon the powers of chastity for support. It is typical of Milton that he should summon physical details of both folklore and pagan myth to give substance to the Christian-Platonic vision of the passage. Here, as always, the poet is implying that the natural world, rightly understood (a proviso that cannot be overemphasized), can be used to grasp the spiritual. Man must see that in the true relationships of the universe, the two realms are in essential harmony. They are harmonious, that is, when natural laws are left to their natural workings: the Elder Brother's vision is antiphonal to the activities of a Comus.

Yet neither boy has a balanced, pragmatically helpful view. That, too, is far from accidental. Both boys are brave and virtuous. Could the Egerton brothers be anything else? However, if the younger lacks philosophical distance and understanding almost completely, the elder has an intellectual awareness that is not dependable in an extraordinary situation calling for greater powers residing in a more experienced head. What is needed is a teacher in the fullest sense. They must look to one who combines virtue and comprehensive skills. So it is that the Attendant Spirit now appears to them. His entry at this point thus fuses the masquing and the actual relationships of the three figures on the stage: it does so through the ideal of the virtuously skilled teacher so familiar to the seventeenth century.

The Attendant Spirit does not speak the truth to the boys any more than Comus had to their sister. Yet his lies, offered partly for reasons of pedagogy, are both good and necessary. In the story, he is the brothers' "defense and guard" (41) as well as the Lady's. Within the private dimensions of the performance, he is their teacher as well. (Thyrsis is, of course, identified with the music of the Egerton household at 493–96.) As a good Renaissance teacher, he wants practical experience to help the process of learning succeed. Under the circumstances, that lesson involves the children's awareness of their own incapacities in a supernatural confrontation. With that focus in their training, no object lesson would be possible, were the boys to be aware of the special aid given them to combat a danger no human could adequately meet alone.[7]

We are not concerned with the identification of haemony, or with the passage (617–47) that presents it. Our interest is in haemony as part of a teaching method. We focus on the lovely myth as it is linked to the difference between moral and physical skills. Especially interesting are the Attendant Spirit's painstaking, explicit instructions to his male charges. Haemony (644–49) can help only to cut through evil disguise; it can offer protection against spells only before they are made. That is what he tells the boys, though perhaps we should more often wonder whether he is telling the truth, or whether, like his disguise, his account of haemony is a lie offered in a good cause. For this teacher, individual virtue must also learn some lessons about the nonmoral sphere. The basically good must become aware of the hierarchical limitations placed on man in dealing with the overthrow of natural law. The Attendant Spirit's instructions (650–56) are similarly framed to give the boys a detailed lesson in how fruitless human attempts may be in areas beyond rightful human undertaking. In the context of the masque, they must see that no amount of learning will help them to conquer the physical powers of a Comus, who practices the things that rightly belong to God. I am sure it is true that Milton intends Christian symbolism for the boys' failure and their need for Sabrina: perhaps he means to indicate man's basic need for grace on both the natural and religious planes of his existence. But there is another meaning connected with the masquing compliment to Lawes. As a bit of private fun so much at home in the genre, the poet wants to indicate that you do not send a boy to do a man's job; that the pupils are both good and valiant, but young and inexperienced; and that, as a result, they still need a teacher, who will therefore step in and resolve all through his extension, Sabrina. In addition to some factors determining Milton's use of Sabrina that will be mentioned later, a basic dramaturgic point may be made here: having allowed his charges to discover through experience that they need their teacher's aid, the Attendant Spirit as a dramatic character could hardly admit that he himself could have released their sister at any time.

The stage direction (between lines 658 and 659) that introduces the scene in Comus' palace is very important. It suggests a kind of dumb show illustrating, in the fashion of *Gorboduc*, one of the main points of the piece, and one central to our concern. The Lady's skills are precisely able to cope with a "Palace set out with all manner of deliciousness; soft Music, Tables spread with all dainties," as well as Comus, his "rabble," and his glass. Gone is the magical subterfuge, the transmutation of physical being symbolized by Comus' now abandoned pastoral disguise. With its departure, the Lady's incapacity has fled as well. She cannot be fooled by an intemperance no longer made to appear innocent through supernatural upsetting of physical identity. Physical ease and comfort

she can and does at once refuse ("he offers his Glass, which she puts by")
when the moral nature attached to them is out in the open. And it is
upon this interaction of skills that Milton now builds the great scene
between Comus and his prisoner. The absolute, consummate art of evil
is revealed as it seeks to use the universe for its own purposes. Antiphonally, we see the quite insufficient art of the virtuous human in the
face of physical entrapment. But the insufficiency is that of a human who
has another skill as polished in her realm of values as Comus' power is
in his.

The opposition is announced in the first spoken exchange of the
pair (659–65): Comus is rejoicing in the control of physical property
symbolized by his wand. We can feel the completeness with which his
disguise has been removed when he says, "Nay Lady, sit; if I but wave
this wand, / Your nerves are all chain'd up in Alabaster." The Lady's
response, equally abrupt and self-identifying, is

> Fool, do not boast,
> Thou canst not touch the freedom of my mind
> With all thy charms, although this corporal rind
> Thou hast immanacl'd, while Heav'n sees good.

Her scorn for him as a fool is central for us. It is much more than mere
angry name-calling. What the Lady is declaring is that her would-be se-
ducer is completely without knowledge, understanding, or discrimina-
tion in the realm of truth and spiritual value. In short, he is totally
unskilled in that context of being where she is herself so fine an artist.

We are not interested in their debate primarily with respect to their
moral positions themselves. Instead, we should see the way in which
everything that Comus says in his two great speeches (666–90 and 706–
55) is part of the vision of one who must see the world in a particular
way in order to control it. As he seeks to convince the Lady that she is
out of step with the rest of creation, he evokes a natural world that is
filled with pressing, demanding loveliness. His approach is due to his
need to produce all the components of the material world in a particular
distortion. The list extends from the delicate "April buds in Primrose-
season," through the "spinning Worms" in their "green shops" and the
"wing'd air dark't with plumes," to the vibrating, insinuating beauty of
"What need a vermeil-tinctur'd lip for that, / Love-darting eyes, or
tresses like the Morn?" It is as if for Comus there is a great scale of being

of a peculiar kind. It is one that omits the spiritual qualities that traditionally gave meaning to the concept and the figure. It is not only that
Milton is characteristically drawing on the Spenserian mode in which
evil at its worst is allied with physical beauty, so that both the temptation and the rejection of it may be meaningful. He wants us to feel something else in compelling detail: we must sense the sheer joy of the evil
artist as he contemplates the puppets over which he has, on one level,
such masterful control. The images pour forth in a profusion of material
delineation and celebration, perversely and exquisitely arranged in order to achieve the effects desired by the magician summoning them.
From stones to man, the scale is present—but there is no spirit, no soul.
The omission is, of course, part of Comus' art. It is also the very seal of
his being. These speeches of the son of Circe thus provide a rich figuring-
forth of virtueless skill, a self-condemning vision. Comus' powers can
operate only when the things of the spirit are suppressed.

And it is on this axis of skill and virtue that the Lady's responses are
made partly to move. Her tone is sharp and her attitude absolute. Yet it
would be an error (as I think it so often has been) to be put off by this
quality in her.[8] We need to experience her lines as, I believe, Milton
intended. They are not only the setting forth of a spiritual opposite to
the essentially Satanic position embodied in Comus' libertine natural-
ism. They are the quintessential demonstration of the Lady's own skills,
which lie in exactly those areas in which Comus is an utter stranger.
With stroke after stroke (690–705, 756–99), she cuts through physical
deception that is not buttressed by a magic that places it beyond the
hierarchically determined sphere of human competency. It was that sorcery that had made his pastoral covering so effective. The point is
brought forward when she herself calls attention to the "credulous innocence" that characterizes her area of inability. On the level of the
masque's moral lesson, to be sure, her impassioned references to temperance, chastity, and virginity place her at the allegorical pole from Comus.
She thus assumes an antiphonal relationship in keeping with Milton's
concepts and in appropriate conformity with a masque's demands for
responsively contrasting elements. But her statements do something else.
They create the universe of the Lady's own powers. If Comus' vision of
things excluded the spiritual, the Lady's (756–99) all but omits the physical. And when the material world does appear in her vision, it is to
demonstrate how it is perceived by the "well-govern'd and wise appe-

tite" of which she had spoken a bit earlier (705). We now have a Lady very different from the one whom we have seen to be weak in a physical context. Now she rejoices in her powers and her skills, just as Comus rejoiced in his own mastery of physical law. "Shall I go on? / Or have I said enough?" she asks. There is something basic in this question, as well as in the repeatedly established tone of superior ability in this passage. Milton intends us not only to consider the Lady a far better moral creature than Comus. He uses the interplay of concepts we have been considering to accomplish another purpose as well: we are to realize that the Lady has finally become Comus' teacher, the superior to him in art, now that circumstances have permitted the moral dimension to become the center of concern. In this area, the formerly skillful Comus has "nor Ear nor Soul to apprehend." Similarly, we must understand Milton to be placing Comus in polar separation from the classical Renaissance ideal of fused virtue and skill, when he has the Lady deride the enchanter's "dear Wit and gay Rhetoric / That hath so well been taught her dazzling fence." Skill is both empty and evil without virtue, a lesson taught by Comus' every word and deed. Later in the poet's career, the concept will be given epic life in the figure of Belial, as Milton singles him out for special scorn in the horrors of Pandemonium.

But Comus' response (800–13) to the Lady's skillful lesson does double duty. Primarily, of course, it shows the validity of the Lady's point, namely, that Comus' soul puts him beyond the appeal of truth. However, it also calls further attention to the Lady's physical need. What interests us directly here is Milton's use of that need as part of the compliment to Lawes. The lessons of the poem increasingly become answers to the needs of the genre: for if the Lady has shown herself to have the skills appropriate for the virtuous, it is nevertheless true that she and all humans exist in the physical realm as well. The "corporal rind" that Comus has managed to affect is the symbol of that plane. And since her physical troubles result from the powers of one able to overturn divinely set natural order, an antiphonal supernatural agency must be used to cure them. Comus is a moral idiot, a truth made almost palpable with his last words to the Lady and to us: "Be wise, and taste." But he has been all too skillful at his own specialty. The physical enchanter's success must be overcome. Otherwise, there can be no fully happy ending based on masquing polarities in final resolution. On the moral level, of course, a happy ending for the Lady was never in question.

Once again, stage directions (between lines 813 and 814) are of great significance. It is the brothers who come in first, and they do so for several reasons. Lawes–Attendant Spirit–Thyrsis gives his charges the chance to demonstrate their bravery. But they also show how poorly they have learned their lesson from their instructor: "What, have you let the false enchanter scape? / O ye mistook" (814–15). The teacher is scolding his students as part of the masquing fun at Ludlow, of course, but they are learning through experience. In the hierarchical nature of things, their material failure was certain—as sure as their sister's moral success.

The closing fifth of the masque is structured to focus on Lawes, and thus keeps building the sense of masquing compliment. By having allowed Comus to escape, the boys have had an object lesson in their need for the great powers of their teacher. In the fable, he offers the resolving fusion of virtue with a skill that embraces both the spiritual and the physical levels of being.

Sabrina, the "other means" to which the Attendant Spirit refers (821), seems clearly to be an appropriate masquing device for the Attendant Spirit himself. Through the Severn references, she provides a compliment to the locale of the performance and the region of the Earl's authority. Milton also surely wished to have another instance of feminine grace and virginal purity in his story, for reasons of balanced coloration.[9] But I think Sabrina is substituted for the Attendant Spirit for another reason, too. It is not only a question of dramatic need, the factor mentioned earlier. By having the final liberation performed by a female character, Milton is able to stress what we have been feeling about the Lady. We sense all the more deeply, that is, the lesson of the Lady's story as it has been blended with her brothers': the physical controls all three children lack, it is right that they lack. Those skills belong to divinity, though they may be usurped by the ungodly. And the concept of a power that is more than human is given greater potency by having it issue from one who in her physical self is so clearly delicate and gentle. The Lady, too, is delicate and gentle, but she is human.

To achieve this effect, Milton joins two great images in the Sabrina episode (820–937). They concern the helplessness of Sabrina's original, human life, and the consummate art and power of her present state. When Nereus' pity led to Sabrina's apotheosis, it did more than save the girl and preserve her forever. It placed her in that realm of being in which girls do indeed control nature and its forces. Furthermore, they do so legitimately: they are allied with the forces of goodness and mercy figured forth in Nereus. They have nothing to do with so dark a supernatural being as Circe, perhaps the greatest classical symbol of disorder and spiritual ruination for the Renaissance.[10] It is far more than only a desire for delightful pastoral decoration that leads Milton to associate Sabrina with a grouping of shepherds and flowers, and especially to praise the help she offers (844–51). She is, let it be remembered, a "Goddess dear," one with a "powerful hand" (902–03). Here, in one of the closing resolutions of the piece, the virtuous, delicate being is also the skilled practitioner in the material world. She is able to overcome the physical impairments wrought by a Comus. She can combat an evil that God has permitted to have power over the workings of nature itself, in order to further His desire for testing in the world. Unlike mere mortals, Sabrina is entitled to such abilities. And so, in the very act of her assistance, she also provides a lesson in hierarchical identity to those she helps.

We are, once again, not concerned with the main thematic and allegorical function of Milton's lines. It seems clear enough, for instance, that he intended the matter and manner of Sabrina's ministrations (910–21) to be suggestive of Christian ritual. We must rather concentrate on this new character as she consciously demonstrates her skills. For the tonal and dramatic reasons I have suggested, Sabrina's performance is made into the purest evocation of fused virtue and physical skill in the masque. In a sense her performance completes the confrontation we witnessed in Comus' palace. There the two antagonists could display their individual powers. Yet there could have been no joining of the Lady's moral skills, her purity, with the supernatural physical controls possessed by Comus. In Sabrina, the extension of the Attendant Spirit, that union takes place. The passage may be Christian ritual in allegorical guise. It may be the poet's delight in providing the formulaic patterns beloved by those given to masquing. But Sabrina's method is also the implicit, warm, and touching reminder that the children's teacher has helped them. He has summoned a goddess, who can aid them in a context of threat in which no humans can physically triumph. It is a lesson given its solid application as each easy and unhesitating step is taken, each confident motion is made. The enchantment is lifted because Sabrina is who she is.

But Milton gets rid of Sabrina as soon as her tonal magic has been injected into the proceedings. Lawes, after all, must have the center of the stage, in a quite literal sense. He may have called upon the nymph temporarily, but it is he who is the real repository of both moral and physical skills in the masque. And it is he who is the object of the masquing compliment. In the final moments of the work the gesture is refined as Milton restricts all verbal activity to Lawes. The musician now moves from the role of guide to the children to that of graceful lecturer to all those assembled. With respect to Milton's deeper lessons in the poem, he is attaching the children's adventures to universal human experience. He is giving the application of the moral. But that is not our concern. The closing lines are also part of the great image of virtue, skill, and of man's hierarchically imposed limitations to which we have been paying attention. And this section also expands the compliment: Milton is careful to shape the end of his masque so that the audience's final memory is filled with the Egertons' tutor.

We may note again that the Attendant Spirit is the "faithful guide" of all three children. It is the trio that he guides out of the wood and presents to their parents (938–75). He identifies the Ludlow setting to which they now come as "holier ground," a place he explicitly (939–43) identifies as one where the skills of a Comus would be hard-pressed to succeed.[11] Now, the ideal fulfillment of the Earl's royal office was of course the nearest earthly approximation of divine order. Many centuries had seen the throne in that way. Or, using the point of view we have been adopting here, it combined the virtue and goodness, justice and mercy, of God, with the practical working out of those qualities on the earthly plane. Milton's artistry thus links the compliment to Lawes and the quite necessary bow to the Earl. Both men are finally joined in the virtue-skill context. The Lord President of Wales might not expect to run into a Comus or other supernatural destroyer of natural order. He would nevertheless, by the quality of his rule, provide the skills that help the virtuous. And they are skills that have been suggested in the figures of the Attendant Spirit and his masquing extension, Sabrina. We need to recall the opening speech of the Attendant Spirit, especially its references (18–36) to the new government in terms of universal law and power. In addition, we must remember how that body of belief was joined to the journey of the children and the mission of the Attendant Spirit himself (36–42). In this way we shall feel the point all the more strongly. We shall hopefully experience something of what the earliest viewers and readers of *Comus* were able to sense in Milton's organic, expansive masquing compliment.

Whatever else it may be felt to accomplish, the Attendant Spirit's epilogue (976–1023) is the final teaching opportunity for Lawes and the last chance for the poet to offer him a compliment. The latter, a demanding pressure from the genre itself, ends and perfects the song of virtue and skill. It is, I think, precisely Milton's extraordinary barrage of natural imagery here that helps us to sense the final unfolding of his gesture to Lawes. And the gesture simultaneously crystallizes the lesson of which it is a part. Finally, these closing evocations of virtue and skill touch upon the new Lord President as well. For one thing, they follow immediately after the introduction of governmental dimensions of which I have spoken. For another, his ordered government and virtuous strength would naturally seem linked to the heavenly realms to which the Attendant Spirit now declares he is returning.

The Attendant Spirit makes clear at once that this ideal level of existence permits free and easy movement in both classical natural loveliness (981–96) and in the warm coloration of British landscape (1013–18). Indeed, his powers are part of the harmonious working of natural beauty. That loveliness, rightly understood and used, is part of goodness (heaven) itself, a union that could not have been part of Comus' libertine understandings. Milton now again turns to water, fertility, and enveloping fragrances. They had been presented as part of Comus' universe of corrupt perceptions. Then, they had been shown to be essentially good by being associated with Sabrina (923–37). Now, with climactic joy, they glow about the Attendant Spirit, who mentions the Venus-Adonis and Cupid-Psyche myths (998–1011). However many other meanings this material may have for the reader, I think it offers a kind of mythological proof of what the Attendant Spirit has been trying to teach all along. The lines concern the need that the virtuous may have for superior kinds of aid when they are faced with extraordinary troubles. These mythological figures, too, have physical griefs requiring intervention by those entitled to correct the interruptions of natural law. To understand this, I believe we must see how Milton presents both Adonis and Psyche as being on the mend. Adonis is, after all, "waxing well" (1000). Similarly, Psyche can, through divine help, look forward to a brighter future (1007–11), with her and Cupid's "blissful twins,"

Youth and Joy, lending exactly the right coloration at this point. Here, the jubilant result of heavenly aid, as it is given to virtuous mortals, is made one with the extraordinary results produced by an extraordinary teacher. In the process, both become part of the demands of the genre and the happiness of the occasion.

In keeping with his principal meanings, Milton has the Attendant Spirit point, of course, to virtue as the greatest teacher in spiritual matters. But the frame of reference is significant for us. With his last breath in the masque, he is dealing with the process as well as the subject matter. He indicates the need for the master to intercede when the going becomes particularly hard. The difficulty may arise because in the nature of the situation no human could do well on all levels, or else because students cannot rightly be expected to do as well as their teachers. The dual possibility is part of the evening's pleasure. That Milton and his age saw such an approach to divinity in the powers of music, the art of Lawes, is an old story. That this body of belief helped to shape the second of the poet's masques is a concept having its own powers to refine our perceptions of the work.

Assumption College

NOTES

1. Although my own study is not directed to these matters, one of these previous treatments should be mentioned. Even though one may not agree with all its assertions, it may be said to have been seminal in *Comus* criticism and to have made Milton's masque perceivable in some of its original terms. The greatness of the study is thus indispensable in one's preparation for dealing with the poem: certainly it has been so in my own. I refer to A. S. P. Woodhouse's "The Argument of Milton's *Comus*," *University of Toronto Quarterly*, XI (1941), 46–71. I share generations of readers' rejection of the awkward *A Mask* as the title for Milton's drama. Throughout my discussion, I shall use the more familiar, if less authentic, designation.

2. The traditions are so widespread in the period that they seem to be part of the very fabric of the age. In particular, however, see Harris Fletcher's illuminating account of the vital importance of Quintilian, who, in Milton's elementary and university training, offered the strongest emphasis on the combination of skill and virtue needed in the ideal orator-teacher: *The Intellectual Development of John Milton*, I (Urbana, 1956), pp. 113–14; II (1961), pp. 205–06. The tradition is that which Quintilian himself had absorbed, that of the *vir bonus dicendi peritus*. With respect to the feelings of Milton's age concerning man's propensity for looking into things beyond his rightful place in the universal scheme, see Howard Schultz, *Milton and Forbidden Knowledge* (New York, 1955), esp. pp. 43–47, which places stress on the linking of

such probings to witchcraft—a connection of special importance in dealing with the deeds of Circe's son.

3. Rosemond Tuve's study of *Comus* is constantly helpful and corrective in its insistence that we must read the poem in the light of the genre to which its creator assigned it: see *Images and Themes in Five Poems by Milton* (Cambridge, Mass., 1957), pp. 112–61. There are also interesting suggestions in C. L. Barber's *"A Mask Presented at Ludlow Castle*: The Masque as a Masque" in *The Lyric and Dramatic Milton*, ed. Joseph H. Summers (New York, 1965), pp. 35–63.

4. As part of his rather inclusive rejections of Milton's poem, Don Cameron Allen is particularly bothered by its intellectual content, finding it in conflict with other aspects of the work. This is a view, of course, quite different from my own. See "Milton's *Comus* as a Failure in Artistic Compromise," *ELH*, XVI (1949), 104–19.

5. My references to the text of *Comus* are from *John Milton: Complete Poems and Major Prose*, ed. Merritt Y. Hughes (New York, 1957). In my opinion, the differences between the 1634 version and the printed text are not great enough to affect my assertions concerning the unfolding of the masque at Ludlow. They therefore also permit us to consider the early viewers and readers together as a body of original perception and reaction.

6. Note may here be taken of the possibility that Milton intended Comus' perversion of dancing, part of the antimasque provided by him and his transformed victims, to be antiphonally corrected by the more traditional, ordered associations figured forth in the good music of Lawes as the Attendant Spirit and Thyrsis.

7. There were many classical and Renaissance precedents for Milton's devotion to the practical as the end of education, and for the precept that the good teacher must allow his charges to learn through experience—considerations that figure in the shaping of the Attendant Spirit's efforts. But perhaps Milton's own *Of Education* is the best commentary on the direct pedagogical relationship between the Attendant Spirit and the boys at this juncture.

8. For an example of this reaction to the Lady, see Allen, "Milton's *Comus*," p. 116.

9. As an example of views that see Sabrina as quite separated from the Attendant Spirit in symbolic function, see Richard Neuse, "Metamorphosis and Symbolic Action in *Comus*," *ELH*, XXXIV (1967), 54–57.

10. The classic and indispensable account of the matter remains that found in Merritt Y. Hughes, "Spenser's Acrasia and the Circe of the Renaissance," *Journal of the History of Ideas*, IV (1943), 381–99.

11. The final setting of the masque receives perceptive and suggestive treatment in Woodhouse's discussion of the three environments Milton provides for his characters. See his *"Comus* Once More," *University of Toronto Quarterly*, XIX (1950), 218–23.